Opera and the City

Opera and the City

THE POLITICS OF CULTURE
IN BEIJING, 1770–1900

Andrea S. Goldman

STANFORD UNIVERSITY PRESS
STANFORD, CALIFORNIA

Stanford University Press
Stanford, California

© 2012 by the Board of Trustees of the Leland Stanford Junior University. All rights reserved.

No part of this book may be reproduced or transmitted in any form or by any means, electronic or mechanical, including photocopying and recording, or in any information storage or retrieval system without the prior written permission of Stanford University Press.

Library of Congress Cataloging-in-Publication Data

Goldman, Andrea S. (Andrea Sue), author.
 Opera and the city : the politics of culture in Beijing, 1770–1900 / Andrea S. Goldman.
    pages cm
 Includes bibliographical references and index.
 ISBN 978-0-8047-7831-2 (cloth)
 ISBN 978-0-8047-9205-9 (pbk.)
  1. Operas, Chinese—Social aspects—China—Beijing. 2. Operas, Chinese—Political aspects—China—Beijing. 3. Operas, Chinese—China—Beijing—History and criticism. 4. Beijing (China)—Intellectual life—18th century. 5. Beijing (China)—Intellectual life—19th century. I. Title.
  ML1751.C58G65 2012
  782.10951'156—dc23

2011047716

Typeset by Bruce Lundquist in 10.5/14 Adobe Garamond

For
my mother, Muriel Goldman,
and in memory of my father, Marvin Goldman (1927–2009),
who nurtured my love for the theater from a very young age.

Contents

List of Illustrations ix
Reign Periods of the Ming and Qing Dynasties xi
Acknowledgments xiii

    Overture   1

PART ONE | AUDIENCES AND ACTORS

1. Opera Aficionados and Guides to Boy Actresses   17
    The Texts   23
    The Connoisseurs   39
    The *Lao Dou* and Other Patrons   53
    Conclusion   58

PART TWO | VENUES AND GENRES

2. Metropolitan Opera, Border Crossings, and the State   63
    The Playhouse   67
    The Temple Fair   87
    The Salon   97
    Conclusion   112

3. Musical Genre, Opera Hierarchy, and Court Patronage   115
    Yabu and *Huabu*   118
    Court Patronage and Regulation to circa 1860   119
    Genre Delineation and the Opera Marketplace   129
    Court Patronage and Regulation after 1860   134
    Conclusion   140

PART THREE | PLAYS AND PERFORMANCES

4. Social Melodrama and the Sexing of Political Complaint 145
   The Garden of Turquoise and Jade and Its Sources 148
   Garden and the Ethics of the Early Qing
   Suzhou Playwrights 155
   Garden on the Commercial Stage 160
   Conclusion 172

5. Sex versus Violence in "I, Sister-in-Law" Operas 175
   The Stories 178
   From Page to Stage 191
   Kunju Performances in Context 205
   Eighteenth-Century Court Appropriation of
   "I, Sister-in-Law" Operas 212
   Violence and the Reinstantiation of Moral Order
   in the *Pihuang* Tradition 217
   Conclusion 233

   Coda 237

Appendices 249
List of Characters 259
Notes 273
Bibliography 333
Index 353

Illustrations

Figures

1	Schematic diagram of the floor plan of a typical Qing-era playhouse	19
2	Outline sketch of the walls of Beijing during the Qing dynasty	70
3	*A Complete Map of the Inner and Outer Cities of the Capital*	71
4	Painting of the Guangqing Playhouse	79
5	Painting of *pihuang* opera performance inside a Beijing playhouse during the Guangxu era	80
6	Detail from *A Pilgrimage to Miaofeng Peak*	88
7	Wall painting of a temple-fair performance at the Jingzhong Temple, Beijing	90
8	Salon performance	99
9	The Qianlong emperor watching plays	100
10	Courtyard stage within the Drenched Fragrance Studio in the imperial palace	110
11	The "Preserved Elegance" stage within the Drenched Fragrance Studio	110
12	Double stages within the Weary of Cares Studio in the imperial palace	111
13	Celebrations for the Kangxi emperor's birthday in 1713	120
14	Cover page of the Sanqing Troupe edition of *The Garden of Turquoise and Jade*	162
15	Cover page of Du Buyun copy of *Tale of the Garden of Turquoise and Jade*	168
16	Table of contents for Du Buyun copy of *Tale of the Garden of Turquoise and Jade*	170

17	Illustration for a set of selected scenes from *Record of the Water Margin* in *The Dark Snow Catalog*	193
18	Illustration for a set of selected scenes from *Record of the Righteous Hero* in *The Dark Snow Catalog*	194
19	Illustration for chapter 5 of *The Prosemetric Plum in the Golden Vase*	195
20	Painting of a scene from the *pihuang* version of the drama "Cuiping Mountain"	229
21	Lithograph print of a scene from the *pihuang* version of the drama "Cuiping Mountain"	230

Color plates (following page 86)

1. Painting of a "flower" *dan* in the *pihuang* opera "Fourth Son Visits His Mother"
2. Painting of a "blue-robed" *dan* in the *pihuang* opera "Fourth Son Visits His Mother"

Reign Periods of the Ming and Qing Dynasties

Ming (1368–1644)

Hongwu	1368–1398
Jianwen	1399–1402
Yongle	1403–1424
Hongxi	1425
Xuande	1426–1435
Zhengtong	1436–1449
Jingtai	1450–1456
Tianshun	1457–1464
Chenghua	1465–1487
Hongzhi	1488–1505
Zhengde	1506–1521
Jiajing	1522–1566
Longqing	1567–1572
Wanli	1573–1619
Taichang	1620
Tianqi	1621–1627
Chongzhen	1628–1644

Qing (1644–1911)

Shunzhi	1644–1661
Kangxi	1662–1722
Yongzheng	1723–1735
Qianlong	1736–1795
Jiaqing	1796–1820
Daoguang	1821–1850
Xianfeng	1851–1861
Tongzhi	1862–1874
Guangxu	1875–1908
Xuantong	1909–1911

Acknowledgments

I have incurred many debts of gratitude in the making of this book. It gives me great pleasure to recount them here. Foremost acknowledgment must go to David Johnson, whose unwavering support and exacting standards guided the project from the beginning; he never doubted that a study on Chinese opera could lend itself to exploration of important historical questions. Other mentors, including Mary Elizabeth Berry, James Cahill, Samuel H. N. Cheung, Carla Hesse, Michael Nylan, Randolph Starn, Stephen West, Wen-hsin Yeh, and the late Frederic Wakeman Jr., shaped the book in inestimable ways through conversations, readings of chapters, and scholarly example.

Along the way, I have received encouragement and advice from friends in the field, many of whom read—in part or in full—various iterations of the project, including Shana Brown, Maram Epstein, Joshua Goldstein, Qitao Guo, Hua Wei, Lindy Li Mark, Keith McMahon, Mark McNicholas, Eugenio Menegon, Tobie Meyer-Fong, Ruth Mostern, James Polachek, David Rolston, Allison Rottmann, Ling Shiao, Joanna Handlin Smith, Matthew Sommer, Catherine Swatek, Sophie Volpp, John Williams, and Judith Zeitlin. John Finlay graciously shared with me his extensive knowledge of Qing court painting, which helped me track down the album leaf reproduced in Figure 9. And my writing group in Los Angeles—Angelina Chin, Natasha Heller, and Georgia Mickey—played a critical role in the process of transforming the manuscript into its final form. This is a better book for all their insights and interventions.

I have been blessed with thoughtful colleagues, formerly at the University of Maryland and now at UCLA, who have been most generous with their time and support. In College Park, Rick Bell, James Z. Gao, Saverio Giovacchini, Clare Lyons, Lisa Mar, and Thomas Zeller offered much-needed perspective on one or several chapters. Martha Burns, my erstwhile neighbor on Capitol Hill, frequently acted as an unofficial colleague and sounding board. In Westwood, Michael Heim, Lynn Hunt, William Marotti, Richard von Glahn, and R. Bin Wong turned their attention and acumen to the manuscript; and Bin, especially, must be thanked for providing incisive comments on the entire work. The two anonymous readers for Stanford University Press sagely prodded me to hone the argument; and Naomi Noble Richard read the entire manuscript and did her best to rein in my penchant for prolixity and alliteration. If the final work does not do full justice to their expectations and exhortations, the fault lies entirely with me.

While conducting research in Beijing, I benefited from the expertise and help of scholars, archivists, and friends too numerous to list, but the contributions of Bi Yuling, Liao Ben, and Lu Yingkun must be singled out for special recognition. Bi Yuling expertly helped recopy by hand many of the scripts that have been so central to this research. Liao Ben, beyond offering guidance and entertaining my many questions, graciously allowed me to reprint several images from his *Pictorial History of Chinese Theater* (*Zhongguo xiju tushi*). Lu Yingkun, in addition to engaging in hour upon hour of discussion about Chinese opera and society (usually over good food), pounded the pavement in Beijing to track down and secure permission for my use of an 1815 painting of a temple-fair performance outside the Great Enlightenment Monastery on Miaofeng Peak, the original of which is housed in the Capital Museum (Shoudu bowuguan).

No less instrumental for being less personal, grants from the following organizations and institutions made possible the completion of this book: a research fellowship from the Committee for Scholarly Communications with China; a Title VI Foreign Language and Area Studies Fellowship (UC Berkeley); the Doreen B. Townsend Center for the Humanities; a China Times Cultural Foundation Young Scholars Award; a Mabelle McLeod Lewis Memorial Fund Fellowship; a Bernadotte E. Schmitt Grant, American Historical Association; a Graduate Research Board Summer Grant, University of Maryland; a Faculty Career Development Award, UCLA; multiple Junior Faculty Research Support grants from the UCLA Department of History; and a generous subvention from the Dean of Social Sciences, UCLA. In addition, a postdoctoral fellowship from the Center for East Asian Studies (formerly the Center for Chinese Studies) at Stanford University in 2005–6 provided the necessary breathing space to rethink the project. Receipt of an Association for Asian Studies First Book Subvention

Prize has facilitated the publication of this book, along with the inclusion of the two color plates.

A version of Chapter 1 was previously published as "Actors and Aficionados in Qing Dynasty Texts of Theatrical Connoisseurship" in the *Harvard Journal of Asiatic Studies* 68.1; I am grateful to the journal for permission to republish it here. The editorial team at Stanford University Press, consisting of Stacy Wagner, Jessica Walsh, Carolyn Brown, and Cynthia Lindlof, attended to the manuscript with efficiency and enthusiasm. Without their expert assistance and meticulous care, this book could not have taken its final shape.

Thanks go, finally, to my family: my sisters Karen and Lauren, my brothers-in-law Craig and Mike, and my nieces Hannah and Abby, who have leavened the years of research and writing with good counsel and pleasant distraction. Playwright and theater director Lauren Goldman Marshall has read (or listened to me read) every word of this book, even in multiple drafts. I couldn't begin to count the times she has pushed me to clarify a point, avoid an obtuse word, or capture the joy and passion of my work in the narrative. She has calmed my doubts and delighted in my discoveries. She remains, as ever, my sharpest reader and my best friend. Fellow Berkeleyan and China historian Qitao has been there to share animated conversations, spicy noodles and organic tomatoes, sweet companionship, and constant support. Simon Zhihong arrived in our lives just in time to add both length and joy to the copyediting process. My parents, Marvin and Muriel Goldman, waited a long time for this book. Although they are no longer able to read it, I dedicate *Opera and the City* to them.

West Los Angeles
July 2011

Opera and the City

Overture

A Chinese comedy sketch from the 1950s commences with two men reminiscing about a day at the opera in times past. "When I was young," says the comic to the straight man, "the theater wasn't nearly so orderly as it is now." The comic begins to narrate the scene: outside the door to the theater stands the barker, announcing the shows and drawing crowds into the semi-open-air playhouse. In a stream of verbal pyrotechnics, the comic imitates the barker's exaggerated description of the day's offerings. "You'll see melodramas and military sagas," he cries; "there's flips and there's fighting—real knives, real spears, real deaths!" But that, the comic claims (back in his own voice), is nothing compared with the chaos inside the theater! Inside, people are milling around looking for seats and locating friends. The opening number has started, but hardly anyone is paying attention. Two men who were listening are now brawling over which of their favorites is the better actor. Vendors are hawking playbills and cigarettes, candied fruits and pumpkin seeds. Table tenders are pouring tea water, and towel servers are dispensing hot washcloths, which they pass out—zip and whoosh—by flinging them through the air across the house. The comic then adopts the voices of two women who have just found their seats and have begun chatting about the weather. "What a nice day it is today," says the first. "Not a cloud in the sky," replies the second, at which both women express surprise at the sudden light rain sprinkling down upon them. There is a pause, the comic looks up, and then, mimicking a woman's voice, calls out: "Hey, you on the balcony, your kid is taking a pee!"[1]

The previous description is exaggerated, as might be expected in a comic sketch. But it probably captures a sense of the excitement and pandemonium that would have been encountered in a theater in Beijing in the first half of the twentieth century, or even earlier, if you eliminate the women, the hot washcloths, and the cigarettes.[2] The anecdote helps us visualize the atmosphere within the playhouses of Beijing in the Qing dynasty and sets the stage, so to speak, for this study of opera in the life of the capital from circa 1770 to 1900. To us the pandemonium presented in the comic routine seems but a gentle send-up of old-style playhouses; but to the Qing court (and others committed to preserving social and moral order) the chaos of commercial opera—both its potential for social disturbance and for conveying subversive messages through the material presented onstage—was no laughing matter. This study of opera in Qing Beijing thus opens a key window onto our understanding of state-society relations and the mechanisms by which ideas and values were shared, shaped, disseminated, and contested.

Before the twentieth century, opera in China was the mass-communication medium of the times, as powerful in shaping and reflecting popular imagination as television and cinema are in our own times. Opera suffused the very fabric of life in late imperial times. It was one of the key mediums through which ideas about the self, family, society, and politics were transmitted over time, over space, and across class. The twenty-volume *All-China Drama Gazetteer* (*Zhongguo xiqu zhi*) lists 394 different regional musical styles of opera, most of which developed and matured during the years 1500 to 1900. The story of how these musical and dramatic subgenres proliferated, interacted, and migrated from region to region can tell us much about trade routes, economic integration, and social interaction in the Qing. My interest lies in examining social interaction and cultural practices. From its emergence in mature form in the eleventh century, at court and in the countryside, opera was intimately connected with religion and ritual, although it also served to entertain. In cities, theatrical performance was mostly spoken about in terms of entertainment and pleasure, although it was never entirely divorced from its ritual origins. Opera was shared across the social hierarchy: for the educated, opera was their entertainment; for the illiterate, it was entertainment and education. In late imperial China, in which perhaps 10 percent of men and 2 to 5 percent of women were conversant with the prestigious high literary tradition, opera was the medium that shaped and expressed most people's understanding of history and culture. Fortunately, sufficient scripts and descriptive records emanating from the performance culture of eighteenth- and nineteenth-century Beijing have been preserved to allow us to penetrate the values of those who otherwise left but minimal traces in the historical record. The opera culture of Beijing evinces a middle-brow urban sensibility, striated with the high literacy of scholar playwrights and patrons and the artistic talents and practical know-how of the debased-status actors.[3]

A growing body of scholarship attests that performance is crucial to understanding culture in late imperial China.[4] To date, much of the English-language use of opera to penetrate the belief systems of semi- and nonliterate Chinese society has focused on rural and ritual performance.[5] As yet little research has examined theatrical performance in relation to urban audiences and to the transmission of cultural values in an urban context. Scholars such as Tanaka Issei have argued that, over the course of the Ming-Qing era, popular (i.e., rural) dramatic traditions were co-opted by local elites, who refashioned them to be palatable to their own sensibilities and at the same time as a means to inculcate proper moral behavior in less educated members of the community.[6] My research, in contrast, by focusing on the understanding of opera by different social constituencies within eighteenth- and nineteenth-century Beijing, has shown that the tale of appropriations and appreciations of opera stories in the Qing capital is not quite so tidy and linear. Rather, opera during the Qing underwent adaptation and circulation, communication and obfuscation, between and among playwrights, court and other elite patrons, elite and commoner audiences, and commercial acting troupes. By examining the context and content of opera in eighteenth- and nineteenth-century Beijing, this work illuminates relationships between culture and power in the Qing dynasty, offering insight into how the state and various urban constituencies partook of opera and the stories played out onstage and manipulated them to their own ends, whether for moral inculcation, for pleasure, for expression of political commentary, or, typically, for some combination thereof.

The eighteenth and nineteenth centuries were a golden age for opera performance in the Qing capital. Many genres of opera, from the elegant Kun operas (*kunju*, written by scholar-poets), to the far less literary "flowery opera" styles (*huabu*), all vied for audiences in Beijing. The Qing capital, with a population of over a million and a thriving economy in the eighteenth century, held out the lure of fame and fortune to opera troupes and individual actors throughout the empire.[7] This same economic vitality brought an increase in domestic trade that was accompanied by the growth of guild associations in Beijing, which further provided a regionally diversified and transregional urban merchant audience receptive to native-place operas of the huabu variety.[8] The capital also became a magnet for well-educated young men from throughout the empire who came to sit for the metropolitan-level civil-service examinations, or who, having passed the exams, waited in the capital for official assignment. To these numbers were added the sons of sitting officials from the lower Yangzi delta—the Jiangnan, or "south of the River" region—who could evade stringent provincial exam quotas by taking their provincial-level exams in Shuntian Prefecture in Beijing, where competition was less intense.[9] While sojourning in the capital, often for months at a time, these would-be officials were avid patrons of the opera styles of their home locales. The high proportion of men from Jiangnan in this highly literate cohort ensured that kunju would be well attended in the capital. Men of the Manchu princely households and the Qing Banner garrisons (the state's chief security forces) stationed in Beijing, both with a surfeit of leisure and wealth, also inflated spectator numbers in the capital playhouses, patronizing commercial opera in defiance of official regulations.[10]

Demographic expansion in the eighteenth century further fueled the development of opera in the Qing capital by supplying a steady stream of unemployed boys (including the children of impoverished families) who were indentured into acting careers.[11]

Even the Qing court furthered development of metropolitan theatrical entertainment by sponsoring operas in the palaces by its own court troupes; it also indirectly prompted diversity of opera style in the capital by requisitioning commercial acting troupes from the central and lower Yangzi regions to perform at elaborate ceremonial occasions, such as the eightieth-year birthday celebration of the Qianlong emperor in 1790.[12] Indeed, the Qing polity, not unlike other early modern states—from Renaissance England and Louis Quatorze France to the sixteenth-century Ottoman Sultanate and Tokugawa Japan—relied on public and theatrical spectacle as a primary medium of power projection.[13] As such, competing theatrical performance, especially in the immediate vicinity of the court, became subject to intense state scrutiny.

The Qing court was ambivalent about opera, especially as performed in the commercial playhouses of the capital. Although it welcomed, promoted, even sought out certain elite genres of opera for its own viewing pleasure, it also fought against the encroachment of what it deemed morally suspect, socially corrosive, and politically subversive popular genres of opera in the city at large. From the late eighteenth into the nineteenth century the court banned performance of huabu opera within the city of Beijing. Actors of proscribed opera genres could be banished from the capital. And all officials above rank seven, as well as bannermen, were forbidden by edict to enter commercial playhouses. Fictional accounts and commonplace-book jottings about opera from the time, however, indicate that such injunctions were routinely ignored. Thus, opera performance—who performed it, what was performed, who watched it, and who policed it—came to be a hotly contested site of state-society friction in Qing Beijing. That the state cared so much about commercial opera in the capital surely attests to its importance at the time—both as shaper of popular sentiment and as catalyst for forms of public association.

Opera in Qing Beijing was not unlike performance in other major urban centers throughout the empire, with the great eighteenth-century entrepôt of Yangzhou bearing the closest resemblance.[14] (With the exception of Yangzhou and Suzhou, much less source material is available for sustained evaluation of commercial performance during the Qing beyond the capital.) Yet Beijing's unique role as the capital shaped opera in distinct ways, since the performance of culture there was more politically charged. The Qing court's fears of social unrest (and ethnic strife) were magnified regarding the capital, in part because Beijing was home to the central state apparatus and disproportionately housed the Banner military regiments and administrative units of the regime. Thus, my narrative is particular to Beijing under Qing rule; and yet, as the capital city, Beijing had an empirewide influence. Because of its importance as the political hub of the empire, Beijing drew educated men (and their favored styles of opera) from Jiangnan, Qing China's economic and cultural center. The analysis of opera and its tensions in Beijing, then, also speaks to larger empirewide transformations under way in the late eighteenth and throughout the nineteenth centuries. In particular, through the prism of opera performance we will see the long-term negotiating of aesthetic taste between Beijing as the empire's political center and Jiangnan as its long-acknowledged cultural heartland.

. . .

This study of opera in the Qing capital offers a new approach to Chinese opera history; it contributes to our understanding of Qing urban culture;

and it employs gender as a critical category of analysis in examining state-society relations under Qing rule.[15] Both Chinese and Western scholars, in writing the history of traditional Chinese opera, have tended to treat the development of Qing performance as in large measure isolated from other social and political transformations, seeking causal explanations for change in perceived aesthetic or artistic deficiencies.[16] Currently few scholars in the West study this very rich period in Chinese theater history.[17] Opera historians in China have tended to gloss over the late eighteenth and early nineteenth centuries, preferring instead to focus on the heyday of Kun opera in the seventeenth century and the rise of "regional operas" (especially Peking opera) in the nineteenth century.[18] Some surveys of Chinese opera history have given short shrift to the period from 1770 to 1900, in part because the multiplicity of genres playing side by side and interacting in the capital complicates a progressive paradigm of historical change, the telos of which is often situated in the triumph of Peking opera as the quintessential national drama (*guoju*).[19] For neat narratives in which one aesthetic style gives way to a new (and implicitly better) one, the hybridity of opera in the capital over these hundred-plus years is problematic. But for my purposes, the very multiplicity of opera types and styles in this era makes it easier to trace competing values and aesthetic practices—and, by extension, patterns and routes of cultural transmission—in the Qing metropolis. In the course of the narration of a larger story about urban cultural transformation, we will see that the eventual success of Peking opera had as much to do with changing court sensibilities and changing political conditions as it did with the genre's intrinsic aesthetic qualities.

If the teleology in the scholarship on Chinese opera history has been implicit, the assumptions embedded in research on Ming-Qing (and Republican) cities have been made explicit by reflection (for over two decades) on the applicability of Jürgen Habermas's concept of the public sphere to Chinese urban communities. In Habermas's historical sociology of seventeenth- and eighteenth-century England, France, and Germany, the urban public sphere is the crucible from which participatory politics and civil society emerged in Western Europe.[20] Noticing strong parallels between early modern Europe and late imperial China—a burgeoning and vibrant mercantile economy, the proliferation of print culture, and new networks of community and sociability in urban centers—a first wave of historians of urban China in the 1980s and early 1990s sought to locate sites analogous to the European public sphere in Qing and Republican cities: guild and native-place associations, chambers of commerce, and fledgling newspaper societies, for instance.[21] As their critics have pointed out, much as these early studies of Chinese urbanism were intent on debunking Max Weber's caricature of China as the moribund, tradition-bound foil to a progressive and rational modern West, they nevertheless still hitched the signifiers of genuine historical transformation to universalized milestones drawn from the particularity of the Western path to civil society and participatory democracy.[22] China historians might better find "public sphere" parallels in early modern Japan, where the "private realm" of art, fiction, and drama—albeit exhibited in public spaces—could become a locus for dissent and polemics, protected from state seizure (if not intervention) by its canny willingness to relinquish any claim to the public realm of social order and hierarchical control.[23]

But that is not to say that urban spaces in late imperial China could not become loci for the germination of horizontally integrated social organization or even political agitation. A second wave of historical scholarship on Ming-Qing Chinese cities has striven to decouple the urban public sphere from the Western development of modernity and civil society, choosing instead to identify urban spaces that might have fostered social community and mobilization not fully subject to state oversight. Ming and Qing cities, in other words, might share early modern characteristics of social and spatial organization without presupposing that these would end (or ought to end) in democratic process. Susan Naquin's study of temples in Ming and Qing Beijing is representative of this trend, identifying an important "public space" in urban temple life and religious associations.[24] More recently Si-yen Fei has posited that in Nanjing during the Ming dynasty there came to be actual and figurative public spaces—if not public spheres—in which residents of the southern capital could appeal for tax reform and protest construction of city walls, as well as shape their own distinctive urban identity through textual discourse.[25] My work on opera in the Qing capital continues in this vein, for though networks of gossip, news, and sociability in eighteenth- and nineteenth-century Beijing did not generate the overt oppositional politics of the London coffeehouse or the Parisian café, they did produce a vibrant "teahouse" culture of ironic play, sentimental excess, and temporary inversion of social norms; perhaps tellingly, the term "teahouse" (*chayuan*) doubled as an elegant euphemism for the metropolitan commercial stage. The commercial playhouse, I posit, poised at the intersection of private fantasy and public space, was the institution most suited to become a venue for the circulation of desires and ideas among audiences differing in status and background.[26]

A third wave of scholarship on the Chinese urban experience has questioned the basic premise of the Habermasian notion of the ideal public sphere. Informed by scholarly reappraisals of early modern Europe, which have criticized Habermas for overemphasizing the rationality of the public sphere, the works of Eugenia Lean and Haiyan Lee on Republican urban culture have argued that sentimentality and sensationalism were central to the coming into being of a Chinese urban public.[27] Lean has proposed that fervent popular consumption of news cycles reporting causes célèbres trials in the 1930s were instrumental in hailing modern publics into existence; Lee has shown that the tear-jerker Mandarin Ducks and Butterfly fiction of the first half of the twentieth century served as a literary public sphere wherein readers, by identifying with the plights of fictional protagonists, came to affirm a new form of subjectivity of self as an integral component of universal humanity.[28] To be sure, the modern infrastructures and technologies of Republican cities allowed this public sphere of sentiment to be maintained over time and distance in radically new ways, but the potent combination of private passion and public display was not new to the urban experience in twentieth-century China. The operas performed in the Qing playhouses, as I will demonstrate, also reveled in this same mix of sentimentality and sensationalism.

The sentimentality and sensationalism or, more simply, the sex and violence, available to be experienced in this "theatrical public space" will be addressed in my examination of attitudes toward gender and sexuality as revealed through the operas performed in the playhouses of the Qing capital. Numerous literary scholars have assessed gender representations in late imperial Chinese fiction and dramatic literature, but there have been few attempts to examine how elite discourses about gender were refashioned when they moved off the page and onto the stage.[29] This has precluded understanding of values beyond those of the high literary elite. The sources on opera in the Qing capital—including diaries of opera fans, guidebooks to the Beijing demimonde, court edicts, descriptions in novels and popular ballads, and hand-copied scripts (which until now have been used only to write opera history)—allow me to attempt to reconstruct performed drama and thence envision imaginings about gender among middlebrow urban audiences.

Representations of gender hierarchies, I find, often became metaphors for articulating other concerns about social hierarchy and political order (or its lack). In particular, the transgressive woman as a literary trope could have very different social meanings depending upon how a play was performed and who was watching the performance. The study of gender representations thus has implications well beyond our understanding of the lived experiences of women and men; gender is intimately associated with concepts of cultural authority and power. As the works of both Matthew Sommer and Janet Theiss have demonstrated, the Qing state (especially under the activist and expansive policies of the Yongzheng and Qianlong emperors) took a proprietary interest in maintaining gender order. Preservation of the normative familial and gender order was vital to the state's civilizing mission, and by extension, its claims to legitimacy.[30] This helps explain, too, the court's active role in policing both the dramatic content and the social context of opera performance, which was rife with gender inversions and transgressions. A cultural equation of sorts is evident in the operas of the playhouses, in which sex and gender transgression stood for subversive sympathies and social discontent, whereas violence represented authority's punishment for violations of the social norms.

This book, then, is an interdisciplinary study of opera history, urban culture, and gender representation. It establishes that the networks of patronage, gossip, and literati connoisseurship, reflected and generated by the opera demimonde in the eighteenth- and nineteenth-century Chinese capital, formed a public space for social critique and sentimental indulgence. Discourses about power (both corrupted and ethical) were often articulated through romanticized representations of gender and class in the dramatic narratives performed in the playhouses and in the writings by literate commentators about opera and actors. Ethnic tensions between the Qing court and the Han (especially Jiangnan) elite—too inflammatory to be articulated openly—were often couched in cultural policy and aesthetic preferences regarding opera in the capital. Yet, as will become evident, this metropolitan space for commentary and complaint never coalesced into a viable challenge to state authority. By the late nineteenth century the Qing court, embracing a petty urbanite aesthetic and moral sensibility, had either co-opted or marginalized literati resistance, thereby neutralizing the oppositional potential of the urban playhouse and its most educated patrons.

The narrative of this book begins roughly in the last quarter of the eighteenth century, by which time the commercial playhouses in the capital were of sufficient quantity and quality to generate a new genre: guidebooks to the actors and ancillary activities of opera in Qing Beijing. This literature, intended to be ephemeral (and often—then and later—dismissed as not worthy of serious consideration), opens up to us an entire world of hitherto unexplored urban culture in the mid- to late Qing. This culture delighted in wit, sex, wine, pretty boys, mooning scholars, good acting, and pushing the boundaries of respectability. Notwithstanding claims to the contrary by opera connoisseurs, it was also hierarchical and exploitative of those who delivered the joy and entertainment—especially the cross-dressing actor youths. Although as social practice this urban culture was a distinct product of the Qing political settlement, its literature shared certain continuities (sometimes consciously so) with cultural proclivities and sensibilities of the late Ming. Indeed, the commercial opera theater of Qing Beijing did much to popularize late Ming intellectual concerns and practices—from the transmission of the gender politics of Ming literati drama to the elite male vogue for boy actresses. Thus, commercial opera served to broadcast elements of late Ming thought to a much wider and more diverse audience than it had reached during the Ming. And, much as the Qing state strove to reestablish neo-Confucian rigor in intellectual discourse and social practice, it was not capable of squelching all expressions of cultural heterodoxy, even in the immediate precinct of the throne.

This culture came to a close by the end of the nineteenth century. The chaos of the Taiping Rebellion (1850–64) radically realigned cultural dynamics in the Qing capital, impacting actors, audiences, and taste in opera. Other more gradual changes, such as the rise of Shanghai and other treaty port cities as centers for entertainment in the late nineteenth and twentieth centuries, fundamentally altered opera in Beijing. The final blow to this mid-Qing urban opera culture came with the occupation of the capital by the troops of the allied foreign powers in the wake of the Boxer Uprising (1900). The fighting disrupted operation of the playhouses and sent audiences (including those at the court) and actors scattering for safety. Although the playhouses later resumed operation, the demimonde culture of opera in Beijing was never quite the same again.[31]

. . .

This book is structured in three parts. Part 1 begins with a literary analysis of a subgenre of writings known as "flower registers" (*huapu*). Comprised of a tangle of biographical sketches, homoerotic poetry, and theater gossip, flower registers also ranked and commented upon the talents of the actor youths who cross-dressed to play the young female (*dan*) roles. The writers of such texts are some of the earliest historians of performed urban opera during the Qing. In conjunction with contemporaneous fictional accounts of the opera theater, I read these sources as embedded in long-standing literati connoisseurship discourses about taste and distinction. While telling us much about the actors, flower registers also fill in the "cast" among the audience, shedding light, especially, on the representations and self-representations of the operagoer par excellence—the dedicated opera fan. Through close readings of these works of opera connoisseurship, I further reconstruct audience expectations and aesthetics. The very act of writing a guide to actors and the opera theater was a way for literate opera enthusiasts to distinguish themselves as true connoisseurs, superior to the mixed clientele of moneyed patrons (some merchant, some official) who haunted the commercial playhouses of Beijing, if only through their virtual reenactment and appropriation of performance on the page. These connoisseurs—the self-styled cognoscenti—were reinventing through literary production and aesthetic taste a status distinction that had become blurred in the socioeconomic realm. Clearly genuinely interested in the practices and players of opera in the city, these contemporary "ethnographers" of the opera demimonde were also drawn to the theater because it offered such rich parables for articulating lumpen literati preoccupations with talent neglected, virtue unblemished, and power resisted.

Without their accounts, too, it would be impossible to reconstruct the social history of opera in the city, which becomes my focus in Part 2. Whereas Part 1 is framed by the concerns of literate opera connoisseurs, Part 2 adds the perspective of the state, especially the Manchu court, necessitating an examination of ethnic tensions as well as tensions of gender and class. Chapter 2 maps out the spatial dynamics of opera within the capital by focusing on three of the key venues in which it was performed: the playhouse, the temple fair, and the salon. Operas, actors, and audiences literally moved from venue to venue, but gender, class, dialect affinity, and ethnicity all in certain ways restricted those patterns of movement and interaction. Opera in the capital, I argue, encouraged multiple boundary crossings—both literal and figurative—making it suspect in the eyes of the state. State regulations attempted to police such crossings to limited effect. Furthermore, the experience of opera connoisseurs mingling with other social classes in the all-male audiences of the playhouses, instead of forging a sense of shared cultural identity, made the cultural critics even more conscious of status distinctions.

Chapter 3 reads opera genre as a contested cultural field in which various agents—the court, Jiangnan music sophisticates, marginalized men of letters, and acting troupes—each held a stake. Whereas the court sought to assert symbolic supremacy in cultural taste and to control social order in the capital by dictating what might be performed, erudite Suzhou scholars of the most elegant (Kun) opera style aimed to rescue their preferred musical genre from "corruption" in the commercial opera marketplace. Meanwhile, down-and-out literate commentators often championed the new and exciting lowbrow genres of opera on display in the capital; and opera troupes and actors struggled to eke out a living in the interstices between court regulation and audience demand. By the end of the hundred-plus years from 1770 to 1900, the opera hierarchy in the capital had been thoroughly reordered. Kunju was on the decline, and formerly proscribed lowbrow genres of opera, such as *pihuang*, had ascended the ladder of cultural taste, in large measure due to court patronage. Taken together, while Chapter 2 charts the court's ineffectual struggle to regulate the locations of playhouses within the city, Chapter 3 shows that, even though the Qing court lost the battle over where opera would be performed, over time it largely won the war on what would be performed.

Against this backdrop of social tensions I reconstruct the performances of specific sets of dramatic scripts in Part 3, tracing the interplay over time between gender and class as markers of moral authenticity and political regeneration in commercially performed operas. Chapter 4 examines the drama *The Garden of Turquoise and Jade* (*Feicui yuan*), written in Suzhou in the early Qing, and its several kunju performance redactions. In the play a poor scholar, an attractive itinerant seamstress, and a bumbling but good-hearted policeman are empathetic and righteous role models fighting against the corrupt power of political cronyism and entrenched masculine privilege. The popularity of this drama onstage reveals that urban audiences identified with the plight of the downtrodden. But whereas in the playwright's script justice prevails at the end through the intervention of morally upright representatives of the state, performance versions typically closed with the protagonists on the run and the mother of the intrepid seamstress dead. This suggests that audiences appreciated (and opera troupes presented) a dose of tragic but heightened realism in their entertainment fare. Commercial Kun opera, with its sympathy for the victimized gender and classes, offered metropolitan audiences not only a space for sentimental escape but also a forum for expression of pointed social complaint.

Moving from a melodrama about raw abuse of official privilege to family romances rife with desire and gender transgression, Chapter 5 centers on a series of performance scripts about adulterous and treacherous women—the "sisters-in-law" (*saozi*) of the chapter title. The plots of these operas all evolved out of the *Water Margin* (*Shuihu zhuan*) story cycle. Although the cautionary message of these operas was never far from the surface, it is clear that in many of the scripts the characters' transgressions—the sex and the violence—were what audiences found compelling. Through contextualized readings of multiple redactions of these operas, I demonstrate that the scripts with greater literary sophistication (i.e., kunju scripts) tended to remold the women of these tales into clever (if comic) and sympathetic romantic heroines. In contrast, scripts crudely cobbled together and directed to less literate audiences (i.e., huabu scripts) focused on the revenge of the male characters and their eventual murder of the licentious woman. The chapter further addresses the "scene selections" (*zhezi xi*) staging of commercial opera, with attention to the way this practice altered the original frame message of the playwright's edition. In the abridged plot sequences of the "sister-in-law" operas in the literate kunju tradition, the focus of the plays switched from the husband's humiliation and revenge to the wife's romantic liaison. The kunju treatments of this material loosely operate within a literary discourse (traceable to the late Ming) in which nubile women and their unbridled passions are imagined as signifiers of authenticity.

The tension between class and gender transgressions so central to these plots was refigured when these tales were appropriated and adapted yet again for performance in the pihuang opera genre in the mid- to late nineteenth century. The pihuang operas of this story cycle evince a romanticized class narrative of male brigandage and brotherhood (with roots also traceable to the late Ming), in which violence wins out over the social disruption of sex and romance. Late Qing court enthusiasm for the populist pihuang opera, I suggest, forged an unlikely marriage between action-play violence and state-promulgated familial and gender orthodoxies. As court patronage elevated pihuang's cultural status, this more misogynistic and moralistic opera treatment came to be embraced by a wider urban audience.

All three parts of this book attest to the place and power of opera in Qing Beijing. Opera had the power to upset social hierarchies: it could make men of means and privilege vulnerable to the charms of lowly cross-dressing boy actresses; it could parody social and cultural norms; or it could be harnessed to the state's civilizing mission. Opera served as a kind of cultural glue—

creating shared repositories of cultural knowledge (if not common cause) across gender, class, and ethnic differences within the Qing capital. The opera theater was a key site of public discourse in the Qing metropolis; and to the extent that it fulfilled that role in the urban community, it was also a site of competition, conflict, and controversy.

PART ONE
Audiences and Actors

ONE

Opera Aficionados and Guides to Boy Actresses

> Ever since the *Orchids of Yan* was registered, spreading tales of gay affairs,
> Year upon year, time after time, a new version is published.
> Be it *New Poems on Listening to Youth* or *A Record of Viewing Flowers*—
> To think that money is actually paid for such frivolous rubbish!
>
> 譜得燕蘭韻事傳，年年歲歲出新編。《聽春新詠》《看花記》，濫調浮詞竟賣錢。
>
> *Bamboo-Branch Ditties from the Capital*, 1814[1]

> Sitting in the balcony of the playhouse, it's so easy to lose one's heart;
> The "old roués" are flush with cash and puffed up with pride.
> Hoping for nothing but a smile bestowed from behind the curtain,
> Even thousands in gold can't buy them the joys of the "exit-door" side.
>
> 茶園樓上最消魂，老斗錢多氣象渾。但得隔簾微獻笑，千金難買下場門。
>
> *A String of Rough Pearls*, 1809[2]

Opera wielded a seductive power over its audiences in late imperial China. As revealed in these two Chinese-style limericks, or "bamboo-branch ditties" (*zhuzhici*), which were recorded early in the nineteenth century, the allure of the world of theater and the charm of its performers could lead literate men to squander their money on doggerel written in praise of actors and could turn wealthy men into pitiful fools for love.

The first limerick offers a tongue-in-cheek assessment of texts known as *huapu*, texts that evaluated the looks and talents of opera actors. *Huapu* came into vogue in the last quarter of the eighteenth century. Part biography, part display of poetic virtuosity, and part assorted trivia about the demimonde of eighteenth- and nineteenth-century Beijing, this genre of writing primarily recorded the skills and exploits of actors who performed the dan role, that is, youths who cross-dressed to play the part of young women characters in various regional styles of opera (or, as I will call them, the boy actresses). This particular limerick not only identifies the huapu genre but also explicitly refers to the first text of its type, *A Brief Register of the Orchids of Yan* (*Yanlan xiaopu*), written by Wu Changyuan and printed in 1785. Yan refers to Yanjing, the name commonly used for Beijing during the Qing dynasty, because Beijing is located in what was once the territory of the ancient state of Yan. "Orchid" (*lan*) refers specifically to the actor featured centrally in *Orchids of Yan* (who was noted as an amateur painter of orchids on folding fans) and alludes more generally to the "flowers"—the cross-dressed boy actresses—of the metropolitan stage. The limerick is simultaneously dismissive of the quality of writing in huapu and revealing of their popularity: these texts were published "year upon year, time after time," and apparently sold very well.

The second limerick caricatures a certain type of opera fan, the "old roué" (*lao dou*), or, more colloquially, the "sugar daddy."[3] The lao dou was characterized as a theatrical patron who had a surfeit of money and time on his hands and who indulged in the pleasures of the theater (including the purchase of intimate relations with boy actresses and entertainment after performances in the winehouses ringing the commercial playhouse district). Not necessarily elderly, he was old relative to the actors he ogled; and the "old" in this appellation is more an honorific (if laced with sarcasm) than a descriptive modifier. Often too, the lao dou is depicted as not entirely in the know when it comes to evaluating the quality of dramatic performances. Rather, he is a bit of a philistine, substituting money for what he lacks in taste and refinement, and easily swayed by immediate sensory perceptions such as pretty faces and revealing gestures. The stereotypical old roué also had a penchant for sitting in the seats facing the onstage exit door (*xiachang men*), what we would call the stage-left balcony seats (Figure 1). Within the commercial playhouse these seats were highly coveted because they afforded patrons the best angle from which to exchange meaningful glances (diagonally across the stage) with actors entering the stage through the entrance door (*shangchang men*), upstage right. As one mid-nineteenth-century huapu author put it: "The most expensive . . . seat is the second one in the 'exit-door box,' as that is a convenient spot from which to intercept

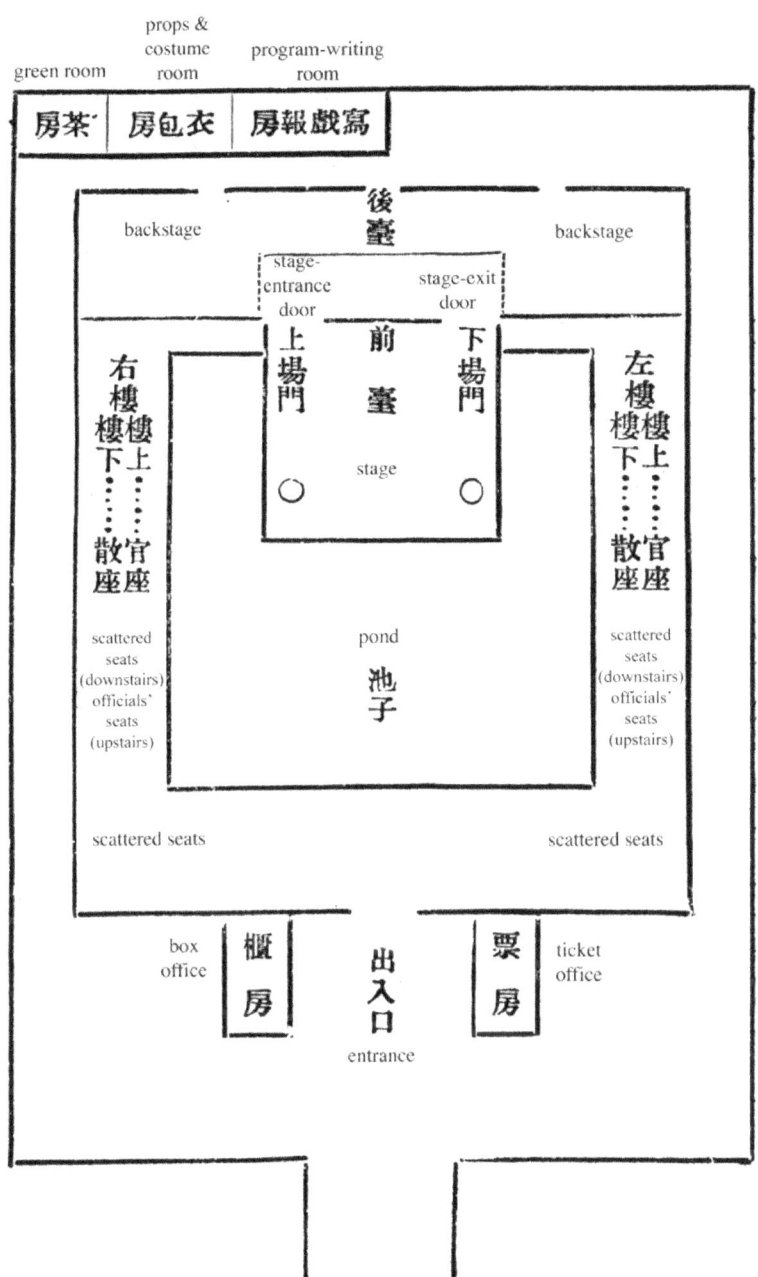

Figure 1. Schematic diagram of the floor plan of a typical Qing-era playhouse. Adapted from Aoki Masaru, *Zhongguo jinshi xiqu shi*, p. 513.

a sign of the heart or the wink of an eye sent as [an actor] pushes aside the curtain to enter. As a bamboo-branch ditty [says]: 'a dizzying glance flies to the balcony above; it clinches a date for dinner tonight.'"[4]

The image of the opera fan, whether the lascivious lao dou or the more sophisticated connoisseur, cannot be separated from huapu, which captured and recorded (sometimes with willful distortion) these characterizations of eighteenth- and nineteenth-century theater patrons. In fact, much of what is known about opera performance in Beijing during the Qing—about actors, about styles of singing and acting, about management of commercial playhouses, or about commonly performed plays—is culled from huapu. Chinese-language scholarship on Qing-dynasty opera has assiduously mined huapu for nuggets of historical fact but has largely ignored them as a literary genre or as a source illuminating the cultural practices of the entertainment demimonde.[5] A recent English-language study by Wu Cuncun has relied upon huapu to reconstruct a history of male same-sex desire in the Qing.[6] But whether writing theater history or social history, scholars have generally looked through—but never at—the huapu.[7] In contrast, I treat the literary claims of the huapu seriously as texts of theatrical connoisseurship; by taking a close look at the various discourses constituting huapu, I aim to gain a more nuanced reading of the social and cultural practices of metropolitan theater in the Qing. The huapu turn out to be as revealing of their author-aficionados as of the actors they wrote about, opening a window onto a middling stratum of literati culture in the late empire.

The production of huapu texts came in two waves. During the second half of the eighteenth century the circulation of huapu in manuscript and in print emerged in tandem with the maturation of a vibrant commercial playhouse culture in the Qing capital. Testament to a metropolitan theater that had become—in the words of its fans—"foremost throughout the realm," these texts were a phenomenon almost exclusive to the capital; although the authors of such texts came from various locales throughout the empire, with few exceptions all huapu or huapu-like memoirs were about the actors and demimonde of Beijing.[8] During the mid-nineteenth century the cataclysmic crises of civil war and foreign aggression slowed the tide of flower-register writings. When huapu production picked up speed again in the 1870s, such texts began to shift their focus from cross-dressing dan actors in a variety of commercial opera genres to critical assessment of a wider array of theatrical role types and increasing attention to northern styles of performance. My readings are based on the extant huapu compiled from 1785 through the first half of the nineteenth century (approximately fifteen works), the first wave of huapu production. These texts especially capture a waggish—even permissive—mood that is rarely associated with Qing intellectual culture, and for this reason, too, are worthy of consideration.

Central to texts of connoisseurship in general and huapu in particular is the concept of evaluative classification (*pin*), used to rank everything from poetry to people. I begin, therefore, with a brief discussion of this concept and the history of its use, showing how allusions to pin enabled Qing theater enthusiasts to position themselves in debates about taste and distinction. Next, I place the Qing-dynasty huapu in the tradition of evaluative biographies of entertainers that dates from Sun Qi's late ninth-century *Chronicles of the Northern Quarter* (*Beili zhi*). Writers of huapu engaged in what I call a "borrowed discourse," invoking the language, imagery, and tone of earlier texts on courtesans and actresses to assess adolescent males specializing in female roles. In appropriating the rhetorical strategies used for courtesan entertainers to record the charms of boy actresses, huapu writers signaled their perception of opera players (especially of the dan roles) as purveyors of erotic as well as theatrical spectacle. Yet I hesitate to cast these chroniclers of the theater in the role of the libertine. Huapu writers stressed that they were seeking sensibility—not sex—and their deft rhetorical positioning signifies their awareness of the stigma associated with the sex trade in boy actresses. Beyond eroticism, the connoisseurs found something deeply appealing about the female gendering of the dan actors: the combined vulnerability and resilience of the imagined feminine subject position spoke to their own senses of self.

Huapu also blended the connoisseurship literature about courtesans with the city guidebook genre. The latter had a venerable history of commenting on the delights of urban theatrical spectacles, beginning with Meng Yuanlao's 1147 memoir of Kaifeng, *A Dream of Splendors Past in the Eastern Capital* (*Dongjing menghua lu*). On the one hand, like guidebooks, huapu served a practical function. They were discursive maps of one segment of the city—the entertainment district—and could be used by would-be audiences to locate the places and people associated with opera in the capital. In this guise, the huapu writer acted as both ethnographer and tour guide, brokering insider knowledge of the metropolitan theater world to outsiders seeking a way in. On the other hand, huapu often exuded a strong sense of nostalgia for cherished places and entertainments. The sentimental, wistful quality of such writings reveals as much about the author and his perceived relation to his object of study as it does about the city and the world of theater itself.

For all the attention that huapu paid to actors and demimonde gossip, the star of such texts was the author. He (and it was always a he) was the opera fan par excellence, the true cognoscente. Through his writings about the theater scene in the capital he could record his aesthetic choices for both his peers and posterity. The voices of these opera enthusiasts ring out the most clearly, whereas the interests and opinions of other patrons and the actors are muted and mediated by the texts that purport to represent them. The writer was often a sojourner to Beijing (frequently from Jiangnan or places farther south), and his prefatory remarks usually traced his trajectory from neophyte to cognoscente. Often depicted as having rejected the "official life," or its having rejected him, the connoisseur drowned his disappointment in obsession with the theater. His dismal prospects in public life—resulting from a lack of recognition of his talent—moved him to identify with the lowly actor and partly drove his interest in recognizing, ranking, and recording the skills of actors. The connoisseur as huapu author was concerned with both the physical charms and the artistic prowess of the actors he cataloged, but he insisted that it was his appreciation of talent that distinguished him from less sophisticated fans.

His protestations to the contrary, the flower-register connoisseur was nonetheless also clearly fascinated with the seedier side of the opera world but cloaked this interest in ethnographer-like comments about the taste of the lao dou, whom he often characterized as "great patrons" (*hao ke*) or "wealthy merchants" (*fu gu*). The huapu writer's distinctions between self and lao dou betray his unease about class and status, likely fostered by the manner in which he partook of the theater. The flower-register literature of opera connoisseurship was a by-product of the mid- to late Qing commercial playhouse. Unlike their late Ming literary exemplars, who mostly experienced and wrote about theater in private settings, the men who chronicled eighteenth- and nineteenth-century opera had to share their experience of it with anyone who could afford the ticket price. This troubled them. By their own accounts, they shared the playhouses with men whom they considered their social and cultural inferiors. Through appropriation and transference of the world of performance to the page, these connoisseurs were reinventing (and reclaiming) a status distinction that was being eroded in the socioeconomic sphere.

The Texts

The introductory passage to Wu Changyuan's *Orchids of Yan* combines a clever mix of whimsy and precision:

> Orchids are not native to Yan, and yet the *Commentary of Master Zuo* [*Zuo zhuan*] records that Consort Ji of Yan had a dream about an orchid in which she was told: "The orchid is the lord of fragrance, and so men are won over to it." Thus, we know that the intrinsic virtue of the orchid has been recognized both in the north and in the south. It was midsummer of 1783; [the actor] Wang Xiangyun had a penchant for making ink-brush paintings of orchids. Because he painted several stems of orchids on a folding fan, I, together with some like-minded friends, took a sudden fancy to elaborate upon this gay amusement by making a record of it. My idle humor not yet abated, I further culled and assembled lore on the best actors to create *A Brief Register of the Orchids of Yan*. This work covers altogether fifty-four actors from 1774 to the present and records 138 poems about them. It also contains a total of fifty entries of miscellaneous verses, anecdotes, and hearsay. It begins with the poems on painting orchids in recognition of its original inspiration. It follows with the entries on the "orchids of Yan," which praise the various actors. It ends with verses on a variety of subjects, which are invested with sardonic words of caution.[9]

In this recollection of a summer's lark Wu's pleasures in the theater and in the literary games of polite society are reined in and ordered by classical allusion, meticulous detail, and numerical particularity. In style, tone, and content this "register" of opera actors ushered in a subgenre of connoisseurship writing about performers, especially about actors playing the dan roles. The three main features of *Orchids of Yan* that he mentions—the use of poems to describe actors, the ranking of highly skilled actors, and the recording of trivia and gossip about contemporary theater—would be borrowed in part or in full by literate fans writing about theater up through the early twentieth century.

The huapu was a relative latecomer to a long tradition of connoisseurship texts that claimed to rank and evaluate things and people. The authors of huapu consciously positioned themselves as the inheritors of that tradition through the use of literary allusion in the prefaces, preambles, and colophons of their texts. As poets, "collectors," and ethnographers of the commercial theater, they presented themselves as the arbiters of good taste. Their writings were virtuoso performances on the page for like-minded opera cognoscenti, and it is clear that many of the huapu writers were in dialogue with each other. Simultaneously they looked outward, capturing the social reality of urban performance; looked inward, writing for the small coterie of social peers who also composed and read such texts; and looked backward, drawing upon a literary tradition that legitimized an interest in things both frivolous and contemporary. I will discuss each of these three perspectives in turn, beginning with the look backward.

RANKING, TASTE, AND THE CONCEPT OF *PIN*

Huapu writers signaled their position within the tradition of connoisseurship through the key conceptual words and generic styles they chose for their writings. One such concept was *pin*, which, like the English word *taste*, refers both to the ability to distinguish flavor and to aesthetic judgment (both meanings are rendered in Chinese as *pinwei*). Unlike the English *taste*, however, *pin* has a broader range of meanings having to do with ranking, classification, and evaluation. It is the combination of aesthetic taste, ranking, and evaluative judgment that gives the term *pin* potency in connoisseurship discourses.

Originally associated with grading men for public office, the term *pin* had, by the Six Dynasties, become an important conceptual rubric in literary and artistic criticism applied to categorizing and ranking poets and artists, poems and paintings. As late as the eighteenth and nineteenth centuries allusions to seminal texts of pin literary criticism could still be found in flower registers, although the immediate precursors of late imperial huapu literary conventions were books that evaluated "literati things," which by the Southern Song had come to include poetry, calligraphy, painting, and other artifacts of scholarly material culture.[10] During the Song catalogs, or "registers" (*pu*), of fashionable collectibles—perfumes, bronzes, wines, rocks, and various kinds of flowers and plants—proliferated. Inherent in the hierarchical distinctions of these catalogs was an expression of literati taste, captured in the evaluation and classification of "sensual things" (*youwu*).[11] The Song horticultural catalogs are the original flower registers, the textual references that Qing chroniclers of actors implicitly invoked when calling their own writings flower registers.

Beginning in the mid-Ming, the concept of *pin* underwent a new development: pin-style evaluation was reapplied to humans, except that the subjects of appraisal were now people at the lowest end of the social hierarchy—entertainers. This reorientation of pin classification from things to "playthings" was facilitated by the lexical slippage between precious things and beautiful women within the Chinese literary imagination. The slippage is graphically captured in the expression *youwu*, which, denoting both "sensual things" and "alluring women," figured prominently in the various genres of "writings on things" (*yongwu*). This literary legacy paved the way for the multiple metaphorical meanings of the term "flower" to refer to women, especially courtesans, and then, through association, to boy actresses. Although never oblivious to the humanity behind the "beautiful creatures" they described, authors of huapu collected and ranked actors and their talents in much the same way they might accumulate or appraise other fine artifacts of literati consumer culture.[12] This commodification of entertainers exhibited in catalogs was part of a larger trend in connoisseurship writings in general.

Literati interest in cataloging fine objects reached its heyday in the late Ming, as the work of Craig Clunas and others has shown.[13] This development—a product of dramatic increases in book publication and growth in markets for luxury goods—was fostered by the rapidly expanding commercial economy in the fifteenth to sixteenth centuries. Writing about objects in the late Ming was a mark of distinction, something that differentiated elite connoisseurs from nouveaux riches merchant-dilettante impostors.[14] As Wai-yee Li has observed, the literatus wrote about objects so as to assemble and order his world; the process, she tells us, "simultaneously pointed inwards and outwards, defining the self at the same time as it ranked and judged the material world."[15] Clunas has further identified late Ming fine-goods catalogs as a site where literati connoisseurs contested for cultural power with merchant upstarts wanting to translate their economic resources into cultural capital.[16]

Similar tensions are revealed in the eighteenth- and nineteenth-century registers of actors. By the mid-Qing, with the emergence of the urban commercial playhouse, the new site of cultural competition had become theatrical entertainment (and the fine youths who brought it to life). In their ranked guides to boy actresses, huapu writers playfully appropriated the pin-connoisseurship tradition as a means of ordering their experiences of the heady jumble of the world of urban performance. In doing so, their catalogs of "sensual things" shared in literati practices of knowing and differentiating the self and the surrounding material world.

BORROWED DISCOURSE

Situated broadly within the pin-connoisseurship literary tradition, huapu writers took their cue more narrowly from one strand within that tradition—

evaluative writings about courtesans and actresses. These, too, afforded an ample supply of literary templates upon which they could draw to legitimate their interests in recording the lives of performers. And they took pains to make the literary genealogy explicit for their readers. In the preface to the first huapu Wu Changyuan staked out his position as the inheritor of that literary tradition:

> Those books by writers past that recognize beauty—*A Record of Southern Flowers in the Mist* [*Nanbu yanhua lu*], *Chronicles of the Northern Quarter*, . . . *Miscellaneous Notes from the Wooden Bridge* [*Banqiao zaji*], and even Zhao Qiugu's *A Brief Register of Foam on the Sea* [*Haiou xiaopu*]—are all about female courtesans and not about boy actresses. Even those actors recorded in the *Blue Tower Collection* [*Qinglou ji*] are female performers of dan roles.[17]

Wu's *Orchids of Yan* is an effort to remedy the exclusion of the male actor—or, more precisely, the boy female impersonator—from this connoisseurship genre.

To educated readers of the time Wu's litany of titles would have been most evocative, conjuring up romantic decadence and the faded glories of famous entertainers of times past. His choice of antecedent texts is particularly studied, embracing broad expanses of history and geography. The first of the titles, *A Record of Southern Flowers in the Mist*, is a highly embellished account of the amorous adventures of the last Sui emperor, Sui Yangdi, on his travels to his provisional palace at Yangzhou.[18] To those familiar with the text (or simply with the "licentious last emperor" lore surrounding Sui Yangdi), the very setting of Yangzhou would have brought to mind "dreams of Yangzhou" (*Yangzhou meng*), which, harking back to an allusion in a poem by the late Tang poet Du Mu, had become metonymic for trysts with courtesans.[19] By beginning with *Southern Flowers in the Mist*, a text that mixes prurient voyeurism with cautionary injunctions against hedonism, Wu implies that his own literary venture shares this conflicted perspective on *its* object of description—the cross-dressing boy actresses.

The next three texts that Wu mentions—*Chronicles of the Northern Quarter*, *Miscellaneous Notes from the Wooden Bridge*, and *A Brief Register of Foam on the Sea*—are also records of famous courtesans. Written in the late ninth, late seventeenth, and early eighteenth centuries as nostalgic memoirs of the pleasure quarters of Chang'an, Nanjing, and Tianjin, respectively, these accounts of courtesans—medleys of biographies, poems, and anecdotes—became the stylistic models for *Orchids of Yan* and other huapu.²⁰ Wu Changyuan's choice of title for his collection—the "brief register" of his *Orchids of Yan*—was surely inspired by Zhao Qiugu's *Brief Register of Foam on the Sea*. Wu himself does not belabor the point; rather, he leaves it to his friend and fellow contributor of dedicatory remarks to the volume, the Raconteur of the Western Hillocks (Xicheng waishi), to alert readers to his inventive—if borrowed—title.²¹

The last title mentioned in Wu's prefatory passage, the *Blue Tower Collection*, by Xia Tingshi (ca. 1316–after 1368), is a mid-fourteenth-century collection of biographies of performers, mostly female, from Yuan-era Dadu (Beijing). Written as a series of short entries, it comments on both the looks (*se*) and artistry (*yi*) of each entertainer, occasionally adding remarks about a performer's familial or artistic lineage and her admirers or patrons. Although *qinglou* in the title (a colorful term for a brothel, which puns on *qinglou*, meaning "tower of desire") clearly links the work to the world of courtesan entertainment, *Blue Tower Collection* had come to be known primarily as a collection of biographies of actresses.²² It wedded courtesan literature to theatrical connoisseurship; and for this reason Wu Changyuan gave *Blue Tower Collection* ultimate pride of place in his list of originary texts.

The works mentioned in Wu's preface are among the textual icons of courtesan literature. Strewn with the phrases and images of earlier prototypes, such texts acquired an ever-increasing density of allusion, as for example, in the preface to Yu Huai's *Miscellaneous Notes from the Wooden Bridge*, which is larded with references to "southern flowers in the mist" (*nanbu zhi yanhua*) and "occasional strolls through the Northern Quarter" (*ou wei beili zhi you*); or, for instance, in the poetic preambles to *Brief Register of Foam on the Sea*, in which the author expresses remorse for his passionate indulgences in language highly reminiscent of Du Mu's poem about his "dream of Yangzhou." Huapu writers borrowed for their own works the highly self-referential and imbricated quality of the language of courtesan connoisseurship literature. Their rhetorical strategies—comparing actors to flowers, projecting an eroticized gaze on the performers, and blending titillation with a tone of *tristesse*—draped metaphors of courtesan beauty and talent onto the cross-dressing boy actresses. By cloaking their records of contemporary actors in the discourses of courtesan literature, huapu authors simultaneously sanctioned and sensualized the huapu, enabling them to tap into the rich repertory of descriptives, metaphors, and allusions to corporeal beauty while obviating the need to talk directly about sex. Such veiled eroticism was part and parcel of the aesthetic appeal both of the eighteenth-century commercial theater and of the texts written about it.

Later huapu took their cues from *Orchids of Yan* in bringing courtesan literature to bear on their comments about actors. *New Odes to While Away the Winter* (*Xiaohan xinyong*), a collection of actors' biographies composed in 1795, compares its project to texts that dwell on "dreams of Yangzhou" and "the ladies of the willowy lanes."[23] A prefatory poem in the early nineteenth-century register *A Brief Register of Songbirds and Flowers* (*Yinghua xiaopu*) explicitly equates its thirteen select dan actors with the Qinhuai district courtesans of late Ming Nanjing.[24] The sixteen-year-old Tianxi, according to one writer, would rival the grace of the Ming courtesans of the Qinhuai were he to exchange his hat for a woman's chignon.[25] And an actor listed in the 1837 *Record of Viewing Flowers in the Capital* (*Chang'an kanhua ji*) is framed by reference to "Zhao Qiugu's *Brief Register of Foam on the Sea*, in which [Zhao] describes [a courtesan as] 'like a bird alighting on one's shoulder' [*feiniao yiren*]." The actor here described, the connoisseur goes on to tell his readers, resembles the courtesan in that he "really moves people with his tender mien."[26]

The writers of huapu, and their friends and commentators, brought literary precedent to bear mostly in the prefatory material. It was as if, to fend off the accusation of dabbling in "frivolous rubbish," huapu authors felt the need to shore up their choice of theme with the cachet of a by-now-respected tradition of courtesan connoisseurship. In the prefaces the flower-register writers strike poses and justify their interests—framing their connoisseurship collections to the outside world. In the body of huapu texts, however, the discourse of the courtesan literature that they have appropriated works somewhat at cross-purposes to the exculpatory tone of the prefaces; the courtesan literature discourse enables opera fans to read the charms of boy actresses as feminine wiles, revealing that, in the minds of male connoisseurs, the performer—and especially the female impersonator—was gendered female.

The rhetorical gendering of the dan performers was achieved, in part, by inscribing metaphors of courtesan beauty onto the boy actresses—foremost among them being the flower conceit. Just a glance at the titles of huapu attests to the ready analogy of beauties to flowers in such texts. *New Odes to While Away the Winter* assigns the name of a flower to each of its actors, and these designated flowers then become the thematic tropes within the poems eulogizing the actors. An afterword to an 1803 huapu, *A Record of Viewing Flowers in the Precinct of the Throne* (*Rixia kanhua ji*), makes the most excessive use of flower imagery:

> A total of eighty-four actors are recorded here.... Nine types are recorded. Why the nine types? Each is according to a category.... Spring flowers are the most beautiful, just like the actor Langyu. And so, beginning with Langyu, there are eight entries for actors of outstanding beauty. Autumn flowers are the most graceful, just like the actor Xiufeng. And so, beginning with Xiufeng, there are nine entries for actors who excel in grace. Between beauty and grace come the warmth of spring and the crispness of autumn; it is hard to capture both qualities in one actor, but doesn't Liuxi capture both? ... In spring, blossoms; in autumn, fruit: plants that flower naturally bear fruit; the blossom must wither for the fruit to be plucked. This is a case of skill surpassing beauty. Of this type there are ten actors, including Gu Changsong.... As for the young kids with their hair still done up in tufts, they are like buds just beginning to open. Whether they possess the intensity of spring or the subtlety of autumn remains to be seen. Those selected for inclusion here all have the potential to become exquisite.[27]

Pin ranking is paired here with the flower as metonym of feminine/actor essence. In this passage, written by a certain Petty Historian Who Feasts on Flowers (Canhua xiaoshi), methodological seriousness is applied to something utterly trivial. A legitimizing, formalistic style is conflated with the sensually indulgent content. Even the author's pseudonym captures this sanction/sensuality duality of huapu writings: he applies the careful methods of the historian to savoring the visual delights of the flower-actors.[28] His fine distinction between types of flowers barely muffles an affective obsession that he can master only through excessive cataloging; and his indulgence in such a scholastic disquisition on flower-actors is what distinguishes him as a true connoisseur.[29]

The eroticized and feminizing gaze on dan actors permeates huapu writings. Throughout these texts actors are compared to crab-apple flowers or to lotuses, or they are described in clichés of female/flower beauty—"so like a pear blossom under the light of the moon" or "with a few plum-blossom freckles dotted upon hibiscus cheeks."[30] Mining the phrasebooks of female loveliness, the texts describe actors as "beauties" (*jiaren*), as having the looks to "topple fortresses" (*qingcheng*), or as possessing "delectable beauty" (*xiuse ke can*).[31] One huapu author comments that "watching new actors take the stage is just like seeing a new bride on the third morning after her wedding;

[they] retain a touch of shyness, which only makes them seem even more lovely."[32] Another enthusiast writes of the female impersonators by using the highly suggestive term *youwu*—creatures of supreme sensuality.[33] In a poem dedicated to the dan actor Fan Rulan, an entranced critic claims, "When [Rulan] has sung through to the red water-flower coda, there's no one who would take him for anything but a girl."[34] The second quatrain goes on to describe the actor's quirky charm, and in midstanza the gaze shifts its focus from Rulan's looks to the effect they have upon the admiring poet:

> His staged smile breaks into a toothy grin, yet still his aspect is fair;
> With such delicate charm, who can tell if he wears a cap or pins in his hair?
> After the lucky scholar is just slightly flushed with wine,
> By the light of a sliver moon, he succumbs to the embrace of rhyme.[35]

In this poem the opera connoisseur flirts with the contrasts posed by the cross-dressing actor who, even offstage, seems more girl than boy. The natural grin, which breaks through the acted smile of the boy female impersonator, only makes him more fair in womanly terms, and his poise and allure blur the distinction between "he," who would wear a cap, and "she," who would adorn herself with hair ornaments. The balance tips toward the feminine side in the poet's mind, where, enhanced by drink and moonlight, the gender transformation finally is consummated.

This verse is just one example of literally thousands of poems about and biographies of actors that delight in this sort of teasing eroticism. Even as late as the 1870s, after huapu authors began to include biographies of actors playing the older male role types into their collections (claiming greater interest in acting talent than in physical attraction), they continued to describe dan actors in eroticized, feminine terms. In his *Record of Cherished Flowers* (*Huaifang ji*), for instance, the author comments: "Su Shi once remarked that tasting [the flesh of the sometimes poisonous] porpoise was worth the risk of death. I say that if [the actor] Qiufu were a woman, and were to become my concubine, that too would be worth dying for."[36] As many such examples illustrate, opera aficionados were well aware that they were watching male youths playing the roles of women. Often the texts remind the reader that analogy, not realism, is at work: they speak about the actor *as if* he were a woman; when in costume, two actors look "*as if* they were sisters, or *as if* they were . . . first wife and consort";[37] or a certain actor makes one "forget that he counterfeits to be a woman."[38] Nonetheless, huapu compilers found these youths attractive even when out of costume. *Orchids of Yan* appreciatively notes of the actor Li Xiuguan: "After he's out of makeup, when he pulls aside the curtain [from backstage] to sneak a peek [at the audience], his wrist and fingers are as if made of jade."[39]

Performing gender with a touch of gender ambiguity was part of the entertainer's appeal. As scholarship on late imperial courtesan literature has noted, it was the literate courtesan—the woman who had mastered the male scholar's skills of literacy and poetry—who held the greatest allure.[40] Her ability to transgress gendered social practices, that is, to play at androgyny, enhanced her charm. Similarly, in mid-Qing texts on dan actors, the way boy actresses performed women teased gender boundaries, and the theatricality of cross-gender performance ultimately was part of the attraction.[41] Rather than being the exact double of the courtesan, the boy actress was the reverse image in the mirror; his appropriation of feminine attributes captured in one persona both hetero- and homoerotic appeal.[42] Borrowing the literary devices of courtesan literature when portraying dan actors helped to put under erasure the overt homoeroticism of the Beijing commercial theater and the huapu.

Flower-register imitation of the tropes and rhetorical strategies of writing about female entertainers, of course, was made possible by the social practices of the Qing entertainment demimonde, in which boy actresses performed the role of courtesan both on and off the stage. Boy actresses could be contracted for sex as well as for their entertainment services, and the business relationship between young actors and their trainers was much like that between prostitutes and their madams.[43] As in the female sex market, talent and the cultural capital it generated could be used as leverage against the sale of sexual services: those actors with the greatest artistic reputations were afforded the luxury to sell their wit, charm, and talent more than their bodies.[44] As with female courtesans, those actors who could preserve their "chastity" in the face of the ancillary depredations and demands of their occupation were praised and celebrated all the more in the biographies written on their behalf.[45] Hence, the image of the spotless lotus growing out of mud was every bit as apropos a metaphor for the boy female impersonator ensnared within the urban opera demimonde as it was for the courtesan in the pleasure quarters.

The parallel circumstances of the lives of actor-catamites and courtesans were reflected as well in the language used to relate these demimonde social practices. The term *lao dou* for wealthy clients or patrons of boy actresses was borrowed from the trade jargon of female prostitution. Like the entertainment services provided by female prostitutes, the after-theater soirées for which boy actresses were hired to sing, pour wine, and play drinking games were known as "tea gatherings" (*chawei*).⁴⁶ The mid-nineteenth-century huapu writer Yang Maojian remarked on the resemblance: "Passing the time in brothels," he observed, "is talked about as 'holding a tea gathering' [*da chawei*]. Visiting the residences of the various actors to engage in lighthearted conversation is also called 'holding a tea gathering.'"⁴⁷ The miscellaneous notes section of *A Record of Tear Stains from the Golden Stage* (*Jintai canlei ji*) further acknowledges the indebtedness of the theatrical demimonde to the language of courtesan culture:

> A prime minister is called an "assisting lord" [*xianggong*], the meaning of which is based on [the duties of those who serve as] lords and officials of state. Scholars are called *xianggong*, the meaning of which is borrowed from the term for a minister of state; this meaning has been in common use for a long time. The city-dwelling men in the north are all called "master" [*ye*]; investigation reveals that their courtesans are sometimes called *xianggong*. City-dwelling men in the south are all called *xianggong*; those in the Wu region also call their courtesans *xianggong*. Those who perform the *dan* roles in the capital playhouses are called *xianggong*. Though I do not know when this practice began, doesn't it signify that this meaning is also borrowed from the term for courtesans?⁴⁸

The commentator's brief history of the multiple meanings of the term *xianggong* indicates that not only is the actor reflective of the courtesan but both actor and courtesan are framed by terms on loan from the world of officialdom. And this, too, is a wholesale appropriation from the discourse of late Ming courtesan culture.

In writing about late Ming pleasure culture, scholars strongly identified with the courtesans they documented. They transformed the courtesan into a signifier for something greater than herself: standing for authenticity—the embodiment of noble passion, or *qing* (despite the obvious paradox of the salability of her love)—the courtesan was the scholar's double, the pathos of her compromised bodily and emotional purity echoing that of the scholar forced to prostitute his talents in the political marketplace. But since the courtesan was often depicted as surpassing the scholar in integrity, she also retroflexively exposed the careerism of the scholar-bureaucrat, thereby iterating through contrast a kind of literati self-reproach.⁴⁹ These tropes were so thoroughly seeded in the literati imagination that well into the nineteenth century they could be applied almost seamlessly to catalogs for boy actresses, that is, if the courtesan pointed to the literatus, then by appropriating the courtesan discourse for actors, so, too, did the dan actor.

Unlike in seventeenth-century writings about courtesans, however, the pointed pathos of actors' lives in huapu was not inflected by the trauma of dynastic rupture. The early Qing courtesan literature harked back longingly to a temporal and political distance that could never be recovered; in contrast, the mid- to late Qing huapu appropriated the longing tone to speak to a more personal sense of anomie. Maybe for that reason—as well as for their homoeroticism—huapu have always been considered less poignant—and less important as literature—than their stylistic antecedents. Nevertheless, the tropes of this literature had been set by the time of the Ming collapse, and by the late eighteenth century it must have seemed natural to borrow the pensive, brooding commentator's voice regardless of the changed social context.

When flower-register writers commented on the parallels between actors' and courtesans' lives, they were careful to distance themselves from the market in male prostitution (and in this respect, too, they differ from earlier biographers of courtesans); their tone switched from enthralled fan to bemused ethnographer.[50] They broached the subject of actors' sex work obliquely, couching it, for instance, in detached philological notes about the term *xianggong*, or tucking it, now and then, into apologetic parenthetical asides in the biographies of skilled performers with "tarnished" pasts. Their coy rhetoric in this regard is reminiscent of seventeenth-century literati writings about male-male desire, which Sophie Volpp has perceptively labeled the "ethnographic mode," a literary manner that decenters and deflects such practices as curiosities always happening elsewhere in time and space.[51] But in contrast to late Ming cultural commentators such as Shen Defu (1578–1642) or even Zhang Dai (1599–1684?), the observers of the mid- to late Qing metropolitan theater come off less as armchair ethnographers; the huapu connoisseurs were writing from *within* the demimonde—their "fieldwork" consisting of, among other things, joining dan actors in postperformance drinking games and poetry parties.

When they did write about their own more intimate engagements with actors, the huapu authors professed to be latter-day devotees of the "cult of qing," in search of the ideal expression of emotive feeling, something that they took pains to differentiate from sexual license. The most sublime pleasure, as one connoisseur put it, is "getting slightly tipsy in the midst of flowers." The author continued with a description of a "tea gathering" with a few friends at the residence courtyard of one of his favorite dan actors on a calm, moonlit night: "Some sipped tea, others played chess, still others ingested the night fragrance or gazed at paintings—each seeking out his own delight. [My friend] the poet tapped out a kun rhythm while the actor Yanxian accompanied him on the flute. At that moment the jade disk of the moon and the jadelike actor vied with each other in radiance. The branches in the courtyard exhaled puffs of perfume as if in counterpoint to the elegant music."[52] This passage emphasizes sensuality rather than raw sexuality. It defines the supreme expression of sensual climax as a chaste—unspent—desire, and this aesthetic preference tempers the homoeroticism of the transvestite theater and its literary chronicles.[53] Flower-register authors might relate gossip about love affairs between boy opera stars and famous statesmen, but often with the stated point of showing actors embodying the ideals of true friendship—loyal to their patrons even after these men of power had fallen on hard times.[54]

The *tristesse* of the actor's plight held a special poignancy for huapu writers. The dan actor as symbol of despoiled purity—compromised both by his occupational hazards and by the passage of time (since flowers wither and die)—spoke to the writers' own sense of personal and temporal loss. It also allowed them to present the charms of boy actresses as informed by more universal concerns with the evanescence of life and beauty. In the words of one huapu preface,

> Ranking actors and distinguishing [literary] talent may seem to be cut from a different cloth but can achieve the same results. In the search for perfection, plain clothes and fine robes are displayed side by side. Suspended between illusion and reality, sadness and joy both mount the stage. . . . Ah, how sad that time passes never to return; the theaters and stages of the past already have been replaced. Know now that this, too, is the fate of men. Have no illusions about what the future holds in store for voice and beauty. The fisherman attempting to return lost his way to the Peach-blossom Paradise. Since the alabaster beauty's passing, the palm-dancing consort of the Shaoyang Palace whirls no more.[55]

The mood of the authorial voice here recalls early Qing memoirs about famous late Ming courtesans, in which, as Wai-yee Li has observed, the "pain of remembrance retroactively legitimizes pleasure."[56] The nostalgic melancholy of the eighteenth- and nineteenth-century flower registers works in much the same way—alternately enhancing and constraining the eroticism of these texts. Thus, huapu writers, when adopting the discourse of courtesan literature to describe boy female impersonators, were borrowing not only literary tropes for categorizing beauty but also strategies for negotiating between pleasurable desire and a desire for respectability.

HUAPU AND URBAN MEMOIRS

Huapu had a practical side, too: they collected and recorded the ephemera of the city; and since actors and the cultural life generated by urban theater were key attractions of eighteenth- and nineteenth-century Beijing, huapu served as a specialized kind of guide to the sights and pleasures of the capital. Combining factual information on how to identify and locate the city's best actors (their names, troupe affiliations, and—sometimes—places of residence) with more subtle guidance on how to recognize artistic excellence and physical beauty (and which actors excelled at which roles), huapu initiated the reader into the domain of theatrical connoisseurship. Balancing the detached eye of the ethnographer with wistful longing for vanished people and things, huapu authors conveyed not only how to watch plays but also how to play the aesthete. In this regard they had a respectable literary tradition to fall back on: the urban memoir. By peppering their texts with the appropriate allusions, they placed themselves within a textual genealogy dating back to the mid-twelfth-century record of Kaifeng, *A Dream of Splendors Past in the Eastern Capital*.

A chatty account of the pleasures of the prosperous capital city of the Northern Song, *Dream of Splendors Past* has been characterized as literate but not highly literary, reflecting the sensibilities of a leisured and educated (but not necessarily officially positioned) urban stratum.[57] The central motif of the title, "dream of splendors" (*menghua*) works as a pun, alluding both to the vibrancy of the metropolis and to the mythical kingdom of Huaxu—an Elysium that one could visit only in a dream. This pun aptly captures the central tension in this work, between the dazzling enumeration of quotidian delights of food, spectacle, and entertainment and cautions about the impermanence of worldly things. Written from the author's refuge in the southern city of Shaoxing some twenty years after the fall of Kaifeng, *Dream of Splendors Past* is intrinsically nostalgic, attempting to reconstruct the lost capital through memory; it compensates for the material loss of the city by capturing, collecting, and classifying its charms in the written word.

As attentive readers of the literary legacy, Qing-dynasty huapu writers found in *Dream of Splendors Past* a ready blueprint for articulating their own fascination with the minutiae of the urban demimonde. The precedent set by this and other nostalgic guides to cityscapes enabled them to cast their own writings as party to a larger endeavor of preserving the ever-vanishing past. The first writer who explicitly linked huapu and the urban memoir tradition was Yang Maojian, whose 1842 text, *Assorted Notes toward a Dream of Splendors Past* (*Menghua suobu*), performed a dual act of obeisance to literary inheritance and of self-flattery via direct allusion to the "dream of splendors." A close look at his literary apology will illuminate other huapu as a subset of this genre.

In the opening passage Yang characterizes his flower register as belonging to the realm of historical discourse, within which he identifies two strains of writing: official history and private history. Both strains, he observes, have long been used to document city life. The official history culminates, Yang writes, in the late eighteenth-century imperially commissioned compendium of the sights of Qing Beijing, *A Study of Ancient Accounts from the Precinct of the Throne* (*Rixia jiuwen kao*).[58] In Yang's words, "This is an enormous compendium, with the likes of which my innumerable jottings could never dare to compare."[59] Though feigning humility before court-sponsored history, Yang clearly identifies with a private scholarly tradition of historical authorship. "Beginning in 1831," he writes,

> I spent eight years as a sojourner [in the capital]. Thinking back on it now, it was like viewing flowers from on horseback; it was all as if in a dream. In the Song dynasty there was *A Dream of Splendors Past in the Eastern Capital*, which recorded the prosperity of Bianliang [Kaifeng]. During our dynasty Sun Chengze wrote *A Record of Remembered Dreams of the Capital* [*Chunming mengyu lu*]. I've secretly cultivated myself in the mold of these writers, desiring to create something comparable. For that reason, I've called this *Assorted Notes toward a Dream of Splendors Past*.[60]

Nearly all huapu authors made some claim to be writing in a historical vein, even if they did not explicitly mention earlier literary guides to cities. As the three compilers of *New Odes to While Away the Winter* state, "We place those who live by mounting the stage and making music into the poet's bag; and we enable those decked out in costume and makeup to ascend the rosters of private history."[61] Mixing self-pity with self-vindication in the preface to his *A Record of Viewing Flowers in the Precinct of the Throne* (*Rixia kanhua ji*), the main author, The Latter-Day Adept of the Iron Flute (Xiao tiedi daoren), complains that he has been "reduced to writing the history of entertainers."[62]

Zhang Jiliang, writing *A Record of Tear Stains from the Golden Stage* under the literary alias Master of Huaxu (Huaxu *dafu*), goes so far as to append personal commentaries to his biographies of actors, all of which begin with the phrase, "The Master of Huaxu says" (Huaxu *dafu yue*)—clearly both a salute to private memoir-style history of the "dreams of Huaxu" variety and an attempt to mimic, and mock, the commentary tradition of "grand history."[63]

The claim to be writing history was both genuine and rhetorical posture; after all, most flower registers were about contemporary or near-contemporary people and things. Nevertheless, the authors envisioned themselves as leaving a record to posterity. The majority of huapu authors writing between the 1780s and the 1840s were historians only insofar as they were biographers. Three flower registers from this period, however, Wu Changyuan's *Brief Register of the Orchids of Yan*, Zhang Jiliang's *Record of Tear Stains from the Golden Stage*, and Yang Maojian's *Assorted Notes toward a Dream of Splendors Past*, made more ambitious claims as works of minor history. And it is these three texts that most closely resemble the urban memoir literature.[64] In the fifth and final *juan* of his *Orchids of Yan*, Wu Changyuan dispensed with actor biographies and instead adopted a rambling, discursive style, loosely stringing together anecdotes and lore related to theatrical performance in the capital. The jottings discuss such matters as musical styles or where certain patrons sit in the audience. "In the past," one entry reads, "when dan actors in the capital imitated [walking with] bound feet, the practice was limited to just a few plays and their movements were always rather tentative. Ever since [the actor] Wei San came to prominence, all [dan actors] use [fake] bound feet when they take the stage; their feet dance and their eyes flash in perfect harmony with the plot."[65]

Half a century later Zhang Jiliang, emulating Wu Changyuan's huapu, appended a volume of assorted notes to his own huapu. These notes record more than thirty items of historical or contemporary lore concerning performances in Beijing—everything from the patois of the opera demimonde to the locations and admission prices of the city's theaters. Zhang's text suggests that he is applying the methods of Qing evidential scholarship to the subject of urban theater. He writes, for example: "Among actors in the south over half of those who play the young female roles are named so-and-so *guan* [*mouguan*]. Based on evidence recorded in *Brief Register of the Orchids of Yan*, it can be verified that in times past this was also common practice among dan actors in the capital. In those days there were also dan actors named so-and-so *er* [*mouer*]. Nowadays that simplicity has been replaced with literary airs. The fashions of our times are truly lamentable."[66] The huapu writers' ethnographic look at capital theater culture is also evident in Yang Maojian's *Assorted Notes*, which devotes an entire flower register to "anecdotes, talk overheard at banquets, self-mocking stories told by those fallen upon hard times, information gleaned from scraps of old paper, and gossip from the alleys—anything having to do with the theater."[67]

Huapu authors appropriated not just the style but also the tone of the urban memoir tradition for their biographies of contemporary actors, invoking the melancholic coupling of personal loss with worldly pleasure, and the Buddhist-influenced trope of the dreamlike quality of all earthly things. In the process, they translated the temporal nostalgia of *Dream of Splendors Past* into figural loss, retaining the nostalgic voice even when writing about the present. The textual preservation of theater sights and the nostalgic framing of such texts were two sides of the same ethnographic-historical project: one a history of the "other"; another, an allegory of the self. If, as James Clifford has observed, ethnography aims to capture on the page a disappearing object, an other who is lost "in disintegrating time and space," employing a tone in which "nostalgia is as much self-definition as memory,"[68] then the nostalgia of the Qing huapu is actually about the evanescence of beauty and talent, where the plight of the actor-object redounds to that of the connoisseur-scholar.[69] In this doubled narrative of self and other, the legitimizing nostalgias of both borrowed discourses—courtesan literature and urban memoirs—merge.

Zhang Jiliang is the most eloquent—if somewhat maudlin—articulator of the centrality of nostalgia and pathos to the historian's calling. Placing himself in a line of chroniclers emanating from Confucius, he prefaces his flower register with the following lament:

> Confucius wept over the capture of the unicorn, and ever since there have been two kinds of tears in this world.[70] Jia Yi [200–169 BCE] of the Han dynasty cried about the times in which he lived. Ruan Ji [210–263] of the Jin dynasty cried over his own lack of career prospects. I have lived in the capital for three years. I have observed closely the present state of the world; I can offer advice about what will benefit it and can cure its ills. But since I had no one to provide me with an introduction, I dared neither to submit suggestions nor to write them in books; hence, I cried bitterly. My family encountered many misfortunes, and lamenting that my talents had gone unrecognized, I cried bitterly again. My friends took pity on me, and fearing that I might grow sick with grief, they frequently sought out youths from

the opera troupes to amuse me with song and wine. Once drunk, I would cry bitterly yet again. Now, I am about to return to my natal home. While sorting through my old clothes, I happened upon a piece still stained with my tears from days gone by. With a sigh I said, "I may have cried the last of my tears, but the stains remain behind." Even so, my fond affections of times past should not be forgotten. And so it is that I composed these ten biographies, fifty-nine poems, three elegies, and thirty-seven miscellaneous entries. Yan [Beijing] has long been a golden site for theater. For this reason I call this collection *A Record of Tear Stains from the Golden Stage*.[71]

The written record is cast as—in the words of another huapu author—an expression of "knotted melancholy" (*chou jie*).[72] The scholar sheds his copious tears more for himself than for his companions in solace—the lowly, unappreciated actors. Likewise, by leaving records of the actors to posterity, he also ensures his own survival in the literary legacy. Neither the nostalgia nor the underlying story of the authorial self necessarily negates the description of the outside world in these records. Rather, the representations of both selves and others in these texts are, to borrow Paul Rabinow's insight about the phenomenology of ethnographic practice, "social facts."[73] The dual narrative of the huapu provides two interrelated histories—one pointing inward to the cognoscenti authors, and one pointing outward to the circumstances of actors, performance practices, and theatrical patronage in Qing Beijing.

The Connoisseurs

Writing and reading huapu demanded two kinds of inside knowledge—fluency in the literary tradition (to appreciate the allusions and import of the poetry and prefatory prose passages) and familiarity with the theatrical practices in the capital city (to decipher the jargon and shorthand for plays, actors, and performance techniques). Mastery of the former required years of training in classical texts; of the latter, residence in Beijing and the leisure and funds to spend one's days watching plays and associating with actors. Possession of both types of expertise distinguished the opera connoisseur.

There is something almost staged about huapu writings, as if through choice of literary styles and motifs the authors were self-consciously performing for literary, aesthetic, and social peers. These literary tours de force usually were not enacted alone. Rather, by contributing dedicatory poems, prefaces, and afterwords, friends and fellow aficionados played supporting roles in each other's flower registers; and these cameo appearances further enhanced the self-image of the opera connoisseur. Always played to that audience of peers (the look inward), huapu reenacted on the page the camaraderie and wordplay exhibitionism of the literary salon. Participation in the creation of flower registers, in other words, both reflected and sustained a belletristic social community.

TEXTUAL COMMUNITY

The printing of Wu Changyuan's *Orchids of Yan* in 1785 established a new tradition of urban theatrical connoisseurship, prompting emulation and the publication of new flower registers "year upon year" and "time after time," as the humorous popular ditty put it. These texts entered into conversation with other contemporary and near-contemporary huapu; their authors were highly conscious of participating in the creation of a new textual tradition. *Orchids of Yan*, the pioneering text of the genre, is often acknowledged in other flower registers, as, for instance, in the following description of an actor listed in *Viewing Flowers in the Precinct of the Throne* (1803): "*Brief Record of the Orchids of Yan* [1785] regarded [the actor Wei] Wanqing as the leading female [impersonator] of his age. The same could now be said of [the actor Gao] Langting."[74] Two nineteenth-century huapu, *Tear Stains from the Golden Stage* (1829) and *Assorted Notes toward a Dream of Splendors Past* (1842), frequently reference *Orchids of Yan*, *Viewing Flowers in the Precinct of the Throne*, and other flower registers in reconstructing the historical practices of opera performance in the capital.[75] Sometimes the nod to textual predecessors is somewhat oblique; surely, The Petty Historian Who Feasts on Flowers was invoking the Wu Changyuan's *Orchids of Yan* in his disquisition entitled "On Orchids" (Lan wen).[76] So, too, the author of *The Realm of Many Fragrances* (*Zhongxiang guo*), who in explicating the motivation for his own collection of poetry about actors claims that "actors as comely as Song Yu become a pretext for these minor verses, the Orchids of Yan a reason to reinvent this brief register."[77]

In other huapu, the authors' recognition of belonging to a textual community is expressed by explicit positioning vis-à-vis other flower registers. Authors often mention having read or consulted contemporaneous flower registers, or they try to explain their own works in contradistinction to other huapu. One huapu writer observed that he disagreed with "a friend's" flower-register ranking of a certain actor in the "the top spot."[78] And the afterword to *Viewing Flowers in the Precinct of the Throne* poses this question: "How does this record compare with others such as *Orchids of Yan*, *Extended Record of Dream Splendors* [*Menghua wailu*], *A History of Flowers in the Phoenix City* [*Fengcheng huashi*], and *A Record of Appraising Flowers of the Yan Stage* [*Yantai jiaohua lu*]?"⁷⁹ Its author, The Latter-Day Adept of the Iron Flute, responds to his own question:

> Last summer by chance I perused several flower registers, but none of them were to my liking. The problem was that their entries were either all based on hearsay and their criteria for selection were erratic, or that those actors who occasionally met with favor did so because the authors were partial and biased. I'm afraid that even after having written my draft volume, *An Occasional Record of Judging Flowers* [*Panhua oulu*], which strove for greater subtlety and was rather pithy in places, I still overlooked orchids in favor of mugwort and discarded jade while retaining common alabaster. For this reason, I had a couple of close friends review it, only then trusting that what lay in my heart day after day was not simply personal whim. Then, after careful revisions, I finished this draft, naming it *A Record of Viewing Flowers in the Precinct of the Throne*.⁸⁰

The Latter-Day Adept was clearly familiar with the huapu genre and drew inspiration from previous works in this style for his own creation. Even his self-deprecatory remarks about his abilities to distinguish talent—the references to orchids and jade—can be read as subtle replies to the images studding the preface to Wu Changyuan's *Orchids of Yan*.

The Latter-Day Adept's comments further underscore that writing a huapu was in itself often a communal endeavor: he needed to verify his own standards of theatrical appreciation against the opinion of friends. According to the postscript to *Orchids of Yan* by the Recluse of the Drunken Bamboo (Zhuhan jushi), this was a common practice. The Recluse writes: "Every time the Mountain Woodsman [Wu Changyuan] finished a draft, he showed it to me for critique, and this has gone on now for many a day."⁸¹ Some huapu were more open collaborations, such as *New Records on Listening to Youth* (*Tingchun xinyong*), which anthologized poems evaluating the talents of dan actors by some thirty different litterateurs.⁸² Soliciting from friends dedicatory poems, prefaces, or afterwords for flower-register collections most openly expressed the participatory quality of the compilation. As one contributor to *Listening to Youth* explained, "The Petty Historian of the Approaching Vernal Pavilion showed me a draft . . . and requested that I add some ink to it."⁸³ Clearly, the huapu authors who read each other's works, and who upon request, "added some ink," were mostly good friends or close acquaintances. From *A Precious Mirror for Ranking Boy Actresses* (*Pinhua baojian*)—the mid-nineteenth-century novel set in the Beijing demimonde—we see that literati social gatherings furnished prime occasions for the creation of huapu.[84] A connoisseur's poem about a favorite actor, then, quite often entailed a literal as well as a literary performance. Wu Changyuan suggests as much when, in commenting on the inspiration for his *Orchids of Yan*, he remarks: "I, together with some like-minded friends, took a sudden fancy to elaborate upon this gay amusement by making a record of it."[85] The flower-register textual community reflected an underlying social network of men of letters linked in part through devotion to opera connoisseurship.

SOCIAL MILIEU AND SELF-REPRESENTATIONS

It is difficult to gauge how large a community of opera connoisseurs existed in mid- to late Qing Beijing. Those who left behind guides to the opera theater were surely a minority; and we know from Qing commonplace books that many educated men, who did not devote whole texts to recording the biographies of popular actors, wrote about performance in passing. Reconstructing the biographies of individual huapu authors can be difficult, in part because writers often did their best to conceal their identities by using pseudonyms, only a handful of which can be matched to historical figures. Of sixteen extant huapu written between 1785 and the 1840s, authorship has been verified for only seven, and four of those are by the same author.[86] For the remaining texts, the most that can be identified is a surname, as in the case of *New Odes to While Away the Winter*, for which we know that the trio of compilers bore the family names Li, Liu, and Chen.[87]

This practice of adopting whimsical pen names further underscores the ambivalence that lettered men felt about being known as creators of such works. Using pen names was one way they negotiated between play and respectability. The huapu, in other words, was intentionally a semipublic text: its content was open to a well-read audience, but the author's identity was veiled—at most, accessible only to the select few fellow connoisseurs who were close enough friends of the author to know his various literary aliases. As one huapu commentator put it: "The point of adopting a sobriquet is to allow one to engage in frivolous writing. Those who know [the author's real name] naturally are in the know, but it is not necessary for everyone to know."[88] Then again, since the turnover of actors in the capital was rapid—

according to one account, a new generation of dan actors came to the stage every five years—these theater guides quickly fell out of date; and few connoisseurs, surely, wished to be identified with old stars and old news.[89] The pseudonym protected the critic's reputation, keeping him as ephemeral as the acting world he described.

Whether or not the huapu authors can be identified, they were all classically trained and some were highly cultivated. Their prefaces and dedicatory remarks show their delight in the conspicuous display of esoteric erudition. Nearly all of the prefatory materials parade the writers' training in parallel prose, a rhetorical craft that demanded rigorous formalistic and thematic pairing of poetic couplets or allusions. At times a literary parlor-game quality creeps into these writings, as, for instance, in the prefaces and poems in *A Record of Collected Fragments* (*Pianyu ji*), in which the first two characters of every phrase or stanza correspond to the first two words of poems by either Yuan Zhen (779–831) or Yuan Haowen (1190–1257).[90]

Literary skill, however, does not seem to have translated into success via the traditional path to bureaucratic advancement—at least, not often. If huapu writers were insiders when it came to mastery of the lettered arts, for the most part they were outsiders when it came to having the social position that theoretically devolved upon those educated in the high cultural tradition.[91] Relegated to the margins of political power, these men devoted themselves—often ostentatiously, even defiantly—to urban theater culture. Here, too, however, the mid-Qing chronicler of actors negotiated a fine line between insider and outsider, using his ethnographic perspective to mark a respectable distance between himself as observer and the theatrical demimonde as observed. This jockeying for position exhibited in huapu—the simultaneous claims to be insider and outsider—captures an analogous concern on the part of the connoisseur to distinguish himself in the social realm.

One of the most successful careers of a huapu writer was that of Wu Changyuan, originally a native of Hangzhou. Beginning in 1783, Wu spent more than ten years in the capital, some of that time serving in a modest post as an editor of imperial documents.[92] He had obtained the highest-level *jinshi*, or presented scholar, degree and was apparently on reasonably good terms with fellow Hangzhou native Yu Ji, since the latter, a Hanlin academician, wrote a preface for Wu's 1788 guide to the sights of Beijing, *A Concise Sketch of the Imperial Enclosure* (*Chenyuan shilüe*). Although little else is known about Wu Changyuan, it is tempting to associate him with the influx of literate men summoned to the capital to work on the *Com-*

plete Works of the Four Treasuries (*Siku quanshu*), on which Yu Ji was active, or on other late Qianlong-era imperially sponsored editing projects. Or, given Wu's authorship of *Concise Sketch of the Imperial Enclosure*, a "pocket-edition" guide to the city, he may have had some role in the imperial publication of *Study of Ancient Accounts from the Precinct of the Throne*.[93]

More typical of huapu compilers, however, were the circumstances of the author of *Record of Collected Fragments*, who mentions in the marginal notes to his biography of actors that he failed the 1804 metropolitan-level examination; or the three authors of *New Odes to While Away the Winter*, who lament that their "ten years of study by the light of the window have been in vain for as many spring and autumn moons."[94] Another author who failed to move up the examination ladder was Zhang Jiliang, author of *Tear Stains from the Golden Stage*. Zhang, a prolific poet from Fujian, in 1825 had traveled to the capital to participate in the metropolitan exams. His literary talent caught the eye of Yao Ying, a former magistrate in Fujian Province, and, as Yao's protégé, Zhang was introduced to various literary salons in the capital, eventually becoming a central figure in the Spring Purification Association (*zhanchun ji*).[95] The patronage networks fostered through such loose associations of scholar-poets, as the work of James Polachek has shown, often served as a conduit for political advancement; when official appointment was thwarted, these groups became the locus of oppositional sentiment—often voiced through aesthetic pursuits.[96]

In Zhang's case, personal eccentricity and failure to curry favor with powerful metropolitan patrons condemned him to perpetual *juren*, or provincial-level examination, status. In 1829 he complained bitterly in the preface to his huapu about being closed out of the world of officialdom. The tears of self-pity induced by his frustrations were channeled into empathy for actors, culminating in the recognition of the talents of the opera world in his *Tear Stains from the Golden Stage*. Zhang also did not shy away from using his record of actors to voice disgust for the hypocrisy of successful bureaucrats. He ridiculed those powerful officials who fraternized with dan actors while publicly mouthing neo-Confucian pieties; and he castigated fellow provincial graduates who, in his view, took advantage of actors.[97]

Zhang's Fujian compatriot Yang Cuiyan, author of *A Collection of Goose-Tracks from the Yan Stage* (*Yantai hongzhua ji*),[98] seems to have taken a somewhat more sanguine approach to examination failure, as is suggested by the long descriptive title to one of the poems in his collection, which explains, "[My friend] Liu Lixian failed the exams and had set a date to return home. Suddenly, he made plans to stay through the summer, at which I was so happy that I sent him this poem in jest. Lixian recently has become close with [the actor] Yang Manqing (Qingxi)."

> A cuckoo caws at the moon and the traveler's thoughts fly home;
> Who would've thought at the moment of return his plans would go all wrong?
> I love the Three Mountains of Fujian and I'm crazy for Little Brother Four (Lixian);
> But half the reason he's staying on is for his willow-flower Yang.[99]

In this instance, examination failure gives would-be officials all the more opportunity to linger in the capital and spend time with their favorite actors.[100] In another poem in the collection Yang describes daydreaming within his examination cubicle about his diversions in the company of actors. Yang Cuiyan's jottings reveal that while in Beijing he boarded at the Jade Antipodes Cloister (Yuji-an), located in the southern half of the city, but once he departs the capital—about late 1831 or 1832—he falls out of the historical record.[101] Whether he was assigned a post in the Nanjing region or was following a relative there is ambiguous.[102] In either case, he fit the pattern of the huapu writer social type, essentially a literary "insider" relegated to the fringes of officialdom.

The carefree tone in Yang Cuiyan's poetry is somewhat unusual. Most huapu writers adopted a plaintive whine, as in the preface by Zhang Jiliang or in the autobiographical musings of Yang Maojian. Something of a polymath, Yang Maojian in his youth had studied under Ruan Yuan at the newly established Xuehai Academy in Guangdong, where he had been trained in evidential scholarship, poetry, and Chinese and Western mathematics.[103] Stationed in Beijing for eight years beginning in 1831, he twice failed the metropolitan-level jinshi exams and was temporarily jailed for having used a taboo character in his replies on the exam the second time.[104] Thereafter doomed to a life of exile, he comments on his fortunes in the opening passage of his *Assorted Notes*: "As a young man, I listened to the rain from inside the opera house; in middle age, I listen to the rain from within the cabin of my traveler's boat; the shadowy illusions of this present world have left me quite out of joint."[105]

Other huapu connoisseurs express even greater resentment at their exclusion from the upper reaches of the political elite, for this affected not only their career prospects but also their accessibility to the opera world. As one writer complained, "From my listening perch behind the thrust of the stage, the song and dance are partly concealed; when it comes time for a moonlight assignation, the double curtain of the secret chamber is not rolled up for me."[106] He continues, "I take advantage of my fleeting glimpse of things ephemeral to tell the tales of actors. My dreams are not careerist like the Dream of Nanke, and my heart goes out to a pretty smile."[107]

The themes that emerge from such writings—the sojourner (usually a southerner) waiting in the capital for his moment of opportunity, the boredom generated by the waiting (which is assuaged by indulgence in the theater), and the lament over his own wasted talent and frustrated ambitions—are brought together most poignantly in the opening passage of the dedicatory remarks to *Orchids of Yan*, in which the commentator, The Raconteur of the Western Hillocks, paints a virtual (self-)portrait of the opera connoisseur-cum-huapu writer:

> The western wind in the trees shakes the leaves downward with a sigh early one morning. The black hat of a recluse visible amid the yellow dust, the sojourner has been detained for so long in his solitude. Watching the boldly passing days, a white frost crystallizes in the hair. Listening to murmuring new voices, Blue Tower Dreams get broken. In the midst of this ennui, one creates some words of fond infatuation. The delighted giggles and the angry curses are written into chapter and verse; the jostle of bracelets and whirl of flowers become one with the World of Brahma. Seeking out singing boys and comparing talents, one occasionally joins actors in casual amusements. The dance stages and the song daises become the stuff of idle chitchat filling the Watery Heaven.[108]

In this verbal tableau the thickly laden imagery of the parallel prose presents the quintessential cognoscente as a world-weary sophisticate suspended in time and place at the autumn of his journey. As if in imitation of the ironic couplings of locutions, the passage portrays the connoisseur as a man who has reached transcendence through (perhaps in spite of) immersion in quotidian pleasures. These images are echoed in the preface to *Viewing Flowers in the Precinct of the Throne*, in which the author writes: "As for me, I am a man with white hairs in the red dust of this world. For three years I have relied on the kindness of others, having squandered everything like whitecaps on a windy sea. All that remains is amusement in dissipating pleasures."[109] As sojourner, bureaucrat, and epicure, the connoisseur-huapu writer is poised on the cusp of an insider-outsider divide. He represents himself as down and out in the capital, and his straitened circumstances confer upon him (he professes) a cool perspicacity with which he eyes the surrounding material world.

The huapu writer's embrace of the world of opera often is presented as a principled stance against careerism; and in this guise—in the deliberate turn from politics to pleasure—the connoisseur willfully adopts the role of the eccentric. Flower registers draw heavily upon imagery and allusions associated with past eccentrics—paragons of talent and virtue who had retreated from politics for less tainted pursuits. They invoke, among others, Qu Yuan (340?–278 BCE), Ruan Ji (210–263), Wang Xizhi (303–361), and Du Fu (712–770)—all literary luminaries left "out of joint" by the times in which they lived.[110] And the Raconteur of the Western Hillocks sums up his dedicatory remarks in *Orchids of Yan* with this analogy: "Should you claim that, upon reaching middle age, Wang Xizhi gave vent to his feelings of sorrow and joy [in his preface to the *Orchid Pavilion Collection*],[111] then, truly, you understand us. If you say that, while at Wu Gorge, Du Fu praised [the unacknowledged virtuosity of Song Yu's rhapsody on] the tryst of rain-and-clouds,[112] then, indeed, this endeavor is just the same."[113]

The allusions and rhetoric displayed here are entirely consistent with the broader aesthetic vogues of literary circles in late eighteenth- and early nineteenth-century Beijing. In his study of early nineteenth-century poetry clubs, for instance, Polachek has shown that the self-identification of a marginalized stratum of frustrated exam candidates with poet-aesthete culture heroes extended beyond the written page. Poetry banquets held by the Spring Purification Association—the literary circle to which the huapu writer Zhang Jiliang belonged—conducted ceremonies to reenact Wang Xizhi's Orchid Pavilion Gathering.[114] And in their emulation of great literati eccentrics this "brotherhood of aesthete-connoisseurs" (as Polachek has called them), took their grandiose vision of themselves and their chosen passion very seriously. For flower-register writers, that passion was opera.[115]

For huapu writers, too, the eccentricity of the true connoisseur was manifest in his actions as well as through his words; he was someone who derived pleasure from violating the proprieties of polite society.[116] Yang Maojian's characterization of one Chubby Zhu the Ninth (Zhu Jiu Pangzi) captures the image of the eccentric opera buff:

> Chubby Zhu the Ninth, grandnephew of the late Grand Mentor, was a peculiar man.[117] He spent his days wandering the opera halls. When people

saw him, they would call out, "Brother Nine, come have a seat," and he would sit right down. If you were to ask him, "Which troupe is performing at which playhouse?" or "Which actor is performing what play today?" the litany would come tripping off his tongue like so many beads on a string. But before a single aria had come to an end, he would have sauntered off. He had something of the aura of the Jin [dynasty eccentrics] about him.[118]

A few pages later, in a description of his own behavior at the playhouse, Yang Maojian casts himself as the eccentric:

> Once at the height of summer I went to the Guangde Playhouse to hear a performance by the Chuntai troupe. It was extremely hot. [My friends] . . . were already at the theater. The red-hot sun had climbed high in the heavens, and there was not the faintest wisp of cloud in any of the four corners of the sky; the sight of it was enough to make my horse pant like a working ox. . . . By the time I arrived, sweat was pouring down my body like sauce. I was uncomfortable, but there was nothing I could do. I leaned against the balustrade of the balcony and cast my eyes downward. From amid the teeming sea of humanity a roiling rumble of chatter and laughter bubbled upward to meet me like steam in a cauldron. [The actor] Qiufang was performing "Selling Rouge," and his acting was incredibly suggestive, which only made me feel all the hotter. On impulse, I untied my belt and draped it over the balustrade. I loosened my summer gown and fanned my bare chest. I caught sight of a watermelon and downed the whole thing, and then, only after quite some time, was I able to cool down. From all over the theater—balcony and house floor—ten thousand eyes stared at me. Acquaintances and strangers alike all exclaimed: "What a wild man this is!" The next day news spread quickly throughout the capital that a bare-chested man had gone into the playhouse. Concerned friends sought to counsel me, saying, "Confucianism has its own realm of pleasure." I laughed, saying, "I may not live among the land of bare beasts, but man, after all, is naked, too. What harm is there in roaming about in the flesh? It's not that I'm wild; it's just that man's nobility lies in his mind."[119]

An eccentric's break with convention could also be conveyed through his aesthetic preference in opera, as Wu Changyuan's *Orchids of Yan* illustrates. One manifestation of Wu's cultural defiance was his eclectic embrace of both the kunju and huabu styles of opera. As a scholar from Hangzhou, he naturally would have been drawn to Kun opera; by the mid-seventeenth century, kunju—originally derived from embellished songs from the Suzhou region—had come to be the opera of choice of the lettered elite. Huabu (a broad category that included most regional musical genres other than kunju) was considered far less refined—both musically and linguistically—than kunju. Lumped under the general rubric of huabu were various forms of *bangzi* opera (*bangzi qiang*, or rhythmic-block melodies), including *qinqiang*—a musical style that had originated in northwestern China and that over the course of the eighteenth century seems to have followed merchant trade routes from Shanxi and Shaanxi into the capital.[120] As if flouting long-standing literati standards of taste, Wu Changyuan gives pride of place to "flowery opera," devoting three of the five juan of his flower register to huabu actors and only one to kunju performers. His valorization of the lowbrow huabu opera would have been read at the time as a bold move.[121]

Just how radical Wu's preference was is underscored by his cautious defense of his focus on bangzi opera actors at the expense of kunju. He explains: "[The qinqiang actor] Wei Changsheng initiated the current style in performance. Though his biography here heaps on him quite a bit of ridicule, nevertheless, his excellence in singing and acting truly surpassed that of others of his time. . . . [Kunju actors] are the old wheelwrights of the opera stage; they do not mingle with the common multitudes. They are all placed in the last volume so as to ensure that . . . one style of singing is differentiated from the other."[122] Further explaining his sequence of the kunju actors within the last juan, Wu remarks: "Northerners do not like kunju-style dan actors. The two actors Wu and Shi also perform bangzi operas. They are listed first following the taste of the times. I end with [kunju actor] Faguan so as to finish on an elegant note."[123] Wu's ordering of his material again reflects his ethnographic outlook—his interest in capturing "the taste of the times" and the tastes of "northerners."

Through his aesthetic eclecticism, Wu, a Jiangnan native, proclaims his rejection of literati mores, while at the same time he can never fully identify with the popular taste of the northerners. Commenting on the bangzi actor Chen Yinguan, he laments: "At those many times when I witnessed exquisite moments, what a shame that I could not bring myself to let out a shout of 'bravo!' [*hao*]"; and "when northerners watch plays, they emit loud shouts of 'hao' at all those moments that really strike their fancy; this is something that my sort [*wo bei*] is unable to do."[124] These comments once again reveal the Jiangnan connoisseur as on the margin—unable completely to cast aside the decorum of men of his standing but envying those who could give full vent to their emotions.

For Wu Changyuan the embrace of non-elite musical styles was but one means of asserting his nonconformism. More broadly, a taste for opera and aesthetics was a way for the connoisseur to distinguish himself—to carve out a niche in which he (and his cohort of underemployed literati) was expert. If huapu writers usually were not guardians of the state, they could at least be minders of artistic excellence, and this self-conferred authority, coupled with the visceral and emotional delight of performance, was salve to their festering political ambitions. Through ranking and cataloging the talent of actors, they restored themselves to their assumed rightful position at the top of a hierarchy of aesthetic discrimination. And the parallels between political and aesthetic ranking were never far from their minds. In the congratulatory opinion of The Raconteur of the Western Hillocks, Wu Changyuan's *Orchids of Yan* was "like filling in a catalog of flowers or seeking out worthies for the ranks of the Hanlin registers."[125] The opera cognoscente's assessment of artistic excellence reinscribed his position in an ideal sociocultural order.

THE AESTHETICS OF THE CONNOISSEUR

Late eighteenth- and early nineteenth-century flower registers judge actors (mostly performers of the dan role) according to three basic criteria: beauty, artistry, and temperament.[126] This last criterion, also sometimes characterized as personality or charisma, was a source of pride for connoisseurs—a standard of aesthetic appreciation that they felt differentiated them from most other opera fans. In the words of the Latter-Day Adept of the Iron Flute, "When I evaluate actors, I don't only consider beauty and talent; I also take into consideration personality, with charisma as its highest expression."[127] Not surprisingly, huapu connoisseurs appreciated those actors who were to a certain extent modeled in their own image. They praised actors who had acquired some literacy, and they expressed sympathy for actors of good family background who, as victims of misfortune, had stumbled into the degraded profession. The actor Wang Xiangyun—the inspirational source for Wu Changyuan's *Orchids of Yan*—was notable in the eyes of the author-connoisseur because he painted ink-brush orchids in a style imitating that of the Yuan dynasty literati painter Ni Zan (1301–74). If the poems about Xiangyun are somewhat patronizing—marveling that an untutored youth could have such talent and cultivation—the actor's mimicry of literati hobbies *and* his less-than-perfect execution of them flatter the self-image of the scholar-patron.[128] One Zhu Fuxi is praised for being "cultured like a student, without the slightest trace of fawning, but also graceful and personable." "When you chat with him face-to-face," the admirer continues, "it's as though he were the son of a good family; and when he waits in attendance upon you, you don't get the feeling that he is an actor."[129] Such comments display a striking dissonance in the connoisseur's expectations—an unspoken contradiction between appreciation of the youth's similarity to himself and preservation of the patron's superior status.

The evaluation of actor temperament was as much about the actors' performance at literati gatherings (or as quasi-courtesan companions) as it was about onstage acting.[130] The two kinds of performance were intimately linked. According to one account, when the eleven-year-old boy actress Zhang Changui sang the emotional highlights from the scene "Hiding in the Boat" (Cangzhou), "tears naturally coursed down his face" and "all who watched sighed in amazement." His stage talents made him a sought-after prize at parties, "a source of pride" for the host.[131] Thus, much as huapu authors claimed that as men of culture they would never dream of defiling the dan actors, they were clearly implicated in the post-performance transactions between boy actresses and members of the audience.[132] Still, in the eyes of the connoisseurs, actor temperament also affected onstage artistry. If the actor's frustration and misery (echoing the scholar's own angst) induced in him a melancholic disposition, that could often be a fortuitous source of emotional authenticity on the stage. Yang Maojian, for instance, writes of one actor who felt trapped, "like a parrot in a cage." Try as he might, the actor was unable to suppress the furrow in his brow, but his dejection translated into exquisite verisimilitude when he performed plaintive heroines, such as Xiaoqing from the drama *Jealousy-Curing Stew* (*Liaodu geng*).[133]

Although any number of actor temperaments had the potential to please huapu connoisseurs, one overriding performance aesthetic emerges from the corpus of flower registers: subtlety—often rendered as *hanxu*, or *qiu dan*.[134] This aesthetic preference, the connoisseurs claimed, distinguished their own taste from that of the popular crowd. In describing the characteristics of an actor who captured this ideal, Wu Changyuan wrote: "Xue Sier: . . . [He] is one of the most winsome graces among the dan of the Western Troupes—slender and delicate, with a face like a flowering lotus. In scenes of romantic flirtation he is rather restrained, so the shouts of 'hao' from the audience are but few. Oh, what a shame!"[135] Rushing to the actor's defense, Wu argues that "pretty flowers are best when only half open; as for the passions of the boudoir, it's the suggestion, not the manifestation, that arouses. Watching 'raw coupling' . . . has no more flavor than chewing on wax."[136] These sentiments are echoed in an assessment of the actor Jiulin in *Viewing Flowers in the Precinct of the Throne*, for which the commentator wrote: "There are those in the audience who feel [his] portrayal [of the White Snake] is too stiff. . . . I say . . . that if the performance is overly slick, it takes on the flavor of chewed wax"; this entry concludes by cautioning other actors against mindlessly imitating the current vogue for excess.[137] Of course, huapu did record actors who rendered more flamboyant interpretations of romantic heroines. Consequently, accounts of such actors as Wei Changsheng and his student Chen Yinguan—who were notorious for their racy performance style—have been preserved in the historical record.[138] Nonetheless, the connoisseur ranked what he watched, placing the half-open flower—or veiled eroticism—at the top of the aesthetic hierarchy.

The huapu aesthetic had less to do with policing morality than with the expression of true emotion (*qing*) on the stage. Overly broad representations of romantic attraction ran the risk of devolving into burlesque, especially when depicted in a transvestite theatrical tradition; although many in the audience may have found the resulting comedic effects entertaining, in the eyes of the cognoscenti broad performances had the potential to undermine the emotional "authenticity" and even the eroticism of certain scenes.[139] In this regard, connoisseurs also expressed strong opinions about the ages of actors playing the dan roles. In the mid- to late Qing most dan actors either stopped performing or switched role types sometime in their midtwenties.[140] Even within the typical range of ages for dan roles, huapu connoisseurs did not fail to make known their preferences. Complaining that the ten-year-old children bought into the profession were too immature to understand the content of their performances, Yang Maojian wrote: "With tender mouths still smelling of mother's milk, they are forced onto the stage. They um-and-ah as if reciting from rote memory. They can barely understand how to respond to the melody or the beat, much less convey an emotionally convincing portrayal."[141] But dan actors at the upper end of the age spectrum were also disparaged by huapu authors. Another connoisseur, writing in the 1850s, commented that watching forty-something actors playing the dan role made him want to vomit.[142] Either age extreme could detract from the emotional and visual integrity of performance. The connoisseurs' taste in opera, then, gravitated to an ideal of immanent sensuality, preserving artistic standards on their guidebook pages that ran the risk of becoming corrupted by the burlesque, the kitsch, and the exploitation of the metropolitan commercial stage.

The Lao Dou *and Other Patrons*

The comments about performance style in huapu reveal more than the cognoscenti's own definition of theatrical excellence; they also transmit an awareness of the tastes and theatergoing practices of other members of the audience. The true connoisseur distinguished himself by constantly contrasting his own likes and dislikes with the tastes of the times, of the crowd, and of the lao dou. If the dan actor was the intended focus of the opera aficionado's critical eye, then other theater patrons, more specifically the lao dou, were the unintended objects of the huapu writer's ethnographic gaze. Especially in recording the practices ancillary to the theatergoing culture of the capital—the drinking parties at winehouses after the performances, the patronage of various actors, the purchase of sexual favors from actors, and so forth—huapu writers devoted considerable attention to what I call the look outward, that is, noticing what other opera fans did. Whereas the actor—his talent, his predicament, and (in spite of everything) his integrity—was often framed in the connoisseur-writer's own image, huapu always presented the lao dou as a figure against which the connoisseur-author constantly measured himself; typically, the lao dou came up markedly short. Echoing such sentiment, "old roués" become a figure of fun in one early nineteenth-century popular ditty:

> His face may be swarthy or pocked,
> Yet always he insists on fancy dress.
> Without millions in golden ingots,
> That old-roué éclat is hard to possess.[143]

As this mocking jingle reveals, the lao dou was distinguished first and foremost by wealth. But two types of theater patrons could fit such a description: powerful officials and rich merchants. Squeezed between these two groups, huapu writers felt themselves to be compromised in relation to both the official elite and the socioeconomic power of merchants. And their anxiety over this interstitial (and often downwardly mobile) condition is reflected in huapu depictions of opera enthusiasts and theater culture. Although the politically well connected became the target of much gossip (so-and-so is infatuated with such-and-such an actor), huapu writers reserved the brunt of their disdain for ostentatious merchants.

Of course, which of the two types of lao dou is being described can be ambiguous, since huapu authors on occasion simply refer to them as "great patrons." In describing the lifestyle associated with theatergoing in the capital, for instance, Wu Changyuan offers the following portrayal of "great patrons" and their interactions with dan actors:

> When the various dan see that their patrons have arrived in the playhouse, either they send over a plate of sweetmeats or they go up to them and curtsy. ... After a short while, before the song and music have even finished, [actor and patron] have left together in the same carriage for the winehouses. Returning home—tongues clucking in drunken speech—it is as though a scene from the [Song-dynasty] Alum-Paper Winehouse were being replayed before our eyes.[144]

According to huapu writers, it was the hao ke or lao dou who patronized the dan actors in their secondary entertainment roles as drinking and sexual companions. A source from the 1820s grumbled, "Successful officials, large-scale tradesmen, and the sons of powerful nobles coerce boy actresses to accompany them to winehouses; they will spend up to several hundred taels on a single banquet. More family fortunes are squandered and reputations ruined by this than by anything else. Yet the customs in the capital are such that nobody thinks it amiss."[145]

The lao dou's money was not always spent in entirely self-serving ways. According to Zhang Jiliang, great patrons sometimes paid up to three thousand taels to purchase a young actor out of his service contract (a practice akin to buying a prostitute out of servitude to a brothel)—although Zhang hastens to add that this usually happened when an actor was in the flower of his youth; after an actor reached maturity, no such benefice was forthcoming.[146] As another anecdote by Zhang reveals, buying an actor out of the profession did not always confer freedom upon him. "Manchu vice minister XX," Zhang further observes, "bought [the actor Quanxi] for the sum of one thousand taels to serve as a page."[147] With perhaps more than a touch of schadenfreude, Zhang ends with the observation that the "vice-minister has since met with political misfortune and been banished to a border region."[148]

More explicit antagonism is directed at lao dou in a comment in Yang Maojian's *Assorted Notes*, which describes men who harass actors by constantly showing up outside their doors to demand a "tea gathering" (*da chawei*) as "having no shame."[149] A passage in *Orchids of Yan* is more explicit still in its contrast between the rich but callow lao dou and the sometimes penniless but always sophisticated connoisseur, claiming with a note of self-satisfaction that the actor Liu Erguan "is petulant in the company of great patrons; but . . . with . . . poor scholars he forms intimate friendships founded on literary elegance."[150] And huapu author Zhang Jiliang writes with palpable admiration (if not vicarious thrill) of the actor Meng Changxi, who, when drunk, had a foolhardy propensity to curse the officials he was entertaining.[151]

Patrons identified as merchants tend to be pilloried in huapu more sharply still. *Orchids of Yan*, for example, records the following story about the relationship between two virtuous actors and their merchant patron from Zhejiang:

> A certain merchant from Xiuzhou was on intimate terms with [Tang Yulin and Fang Lanru]. He squandered all his business capital on the pleasures of wine and song. Later the merchant was arrested for defaulting on his loans. The two [actors] reported this to the merchant's friend. They said, "You know what has happened to him. If we can enlist your support to get him out of trouble, then we will contribute two thousand taels so that he doesn't lose everything he owns." Moved by their words, the friend intervened to settle the lawsuit. . . . Not long afterward the merchant took up with a different actor. In disappointment the two actors said, "You can't save a drowning man! We did not fail the merchant, but the merchant has failed us." Thereafter, the merchant depleted his entire fortune.[152]

In the process of celebrating the generosity of the actors, the story portrays an ungrateful, profligate merchant. In another anecdote, the merchant is presented less as the villain than as the dupe. Wu Changyuan regales his readers with the story of "a certain rich merchant from Jinling [Nanjing] who in 1773 used his wealth to purchase a post as a department vice magistrate." The story continues:

> On first arriving in the capital, the merchant had a fancy for jade vessels but no other indulgences. In a matter of a few months he met two men at a playhouse who were—to use the colloquial term—"go-betweens." They invited actors to his lodgings, increasingly with each passing day. The merchant's domestics viewed these two men as devils, [but] the rich merchant's magnanimity was aroused and he began to spend lavishly on wine, delicacies, carriages, and horses. He spent his days in opera halls and winehouses, and he spent his nights drinking and gambling. Every evening he would retain a dan actor to lie with him through the night. He went on to arrange marriages and purchase houses for the actors, complete with clothing and household items—spending more than a thousand taels per actor. In just

five months he had arranged marriages for three of them. Having depleted the funds he had brought with him to the capital, the merchant sent home for more. His son came to the capital and urged him to return south, but he would not listen. Still, his money was not so plentiful as it had been before. Sometime later an actor came to him to borrow three hundred taels in silver. The merchant agreed to provide the money in a few days but then was unable to make good on his promise. The actor cursed out the merchant at the door to his lodging; this was one of the actors whom he had previously set up with a wife. On hearing the actor's curses, the merchant was overcome with remorse and chagrin. That night he hanged himself. In less than a year the merchant had spent more than ten thousand taels. His son wanted to bring a suit [against the actor], but hometown natives [in the capital] cautioned him against broadcasting his father's vices. So all the son could do was swallow his cries and conceal his tears. Alas! In truth, who was it that brought him to such an end? It was all the fault of those two devils! Those who take up residence in the capital cannot be too careful when it comes to making friends! I heard this from the rich merchant's neighbor who saw everything with his own eyes. Though I have concealed the merchant's true name, I record this as a warning to others.[153]

These and many other anecdotes recorded in huapu have the ring of cautionary tales.[154] But that was precisely the point. Working with the rumors generated by the metropolitan gossip mill, huapu writers embellished and shaped their stories of the theatrical demimonde in familiar patterns; in the process they cast the lao dou as nouveau-riche naifs—lacking both the refinement and the savvy to be true aficionados.

Ultimately, what really distinguished the merchant lao dou from more cultured opera patrons in the eyes of huapu connoisseurs was his lack of aesthetic sophistication—as evident even in his choice of winehouse. Another anecdote, this time provided by Yang Maojian, makes a not-so-subtle dig at the taste of lao dou merchants:

> The Pork Market district has the largest concentration of winehouses; the smell here is most odious, completely incompatible with the clientele. I have always said that taking beauties to the Pork Market district to drink and dine is tantamount to burning a zither for firewood or boiling a crane for food. Just south of there is the Jinyuan Winehouse. It's a place where merchants from the western regions gather. It doesn't have second-story private guest alcoves; actors won't set foot in the place. In the playhouses, when the actors ask, "Where will the feast be held tonight," if the response is, "Jinyuan Winehouse," they shake their heads and walk away.[155]

Yang's anecdote, aside from being remarkable for the sense of agency it accords to the actors, once again exposes the connoisseur's subliminal preoccupation with hierarchy and ranking—in this case, of patrons.[156] The implicit highest rank is reserved for the true cognoscenti—such as Yang himself—who would not dream of subjecting favorite actors to the smelly winehouses. The next level down in the hierarchy is revealed by adopting the perspective of the actors, especially the highly successful and popular ones, who, like the connoisseurs, ranked the lao dou by the winehouses that they visited. In Yang's view the "merchants from the western regions" are relegated to the bottom rung of the hierarchy of patrons; even the actors, he implies, exploited as they might be, will not demean themselves by frequenting the second-rate winehouses.[157]

Even more telling was the lao dou's aesthetic preference in opera. Some huapu writers simply allude to this as "the taste of the times," which they always classify as inferior to that of the connoisseurs.[158] A number of huapu writers express regret that a favorite actor has changed his performance style to cater to the taste of the times. "Several years ago," Tieqiao shanren writes, "Yuling . . . was quite proper and demure, but later he poured all his effort into flirtation plays; I think he must really have wanted to make a name for himself, so he did this to appeal to the taste of the times."[159] *Viewing Flowers in the Precinct of the Throne* similarly critiques the actor Cai Sanbao.[160] Behind the phrase "taste of the times," however, is also recognition that the connoisseurs and the lao dou were watching (and patronizing) essentially the same actors. This is confirmed by other comments in huapu. Zhang Jiliang, for instance, admired the actor Feng Hongxi for his outspoken personality and his fondness for wine; and according to Zhang, Feng was also especially popular with merchants.[161] Huapu present merchant lao dou as uninterested in kunju;[162] and they characterize bankers from Shanxi and Shaanxi as particularly fond of qinqiang and bangzi opera.[163] For connoisseurs such as Wu Changyuan to take an interest in bangzi opera was presented as a mark of eccentricity (and thus distinction); for merchants to like such plays was expected, and therefore simply common.

In the end, it was the proximity of taste and theatergoing practices in the capital that prompted the connoisseurs to differentiate themselves. Since in practice the connoisseurs and the lao dou all watched much the same actors and plays in the same commercial playhouses, ultimately what really distinguished the connoisseurs from the lao dou were their methods of opera consumption and connoisseurship. Lao dou expressed their appreciation of actors through direct patronage, whereas huapu connoisseurs did so by patronage (when they could afford it) and by cataloging the actors and their talents through the written record. What marked someone as a true cognoscente, in other words, was the very act of writing a huapu.

Conclusion

The derivative or appropriated nature of the many literary tropes in flower registers tends to mask just how new the experience of commercial opera was in High Qing Beijing. Development of the full-fledged commercial playhouse during the eighteenth century widened the circle of audiences who attended opera performance in enclosed theatrical venues (outdoor and festival opera continued apace). On the one hand, the commercial playhouse extended a proximate experience of the select and elegant mandarin's salon to anyone with the means to buy his way in, and quite likely many of the anonymous and marginal literati who wrote huapu would not have had such ready access to urban opera otherwise.[164] On the other hand, the lowered (and now purely monetary) threshold of exclusivity of the commercial playhouse prompted a desire on the part of literate fans to inscribe new boundaries—boundaries founded on the intangibles of culture and sensibility instead of on power and money. The expanded economic possibilities (both upward and downward) of the High Qing fostered greater anxiety about one's place in the changing social arena—especially for men with education but neither official status nor mercantile wealth. These concerns were refracted in texts about theater in the capital. Huapu writers turned their wits and passions to the demimonde when the path to and through the "monde" was often blocked and treacherous. The gender-bending practices and evocative metaphors of the metropolitan acting world, in which playing the dan and the experience of being "feminized" were valorized, generated potent stuff out of which to craft morality tales about integrity under duress and talent in the face of adversity.

The anxiety about place—place within a long historical and literary legacy, place among contemporary peers, and place within the slippery social hierarchy—is reflected in the three intertwined looks of the huapu. The look backward involved a conscious deployment of concepts and allusions drawn from the rich corpus of antecedent connoisseurship literature to frame huapu writers' interest in contemporary opera and actors. If display of familiarity with the classical tradition was a way of legitimating what they themselves sensed (and sometimes even acknowledged) was a frivolous literary endeavor, it was also a way of demonstrating that they alone were truly equipped to be the arbiters of aesthetic excellence. The look inward spoke to and for a small cohort of like-minded and similarly situated men who took delight (and sometimes emotional refuge) in opera performance. But there was considerable overlap between the look inward and the look backward, since one of the means by which huapu authors laid claim to be members of this exclusive group of literary and theater sophisticates was through facility in classical genres and allusions. The look outward was a necessary precondition of the look inward, for self-definition of the true cognoscenti was always predicated upon the observation and recording of actors (and the theatrical demimonde) and the contrast with other (in their eyes) less cultured members of the audience. The exclusivity of the connoisseur's aesthetic and social vision could only be fully articulated against a backdrop of vulgarity—whether the taste of the lao dou, the taste of merchants, or, more broadly, the "taste of the times."

. . .

To understand the impact of the flower registers, we must turn briefly from the writers to their readers. Readers responded differently to the three looks of the huapu. The look backward, which I locate primarily in the prefaces, postscripts, and dedicatory essays and poems that frame the huapu, would have had the most selective audience. The language of these passages, though full of mea culpas and self-justification, was also the least accessible. If we can judge from the comments put into the mouths of characters in the late Qing novel *A Precious Mirror for Ranking Boy Actresses*, probably most readers just passed over the highly literary and exceedingly ornate prefatory statements to get to those parts of the huapu that actually described actors and operas. In the opening chapter of the novel, for example, when an uninitiated young scholar picks up a huapu for the first time, he notices "several prefaces, which were none other than four-six parallel prose"; and he is told by his sophisticated friends (including the author of the huapu) to "skip those" and get on to the biographies of the actors.[165] In actuality, then, readership for such abstruse passages may well have been restricted to the author, his immediate circle of highly learned friends and patrons (who had been asked to respond to the compilation with dedicatory remarks), and later huapu writers. And reading this material was probably not the point;

its presence as a frame for the text sufficed to lend the desired imprimatur of high belles lettres and connoisseurship.

A likewise educated but somewhat wider readership would have been drawn to the look inward, which permeated the core of huapu and their framing texts. This was the look that spoke to fellow connoisseurs and social peers, and it engaged sympathetic opera buffs in a conversation about beauty, authenticity, and standards of moral integrity and theatrical excellence. Entry into this conversation required knowledge of the language of the theater as well as some classical erudition, but presumably one could accrue familiarity with the jargon of performance through frequent visits to the playhouses and not just via book learning; thus, even a man of modest letters could become well versed in opera lore. Still, maintaining a threshold of exclusivity would have been important to preserving huapu claims to true mastery of connoisseurship skill, paradoxically delineating insiders from outsiders, and thereby accentuating the appeal—and the marketability—of such texts for readers desiring to acquire a semblance of insider knowledge.

It was via the look outward, as guidebooks—as primers to playing the connoisseur and as aids to finding the best actors in the capital—that flower registers would have attracted the largest and most heterogeneous audience. As one nineteenth-century observer put it: "Sophisticated dandies write 'rosters of the famous flowers in the precinct of the throne,' recording their places of residence and names; they evaluate their beauty, artistry, and temperament. . . . Those in search of romance have but to glance at [a guidebook] and they will find it."[166] Surely, then, it was the allure of opera in the capital—and the resulting demand for and interest in these guides to popular actors—that enabled flower registers to be published "year upon year" and ensured that "money was actually paid for such frivolous rubbish."

PART TWO

Venues and Genres

TWO

Metropolitan Opera, Border Crossings, and the State

> You steal some time and off to the playhouse you go;
> But you've forgotten to bring your reentry ticket stub.
> Suddenly, a whole lot of people shout out bravo!
> Don't know why, but you nod along to the hubbub.
>
> 偷得功夫上戲樓，寫來長票不持籌。忽然喝采人無數，未解根由也點頭。
> Zha Kui, *One Hundred Jingles for the City of Yan*, ca. 1800[1]

> They sit with both legs tucked up under them on their seats,
> The day's plays written down on a narrow, red-paper bill.
> Arrayed left to right, shoulder to shoulder, men as pretty as jade,
> No one in the house even bothers to look at the stage.
>
> 坐時雙腳一齊盤，紅紙開來窄戲單。左右並肩人似玉，滿園不向戲臺看。
> *Bamboo-Branch Ditties from the Capital*, 1814[2]

Eighteenth- and nineteenth-century sources reveal that a day at the opera could be a raucous, even rowdy, event. The theater was hectic: audience members came and went at whim; table tenders and vendors circulated through the house; and actors not onstage came out into the house to hobnob with potential patrons. The theater was noisy: audience members chatted with friends and other actors whenever the performance did not capture their attention; and they expressed their approval of good acting by punctuating the singing with shouts of admiration, typically a shout of "hao!" But none of this seeming chaos detracted from audiences' enjoyment of what they viewed on the stage. Chinese travelers to Beijing in the eighteenth and nineteenth centuries raved about the theater in the capital. Its splendors, they claimed, "were foremost throughout the realm."[3]

These splendors could be experienced in any number of venues within the capital city. Yet, as much as the opera theater had its enthusiasts in the eighteenth and nineteenth centuries, it also had its detractors. Commercial opera in the Qing metropolis was thus a contested realm. This chapter introduces the characteristics of opera in Beijing circa 1770–1900 and analyzes the spatial and social dynamics of performance in three main venues: commercial playhouses, temple fairs, and private salons. Operas, actors, and audiences moved from venue to venue, though not entirely without barriers: ethnicity, class, and gender all placed certain restrictions on the patterns of movement and interaction. In state-society tensions over who could watch opera in the capital city (and where), one of the key "actors" was the Qing court, which took upon itself the prerogative to police opera, especially commercial opera, in Beijing. The court's interventions were prompted by state concerns to preserve ethnic sovereignty and social control. But the allure of opera entertainment was so great that it often thwarted state design. And the state, though a primary player in negotiations over opera in the urban space, was not the only force monitoring ethnic and gender boundaries; other social conditions as well constrained audience constituency in the various performance venues within the capital. The push and pull of these many forces will be evaluated venue by venue.

The commercial playhouse was an institution that came of age during the eighteenth century. Although the playhouse is by far the newest of the venues under scrutiny, I examine it first because it was both the most distinctively urban of the venues, and to the extent that any of these sites created a public space for the expression of sentiment and a locus for interaction and negotiation among peoples of different social background in mid- to late Qing Beijing, that role fell to the playhouse. Because of these potentials, among others, the playhouse was subject to close scrutiny by the Qing state. Playhouses were tolerated but regulated. By imperial order commercial theaters were forbidden within the Inner City; as a result, until the late nineteenth century commercial playhouses were clustered almost exclusively in the bustling shopping and entertainment district located just south of the three southern gates to the Inner City. Other efforts by the Qing court to orchestrate public order and morality in the capital—everything from curfews to prohibiting high-ranking officials and bannermen from visiting playhouses—had both direct and indirect influence on who attended what and where. Admission prices established an economic threshold to consumption of entertainment at commercial theaters. And women were forbidden in playhouses in Beijing until the early twentieth century. All of these regulations, whether written or customary, influenced the manner in which opera was performed and patronized in the city.

The venue with the fewest restrictions on what might be performed and who might attend was the temple fair, one of the oldest sites for theatrical display in China. During the Qing, opera performance at temple stages in the city and suburbs of the capital had the potential to accommodate the most socially heterogeneous audience, including women and the urban poor. As in the playhouse, the public nature of performance at the temple fair—and the resulting mix of occupational and gender constituencies—incurred the watchful eye of the state. The religious function of the temple fair restrained the Qing court from banning such performances outright, and so it settled for edicts pleading for restraint and for crackdowns on individual cases of crime or social disturbance. Court meddling in both playhouse and temple-fair performances waned steadily over the years from 1770 to 1900, a result of changed attitudes among powerful figures within the royal family and state preoccupation with more pressing "theaters of social unrest" in the late nineteenth century.

The third venue for theatrical production—the salon (*tanghui*)—was also a venerable institution that existed well before the Qing. The heyday of salon-style performance came in the Ming, although the practice of inviting troupes for performance in private residences or native-place lodges (*huiguan*) before select guests continued in the Qing. The salon offered a somewhat different dynamic from that of either the playhouse or the temple fair. Though it often bent protocol to allow attendance by women, the social composition of its audiences was otherwise even more exclusive and homogeneous. Official interference did not (and could not) penetrate so easily into the salon. Theater within the Qing imperial palace can be considered an extreme expression of salon performance. Notwithstanding that much of court-sponsored performance was akin to the Jacobean masque—an ideologically charged display of court ritual and power before large numbers of courtiers and high officials, intended to exalt the glory of the dynasty—the palace was home to more intimate settings for opera watching, too, which more nearly replicated the private salon experience.

Analysis of these three venues demonstrates that urban opera performance in Qing China involved many kinds of border crossings—both literal and figurative—among ethnicities, classes, and genders. Urban performance created a bridge between Han and Manchu identity, allowing Manchus and bannermen to participate in and appropriate for their own uses the lore of the Han-identified and Han-dominated historical and dramatic tradition. The mixed social makeup of audiences enabled mingling across economic and occupational levels—which seems to have made some opera patrons more rather than less aware of social difference. And the transvestite theater of the Qing, in which boys cross-dressed to play the roles of women, allowed for gender boundary crossings. In the sex-segregated commercial playhouse, however, this erotically charged seeming transgression was not particularly threatening to social norms, since it merely imposed gender hierarchy onto preexisting status hierarchy. In other words, the low status of the actors relative to their audiences accorded perfectly well with their assumed female identities both on and off the stage. Each venue enabled a different combination of these border crossings. To the spectators, most of these "transgressions" were playful and innocuous. To the state and other defenders of prescribed social norms, some of them were potentially subversive.

The cumulative effect of the movement of people and plays throughout the city reveals commercial opera in Qing Beijing to be the locus of one additional border crossing; it became a threshold between public and private life. It was in the public setting of the playhouse that audiences indulged in and gave vent to private passions. The playhouse carved out a niche within urban society for release of a range of sentiments, which could not be fully gratified—or necessarily found—even within the privacy of family life. For that reason, the theater was utterly beguiling: it was exciting, sexy, inspiring, and funny. And for that reason, and for the tendency of private passions to spill over into the public arena, the theater was also potentially volatile. The ethnic and social mix within the Qing playhouse made the contagion of the public by the private that much more fraught with political and social undertones.

The stages within the imperial palaces were the only sites for opera in Beijing that were relatively sheltered from boundary crossings circa 1770. Although the court was the greatest single patron of opera in the capital throughout the Qing, its entertainment practices for the most part were not continuous with those of the city at large; the court commissioned its own grand multiday spectacles and ritual dramas, it kept its own companies of actors (distinct from those in the commercial realm), and, naturally, it determined the audience for such occasions. Part of the narrative of this book is the story of how that relatively unbreachable boundary between court and commercial performance broke down by the end of the nineteenth century, at which time the operas and actors—if not the audiences—at court had become nearly indistinguishable from those at commercial playhouses, temple festivals, and private salons within the city.

The Playhouse

Playhouses were most commonly designated in eighteenth- and nineteenth-century records by the phrase "tea garden" (*chayuan*). The term was an elegant euphemism, since, as commentators of that time reveal, "those places where one goes for the sole purpose of listening to songs and where no meal is provided are called 'tea gardens.'"[4] "Tea garden," while perhaps the most flowery of names for this establishment, was just one of many used to describe a commercial space for watching operas; others included "song hall" (*geguan*), "play garden" (*xiyuan*), and "play hall" (*xiguan*).[5] To reflect in English the full range of its social functions, I call this entity the "playhouse."[6]

Public forums for theatrical presentation have a long history in China, dating from the mid-eleventh century, but the playhouse differed from earlier theaters in several important respects. Unlike the earliest urban theaters, the state-sponsored "tent-arena" (*goulan*) theaters, which flourished circa 1050 to 1450, Qing-era playhouses were privately run commercial establishments. Unlike outdoor temple stages, which also emerged during the Northern Song (ca. eleventh century), the playhouse was a fully enclosed and (usually) completely roofed two-storied structure. Unlike either the temple or guildhall, which attracted audiences in part by spiritual, native-place, or occupational affinities, there was no identifiable marker of community to the playhouse audience. To the extent that the playhouse created an audience community, it was based on ability to pay and a shared interest in watching performance. Theater in the playhouse, in other words, was more commercial and more about entertainment.[7]

A mix of institutional and social developments contributed to the rise of the eighteenth-century playhouse. Inspiration for a structural enclosure devoted almost exclusively to the presentation of opera was likely fueled by the proliferation of native-place lodges and guildhalls in the Qing capital. During the mid-Qianlong years, as many of these lodges underwent reconstruction, permanent stages were added to the structures.[8] Parallel to this development, winehouses (*jiulou*) or restaurants (*fanzhuang*) featuring theatrical entertainment proliferated in Beijing beginning in the late Ming. During the mid-eighteenth century, as the research of Liao Ben has shown, these venues for occasional performance began to transition toward offering theatrical fare on a regular basis, hence the distinction made in accounts of the time between the earlier culinary establishments and the later tea garden playhouses, at which the only refreshments were tea and light snacks.[9]

Broader political and socioeconomic trends further spurred the rise of the playhouse as a site for social congress and conviviality in the mid-eighteenth-century capital. The early Qing state publicly discouraged lavish expenditure by officials on private family troupes.[10] The projected austerity of the early Qing state may have constrained some families of means and privilege, who might otherwise have invested in a household troupe, to seek out less ostentatious sources of entertainment. The commercial playhouse offered one such alternative. Then, too, the social and military chaos of the dynastic transition in the mid-seventeenth century temporarily dispersed much of the wealth of certain great gentry families of the lower Yangzi River delta (Jiangnan region) who had been the foremost patrons of private opera troupes.[11] Although by the eighteenth century private troupes had reappeared in major metropolitan centers such as Beijing and Yangzhou, they were far fewer, even among elite families, than before.[12] As a result, opera patrons who might have preferred entertainment in the privacy of their own villas were reoriented toward the commercial playhouse. A final spur to the growth of playhouses in eighteenth-century Beijing was (as noted earlier) the pull of the capital for men of talent throughout the empire: to work on the massive imperially sponsored literary projects of the eighteenth century; to sit for the metropolitan exams and then to await or take up official appointment.[13] It was largely this cohort of men who became the main commentators on commercial opera in the Qing. The maturation of the playhouse and renewed interest in commercial theater on the part of the educated seem to have acted as mutual catalysts in the second half of the eighteenth century: the quality of commercial theater in the capital attracted educated audiences; and elite patronage of the playhouse contributed to its commercial viability.[14]

To appreciate the social and cultural roles of the playhouse in Qing Beijing, we must first understand the particular politico-ethnic demands on urban geography under Qing rule and the resulting impact on social and spatial organization in the capital city. The Qing state was essentially an apartheid regime, in which the Manchu imperial household and a relatively small mixed bureaucracy of Manchu, Mongol, and Han courtiers and officials governed a predominately Han population.[15] As the work of Mark Elliott and others has shown, the impact of Manchu apartheid in garrison cities—of which the capital at Beijing was the preeminent model—was felt most immediately in the realm of spatial segregation.[16]

This feature of Qing urban planning was reinforced by the city walls. Spatial barriers in the form of massive walls replicated and reiterated customary, legal, and symbolic notions of ethnic difference (Figure 2).[17] In the center stood the imperial palace (also known as the Forbidden City), the ritual hub of the state, locus of the court, and home to the emperor, his immediate family, and an expansive imperial household retinue. The palace was surrounded by the Imperial City, the site of official organs of state power. This in turn lay within the Inner City, the preserve of residences for officials and the Banner garrisons.[18] Together these areas made up the northern portion of Beijing, which was disproportionately Manchu in ethnic composition and almost entirely in direct service to the court, as the imperial residence, as the site of bureaucratic offices, or as the living quarters of Banner populations. The walled and ritually invested layout of the capital was not a Qing invention; rather, what was new under the Qing was the division of the urban space into Banner and non-Banner populations, a division that largely recapitulated ethnic differentiation.[19]

A mostly walled rectangle jutting south from the Inner City circumscribed the Outer City, over 90 percent of whose residents were of Han ethnicity.[20] The Outer City became the commercial heart of Beijing under the Qing. Playhouses, winehouses, and brothels for boy actresses clustered just outside the three southern gates in the wall of the Inner City. According to stele inscriptions in the Jingzhong Temple (which doubled as the site of the local actors' guild), by 1792 there were at least eight major playhouses in this area; the turn-of-the-century anonymous diary *Playwatching Journal* (*Guanju riji*) adds yet another four theaters to that list; and within just thirty years the number had grown to at least twenty.[21] An 1829 source notes one playhouse located just outside the Xuanwu Gate, another just outside the Chongwen Gate, and a total of eleven dotting the eastern and western parts of the region just beyond the Zhengyang, or Front Gate. Of those eleven playhouses, five were located in the Dashalar neighborhood, the busiest shopping district in the capital.[22] These sites were "ringed by winehouses and restaurants" (Figure 3).[23]

The spatial positioning of commercial theaters in Qing Beijing is telling. Reflective of the larger significance of dramatic performance in urban life in general, the playhouse was at once both marginal and central. It lay smack in the center of the milieu of urban business and entertainment. It was literally situated on the margins of—or just over the border from—the spatially demarcated realm of officialdom. This border was policed; yet as much as the court tried to confine commercial theater to the margins of political space and culture, it kept coming back front and center.

Beginning in the late seventeenth century and lasting well into the nineteenth, the Qing court adopted a containment policy with regard to com-

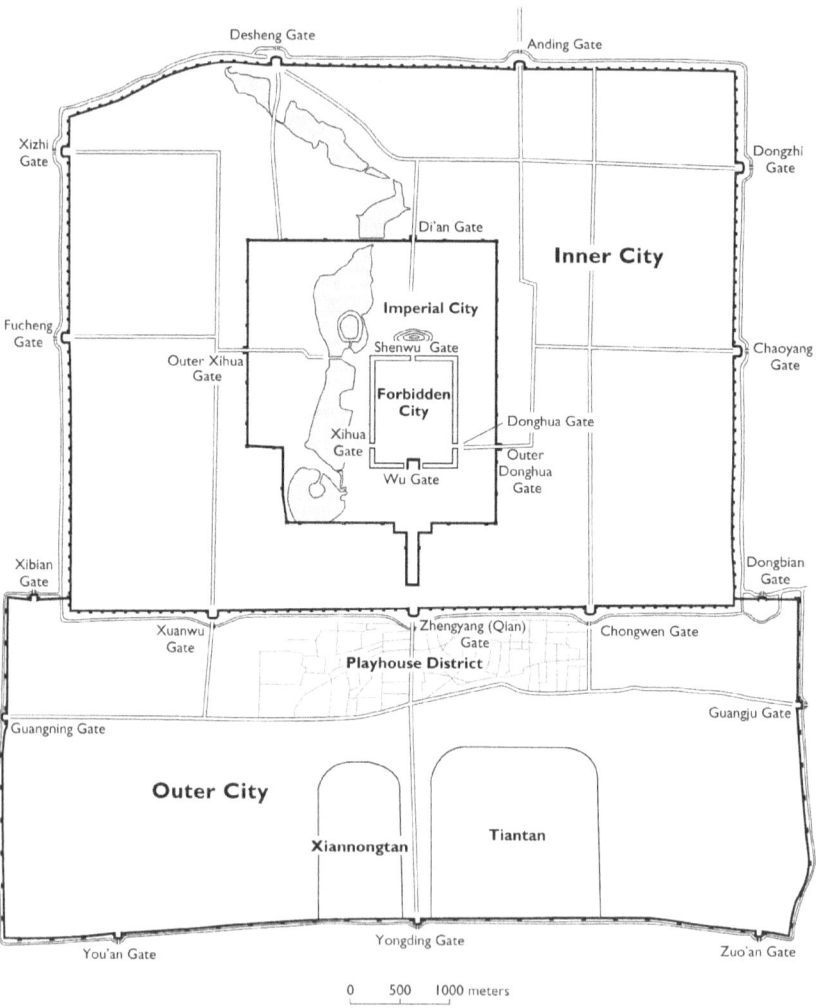

Figure 2. Outline sketch of the walls of Beijing during the Qing dynasty.

mercial theater. Playhouses were tolerated so long as they were confined to the Outer City. They were not permitted to operate within the Inner City, and high officials (whether Han, Manchu, or Mongol) and Bannermen were forbidden to attend performances in commercial theaters. The first such edict, issued in 1671 by the Kangxi emperor, explicitly stated: "Within the Inner City of the capital it is not permitted to establish theaters. This ban

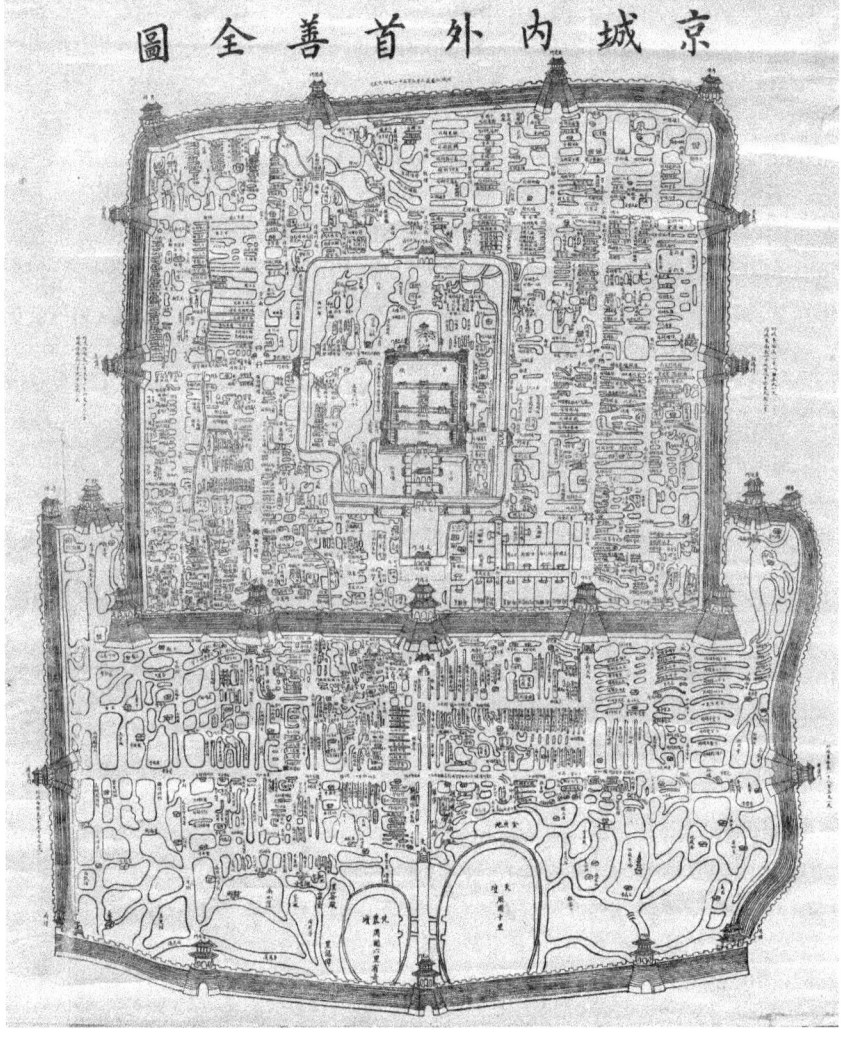

Figure 3. A Complete Map of the Inner and Outer Cities of the Capital (Jingcheng neiwai shoushan quantu). Lithograph. Beijing [s.n.], between 1875 and 1911. Courtesy of the Harvard-Yenching Library.

is to be implemented permanently. As for those theaters in the Outer City, should malicious ruffians use them as a pretext for creating disturbances, let officials of those districts seek out and detain them and punish their crimes."[24] But, as is clear from the cascade of similar warnings issued again in 1775, 1799, 1803, 1813, and 1824, the court was hard pressed to enforce these boundaries.[25] In fact, the very frequency with which such prohibitions were reiterated reveals that throughout this period there was persistent playhouse creep into the Manchu-identified space of the Inner City.

In 1806, for instance, a scandal involving an imperial censor and his overzealous patronage of the theater brought to the emperor's attention the existence of a playhouse in the Xidan Arch section of the Inner City.[26] Smaller playhouses, known as "variety-skit houses" (*zashua guan*), which featured various kinds of storytelling and opera scenes by small, lesser-known troupes, seem to have escaped the detection of authorities more easily than larger houses. A source from 1842 notes that "within the Inner City it is forbidden to establish playhouses, [so] there are only variety-skit houses there."[27] This same informant nevertheless observed that small playhouses were located just outside three of the gates to the northern portion of the Inner City: the Fragrant Flowers Playhouse (Fangcaoyuan), which was just outside the Qihua Gate in the eastern quarter of the city; the Prosperity Playhouse (Fuchengyuan), just outside the Pingze Gate in the western quarter of the city; and the Victory Playhouse (Deshengyuan), just outside the Desheng Gate on the northern edge of the city.[28] By the 1860s the court acknowledged that, in defiance of the prohibitions against playhouses within the Inner City, "recently a Great Resplendence Tea Bower [Taihua chaxuan] has appeared in the Dongsi Arches area and a Scenic Greatness Tea Garden [Jingtai chayuan] in the Longfusi Alley, both of which put on plays. Furthermore, even on ritually proscribed days, they openly perform."[29] Unable to keep the playhouses from infiltrating the Inner City, the mid-nineteenth-century court edicts (while not entirely conceding defeat) sound more resigned, urging moderation and restraint—no performances on ritual fast days, no night performances, no women's seating sections—rather than issuing yet more prohibitions.[30]

Over the course of the eighteenth and nineteenth centuries, even as playhouses crept into the Inner City, high-ranking officials and bannermen crept into the Outer City playhouses. As one early nineteenth-century commentator remarked, "At the striking of the first note of the music of the 'middle scene-set,' the officials and notables arrive. Just about all the luminaries of the capital hide their brilliance in the face of the restrictions"; the author explains parenthetically, "when officials above the sixth rank enter playhouses, they first remove and hide their officials' hats."[31] To avoid detection, in other words, they had to hide their insignia of office. Hats or no hats, it was still perfectly possible to identify not only an official but even his rank among the playhouse visitors. Quoting a bamboo-branch ditty from the early nineteenth century, the mid-nineteenth-century opera aficionado and historian Yang Maojian described the seats within the playhouse as "covered with cushions—a swath of red," to which he added the notation that red cushions were used only for the highest (ranks one and two) officials; all other patrons were provided with blue seat cushions.[32]

The practice of "disguising oneself and sneaking into the theaters" was also noticed with alarm by the court and became the subject of additional imperial injunctions. In 1724 the Yongzheng emperor issued a ban on patronage of Outer City theaters by bannermen, warning that hitherto unenforced infractions would be added to all newly committed offenses in assigning punishments.[33] In 1762 the Qianlong emperor fulminated about the doubling of the number of playhouses and winehouses in the Front Gate district and the frequency with which bannermen and officials visited such places.[34] Clearly, such imperial concern fell on inattentive ears, since in 1803 the Jiaqing emperor had again to remind his capital policing corps:

> Hereafter, let the roving censors of the five wards of the city within the Office of the Captain-General of the Gendarmerie conduct regular inspections at those places in the Outer City where winehouses and playhouses are in operation. Should there be officials and others who have disguised themselves and furtively gone there, and who for no good reason are found dallying and feasting at a certain establishment or restaurant, investigate and impeach them according to the facts. Do not entertain any notion of covering up even for princes and high officials.[35]

As the 1806 scandal involving a playgoing imperial censor reveals, even such imperial tirades could not diminish the lure of the commercial playhouses for those in official position. The scandal first came to the attention of the court in November 1806, when a certain citywide roving censor by the name of Hexun petitioned the emperor with a complaint against six bannermen who had been discovered frequenting commercial playhouses and performing onstage alongside career actors.[36] When the court pressed for more details about the culprits and for evidence of how this transgression had come to light, Censor Hexun was unable to keep his story straight, claiming both that "he had observed the bannermen in the playhouse from a distance while riding by on horseback," and later that "his household servants had observed them while inside the playhouse."[37] After further investigation, Wang Da, a table tender from the playhouse, was summoned to make a statement. Wang Da asserted that Censor Hexun was a frequent patron of the playhouse and that the censor had gotten into a turf war with other patrons (the other six bannermen whom Censor Hexun had originally reported to the throne) over the right to sit in the coveted exit-door seats. Wang Da's version of events was confirmed when he was able to pick the censor out of a "lineup" of officials. The deliberating council concluded that Hexun had "secretly gone to the playhouse to listen to operas," his memorial to the throne was "nothing but a private vendetta arising out of the fight over the seats," and his actions had been "sordid in the extreme." "If all officials were to lodge accusations against each other in this manner," the emperor cautioned, "would that not be following in the footsteps of the evil habits of the Ming?!" Hexun was dismissed from his post, and the case was handed over to the Grand Secretariat and the Board of Punishment for sentencing.[38] The perfidious Hexun shows just how far officials were willing to go in defying the court when opera in the playhouses was the prize.

The Qing court's interest in containing commercial playhouses within the Outer City and in policing patronage of such theaters by high officials and bannermen was part of a battle that it fought on two fronts: one against encroachment onto Manchu space by Han-identified cultural practices; the other against contamination of the core group of the regime's bureaucratic support staff by the perceived "corrupting influence" of Han—even Ming-dynasty—ways. And both of these battles were designed to prevent a dilution of the "Manchu Way."[39] This tension over where opera could be watched and who could watch it, in other words, was one expression of a larger anxiety of Qing rulers throughout the eighteenth (and into the nineteenth) century over a perceived threat of sinicization and consequent weakening of martial sinew. The example of commercial theater in the Qing shows that this was a cultural battle the state lost. To the Qing court, even as late as the eighteenth century, when most Manchus and bannermen in Beijing had been living and breathing Han culture for more than a hundred years, cultural appropriation was still supposed to go in only one direction. It was fine (or at least more acceptable) for the court and Manchu princes to bring Han performance into the privacy of their own palaces and mansions, that is, to shape Han cultural practices to their needs. The reverse, however, was forbidden: bannermen and high officials crossing into Han-identified public space, where they engaged in Han cultural practices side by side with people of mixed ethnicity and class, was highly suspect.

This anxiety over the ebbing away of a normative Banner identity can also be corroborated from the punishments proposed for bannermen who violated the court prohibitions. Official proclamations decried bannermen who "visit the playhouses at will, squandering their savings and growing more dissolute by the day."[40] Hexun's scandal of 1806 generated a slew of court documents, many of which lamented the current trend among the "scions of the Eight Banners" (*baqi zidi*) to have become infected by Han customs and airs (*hanren xiqi*) and to be unwilling to steel themselves in the practices of the Manchu language, riding, and archery.[41] As punishment for his crimes Censor Hexun was sent north to the frigid Manchurian heartland of Jilin, where under military surveillance he was to undergo training in the Manchu tongue and in martial skills.[42] Kun-du-le, a prince of the imperial household who had also been caught sneaking into commercial playhouses, was banished to Shenyang, where he, too, was to study the "state language, riding, and archery" and was ordered to rid himself of his "rich playboy-like habits."[43] The potential for social unrest posed by public performance had been of concern to officialdom long before the establishment of the Qing. Under the Qing, however, underlying tensions regarding ethnic identity, coupled with the regime's investment in mapping ethnicity onto the geography of the capital city, made patronage of commercial theater doubly sensitive: in Beijing, where performance took place and who attended it became a touchstone for larger issues of social control and political transgression.[44]

Given the proven inefficacy of repeated court restrictions, we might wonder how serious the court really was about containing theatrical performance and restricting access to it. Were these edicts simply rhetoric without any real intent to enforce, promulgated to depict the state as defender of social morality? If the court had truly desired to eradicate "evil Han customs"—theatergoing being a prime instance—would the state not have allocated serious resources and police power to that end? The expression of Qing state power as demonstrated through morality campaigns was never constant. Rather, as others have long since recognized, the power of the state was not only overextended by the sheer extent of the territory to be administered but also subject to individual imperial whim. At times the regime struck out at perceived threats ferociously; at others, it was indifferent to those selfsame dangers.⁴⁵ When the state pendulum swung toward indifference, illegal playhouses were established and proscriptions flouted with impunity. Moreover, the very persons relied on to enforce restrictions on playhouses and playhouse attendance were in large part officials and Banner commanders thoroughly besotted with the pleasures of the playhouse. So it is not hard to comprehend why the regulations were so often reiterated and with such ever-diminishing effect.

. . .

Most bannermen and officials sneaking into the playhouses were probably less bedeviled by awareness of spatial and ethnic transgressions than by more practical considerations, such as not getting caught in the playhouses and getting back into the Inner City before the gates were locked at night. Bannermen and high officials were not the only operagoers who had to be on the alert. A ditty from an early nineteenth-century collection of odes to the city colorfully describes a real-life border-crossing predicament facing lower-ranking officials who had stayed out too late:

> The newly arrived purchased-post officials are delighted to do the sights.
> First the playhouse and then much drinking long into the night.
> They use the money they've now earned to buy some song and dance;
> Finally heading home, they ford the moat under cover of the night.⁴⁶

Reaching the gates after curfew meant spending the night exposed to the elements in one of the gate stockades located inside the three gates between the Inner and Outer cities, or getting caught out and paying a fine for the curfew violation, or, apparently, "fording the moat."⁴⁷

From all the previous examples, we can see that the spatial and ethnic border crossings encouraged by playhouse performances could have real political, legal, and socioeconomic repercussions, both for individuals and for the larger polity. But we can also see that the seemingly solid boundaries of space and ethnicity that the Qing rulers wished to keep intact were by the late eighteenth century rather permeable. By the mid- to late nineteenth century, the breaches were acknowledged and essentially ignored.

Yet another potentially fraught set of border crossings attended the social mix within playhouse audiences. Officials and bannermen were not the only patrons drawn to the eighteenth- and nineteenth-century playhouses. The playhouse was also a favorite pleasure spot for examination candidates. These would-be officials came to the capital from around the empire to prepare for, take, and then await the results of the regional- and metropolitan-level civil-service examinations.[48] The same informant who commented on the manner in which the "luminaries of the capital" sneaked into the theaters also noted that "would-be dragons from the coastal regions come to release their surfeit of emotion in tears," adding the explanation that "those who fail in the examinations always go to the playhouses after the results have been posted."[49] A poem by the Fujian literatus Yang Cuiyan, entitled "Thinking of the Various Actors from inside the Exam Cubicle" (Wei zhong huai zhu xiaoshi), further attests to the lure of the theater to these examination contenders:

> A low hut opens on a tiny sliver of an alley;
> In here, it's hard to chase the carousing from my mind. . . .
> The dim candlelight above my head rouses my ruminations;
> And the colors and forms in my dreams stir my imaginings.
> I rub my bleary, heavy eyes—how hard it is not to doze,
> Surprised to find that the beauties vanished when the moon rose.[50]

This was a lure so strong that it threatened to distract one examinee from the primary purpose of his visit to the capital.

The Outer City playhouses were recognized far and wide as one of the common tourist destinations in the capital, along with other must-see sights such as the Altar to Heaven (Tiantan), the Altar to the Earth (Ditan), and White Stupa Monastery (Baitasi). When the Kaifeng native Tan Shaowen, the protagonist in the late eighteenth-century novel *The Lamp at the Fork in the Road* (*Qilu deng*), arrives in the capital to study at the National University (Guozi jian), the first places he visits after calling upon native-place elders in the city are the playhouses and variety-skit houses to see "the debut performance of a new troupe on a certain day, the noontime plainclothes storytelling and vaudeville of a certain troupe on a certain day, the knife-swallowing, fire-breathing, and somersaulting with spears of a certain house on a certain day."[51]

The Raconteur of the Western Hillocks, a contributor to *Brief Register of the Orchids of Yan*, describes the process of his own increasing attraction to commercial opera while sojourning in the capital. In his "Dedicatory Remarks" to this earliest of flower registers, he writes: "I was a native of Suzhou and had never known the pleasure of women. When wishing to rest my eyes from books, I made frequent visits to the Zha Playhouse.[52] Occasionally diverting my money from scholarship, I sometimes pressed it upon the Chrysanthemum Quarter.⁵³ After amusing myself there several times, I came to appreciate its true flavor."⁵⁴ Yang Maojian, writing in the early 1840s, comments:

> Every year after the regional and metropolitan examinations are over, without fail all the playhouses put on "Wang Mingfang Ascends Three Consecutive Ranks" (Wang Mingfang liansheng sanji);⁵⁵ and the painted-face roles perform "Explicating the Question" (Shuotijie) as an amusement; it is rather irreverent of the teachings of the Sage. . . . The best of these scenes is "The Schoolroom" (Guishu) from *The Peony Pavilion* (*Mudan ting*). Du Liniang comes onstage and says: "Wine is the teacher's sustenance; woman is the gentleman's primer." [The audience] doubles over in laughter, and it is truly sublime.⁵⁶

The plight of the downtrodden scholar and the satire of classical allusion presented in such farces surely appealed to students who had trained long and hard for the examinations.

Not all playhouse patrons were scholars and would-be officials. As discussed earlier, flower-register writers were highly conscious of the presence of wealthy merchants among the crowds of playhouse attendees, and they took pains to distinguish their own taste in performance from that of the mercantile profession. In the novel *Precious Mirror for Ranking Boy Actresses*, the predatory operagoers who haunt the Outer City playhouses and abuse the boy actresses include Xi Shiyi, the rich son of an official (who is in the capital waiting for an official appointment); Ji Liangxuan, Xi's unscrupulous personal secretary; and Pan Qiguan, a wealthy banker from Shanxi.⁵⁷ This description of the motley social makeup of audiences—if not their individual personalities—meshes with records in Qing-era flower registers.

Finally, there were the audience members who sat in the cheapest area, the pond seats located directly in front of the stage. These people were characterized by accounts of the time as "butchers, inn-keepers, and carriage drivers."⁵⁸ Although the chroniclers of commercial theater at the time did not spill much ink over these poorest of fans, we can infer that these are the audiences whom Wu Changyuan, the literate opera connoisseur from Jiangnan, obliquely describes as the "northerners" who lustily shout "hao" at moments of singing that thrill them.⁵⁹

Even though the commercial theater brought together audiences of disparate social and occupational backgrounds, status and economic standing within the playhouse were still markedly differentiated by the type of seat purchased: the benches in the "pond" (*chizi*); the stools arranged around tables in the "scattered seats" (*san zuo*) section; or the boxes, or "officials' seats" (*guan zuo*), located on the balconies. Playhouse stages were constructed as raised platforms in three-quarter-thrust design, with the audience on three sides on both the floor and balcony levels (Figures 4 and 5). Nineteenth-century sources suggest that playhouses could hold anywhere from several hundred to a thousand people, numbers that few other public spaces supported.[60] The pond benches, located on the ground floor of the playhouse directly in front of the stage, were lined up perpendicular to the stage alongside long shared tables upon which theatergoers could place

Figure 4. Painting of the Guangqing Playhouse. Qing era. Reprinted with permission of Liao Ben, *Zhongguo xiju tushi*, p. 479.

Figure 5. Painting of *pihuang* opera performance inside a Beijing playhouse during the Guangxu era. Qing era. Reprinted with permission of Liao Ben, *Zhongguo xiju tushi*, p. 482.

teacups and playbills. "When one leaned against the balcony balustrade and looked down on the world below," one opera enthusiast noted, "the long tables were arrayed like lines on a chessboard, [and the people were] very much like pawns lined up in military formation, their necks stretched out as if poised in readiness." "The only difference," the author went on to complain, "was that there were no reed stalks gripped between their teeth to keep them quiet."[61] The scattered seats consisted of stools arranged around rectangular tables located on the two sides of the hall directly underneath the balconies. Behind them, against the walls of the playhouses, were slightly raised stools; their elevation helped patrons seated there to see the stage.[62] More scattered seats were arranged in rows on the stage-facing balcony, and "their price decreased with the distance from the stage."[63] The richest patrons sat in the officials' seats, essentially boxes separated by screens, three or four of them located on the left and right side-facing balconies.[64] As we have seen, the seats in the second box on the exit-door side were considered the best in the house.[65] One final category of seats was not usually available for purchase: the "reverse officials' boxes" (*dao guanxiang*), which were located to the rear of the stage thrust on the side-facing balconies and were reserved for playgoers who—through either special clout or personal connection—might enter the playhouse free of charge: eunuchs from the Bureau of Ascendant Peace (Shengping shu), runners from the local yamen, and friends and relatives of the playhouse owner.[66] If a performance was especially in demand, these seats could also be sold.[67]

According to one opera enthusiast writing in the 1820s, the price of a seat in the scattered-seats section was one hundred copper coins. The cost of officials' seats was seven times that, but it may also have included the price of the extra spaces at which off-duty actors could perch while chatting with their patrons.[68] A partial price list compiled by a Russian envoy stationed in Beijing in the 1820s provides scanty but valuable consumer goods comparison costs. For the cost of a scattered-seats ticket one could buy two catties of pork, close to four catties of top-quality wheat flour, or approximately thirty catties of cabbage.[69] A day of watching multiple scenes at the playhouse cost more than the basic necessities but less than a small luxury such as a cheap amber snuff bottle, which, according to one account, might sell for four hundred copper coins.[70] Other sources estimate monthly wages for a servant in a "second-class" household to be one thousand to fifteen hundred copper coins, which would mean that one visit to a playhouse would have consumed roughly one-tenth of that monthly income.[71] For many people even a pond seat was probably a luxury not often affordable.⁷² Opera buffs lacking the means to attend opera at the city playhouses had recourse primarily to variety-skit houses, storytelling teahouses, temple festivals, and itinerant street performances. Then again, truly devoted fans who lacked resources to indulge their operagoing habits might resort to almost anything to get into the theater, or at least to snatch an after-show drink with the boy actresses, as captured in the following wry ditty from the early nineteenth century:

> Clothes pawned till he has nothing left to wear, yet still his passion runs high;
> At thirty percent interest and ninety percent return, he borrows just to get by.
> The money from his pawn tickets has all been spent—how sad;
> In a pinch tonight, this once he'll stiff the actors—like a cad.⁷³

Cost dictated who could afford to sit where in the playhouse, but it was not the sole determinant of where one actually did sit. Sitting in the pond was so stigmatized that "not only literati and officials but even relatively well-off merchants were unwilling to sit there."⁷⁴ Even the view-restricted reverse officials' boxes were considered preferable to the pond. The view from the reverse boxes is captured through the eyes of the Shandong yokel Deng Jiugong in the late nineteenth-century novel *A Chronicle of Lovers and Heroes* (*Ernü yingxiong zhuan*). Complaining about his miserable visit to an Outer City playhouse, Deng Jiugong relates that his guide to the theater—a monk with the dharma name of "Un-void" (Bukong Heshang)—"was in the know in all these matters." Deng continues: "After going inside, he insisted on claiming one of the exit-door balcony boxes. But they were already taken, so we had to make do with squeezing into the reverse balcony box seats running parallel to the stage. When we finally sat down, I looked down thinking to watch the show, but all I could see was the actors' spines."⁷⁵

The ranking of seating areas within the playhouse ensured that awareness of the economic and social status of one's fellow playgoers was always a part of the play-watching experience—an awareness that was parlayed in writings by educated (but not necessarily wealthy) connoisseurs of opera into anxieties over aesthetic taste. In other words, although the commercial playhouse was open to people of various social standings and occupations, the experience inside, rather than bridging social and economic divisions, tended to exacerbate consciousness of those distinctions.

Regardless of economic means or social status, women could not enter the commercial playhouses. That proscription in the capital was made official at least as early as the third quarter of the eighteenth century. The exclusion of women by means of both custom and law seems to have emerged in tandem with the maturation of the playhouse as a commercial institution in the eighteenth century. These regulations remained in effect in Beijing throughout the nineteenth century.[76] As with the exclusion of playhouses from the Inner City, by the mid- to late nineteenth century the restriction on women's attendance was not always fully enforced. Court edicts reveal that the restriction first broke down in the illicit Inner City theaters, suggesting that in the late nineteenth century Banner women would have had greater access than their Han counterparts to performances at commercial venues.[77] In general, however, the laws and customs that barred women from commercial theaters in the Outer City were not suspended until the early twentieth century. Even when women began to gain entrance into playhouses, they were still seated in segregated viewing areas.[78]

Within the all-male environment of the playhouse, biological women were supplanted by performed women, that is, by the youths impersonating the female roles. Women's exclusion from the playhouse venue helped create a unique performance atmosphere in two ways. First, it freed men of all status backgrounds from social inhibition, since they were no longer constrained by prescriptive social and moral codes on interaction with proper women, thereby giving greater license to emotional indulgence; they could shout, they could flirt with the actors, and in summertime they could even, like Yang Maojian, unfasten their robes to relieve themselves from the stifling heat. Second, it facilitated the creation on the transvestite stage of the ideal woman, in turn helping to preserve the illusionary world of the theater. These gender dynamics could not be reproduced quite so effectively in other performance venues.

In order to better evaluate these audience-actor dynamics, we must turn to analysis of how plays were performed within the playhouse. With few exceptions, playhouse performances took place in daytime, allowing patrons from the Inner City to view a day of performances and return to the Inner City before the gates closed.[79] Typically, operas began at noon and lasted until about five or seven in the evening, stopping before dark.[80] Professional opera troupes rotated through the various playhouses, performing at a given site for three to four days before moving on.[81] The musical styles of the operas varied, depending on the troupe performing. In general, the troupes singing Kun opera, a blend of Kun and Hui melody (*huidiao*), and, later, pihuang opera got billing in the larger playhouses. Writing in the early 1840s, Yang Maojian observed that "the large playhouses such as Guangdelou, Guanghelou, Sanqingyuan, and Qingleyuan . . . primarily showcase the Hui Troupes" (which then still performed much of their repertoire in the kunju style).[82] Qinqiang and other bangzi-style opera troupes, which tended to attract less literate audiences, ran the circuit of the smaller houses. Again, Yang explained: "The Hui Troupes do not frequent the smaller playhouses in the Outer City; rather, on different days [these houses] offer plays by the western [i.e., qinqiang and bangzi troupes] and minor troupes. If that is not sufficient [to fill the schedule], they supplement it with variety skits. So there are also many variety-skit houses within the Outer City."[83]

The plays performed in the playhouse venue—especially those from the Kun opera repertoire—typically consisted of excerpted scenes from longer *chuanqi*-style dramas. One early nineteenth-century observer commented: "When the acting troupes of the capital mount the stage, they first perform three to four independent scenes, after which they perform three to four connected scenes, called the 'middle axle.' Then they again perform one or two independent scenes, followed yet again by three to four connected scenes, called the 'big axle.' And before you know it, the sun is setting."[84] Especially in romantic comedies or seduction-and-revenge operas—and many of both kinds were performed—the scenes presented emphasized emotional highlights of flirtation and seduction, omitting the cautionary moral message that often bracketed such scripts in their full written editions. Alternatively, the selected scenes concentrated on acrobatics and comedy[85]—supplemented with a healthy dose of camp and spectacle.[86]

. . .

Within the commercial playhouse there was always a marked status differential between audiences and actors. Audiences were relatively elite; actors belonged to a degraded status group.[87] The young boys who cross-dressed to play the young female roles onstage were particularly vulnerable. These boys were often sold into the trade by destitute parents, essentially indentured to an opera troupe master until they came of age or were able to purchase their freedom.[88] In the words of opera aficionado Zhang Jiliang: "Nowadays [the actors] all come from Suzhou, Yangzhou, and Anqing at the age of eight or nine. The teacher gives money to the parents, and a contract is drawn up for the years [of service]. They are coerced into coming to the capital, where they are taught pure singing and are decked out in pretty clothes. They are sent dashing here and there to entertain guests with music and wine for [the troupe master's] profit."[89] Even foreigners noticed the cross-dressing and attendant eroticism of the Chinese theater. One commentator observed: "The female parts are performed by youths who act so well that it is not easy to distinguish them from young women. They are very much encouraged by the wealthy Chinese."[90] A ditty from the early nineteenth century confirms the link between acting and sex work:

> The actors of the Hui troupes are sold as male companions.
> All powdered and perfumed, they perch by their patron's side.
> Destined to be your cursed-love, he's a curse through and through.
> All on account of him, you've got sores up and down your hide.[91]

Not all commentators writing about boy actresses were quite so cynical. As we have seen, the constructed woman of the boy actress on the stage was exalted by sophisticated opera aficionados in catalogs devoted to recording actors' talents and charms. And the half-mocking, half-admiring biographies and poems written about actors in such texts compared them to flowers and birds, invoking tropes and metaphors for female beauty that had a long history of use in evaluating courtesans. The eroticized gaze of the male opera fan on the boy actor as "actor-playing-woman" intensified the already suggestive content of the abridged romances and social melodramas of the playhouse repertoire. Though by no means the sole attraction, that frisson was one of the major enticements of the commercial theater (Plates 1 and 2).

The transvestite theater of the Qing era can be seen as a border crossing of sorts. Yet, at least within the culture of the commercial playhouse, this erotically charged apparent transgression was not particularly threatening to social norms. In essence, the gender of the performer—whether boy or woman—was always tagged as female. Although titillating and the stuff of imaginative play in the minds of opera devotees, cross-dressing onstage posed no real challenge to existing social hierarchies.

The eroticized gaze of male opera fans on the female impersonators, written about in texts of theatrical connoisseurship, could at times be disconcerted by the reality of performance within the commercial venue. Whereas on the written page of the flower register the gaze was wholly that of the aficionado trained on the boy actress, within the space of the theater, where flesh-and-blood actors moved about freely among the patrons in the house, as well as onstage, the dan actor was not necessarily a passive recipient of the gaze. He could respond to it; and when he did, there was always the potential for mimesis and suspension of disbelief to be exploded. Numerous nineteenth-century sources and literary representations of the commercial theater note the squalor of the Outer City entertainment quarters and the poverty of many actors, which tarnished the idealized image of the delicate and alluring "flowers" of the stage. Even the novel *Precious Mirror*, which largely participates in the discourse of the flower registers, pokes fun at its own idealization of the boy actresses, occasionally presenting them as sniveling ragamuffins who latch on to any potential old roué patron as a ticket to a free meal.[92] Even when the gaze of patron on boy actress remained intact, the heightened passions of the theater could subtly redistribute the actor/audience power imbalance, making wealthy patrons feel emotionally vulnerable, notwithstanding their social and economic superiority.

Furthermore, as suggested by the ditty about the wealthy youths—"pretty as jade"—who frequented the playhouse, the dan actors were not the only people subjected to a gaze within the commercial theater. There was much to look at within the playhouse, and the performances onstage sometimes had to compete for an audience with the social dramas unfolding within the house. The messiness of the gaze and of power hierarchies within the playhouse may explain some of the appeal of the huapu. These texts fixed—even perfected—the patrons' gaze and in doing so securely empowered the writer/reader (in all his magnanimity) vis-à-vis the female-identified boy actors. Thus, the "virtual" theater experience of the huapu might be considered even more sublime than that of the actual playhouse. In contrast, it was precisely the unpredictability of *performed* literary culture—and its potential disruption of accepted hierarchies—that made the playhouse suspect in the eyes of the state and other self-appointed guardians of social and moral order.

It is clear that court circumscriptions on the locations and patronage of playhouses waned over time. Within that venue, however, transformations of the internal social dynamics did not occur at a steady rate; some were slow and gradual; others, at the end of the nineteenth century, relatively abrupt. The mix of Han and Banner patrons in the commercial theaters persisted; indeed, by the late nineteenth century infatuation with even opera came to be tagged as a particularly "Manchu" characteristic.[93] But, as suggested by the decrease in court documents on such matters, this no longer so threatened the state. The mix of class constituencies within the playhouses remained essentially unchanged, with admission prices still keeping

Plate 1. Painting of a "flower" *dan* (*huadan*) in the *pihuang* opera "Fourth Son Visits His Mother" (Silang tanmu). The painting depicts a boy actress performing the role of Eighth Sister (Bazi). Painting commissioned by the Qing court, ca. late nineteenth century. Courtesy of the Zhongguo yishu yanjiuyuan Library, Beijing.

Plate 2. Painting of a "blue-robed" (*qingyi*) *dan* in the *pihuang* opera "Fourth Son Visits His Mother." The painting depicts the character Empress Dowager Xiao (Xiao Taihou) and is likely a rendering of Mei Qiaoling in this role. Mei Qiaoling was the grandfather of Mei Lanfang, the most famous *pihuang* opera female impersonator of the twentieth century. Painting commissioned by the Qing court, ca. late nineteenth century. Courtesy of the Zhongguo yishu yanjiuyuan Library, Beijing.

out the urban poor. Immediately after the end of the nineteenth century, however, women of means did begin to gain entrance to playhouses; surely, this reflected the influence in Beijing of new practices introduced in Shanghai theaters in the latter part of the nineteenth century.[94] To the extent that we can detect other diachronic changes in the second half of the nineteenth century, texts commenting on the commercial theater began to pay greater attention to actors other than the dan role type—especially to actors specializing in male heroic roles. The changing audience that this reflects may also help account for the state-sanctioned dismantling of brothels for boy actresses immediately following the fall of the dynasty.[95] Although the ethnic and gender tensions of the playhouse venue were largely defused by the end of the dynasty, it is clear that contemporaries still recognized an implicit link between cultural and political performance within urban commercial theater: by the first decade of the twentieth century capital playhouses became popular sites for staging lectures about social reform, and many new-style intellectuals looked to opera as a medium for fomenting "enlightenment" among the lower classes.[96]

The Temple Fair

Since the eleventh century, the venue at which the vast majority of Chinese—rural or urban—have viewed opera has been the temple fair.[97] Performances at temples in the city and suburbs of Beijing much resembled those at village temples throughout north China, the primary difference being the more urban clientele attracted by their proximity to the capital. Suburban and urban temple fairs presumably profited from the relative wealth of their urban location.[98] Further, temple-fair audiences in and around Beijing would have been more ethnically mixed than the typical opera audience in most rural communities in north China.[99] Finally, relative to the playhouse the temple-fair venue exhibited less obvious transformation over time, at least until the twentieth century, when competing and secular sites for popular and mass entertainment reduced the importance of temple stages within the urban space.

Although temple-fair performances were occasional in nature, the ritual calendar of temples within the environs of Beijing ensured that festivals occurred throughout the year on a fairly regular schedule. In her study of temples in Ming- and Qing-era Beijing, Susan Naquin has identified permanent stages in twenty-two temples, most of which were constructed dur-

Figure 6. Detail from *A Pilgrimage to Miaofeng Peak* (*Miaofeng shan jinxiang tu*), a painting of a temple-fair performance at the entrance to the Great Enlightenment Monastery (Dajuesi) at Miaofeng Peak in the Western Hills outside Beijing, 1815. Courtesy of the Capital Museum, Beijing.

ing the eighteenth and nineteenth centuries.[100] A permanent stage was not necessary, however, to host performances. Makeshift stages could be erected when needed, and the open space within temple courtyards and in front of temples became a common site for performances by itinerant opera troupes, storytellers, and troubadours. The painting in Figure 6, for instance, depicts a performance by traveling players on the grounds before the Great Enlightenment Monastery (Dajuesi) in the western suburbs of Beijing. The Protect the Kingdom Monastery (Huguosi), located north of the Xisi Arches within the Inner City, held fairs regularly on the seventh, eighth, seventeenth, eighteenth, twenty-seventh, and twenty-eighth of each month; the Abundant Blessings Monastery (Longfusi), situated in the eastern half of the Inner City, sponsored its fairs every eight days beginning on the first and second of each month. Throughout the Qing both of these temples were known for their entertainments as well as for their periodic markets; the Beijing copyist-publisher of opera and storytelling libretti, Hundred-Books Zhang (Baiben Zhang), regularly sold its scripts to opera fans at these locations.[101] The Medicine King Temple (Yaowangmiao) in the Outer City was equipped with a stage, and the Fire God Temple (Huoshenmiao) located nearby was known for its storytelling teahouse and other entertainers.[102] These temples, too, conducted twice-monthly fairs. Many other temples in the Beijing region sponsored seasonal or annual festivals, with the cumulative result that a temple fair occurred on average at least once a month.[103]

Though often the occasion for temple performance was a celebration of a god's birthday or some other seasonal or annual rite, the content of the opera performed on such occasions was not necessarily directly related to the religious content of the festival. According to the entry in *Playwatching Journal* of 18 December 1797, for example, operas performed at the (Jiangnan) City God Temple (Chenghuangmiao) on Nanheng Street in the Outer City included a handful of kunju scenes from the longer dramas *Jealousy-Curing Stew*, *The Thorn Hairpin* (*Jingchai ji*), and the scene "Flirting with Brother-in-Law" (Xi shu) from *The Righteous Hero* (*Yixia ji*). The only ritual play among the selection was the initial scene, "Dispensing Blessings" (Cifu), which was commonly used on auspicious occasions as the opener for a series of connected scenes.[104] The remaining scenes were no different from a selection typical at an Outer City commercial playhouse. In fact, many of those same plays had been performed by the same troupe of actors at the Qingchun Playhouse just seventeen days earlier.[105] On the occasion of the 18 December performance all the opera scenes were presented by the

Figure 7. Wall painting of a temple-fair performance at the Jingzhong Temple, Beijing, which doubled as the site of the Actors' Guild in Beijing, Qing era. From *National Opera Pictorial* (*Guoju huabao*) 8 (11 March 1932): 29. Photograph by Qi Rushan.

Sanduo Troupe, meaning that the temple or, more likely, a rich patron on behalf of the temple, had hired this commercial troupe to perform at the City God Temple.[106] For the latter occasion, the plays chosen for presentation were all from the Kun opera repertory. Presumably, at most temple-fair performances in the capital city more local styles of opera—whether "capital melody" (*jingqiang*) or some iteration of bangzi opera—would have predominated, a further indication of the humbler social and occupational backgrounds of the temple audience.

The main difference between the audiences for temple fairs and those of the playhouse was that the former encompassed an even broader social constituency—including women and the urban poor. One early nineteenth-century assessment of Beijing temple festivals encapsulates the experience with the following rhyming quatrain:

> Everyone says that going to the actor fair is a must.
> The banners on the stages make such a splendid sight.
> With thugs and harlots edging through the crowds,
> It would be odd if it didn't lead to some kind of legal fight.[107]

A somewhat later and more genteel depiction of temple festivals explains:

> The halls and stages of the Tianling [*sic*] Monastery are so fine.
> Every year in late autumn the chrysanthemums bloom anew.
> It's enough to get the carriages moving throughout the whole city.
> Coming to see the flowers, they bring along the ladies, too.[108]

An early twentieth-century commentator confirms women's attraction to plays at temples: "In times past, women did not have opportunities to watch plays [outside the home]; monks and nuns in their temples used ceremonies to the Buddha as an excuse to put on plays, at which seats could be sold to women patrons."[109] Women of various social standings were among the key constituents of audiences for performances at temple stages.[110] This is confirmed by pictorial as well as textual sources, as seen, for instance, in a nineteenth-century wall painting from the Jingzhong Temple in Beijing, which depicts the segregated platforms on which women spectators could stand (Figure 7). Temple fairs were particularly significant to women since temples were one of the few places to which respectable women could legitimately travel outside the home.

The presence of women at temple fairs, and especially the mingling of men and women there—a breach of gendered spatial segregation—considerably perturbed the state, which treated the matter much as it did the existence of playhouses: it was tolerated but policed. Temple festivals, partly due to their public character and the perceived risk of social disturbance and moral turpitude posed by the heterogeneous crowds drawn to them, generated persistent state regulations and admonitions. In 1762, for example, the Qianlong emperor approved a memorial prohibiting clerics at temples within the Outer City from sponsoring plays, claiming, "The monks and nuns of the temples within the five wards of the city sponsor plays. Men and women must all contribute money, and this is called a 'holy festival.' This mars morals and wastes funds; it is not a trifling matter."[111] Attempts by the Qing court to restrict temple performances continued well into the nineteenth century on the grounds that they "encouraged men and women to mingle indiscriminately" and "were seriously injurious to morality."[112] In 1869 an edict specifically targeted the commotion caused by groups of women spectators watching plays at the Longfu and Huguo monasteries within the Inner City.[113]

These regulations, however, seem to have been honored more in the breach than in practice. Qing court enforcement was never too zealous out of concern that yamen runners might "use this as an excuse to disturb the people," thereby inciting even greater social disturbance.[114] The court sought to strike a balance between stringency and laxity, with the result that enforcement tended to be ad hoc, and only when a particular temple became a haven for illicit activities.

An incident that transpired in October 1838 at the Temple to the Divine Agent (Lingguanmiao), located in the eastern suburbs of Beijing, affords us an example of state interference with temple performances in the environs of the capital. This one incident encapsulates state concerns over perceived ethnic, class, and gender transgressions in the temple-fair venue. In addition, we are fortunate to have three different accounts of this same incident: (1) the paper trail left by the court in its efforts to prosecute the crimes committed at the temple; (2) a narrative description in the "scions' tales" (*zidi shu*) storytelling genre of these very festivities; and (3) an early twentieth-century retelling of the incident by the Mongol bannerman Chong Yi (ca. 1850–1930) in his *Miscellaneous Records from Court and Society since the Daoguang and Xianfeng Reigns* (*Dao Xian yilai chaoye zaji*).

According to an edict dated to 21 October 1838, eight high officials, including three princes of the blood, were apprehended on various charges ranging from smoking opium and escorting prostitutes to a temple for the purpose of performing songs to "lack of self-restraint" and "inappropriate" behavior. The imperial relatives were stripped of their titles, banished, and handed over to the Court of the Imperial Clan for punishment, and the officials were removed from their posts. Three of the officials captured in the raid on the temple aggravated their punishments by giving false identities to those who had first apprehended them.[115] The edict is quite specific in identifying the ranks and positions of the various culprits but reveals little about the circumstances of the arrest, mentioning only that the infractions had occurred at a birthday celebration in honor of the prioress (named Guangzhen) of a certain temple.

Fortunately, some of the details of the incident can be found in the two-part scions' tale, "The Temple of the Divine Agent" (Lingguanmiao) and "Sequel to the Temple of the Divine Agent" (Xu Lingguanmiao). Although we know almost nothing about the author of "Divine Agent" and its sequel (except his pen name, Master of Hidden Talent, or Yundu shi), we can be sure that the two pieces were not created prior to the arrests in 1838, and fairly certain that they would have been written within, at most, a year or so afterward—when the incident was still fresh in the public imagination.[116] According to Chong Yi, this incident became a cause célèbre, not only at court but also with "busybodies who made up song lyrics about it and sang them everywhere," surely a reference to the scions' tales.[117] It is these lyrics that tell us

> This priory was located beyond the Chaoyang Gate in Shuntian Prefecture of Northern Zhili,
> [And] it had a prioress whose name was Guangzhen . . .[118]

> The Middle Primordial already had come and gone; it was neither too cold nor too warm;
> Sister Guang[zhen] set out a feast at the Temple of the Divine Agent to celebrate her day of birth.[119]

In contrast to the imperial edict, the scions' tale does not name names, but in many other ways it identifies much more explicitly the participants at this temple fair:[120]

> Those invited were the powerful and the prominent at court;
> And also their wives, who frequently busied themselves there.
> There were also princes and officers dear to the throne, founders and pillars of state;
> There were also civil officials whose families for generations had drafted the laws.
> There were merchants with fortunes in the millions;

> There were runners, those friends from the yamen.
> And then there were monks, boy actresses, and prostitutes;
> All of them were Guangzhen's benefactors, a band of happy penitents.[121]

"Temple of the Divine Agent" goes on to describe a veritable orgy at the temple: a vegetarian feast (the only religious prescription properly observed), followed by entertainment from singing girls and boy actresses, gambling, boasting, drugs, and both male-female and male-male sex. We are told of the patrons at the temple:

> They evaluated the relative merits of the boudoirs of the boy actresses beyond the three gates.
> They evaluated the womenfolk of their superiors in the five offices and the six bureaus.
> And they talked about so-and-so who'd been promoted and who it was who'd helped him out.
> And they talked about what's-his-name who had run into trouble and who it was who'd lent a hand.
> This one said: "That little nun likes me the best."
> That one said: "Old Sister Guang[zhen] is really good to me."
> This one said: "My wife often spends the night at the temple."
> That one said: "Because of my daughter's illness, we've pledged to have her become a nun here."
> As for those who preferred quiet, some smoked opium inside the prayer hall;
> Others brought the little nuns to private rooms where they could be intimate.
> And then there were those who preferred it rowdy: some mingled among the wives, telling stories and jokes;
> Others held prostitutes in their arms, but said "my dearest" while looking at the wives.
> Those who fancied the male persuasion led boy actresses to secluded spots, where they frolicked in the rear garden;
> Those saps who couldn't hold their liquor had long since fallen asleep on the prayer mats.[122]

"Divine Agent" ends with a description of the official crackdown on the temple: "It must have been that the several dozen years of bad karma of the lot had run their course, and only thus were they discovered by the roving city censor. Just after sundown, he led a group of soldiers with hooks and crooks, with ropes and locks; with a single shout the soldiers surrounded that ancient shrine, barricading the doors to the Temple of the Divine Agent."[123] Like so many of the "slice-of-city-life" scions' tales, the tone of these pieces is both cautionary and salacious—lamenting the collapse of social morals while vividly cataloging the illicit pastimes of the rich and powerful and ostensibly pious.

Even allowing for hyperbole and literary license, these scions' tales help explain the severe reaction of the court in 1838. The goings-on at the temple reinforced the Qing court's very suspicions regarding temple fairs—that temples tended to attract highly heterogeneous crowds, to encourage the mingling of men and women, and to serve as magnet sites for dissipation and vice. These were some of the same qualms that the court had about commercial playhouses—only the transgressions at the temple were considered even more odious because of the mixed gender of the perpetrators. The only people mentioned in the edict of 21 October 1838 are Manchu nobles and high officials. Were the yamen runners and wealthy merchants who attended that fateful birthday celebration (if we can trust the description in the scions' tale) treated with greater leniency because they were lower in the social and occupational pecking order, or on account of their Han ethnicity? Or was it just that their infractions did not warrant the attention of the central authorities, so the prosecution of their crimes has fallen out of the historical record? These questions cannot be answered definitively, but I suggest that the court's attempts to contain both playhouse and temple-fair venues reveals a state that felt a need to guard what it saw as potentially corruptible groups against moral, ideological, and physical contamination, thereby maintaining ethnic (i.e., Manchu) purity and preserving the integrity of the family. The higher the status of the corrupted, the greater would be his or her fall from grace. As the disdain expressed in the scions' tales indicates, however, the court was not alone in its civilizing project; clearly, at least one literate bannerman shared its views.

. . .

Not all temple-fair performances (or their textual representation) were necessarily so anarchic and vulgar. Nor did women's presence in audiences for operas at temples necessarily heighten the eroticism of the experience. A much more forgiving literary representation of one Manchu woman's experience of opera in the temple-fair venue is provided in another early nineteenth-century scions' tale, "The Wealthy Young Mistress Goes to the Holy Festival Plays" (Kuoda nainai ting shanhui xi).[124] The ballad begins with a long description of the woman's preparations for the outing. Eventually arriving at a Daoist temple, there she is treated as the principal guest of honor on account of her elevated social status (and perhaps ethnic identity). The narrative continues:

> In no time at all, the drums and cymbals sounded, announcing the beginning of the plays.
> It turned out to be a joint performance by the Xinxing and Jinyu troupes.[125]
> Plays were often performed in the wealthy young mistress's home, [so] she was familiar with the names of quite a few of the actors.
> A couple of them came down from the stage, curtsied, and handed her a program.
> "Would it please your ladyship to select some plays for your amusement?"
> She chose the scene "Bizheng Steals the Secret Poem" just to tease the nuns.[126]
> What's more, she chose the actor Cuilin for the lead role, for he was so good at expressing feelings.
> She also selected Sanlin's "Tale of the Jade Bracelet" and Lanling's "Twelve Tael Dowry."[127]
> Indeed, the actor's jadelike bodies danced about and flute music filled the ears.
> Their mellifluous and delicate voices were so delightful to hear.
> This beautiful lady, listening with a smile, suddenly said:
> "Give them some packages of largesse for this pleasurable indulgence."
> The several actors all curtsied, thanked her for the gift, and made their exit.
> In no time at all, treats and wine were set out and she drank with actor Liu by her side.[128]

In this representation the listed plays from which the woman is to select are all flirtatious romances. Her familiarity with the actors and dramatic repertoire is explained with the phrase "plays were often performed in the wealthy young mistress's home," suggesting that the circulation of actors and operas through the various performance venues of the city created a shared repertoire of cultural knowledge that transcended gender boundaries.

The woman's rank and wealth privilege her not only to choose the plays but also to dispense the largesse to the cross-dressing boy actresses at the end of their performance. After the performance the woman invited one of the actors to sit and sip wine with her. This was a common gesture among wealthy male patrons, but the only reference I have found to a wealthy woman imitating this elite male practice. The woman's elevated status relative to that of the actors allowed her to transcend gender hierarchies. In other words, sex did not bind the gender identities of either spectator or actor, for she got to play the "male patron" to the actor's "constructed woman." Social standing trumped the gender hierarchy. Finally, even though the female protagonist is watching romantic comedies, at least in this one representation of a woman's appreciation of theatrical performance, there seems to be a softening of the erotic gaze of the transvestite theater. The narrative of the ballad splits the gaze between the wealthy young mistress and the pretty youths she is watching.

To understand how women such as the one represented in this ballad might have become so worldly wise and so attuned to the popular actors and operas that were in circulation in mid- to late Qing Beijing, we must turn to the last of the three venues, the salon; it was in this private setting for entertainment that most women of means "attended" opera. The porousness of boundaries between venues in the capital city ensured that even when barred from the playhouses, urban women could share the cultural knowledge of play repertoires and actors regardless of gender.

The Salon

Salon performance, my translation of the Chinese phrase *tanghui yanchu*, designates operas performed for an audience of invited guests. The sponsor of the performance was the host, and the guests tended to be the host's social peers. As at the temple-fair venue, salon performances were occasional, meaning that most often they were convened to commemorate a ceremonial event: a holiday, a birthday (of a person or a god), a wedding, a wake, or a reunion among fellow tradesmen or people who had come from the same native-place.

The salon was one of the earliest types of performance environments, evidence for which can be traced at least as far back as the first century BCE.[129] It predated the formal development of Chinese drama and theatrical stages by well over a thousand years. With the emergence of full-fledged dramatic skits during the Song and Yuan, plays began to supplement and even supersede acrobatics and musical-song performance within the salon setting. Salon performance reached its zenith in the late Ming, when it became the fashion for prominent, wealthy families to occasionally sponsor or even permanently maintain their own theatrical troupes. The list of families who owned private troupes in the sixteenth and seventeenth centuries reads like a who's who of the social and cultural luminaries of the age—Li Kaixian, Wen Zhengming, He Liangjun, Shen Shixing, Feng Menglong, Shen Jing, Tu Long, Ruan Dacheng, Qi Biaojia, Zhang Dai, Mao Xiang, and Li Yu—to name the most illustrious of them.[130] This practice of owning private troupes continued as a marker of social distinction into the Qing and is amply documented in commonplace books and novels from the seventeenth through nineteenth centuries. As late as the eighteenth and nineteenth centuries, elites still considered the salon the most elegant setting in which to view theater.[131]

During the Qing, salon performances could occur in both the Inner and Outer City. Typically they were held in the private homes of the wealthy, in guildhalls and native-place lodges, or within the residential and recreational quarters of the Qing palaces. On occasion, restaurants or playhouses would be rented by the host for a private theatrical salon. Sponsorship could be familial or corporate (as was often the case with guild-sponsored performance).[132] The socially homogeneous audience for the typical salon performance did not threaten boundaries of status and class.[133] The private nature of the setting meant that urban spatial divisions and their corresponding ethnic reverberations were never at issue. The scale of the salon could vary dramatically, from an intimate party with a few close friends at home (Figure 8) or at the yamen office to a gala event before the emperor at one of the three-tiered stages in the palaces, with officials as the invited guests (Figure 9). Han, Banner, and Manchu households all hosted salon performances, the sole criterion being sufficient means.

To the extent that the court influenced salon performance, its concern was directed toward exhorting frugality among Banner (especially Manchu) households and official misappropriation of public funds for private entertainment. A handful of edicts from the early eighteenth through the early nineteenth century forbade officials to maintain private acting troupes.[134] Nevertheless, as veiled autobiographical evidence from the novel *Dream of the Red Chamber* (*Honglou meng*) suggests, even in the mid- to late eighteenth century wealthy bond-servant families such as the Cao household bought poor children, who were then raised as servants and trained to perform for family ceremonies. In the eighteenth and nineteenth centuries the princely households were among the few who had the economic means to support their own private troupes, as well as the social standing to flout court proscriptions.[135] Rumor had it that the actors cultivated in the mansions of Prince Gong (Yixin) and Prince Chun (Yihuan) in the second half of the nineteenth century were better than those belonging to the troupes within the imperial palace.[136] Even when state injunctions made raising one's own troupe of actors illegal and cost made it prohibitive, except for ritually proscribed mourning periods, there were no restrictions on wealthy families hiring professional troupes to perform for the occasional salon gathering.

One glimpse of the proceedings of an intimate salon party in an elite Manchu household is provided in an anonymous nineteenth-century scions' tale entitled "Pleasures in the Family Garden" (Jiayuan le). The piece relates the events of a single night in the household of a retired official, possibly a

Figure 8. Salon performance. Republican-era reproduction of an album leaf from a late seventeenth-century illustrated album based on *The Prosemetric Plum in the Golden Vase* (*Jin Ping Mei cihua*). Illustration for chapter 63. In *Two Hundred Illustrations of Beauties from the Rare Collections of the Qing Court* (*Qing gong zhen bao Bi mei tu*), China: [s.n.], ca. 1911–49. Courtesy of the Harvard-Yenching Library.

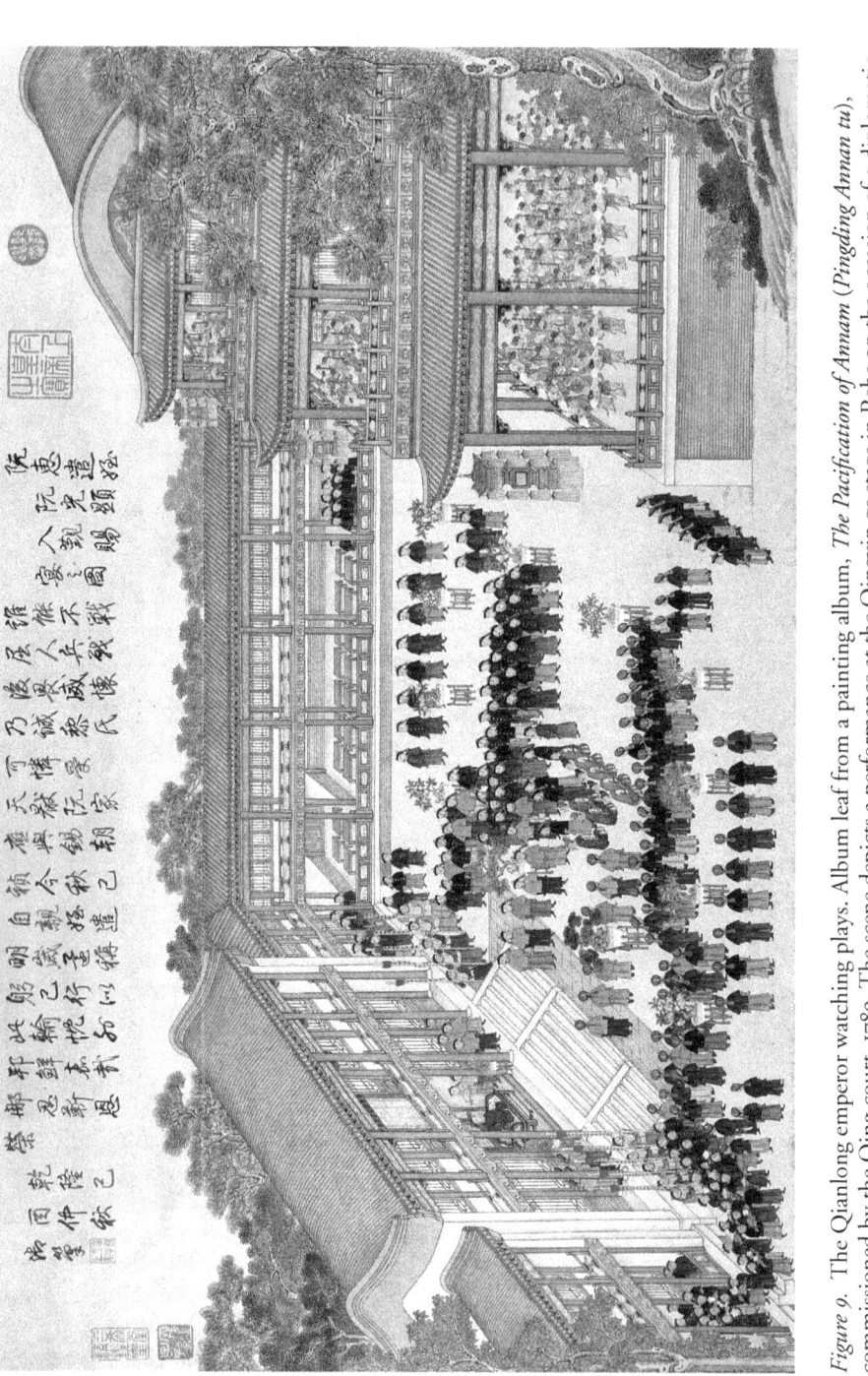

Figure 9. The Qianlong emperor watching plays. Album leaf from a painting album, *The Pacification of Annam* (*Pingding Annan tu*), commissioned by the Qing court, 1789. The scene depicts a performance at the Qingyin ge stage in Rehe on the occasion of a diplomatic visit from an emissary from the newly established Nguyễn dynasty in Vietnam. The Palace Museum Collection, Beijing. Courtesy of the Palace Museum.

prince of the blood. The sixty-something man is the proud father of three sons and is blessed with many grandchildren and two devoted concubines. The ethnicity of the family is only obliquely marked by the use of one or two Manchu phrases, such as the term *a-ge* to refer to the man's sons.[137] On a certain moonlit evening the elderly gentleman calls for the tutor of his adult sons to join him for some wine and cakes in the garden.[138] Together they observe the beauty of the evening, admire some calligraphy written on lanterns displayed in the garden, and quiz the sons on their ability to compose verse. Wishing to prolong the pleasure of the evening, the host makes a suggestion:

> "Tonight, why don't we call out for some plays by a theatrical troupe;
> The womenfolk can also come out to listen."
> He quickly ordered his servant to send out the call:
> "Just say that I want to listen to some plays tonight; and I definitely will give them a bonus."
> He turned back to the tutor and said:
> "Crass as it may be to speak that last phrase, still, you can't not mention it."[139]

The garden is selected as the location for the performances. The host orders his servants to hang a screen-curtain from the eaves from behind which the women of the household will be allowed to watch the show. The narrative continues:

> In no time at all, the troupe players all entered the garden.
> They held out an ivory tally-placard and beseeched the host to select some plays.
> The first play selected was "The Three Top Candidates Make the Grade."[140]
> The second play was "Departure of the Soul" and "Awakening from the Dream," chosen so as to watch the lantern-dance.[141]
> "You arrange the other plays to be sung;
> We want the star actors and the showy plays."[142]

The performances are interrupted when it is announced that one of the daughters-in-law of the host has just given birth to a baby boy. The actors receive their money and leave, but not before congratulating the host and putting in a pitch for being invited back to perform for the customary first-month celebration for the newborn child: "The players said, 'When the mistress has completed her first-month seclusion, we'll come again to be at your service. Tonight, in your very presence, Your Honor, we openly request to reserve the date.'"[143]

In this tale, an ideal imagining of a salon, to be sure, the composition of the audience, the timing of performance, the negotiations over the hiring of the actors, and performance protocols are revealed in just a few short lines. The women of the household are allowed to watch the performance, although they are sequestered from the men by a "screen-curtain." The performance occurs at night—common for salon performance but almost unheard of in the commercial playhouse. The family hires an outside troupe of players, and it is hinted that there will be some haggling over the price—at the very least, an additional fee for requesting the actors to perform at night. The conversations between the troupe and the host—including everything from selection of plays to payment of the actors and the troupe's leave-taking—only barely veil savvy attempts by the actors to ingratiate themselves with their host and set up future engagements. Finally, the descriptions from this tale confirm that salon performances in Manchu households were conducted in roughly the same manner as in Han families.[144] In Han households, too, women were often permitted to view the plays so long as they were segregated from the men. Figure 8, from an early Qing illustrated edition of the novel *The Plum in the Golden Vase* (*Jin Ping Mei*), offers a visual representation of women enjoying dramatic performance within the home.

Manchu aristocrats were not the only elites drawn to salon performance. Salon opera thoroughly permeated official culture. Wu Tao, writing about his experiences in the capital in his *Old Talk about the Pear Garden* (*Liyuan jiuhua*), observed:

> Every year I had to attend twenty to thirty salon performances. As soon as the season began with the breaking of the seals,[145] every department, every province, and every yamen would all hold reunion gatherings at which plays were performed; whenever the governors-general, governors, or regional commanders . . . came to the capital, their native-place compatriots and subordinates in the capital would entertain them with music and feasting; and in years when the metropolitan examinations were held, when the new "recommended men" [*juren*] candidates from each province arrived in the capital, there were always banquets thrown at which they were made the guests of honor.[146]

. . .

Within the salon setting, as in the playhouse venue, actors were still the status inferiors of hosts and their audiences. Their subservient status was marked by many of the intricate protocols that developed surrounding play selection and payment. As seen in the passage from the scions' tales, audience members were asked to participate directly in selecting the plays to be performed. The troupe master or lead actor of a hired troupe would come down into the audience with a list of the plays in the troupe's repertoire. The host or guests of honor would then be asked to choose from among them. This practice also is depicted in a passage in the mid-eighteenth-century novel *The Scholars* (*Rulin waishi*). The setting is a salon performance at the home of a certain Secretary Wan:

> Dressed in colorful costume, the older male lead came forward holding a program. He bent down on one knee and said: "Would it please Your Honor to favor us with the selection of two plays?" Secretary Wan first deferred to [his guests] Academician Gao and Censor Shi, and then selected "Invitation to the Banquet" and "The Farewell Feast."[147] Censor Shi then selected the scene "Meeting at Wutai Mountain. . . ."[148] The male lead marked these down on the program placard and took it backstage to get ready.[149]

This ritual gesture, embraced by both actors and audiences, flattered the patron by publicly marking him (or, in some cases, her) as someone of taste. It also served to veil embarrassment over what was known to both parties as a pay-for-service exchange.

After performances the host and/or guests of honor distributed packets of "thank-you" money, or largesse, to individual actors, essentially bonuses on top of the price already paid for the troupe's services. If a patron really liked the performance of a particular actor, the actor would be invited to drink some wine at the banqueting tables. Within the salon setting, just as in the playhouse, the dan actor was expected to do more than just perform onstage. He was also expected to pour wine for the wealthy host and his guests and generally entertain them in witty conversation and drinking games—an expression of his courtesan-like identity and status. Again, some of the best descriptions of these practices come from literary sources. In the novel *Lamp at the Fork in the Road*, when a troupe of actors arrives to prepare for a performance at the Sheng mansion, the master of the household orders his family steward to "take out two thousand-piece strings of coins, one string for all the actors of the troupe, and one string just for Yuhuaer [the youth playing the dan role]."[150] In *Precious Mirror*, even at the garden parties hosted by refined young gentlemen (who profess to be uninterested in status distinctions and who treat the boy actresses with respect), it still falls to the actors to pour the wine for the guests.[151]

Remuneration for performing and its attendant services was on average much better at salons than in the commercial theater. One observer in the late seventeenth century wrote, "The largesse for actors in the past was only about one to two hundred copper coins; nowadays it is very common to give one thousand copper coins; and the powerful and eminent give as much as a whole tael of pure, engraved silver."[152] In the novel *Precious Mirror* actors pouring wine for and playing drinking games with patrons at salons in the homes of the wealthy are described as receiving "several dozen taels of silver for a day's activities."[153] In the same novel, actors' entertainment services in the theater district winehouses are recompensed with only five strings of copper coins.[154] Wu Tao, writing toward the end of the nineteenth century, maintains that the average cost for wine, food, and performance at a salon banquet held by an official (or officials) could come to as much as two to three thousand taels of silver. If the money for the event did not come out of public coffers, then each audience member contributed two to three taels of silver for expenses.[155]

Since a salon event was far more lucrative for actors than routine repertory performance within the playhouses, a commercial troupe would sometimes accept a salon engagement even if it meant leaving in the lurch the playhouse where they were booked, which might have to close during their absence if the troupe had insufficient actors to cover both venues.[156] The effect of this practice on performance in the commercial milieu is captured in a mid-nineteenth-century ditty. The song complains:

> It's the minor playlets that are popular these days.
> The standing of the four great Hui troupes has begun to fade.
> And so it goes that the theaters can't sell a full house.
> The reason? At the salon, there's more money to be made.[157]

The private and occasional nature of salon performance meant that it was not bounded by temporal factors such as playhouse operating hours or urban curfews. Operas could be presented by day or at night.[158] Thus, while selected scene performance was still common in salons, it was also more possible to perform full or nearly full versions of chuanqi dramas. If the salon were to run for several consecutive days, a long multiscene play could also be enacted in installments.

Reminiscing about performance in Beijing at the end of the nineteenth century, the opera critic Qi Rushan has observed that women tended to talk about opera in terms of the content of the plays, whereas men talked about opera in terms of the skills of the actors.[159] These observations may relate to where men and women typically watched plays. The playhouses, which featured little besides selected scenes repeated again and again in the repertoire, pushed both actors and audiences in the direction of technical expertise. Patrons who had seen these scenes many times were not watching them for story content. And if the actors wanted to be successful with a dramatic corpus that their audiences already knew so well, they would have had to distinguish themselves, primarily through looks and skill. The culture of the (educated) male fan, as we have seen, was fixated on cataloging the talents of actors. This practice was the connoisseur's way of both sublimating desire into possession and compensating for the fleeting quality of live theater through fixing it in the written word. Women were not privy to this playhouse-centered culture of the male opera connoisseur. In the settings in which they were allowed to watch opera, they sometimes had occasion to view full-cycle dramas.[160]

The presence of women in the audience did not necessarily preclude the playful eroticism of the playhouse in the salon setting. A cautionary instruction about the deleterious effects of women watching plays, written by Qian Decang in the eighteenth century, makes this clear. Women's presence at salon plays stoked his agitation:

> Plays performed by actors should only be shown as entertainment for [male] guests. When women watch from behind a curtain, the fragrance of their face powder permeates the air; they crowd in close behind the curtain, their stockings and tiny shoes ever so faintly revealed below the partition. Sometimes the women even comment on the visiting guests in loud voices and with lots of giggling. The gaze of the actors penetrates right into their midst, and the thoughts of the guests keep drifting back behind the curtain. But that is all of secondary importance. There are few plays that deal with loyalty, filiality, chastity, and righteousness. There are many that dwell on illicit love and provocative flirtation. When women watch such plays, they get excited and their hearts are stirred. This is not a trifling matter. Be careful.[161]

Here Qian sounds like so many other theater nay-sayers of the late imperial era. But unlike those others, Qian was not just any neo-Confucian moralist. He was a compiler of the multivolume *A Cloak of Patchworked White Fur* (*Zhuibaiqiu*), the largest anthology of drama scenes heretofore published in the eighteenth century.[162] Qian's intimate participation in the publishing of drama makes it clear that he was not opposed to opera in principle, just to the mix of women and opera. His main objections are twofold. First, the content of the plays had the potential to corrupt the morals and conduct of the elite women who watched them. Second, and apparently even more upsetting, boundaries were being crossed—both literally and figuratively. The smells, sights, and sounds of the women could not be contained by the separating curtain. Nor could the curtain keep out the straying thoughts of the male guests or even the wandering eyes of the male actors. If the boy actress is usually the object of the male patron's gaze, with women in attendance a multitude of gazes confuse gender and status distinctions. Women are eyeing and assessing their male peers as well as the pretty boy actors. The attention of the male guests wanders between the stage and the partitioning curtain (perhaps upsetting the delicate balance needed to maintain the "constructed woman" onstage). And maybe most distressing of all to the elite male writer, the power hierarchy is disrupted by the actors' gazes on women considered their social superiors. Although it is possible that Qian—compromised by his participation in the compiling of *Cloak*—vented this screed to bolster his image of peerless rectitude, his comment nevertheless reveals that even avid male devotees recognized the socially transgressive potential of opera.

. . .

So long as theatrical spectacle remained under the panoptic eye of the Qing court, its various boundary crossings could be tolerated. Court performance was an expression of the theatrical salon writ large. The imperial household was the greatest patron of theatrical performance throughout the Qing, and that patronage was most extravagant under the Qianlong emperor and later under Empress Dowager Cixi. By the latter half of the eighteenth century the Nanfu—the office within the Imperial Household Department in charge of court theatricals—governed close to fifteen hundred actors (organized into an assortment of "inside" eunuchs and "outside" recruited acting troupes).[163] In addition to hosting birthday performances, every year on the fifteenth of the first month the Qianlong emperor "summoned all his ministers to the Garden of Communal Joy [Tongle yuan] to watch plays . . . and enjoy a meal of fine delicacies."[164] Over the course of his reign the Qianlong emperor also commissioned several lengthy and elaborate grand operas (*da xi*) to be performed at court, including opera versions of the Mulian story cycle (*Quanshan jinke*), the Three Kingdoms saga (*Dingzhi chunqiu*), and the legend of the Water Margin rebels (*Zhongyi xuantu*).[165] Each of these scripts comprised ten books with twenty-four scenes per book; a full presentation of one such grand opera took several days.

The most exaggerated expression of salon performance at court was the imperially sponsored birthday celebrations—for the Kangxi emperor in 1713, for the Empress Dowager Xiaosheng (Hongli's mother) in 1752, and for the Qianlong emperor in 1790—during which raised platform-stages were erected citywide along the roads stretching from the western gate of the palace to the imperial retreats in the suburban western hills. For the latter two occasions, command performances, which lasted for several days, acting troupes were requisitioned from Yangzhou and elsewhere.[166] In these grandiose gestures the emperor turned the whole of Beijing into his salon within his imperium. Officials and the people of the city, the emperor's minion-subjects, became his invited guests. Zhao Yi was present in the capital for the sixtieth-birthday celebration of the empress dowager, and he has left a record of his impressions:

> The empress dowager's birthday fell on the twenty-fifth of the eleventh month [11 January]. In 1752, on the occasion of Her Highness's sixtieth birthday, central and provincial officials all rushed to the capital to participate in a huge celebration. For several tens of *li*, from the Xihua Gate to the Sorghum Bridge outside the Xizhi Gate . . . every dozen steps or so a stage had been set up on which was performed all the music of the four directions—from southern tunes to northern melodies. Young boys and pretty singing girls sang and danced; one troupe had barely finished before the next rushed on to begin. . . . A festival of this magnitude does not come around more than once in a millennium. Was it not my great privilege to get to see it in person! . . . On the occasion of the eightieth birthday of the emperor, I heard that the lavish celebration was no less magnificent than that of 1752. But I had already left the capital, so I did not have the chance to see it with my own eyes.[167]

Visual as well as textual records speak to the grandiosity of such performances. The court-commissioned album-leaf painting shown in Figure 9 depicts a celebratory performance before the Qianlong emperor and his guest, an emissary from the new king of the Nguyên dynasty in Annam, at the Pavilion of Pure Sounds (Qingyin ge) in the palace at Rehe (Jehol) on the occasion of the Mid-Autumn Festival in 1789.[168] This was the largest of the Qing court's three-tiered stages, informally referred to by eunuchs as "the big master" (*daye*).[169] The massive scale of production on one such occasion is recorded by Zhao Yi, who in 1756 and 1757, during the course of his long career as an official in the capital, had the chance to view performances on "the big master." He once traveled to Rehe as part of the imperial entourage for the autumnal hunt; on that occasion, he observed:

> The various Mongol princes all came for an audience [with the emperor]. The emperor's birthday fell two days before the Mid-Autumn Festival, so beginning on the sixth of the month and lasting until the fifteenth, grand operas were performed. The plays performed were all selections about gods and demons from the novels *Journey to the West* [*Xiyou ji*] and *Investiture of the Gods* [*Fengshen zhuan*]. They excerpted the most fantastical parts, stories that did not run the risk of broaching taboo subjects, which they could embellish upon more out of thin air and further make use of hosts of actors to create a bizarre and variegated spectacle. The stage was nine mats wide and had three levels. Some of the demons depicted onstage descended from on high, others popped out from below, and still others even appeared mounted on camels and riding horses from behind the audience seats on either side of the stage so that even the courtyard in front of the stage eventually was filled. At times, when all the gods and demons were gathered on the stage, you could literally see thousands of masks, yet there was not one duplication. . . . On the day that the monk Tang Xuanzang reached the Leiyin Monastery, when the Rulai Buddha mounted the throne, nearly a thousand disciples and arhats . . . from top to bottom were arrayed seated on nine levels, yet there was still plenty of room left on the stage.[170]

These massive productions were orchestrated to instill awe in spectators, and apparently they succeeded. In addition to the descriptions left behind by Zhao Yi and Zhaolian, envoys to the Qing court from Joseon Korea commented on the magnificence of these performances. So Hosu, a member of the 1790 Joseon embassy to the Qing capital, marveled in his diary about the entertainments featuring gods and immortals: "The gods of the River and the ghosts of the Ocean presented their banners of waves, marching in circles: group after group, waving and shaking, their energy rising and surging! The various immortals came to disport themselves on the boundless expanse, riding on dragons and whales, seated on rafts and cranes. Dragons leapt up and whales jumped about, spouting water like rain!"[171] In 1793 even a skeptical Earl George Macartney, in the audience for the Qianlong emperor's birthday celebrations, was moved to admit: "However meanly we must think of the taste and delicacy of the Court of China, whose most refined amusements seem to be chiefly such as I have now described, together with the wretched dramas of the morning, yet it must be confessed that there was something grand and imposing in the general effect that resulted from the whole spectacle."[172]

Had Macartney lived a century earlier he might have thought much less "meanly" of such exotic sights, for not unlike the masques of Jacobean and Caroline England, these mid-Qing pageants were ideological—paeans to the glory of the dynasty—and relied as much on spectacle as on plot.[173] Whether through mastery of technological wonders (water-spouting whales and stage trapdoors) or through the sheer number of actors mustered for such occasions, these elaborate displays were calculated to project the power of the regime, becoming an integral facet of interdomainal and intra-Asian Qing diplomacy.[174] Documentation of such events—whether in the form of the auspicious scripts left behind, commentary by observers, or the court preservation of such celebrations in its commissioned paintings (see Figure 9)—speaks to the court's mastery of control. Under court orchestration the social boundaries between players and spectators and the moral messages of plays could be fixed, making opera an important tool of state ideology. Such control eluded the state when opera was mounted in the metropolis at large.

If the court grand operas seem overly extravagant to have had much bearing on the salon experience, the court also had more intimate settings in which to enjoy opera performance. The imperial palaces were home to many midsize and small theaters. The Drenched Fragrance Studio (Shufangzhai), the former princely apartments of the Qianlong emperor, housed two stages, one in the central courtyard and the other within its western anterior hall, both of which date from the early years of the Qianlong reign (Figures 10 and 11).[175] Yet another pair of stages was built in the Weary of Cares Studio (Juanqinzhai), intended, as the name suggests, for amusements to entertain the Qianlong emperor in his retirement (Figure 12).[176] The single-story stage located in the western wing of the building directly opposite the Pavilion of Joyful Sounds (Changyin ge) stage within the Ningshou Palace was the favorite opera-viewing location of Empress Dowager Cixi, reputed to be an avid enthusiast.[177] These stages more closely approximated the scale of performances both within salon settings outside the palace and in the commercial playhouses. These more modest stages were also the most used.[178]

It was in these spaces, too, where members of the imperial family often indulged a double standard—privately viewing some of the very story material that they deemed inappropriate for public consumption. As with salon performances in the homes of the wealthy, the familial hierarchy and supervision mechanisms within the imperial palaces could always determine who saw what, making this permissible. The operas mounted on

Figure 10. Courtyard stage within the Drenched Fragrance Studio (Shufangzhai) in the imperial palace. From *National Opera Pictorial* (*Guoju huabao*) 39 (14 October 1933): 153.

Figure 11. The "Preserved Elegance" (Fengyacun) stage within the Drenched Fragrance Studio (Shufangzhai). Stage dimensions: 3.9 m wide; 3.5 m deep; 2.2 m from the stage floor to the ceiling. Dimensions from Liao Ben, *Zhongguo gudai juchang shi*, p. 138. The Palace Museum Collection, Beijing. Courtesy of the Palace Museum.

Figure 12. The recently refurbished double stages within the Weary of Cares Studio (Juanqinzhai) in the imperial palace. These stages were built for the amusement of the Qianlong emperor upon his retirement in 1796. Dimensions of the roofed stage: 3.7 m wide; 3.4 m deep; 2.2 m from the stage floor to the ceiling. Dimensions of front stage: 2.3 m wide × 3 m deep. Dimensions from Liao Ben, *Zhongguo gudai juchang shi*, p. 138. The stage was only large enough to support solo and duo performances. It was also used for magic shows and other variety-skit acts. The Palace Museum Collection, Beijing. Courtesy of the Palace Museum.

smaller palace stages tended to be drawn from the same dramatic repertoire as those performed beyond the walls of the imperial residences, including both selected scenes and full plays from well-known dramatic story cycles, in addition to the ritually prescribed fifteenth-of-the-first-month and birthday-felicitation operas.[179] All scripts to be performed before the emperor or members of the imperial household were subject to scrutiny. A special palace repository copy (*andian ben*) of each playscript was submitted for approval prior to performance and was made available for the emperor or empress dowager to consult during the performance.[180] Many of these scripts are marked with corrections in the vermilion ink of the imperial hand, indicating that the emperor and his surrogates took their surveillance of entertainment seriously.

Imperial interest in opera waned steadily after the Qianlong reign. During the subsequent Jiaqing reign the number of actors employed at court was reduced by nearly half. The Daoguang emperor economized even further; in 1827 a major reorganization of the palace entertainment corps was undertaken (the bureau in charge of actors was renamed the Bureau of Ascendant Peace), by which time most of the "outside" recruited actors had been dismissed and allowed to return to their native locales.[181] The Daoguang reorganization represents the last major attempt by the Qing court to assert clear boundaries between the entertainments at court and in the capital at large. In the late 1800s, at roughly the time that the court relaxed its vigilance over the locations of playhouses within the city, a new generation of monarchs, princes, and their consorts revived court patronage of opera, building to a second crescendo during the watch of Empress Dowager Cixi. These members of the royal family no longer kept commercial opera at a distance; rather, they invited commercial troupes and actors to perform within the walls of the palace. Through this embrace of commercial opera, ironically, the court exerted far greater influence upon the shape of opera culture in the capital.

Conclusion

From the late seventeenth through the middle of the nineteenth century the Qing court actively attempted to police opera performance in its capital city. State proscriptions, often couched in the language of morality, at heart were about preserving social order within the city. Commercial theater especially was suspect because it defied state attempts to maintain boundaries of ethnicity, class, and gender. Indeed, in all three venues—the playhouse, the temple fair, and the salon—participation in opera in Qing Beijing encouraged many kinds of border crossings. Those border crossings that went against the grain of existing political, social, and gender hierarchies were perceived as transgressive by the state and by some elite champions of orthodoxy, whereas those crossings-over that simply reinforced or were mapped onto preexisting hierarchies were tolerated, even indulged.

The ethnic and social heterogeneity of the crowds in the commercial playhouse caused anxiety in the eyes of the apartheid regime—a regime that viewed Manchu difference (and hence purity) as central to its claim to legitimacy. But as we have seen, over the course of the eighteenth and nineteenth centuries attempts to preserve ethnic and spatial segregation—at least in the audiences of commercial theater—gradually broke down and were abandoned. Likewise, in the writings of some of the educated men who frequented the commercial theaters there is clear discomfiture at the mix of humanity among the patrons, but also clear evidence that mingling with merchants and pond-seat crowds was not enough of a deterrence to stop them from attending the public theaters. Those truly disgusted by playhouse crowds could always find their dramatic entertainment in the relative insularity of the private salon, at least so long as they had the financial means or social connections to do so. The gender reversals of the Qing-era opera theater, rather than being transgressive, satisfied a pervasive awareness of the debased status of the entertainer and enhanced the allure of the transvestite stage. And women's exclusion from the commercial playhouse seems to have worked as an unwritten, unstated social pact, defusing official anxiety over the public mingling of men and women, while at the same time perfecting the erotic gaze on the boy actress as woman.

Women did have ready access to the temple fair, the most accessible of the three venues. This venue had the most socially diverse audiences, and as with the playhouse, the mix of crowds at the temple fair was cause for alarm to and intervention by the state. The state seems to have been particularly concerned to protect Manchus, Banner affiliates, and women from the deleterious effects of temple-fair entertainments. Unlike the playhouse, however, the temple fair was not solely devoted to theater. Its legitimate religious and economic functions sheltered it from both the number and harshness of the proscriptions directed at the commercial playhouse. Again, in contrast to the temple fair, the compromise of the commercial playhouse becomes more obvious. By excluding women from the playhouse venue, one additional potentially disruptive element was removed from the mix, thereby making the playhouse less suspect in the eyes of the state.

Court policy toward salon performance shows that the court had little desire to police its own leisure, nor did it have the will or ability to intervene very much in the entertainments of other elites in their own homes and private associations. The familial economy of the salon preserved hierarchies of social class and status. In the salon venue, the only potentially transgressive border crossings arose when elite women joined the audience, although the extent to which men found this troubling seems to have varied, as did house rules on the matter. However much some commentators fretted about women from good families getting the wrong ideas from plays, as long as gender heterogeneity was not compounded with class heterogeneity in the audiences, women's attendance at performances was for the most part accepted. The private nature of the salon made this possible.

Among the three venues, then, the playhouse was unique in that it was both public and exclusively devoted to performance. This was the venue that generated the demimonde associated with commercial opera. Notwithstanding the curbs that ticket prices and the exclusion of women exerted on audience constituency, this was the venue most apt to become a site for the circulation of ideas and sentiments among patrons of varied status. But the playhouse was not just a space for exchange of ideas; it also was a site of passion and private desires. In other words, commercial opera had the affective power to move audiences, and the sentiments thereby generated might be played out within the public space of the city. It was precisely this mix of public and private attributes that made the playhouse at once so attractive to audiences and so potentially threatening to the Qing state. Clearly, the Qing court failed in its efforts to spatially contain commercial playhouses in Beijing from circa 1770 to 1900. By the end of this era, however, it proved much more successful in shaping the content of what was performed in the theaters. The key element in the court's successful intervention was its sanction and patronage of particular genres of opera music.

THREE

Musical Genre, Opera Hierarchy, and Court Patronage

> Hereafter, for all opera troupes in the Outer City, only those singing *kun* and *yi* melodies will still be allowed to perform. Those troupes singing *qin* melody are to be notified by the Office of the Captain-General of the Gendarmerie of the Five Wards of the City of a prohibition against such opera. Current actors of such troupes are ordered to resume the *kun* and *yi* styles of singing. Those who are unwilling to abide by this should seek out alternative means of livelihood. Those who obstreperously refuse to obey should be arrested and handed over to the aforesaid Office for punishment, and thence deported back to their provinces of origin.
>
> 嗣後城外戲班，除崑弋兩腔，仍聽其演唱外，其秦腔戲班，交步軍統領五城出示禁止。現在本班戲子，概令改歸崑弋兩腔。如不願者，聽其另謀生理。儻有怙惡不尊者，交該衙門查拏懲治，遞解回籍。
>
> Edict of 1785[1]

The Qing court may have lost the battle over where opera was performed in the capital, but it was considerably more victorious in influencing what was performed. By patronizing some musical genres and forbidding others, the court became an active agent in shaping opera taste in Beijing.

Since the late Ming, taste in opera had conformed to the aesthetics of the lower Yangzi delta (Jiangnan) elite, who esteemed above all their local, Suzhou-identified Kun opera. Their estimation, bolstered by the long-standing economic and cultural preeminence of the region, quickly made Kun opera fashionable throughout the realm, preferred by both scholar-official and mercantile elites. The dynastic transition in the mid-seventeenth century had done little to shake kunju's supreme position in the opera hierarchy. Early Qing rulers publicly endorsed the cultural matrix of the Han elite in all fields of the arts, including opera, although in the privacy of the palaces they gave rein to somewhat more eclectic tastes.[2]

By the late eighteenth century the capital had become host to a rich assortment of opera genres—from the Jiangnan-derived kunju to northern variants of Yiyang melody (also called *yi* melody, capital melody, or jingqiang) and northwestern bangzi operas such as qinqiang.[3] This diversity of genres was supported by the heterogeneity of subcultures within the city, in which Banner institutions rubbed shoulders with the aesthetics of the Han bureaucratic elite, and merchants from all around the empire gathered, whether as transients or transplants, in the precinct of the throne. Each constituency favored its own local opera, while potentially open to any other performance genre the capital might have to offer. These genres were informally but implicitly ranked by both connoisseurs and the court, with kunju exalted as "elegant opera" (*yabu*), and with all other genres categorized as huabu, or, more dismissively, "chaotic strumming" (*luantan*).

Through both symbolic and practical means, the court attempted to dictate the variety of opera available to audiences in the capital.[4] On a symbolic level, at the same time that the Qing court corroborated the dominant Han taste, it also competed with that elite in defining knowledge about opera. By publishing court-sponsored research on dramatic prosody (among other topics), such as the *Great Compilation of Musical Scores from the Southern and Northern Arias in All Nine Modes* (*Jiugong dacheng nanbeici gongpu*), the state aimed to assert cultural preeminence. Like other knowledge-production compendia of the era, *All Nine Modes* was encyclopedic in scope.[5] It exemplifies the Qianlong court's ambition to catalog—and by cataloging to constrain—all Han culture under its watchful gaze.

In terms of the practical side of Qing court policy, even when the Jiangnan elite set the cultural norms, the state enforced them through regulation. By imperial fiat the only sanctioned styles up through the mid-nineteenth century were kunju and Yiyang melody. Certain huabu styles, such as qinqiang, became the target of state proscription. The court framed such interference in commercial opera as an aspect of the state's proprietary concern to preserve public morality, and since huabu opera was reputed to be lewd and crass, it received the brunt of the court's wrath. Arguments about indecency or morality alone, however, are insufficient to explain the court's favoritism of kunju and Yiyang opera. The court was at least equally concerned with monitoring and maintaining social order in the capital. Audiences responded to qinqiang and other new huabu styles of opera with highly emotional outbursts, which traversed class and regional boundaries (appealing to men of power and means as well as local constituencies within the capital) and threatened to disrupt orderly conduct within the city.

Qing policing of opera genre—as of opera location—was at best partly effective. Commercial opera troupes, too, were critical players in the contestation over what would be performed in the capital city. Troupes and actors modified their styles of performance to adapt to and evade official regulations—simultaneously censoring themselves and eluding proscriptions. This process considerably hybridized the various opera styles; and thus, performances often defied neat genre classification.

Educated audiences responded to the resulting mélange of styles that emerged in commercial playhouse performance in the mid-Qing in essentially two ways. On the one hand, some connoisseurs of highbrow opera attempted to wrest kunju away from commercial performance (and genre contamination) so as to fix its elegant quality. Late eighteenth-century anthologies of Kun arias, such as Ye Tang's *Musical Scores from the Last Word Studio* (*Nashuying qupu*), were compiled to valorize the songlike expression of the genre over its theatricality. In consciously attempting to preclude Kun opera from commercial performance, these musical sophisticates (or genre "purists") were defending the emergent concept of elegance.[6] Such private literati anthologies reflect an awareness of the court-sponsored *All Nine Modes* compendium and suggest their authors' intent to carve out a cultural space distinct from both state recognition and urban commercialism. On the other hand, some marginalized literati enthusiasts made a point of expressing their eccentricity and individuality by championing the popular huabu opera. For the most part, however, until the second half of the nineteenth century, most of the elite considered huabu opera lowbrow.

In spite of court regulations and a lingering elite preference for yabu opera, by the early nineteenth century a bowdlerized, commercial kunju, as well as huabu opera, were on the ascendance in the capital playhouses. This trend—including the blending of musical styles—would culminate in the eventual rise of pihuang opera.[7] In response to the vibrancy of these new opera styles, a marked shift in court sensibilities transpired in the second half of the nineteenth century. A new cohort of Manchu rulers, while never rejecting kunju, came to actively embrace lowbrow opera such as pihuang, thereby helping lend to it the patina of high culture; and new court oversight of the Beijing Actors' Guild put curbs on public urban performance in novel ways.

Opera genre thus became a cultural field in which both the Manchu court and Han connoisseurs sought to assert authority—at times in concert, at times in competition.[8] The lead in defining opera taste changed hands over time, with Jiangnan elite sensibility largely ordering the opera hierarchy through the mid-nineteenth century, and the Qing court thereafter. An urban audience public—not always fully literate and thus not often reflected in textual sources—participated in this cultural contest by "voting with their feet" on plays and actors. Finally, acting companies in the Qing metropolis responded creatively to their two masters of state interdiction and economic livelihood. Untangling the shifting hierarchies of musical genre and audience patronage in eighteenth- and nineteenth-century Beijing reveals a larger story about state-society tension, negotiation, and accommodation as played out in the cultural realm.

Yabu *and* Huabu

The classical opera music of the late Ming and early Qing originated in Kunshan, neighboring the great late imperial city of Suzhou. Suzhou gentlemen of the sixteenth century adapted local tunes into a musical system for use in dramatic composition, which became known as the "melody of Kunshan" (or Kunshan *qiang*). Wei Liangfu (1489–1566) is credited with having spent more than ten years perfecting Kunshan qiang into its mellifluous and distinctive "water-polished melodies" (*shuimo qiang*), which quickly gained (and long retained) wide favor throughout the realm. The principal melodic instrument for Kunshan qiang has always been the horizontal flute (*di*). Aria lyrics are poems composed of lines of uneven length, set to preexisting melodies arranged in set patterns, or suites. Writing the poetry for dramas to be set in the Kunshan melody took considerable erudition and soon became the subject of scholarship, including a prodigious output of works on dramatic prosody. The original name of the musical genre came to be abbreviated as "Kun melody" (*kunqiang*); persons choosing to emphasize the music of this dramatic tradition have referred to it as *kunqu* (*qu* meaning "song"); those focusing on the theatrical totality of Kun opera have called it *kunju* (*ju* marking its staged expression).[9] By the early Qing, as both scholar-officials and the court granted Kun music the canonical position within a wider field of melodic systems, it came to be identified by the term *yabu*.[10]

Yabu implicitly was a relative term; its antonym, coined in the late eighteenth century, was huabu.[11] Musically, huabu operas differ from kunqu in having simpler lyrical phrasing (arias are made up of couplets of even line length) and noisier, percussive instrumentation (including heavy reliance on cymbals, drums, and rhythmic wooden blocks). Huabu music was loud, busy, colorful, and bold. Many musical styles fall within the huabu (or luantan) category, key among them *qinqiang, bangzi, erhuang, xipi,* and *pihuang*. Present-day readers are not alone in finding this welter of genre labels confusing; even during the Qing dynasty the various names denoting subgenres of huabu opera could be daunting. A nineteenth-century comic scions' tale entitled "The Lament of the Fake Lao Dou" (Jia lao dou tan), about a would-be opera sophisticate, portrays the title character's utter befuddlement: "Although he called out, 'What a sight, what sounds!' he didn't understand a damn thing; 'what is this erhuang, this xipi, this bangzi, which are also called luantan?'"[12] Whatever their names, these subgenres of huabu styles had one thing in common: all were considered "vulgar" (*su*), in contrast to the "elegance" (*ya*) of yabu.

Past scholarship on Chinese opera history has tended to treat *yabu* and *huabu* as fixed categories. Instead, I suggest that application of these terms was a response by educated observers of the time to the multiplicity and fluidity of performance styles in the urban opera marketplace. As such, these labels—whether deployed by the court or by literati commentators—attempted to impose a modicum of stability upon the contested cultural field of opera genre.

Court Patronage and Regulation to circa 1860

References to Qing court performance are scanty prior to the late seventeenth century. The fledgling Qing state modeled its palace entertainment bureau after the Office of Music (Jiaofang si) of the Ming dynasty, which was staffed by male and female performers who belonged to households that owed hereditary obligation to serve the court in this capacity. By the Kangxi reign women had been eliminated from palace performance, and court acting "schools," comprising both palace eunuchs and commercial actors requisitioned into palace service, had come under the jurisdiction of a new agency known as the Nanfu.[13] The Nanfu trained these actors in the kun and yi musical genres of opera for performance at court.[14]

From the 1680s on, when court patronage of opera does begin to appear in the historical record, it invariably is linked with public demonstration of Qing authority and dominion. The first court "grand occasion" to include opera performance was held in 1683 to celebrate the suppression of the Rebellion of the Three Feudatories, at which enactment of the ritual Mulian drama cycle was staged, using live tigers and elephants.[15] The "elephantine" scale of such celebrations was meant to awe. In 1713, upon the Kangxi emperor's return from the imperial hunt and to commemorate his sixtieth birthday, a lavish citywide festival was held featuring at least forty-nine temporary stages, which stretched from the Shenwu Gate of the Forbidden City to the imperial pleasure gardens in the western suburbs of the capital; most of these stages hosted kun and yi melody performances (Figure 13).[16] Thereafter, as discussed earlier, sixtieth and eightieth birthdays of emperors and empress dowagers became occasions for the court to hold flamboyant theatrical spectacles in the capital.

Court patronage of opera was further closely entwined with the many imperial southern tours, for it was on these ambulatory demonstrations

Figure 13. Woodblock print of the elephantine celebrations for the Kangxi emperor's birthday in 1713. Detail from *Draft Edition of the Imperial Birthday Celebrations* (*Wanshou shengdian chuji*). Reprinted from *Siku quanshu*, ce 653, juan 41, p. 19.

of dynastic power, many of which paraded through the heart of Jiangnan, that emperors became especially enamored of the sights and sounds of Kun opera. According to one account: "When the Kangxi emperor toured the south, the commissioner of the Jiangsu Imperial Textile Manufactory arranged for the Hanxiang, Miaoguan, and other troupes to perform for the traveling entourage, and they were met with lavish praise and reward. Two to three people were chosen from each troupe to serve within the palace."[17] As attested by some of the earliest private communications between the Kangxi emperor and Suzhou Textile Commissioner Li Xu (1655–1729), the Imperial Textile Manufactories, which were responsible for hosting the Kangxi emperor on his tours through Jiangnan, served as the conduit through which non-eunuch actors were funneled into the court.[18] Gu Lu, writing on the customs of Suzhou, confirms that this agency continued to supply the palace with actors for Kun opera into the nineteenth century: "The Laolang Temple serves as the central guild for the [players of the] Pear Garden. All who are registered as actors must submit their names to the Laolang Temple. The Temple is under the administration of the Imperial Textile Manufactory; when actors are needed to serve in the Nanfu, . . . they must all be selected through the Textile Manufactory."[19] Beginning with such encounters in the 1690s, the state both appropriated Jiangnan opera (and actors) for its own uses and vied with the Han elite to be the foremost patron of the dramatic arts. The late Kangxi era thus marks the time when Qing rulers began to exhibit state power through conspicuous cultural patronage.[20]

Beyond citywide celebrations and imperial touring, sponsorship of scholarly research—from dictionaries to histories and encyclopedias—was equally important to the state's claim to cultural hegemony.[21] By the Qianlong era the emperor was envisioned, in Pamela Crossley's words, as "a paragon of omniliteracy, the esthete of all cultures."[22] Music was among the first of the fields of study tagged for court surveillance and mastery. In 1742 the Qianlong emperor launched preparation of a comprehensive concordance to entertainment music, which was completed in 1746 and came to be known as *All Nine Modes*.[23] In eighty-two volumes, *All Nine Modes* was designed to record and (re)categorize all known scores for lyric song suites and arias from Tang times to the date of commission. The work drew liberally from privately produced collections of northern- and southern-style scores for drama such as the late Ming *Expanded and Corrected Scores for Northern Lyrics* (*Beici guangzheng pu*) and the early Qing *Established Pitches for Southern Lyrics* (*Nanci dinglü*).[24] Whereas these and earlier private compilations focused on either the heptatonic northern music or the pentatonic southern music, the court production, aiming to be comprehensive, combined knowledge about both musical systems into one text. Like so many other, later Qianlong literary projects, *All Nine Modes* was a product of collaboration between Han literati under the supervision of a Manchu prince, in this instance Yinlu, uncle to the Qianlong emperor.[25] The team of courtier-scholars who worked on this massive compilation—Zhou Xiangyu, Zou Jinsheng, and others—also penned many of the mid-Qing auspicious plays and grand operas performed exclusively for the court.[26]

Theories of Chinese statecraft had long associated political order and canonical music, a principle not lost on the Qing and alluded to in the preface to *All Nine Modes* by its editor-in-chief, Yinlu:[27]

> Many are those who have mistaken the key for the mode or the mode for the key, causing vain controversy; or they have confused the beat for the melody or the melody for the beat, making matters even more perplexing. With the protocols lost, confusion and mistakes ensued; with no standard to follow, everyone became teacher to himself. Entering this era of joyous peace, and being situated as well in this beautiful imperial capital, I was directed to oversee this matter, and thus this book was brought to fruition. . . . From the completion of this work, the emperor desires to return the pitches to harmony. . . . When the fall of the *jue*-note is clarified, bright air rises up to the skies, and when the playing of the *shang*-note is clarified, wind and rain pour down from on high.[28]

The clichés about musical and political harmony—boilerplate, perhaps, for prefaces in imperially issued encyclopedias—nevertheless reveal a clear link in the imperial imagination between auspicious music and efficacious rule.

The comprehensiveness of the collection, in and of itself, was key to Qing assertion of cultural supremacy. *All Nine Modes* was intended as the final word on musical prosody. It was the court that took it upon itself to end the various divergent interpretations of musical composition, to patch over the sonic north-south fault line, and to arrive at a new synthesis. In the words of one of the editors,

> That the discourse of music is difficult is not because music itself is hard to speak of, but rather it is the fault of those who [in the past] have spoken about music. When scholars discourse on music, their emphasis is on theory. Though their erudition may be great, it is hard for them to harmonize theory with practice. The art of practitioners suffers from their mode of [oral] transmission and is often at odds with theory. These two approaches being at odds

has led to the obfuscation of our understanding of music. . . . This compilation traces pitches back to their origins, it covers all possible variations of the modes, it rectifies the transmitted errors, and it collates the complete northern and southern modes.[29]

The title of this multivolume work, by invoking the term *jiugong*, or "nine modes," seems to place the encyclopedia in a long line of scholarly manuals on musical prosody dating back as far as the Song dynasty. In fact, however, *All Nine Modes* departed significantly from earlier classificatory schemes; it subsumed the nine modes within a new organizational division based on the seasons (and months) of the year.[30] In ordering the musical systems according to the calendar, the collection gave priority to the ritual uses even of entertainment music. *All Nine Modes* was also the first work to record the music for auspicious plays and grand operas created especially for court consumption among its scores. Whether or not *All Nine Modes* worked as a new theoretical basis for a comprehensive musical system encompassing northern and southern styles, it was a conceptual construct well suited to the Qianlong-era political climate. Although the new compendium could not erase earlier scholarship on the topic, the cumulative effect of its innovations was to place a singularly Qing imprint on the organization of knowledge for dramatic music. Henceforth, according to Yinlu, *All Nine Modes* would "be sufficient to let the players of Qi and the harps of Zhao spread their brilliance across the stretches of time; the beauties of Yue and the songs of Wu will lose some of their evergreen luster in compare."[31] Here, the allusion to Qi, Zhao, Yue, and Wu—all ancient Chinese kingdoms—is an oblique way of comparing the music of the north (Qi and Zhao) with that of the lower Yangzi delta (Wu and Yue), with the implication that the efforts of the dynasty in the north can outrival those of Jiangnan.

It is hard to discover just how widely *All Nine Modes* was disseminated beyond the court, but excerpts from the compendium were published in 1757 and 1844 under the respective titles *Music Scores from the Studio of Self-Amusement* (*Ziyixuan yuepu*) and *Golden Fragments Lyric Scores* (*Suijin cipu*).[32] In addition, as will become evident, experts on Kun opera music, such as Suzhou native Ye Tang, were aware of *All Nine Modes* as a new standard of authority on drama prosody. The Qing challenge to Jiangnan supremacy in cultural matters was clearly recognized, if not openly acknowledged.

Just as the Qing court strove for total mastery when it arbitrated guidelines for composition of dramatic music, it sought total control when it intervened in the practices of opera within the capital. Total control was unachievable, but the state did manage to curb certain types of opera. Although the court issued edicts restricting the *location* of playhouses within the city as early as the 1670s, those targeting certain *genres* of opera commenced only in the last quarter of the eighteenth century, roughly concomitant with the rise in popularity of huabu opera, and especially of qinqiang. Qinqiang, an amalgamation of various bangzi melodies originating in the Sichuan-Shaanxi-Shanxi region, had been brought mostly by traders along trade routes into the capital.[33] In the capital its practitioners became known as the players of the "Western Troupes."[34] By all accounts, the Western Troupes took the capital by storm in the 1780s. In response, the court did its best to suppress qinqiang within Beijing.

To better understand why the court acted with such alarm to the introduction of this musical genre into the capital, we can look in some detail at the career of qinqiang's most famous eighteenth-century actor, Wei Changsheng (1744–1802). According to one account,

> In 1779 he followed others to the capital. At that time the Shuangqing Troupe was not popular; no one even bothered to note them in the singing halls. Changsheng [approached the company and] told its members: "If you allow me to join your troupe, if within two months I do not improve your reputation, I shall willingly accept punishment with no regrets." Thereupon, with his rendition of the scene "Rolling in the Loft" [Gunlou] his fame shook the capital.[35] More than one thousand spectators came to watch every day, and the six great troupes lost some of their appeal in comparison.[36]

Wei made a name for himself as a female impersonator in sexually suggestive romantic comedies. His signature opera scene, "Rolling in the Loft," another observer claimed, "made him all the rage throughout the empire."[37] He is also credited with popularizing the practices of wearing long-haired wigs and walking on raised-platform *qiao* shoes (which approximated the look of walking on bound feet), both of which greatly enhanced his femininity in the dan role. These innovations were considered racy at the time, eliciting powerful audience responses.[38] According to one observer, when Wei's student Chen Yinguan took the stage, butchers and carriage drivers in the audience erupted into banging on the tables and hooting wildly.[39] Another wit wagged in verse about Chen's rendition of the opera "Saved by the Fire" (Kao huo):

> Head bowed low, s/he pleads piteously, much to our delight;
> And walking on those *qiao*-shoes, s/he's really quite a sight.

No wonder the whole house yells "hao!" at all these goings on;
Today's "Saved by the Fire" would be nothing without Yinguan.[40]

The appeal of qinqiang did not rest solely on story content and costuming novelties. The music, too, was compelling. In Zhaolian's recollection, "Although the lyrics were rustic, there was an urgency to the music, and its throbbing wails moved people."[41] Zhang Jiliang observed that the singing—in short, choppy patter—was a lot like speech.[42]

The popularity of qinqiang seems to have spooked the Qing court. Most commentators have pointed to the prurient stories of qinqiang opera to explain the court reaction, yet that, while surely part of the reason, seems only part. After all, qinqiang was hardly the only opera genre that trafficked in titillating plots. Kunju, the "classical" opera genre, was rife with romance and sexually explicit plays too. Perhaps the clarity of the lyrics in qinqiang—"a lot like speech"—made the same story material more readily understandable and hence more problematic in the eyes of the state.

Social control (or its lack), however, seems to have been equally at issue in the court response to qinqiang. The prevailing assumption was that the educated enjoyed kunju whereas huabu appealed to more benighted audiences. It was also assumed that the literati would and could control themselves in public settings; the court was not so sanguine about the capacity of crowds of "butchers and carriage drivers" to do the same. But audience response to Wei and his fellow qinqiang actors defied expectations—blurring aesthetic and social boundaries—and this may have been even more worrisome for the court.[43] Accounts from the time reveal that "men of wealth and status swooned for him; for a time in the singing halls the audience crowds were as thick as walls."[44] Zhao Yi confirms that wherever Wei went, "Everyone was smitten with him; princes and officials frantically vied to seek him out."[45] Zhaolian, writing in the early nineteenth century, echoes this observation: "From princes and nobles to Hanlin academicians and ministers of the boards, not a one did not spend several thousands in silver on him. For a time, whoever had not had the chance to make Wei's acquaintance . . . could not hold up his head in public."[46] Actors of other genres, too, gravitated to Wei and the performance styles of the Western Troupes. According to Li Dou, "When Wei Changsheng entered the capital with qinqiang, in beauty and talent he surpassed that of [those in] the Yiqing, Cuiqing, and Jiqing [Troupes], and so the actors of the capital melody troupes imitated him."[47] Wei's popularity was such that even kunju actors from Suzhou studied his style.[48]

From the court's perspective, in other words, the problem may have been that *everyone*—high or lowly, Manchu or Han, Yiyang or kunju performer—was taken with qinqiang. Crowd control alone, even allowing for exaggeration in reports of "spectators in the thousands" and "crowds as thick as walls," would have been a security concern for the state in the capital. Moreover, the sensation caused by the qinqiang performers and their music and new costuming techniques threatened to erase important social and artistic distinctions—a border crossing that gave the court further reason for anxiety.

Anecdotal evidence also reveals that Wei's meteoric rise threatened the livelihood of the "six great troupes" (*liu da ban*). These six acting companies specialized in capital melody, or jingqiang (a variant of Yiyang melody), and, according to one account, half of them were sponsored by princely households.[49] The entrance of Wei and the qinqiang actors into the capital realigned the popularity of the existing acting companies, causing the earlier troupes either to fold or to remake themselves in the likeness of qinqiang troupes. This process may have attenuated the authority of princely oversight, as the urban opera troupes moved further in the direction of private commercial enterprise. Increasingly, by the end of the eighteenth century, troupes became more beholden to public audiences than to noble patronage, and so the court acted, first by exiling individual qinqiang actors and, when that proved insufficient, by issuing a blanket prohibition of the genre.

In 1782 Wei was forbidden to act in the capital.[50] Shortly thereafter he left the capital for Yangzhou, where, beyond the immediate purview of the court, he again found a welcoming audience for his talents.[51] But Wei, while perhaps the most notorious of the qinqiang actors in the capital, was by no means qinqiang's only practitioner there. As amply documented in the actor biographies collected in late eighteenth-century flower registers, Wei's students as well as other qinqiang performers kept up the fashion. Wu Changyuan records that "various actors, such as Wang and Liu, have inherited his performance style; they also copy his disgraceful ways so as to run with the taste of the times."[52] The 1785 edict outlawing all performance of qinqiang in the capital was a response to the genre's continued acclaim.

In contrast to court regulations regarding the location of playhouses within the capital, the very frequency of which indicates that they were never really effective, prohibitions aimed at opera genres seem to have been more potent. Wei, after all, was compelled to leave the Beijing stage for many years, and when he eventually returned to it in 1800, he is reputed to have censored himself, gravitating to less provocative story material.[53] Wei's most famous disciple, Chen Yinguan, also ran afoul of the authorities; in 1786 he was banished to Sichuan, likely for flouting the 1785 decree. Zhaolian, writing in the early nineteenth century, claims that following Chen's expulsion from the capital, the craze for qinqiang subsided.[54] Although this assertion is partly contradicted by other evidence in guides to actors from the late eighteenth century, the last major court pronouncement on qinqiang dates from 1798, when a stone stele reiterating the prohibition was erected on the site of the Suzhou Actors' Guild (Laolang Temple), further indicating the reach of qinqiang beyond the capital to the Jiangnan region.[55] Thereafter, calls for a moratorium on qinqiang ceased, suggesting that the eradication campaign had had some success.[56] If nothing else, court policing of opera genre directly affected how actors characterized their performance styles. Troupes in the capital stopped calling their style qinqiang.

. . .

In response to court regulations, actors found ways to give audiences what they wanted while still obeying the letter—if not the spirit—of the law. Often, it seems, they simply renamed the opera genre they performed, while continuing to enact the same styles and plays that had brought them popularity. Wei Changsheng, for instance, in response to the ban on qinqiang is said to have "changed the name of his troupe from Shuangqing to Yongqing, which specialized in the capital melody style; he and his fellow qinqiang performers quickly switched to singing kun and yi [capital] melodies."[57] A list of the plays performed by the Yongqing Troupe in Beijing on 16 July 1797, however, reveals that the company offered a selection of plays sung in both kunju and huabu style on any one day.[58] The forbidden qinqiang, in other words, was subsumed under other genre labels, first capital melody and, later, the various singing styles of the so-called Hui troupes (Huiban). After Wei entered the capital in 1779, Li Dou observed, "There came to be no difference between capital and qin [melodies]. . . . Later Gao Langting entered the capital with his flowery opera troupe from Anqing. He combined the capital and qin melodies and named his troupe Sanqing."[59]

Both in their ability to perform multiple musical styles and in their blending of various opera traditions, the Hui troupes best reflect the growing hybridity of opera genre within the capital. The Sanqing Troupe cited by Li Dou is reputed to be the first of the Hui troupes to have arrived in the capital. These Hui troupes flocked to Beijing from Yangzhou beginning in 1790, drawn by the festivities for the Qianlong emperor's eightieth-year birthday.[60]

So named because they were originally sponsored by wealthy Huizhou merchants residing in the city of Yangzhou, the Hui troupes were associated with the music and performers of the Anhui region; they specialized in a melodic style known as *erhuang*. It is clear, however, that qinqiang acting techniques and play repertoires were incorporated into Hui troupe performances, although the name qinqiang was being invoked less frequently by the nineteenth century. Liu Langyu, for instance, an actor with the Sanqing Troupe circa 1803, had trained with Wei Changsheng; Liu, like Wei's qinqiang disciple from Sichuan, Chen Yinguan, specialized in the play "Saved by the Fire."[61] "Langyu's plays," one fan mused, "truly captured the bygone style and spirit of his teacher."[62] From their arrival in the capital into the early decades of the nineteenth century, the Hui troupes adopted and blended the best singing styles that Beijing had to offer, including qinqiang, xipi (thought to be related to qinqiang),[63] erhuang, capital melody, and kunju.[64] A synopsis of this complex musical history is encapsulated in the preface to opera connoisseur The Latter-Day Adept of the Iron Flute's guide to actors in the capital:

> Formerly, there were the six great troupes, all of comparable talent, . . . who for a time were all the rage. Then came the stars among the Sichuan actors who, by means of platform shoes and long-haired wigs, bested others in skill and beauty; . . . they dazzled the eyes and changed the fashion. Next came the rise of the Hui Troupes, who in succession added to the splendor; actors floated between opera genres, melding the music of the five directions and blending it into a coherent style of music and dance; and so the taste of our times is again different from that of thirty years ago.[65]

Thus, through creative adaptation, opera troupes in the capital were able to avoid state proscriptions while still catering to popular demand. The effect of such tactics ensured that in spite of the court's crackdown on huabu opera, "these tunes in the end could never be stopped."[66] By the early nineteenth century, through the resulting "melding of the music of the five directions," the various musical components of what would coalesce into pihuang opera were in place.[67] Indeed, the neologism *pihuang* is a contraction of the terms *xipi* and *erhuang*, the two main melodic styles that formed the musical armature of this nineteenth-century huabu genre.[68] Most elites still considered pihuang a lowbrow genre of opera, however. Only in the second half of the century, when a new generation of royals receptive to the sounds of huabu music turned to co-optation instead of interdiction, would pihuang ascend the opera hierarchy.

Genre Delineation and the Opera Marketplace

Opera troupes in the Qing capital from circa 1770 to the mid-nineteenth century, as we have seen, mixed genres freely: kunju actors borrowed from qinqiang practitioners; capital melody and qinqiang became nearly indistinguishable; and some qinqiang actors even performed plays from the kunju repertoire.[69] The Hui troupes performed some of everything.[70] Through the mid-nineteenth century, even as the originally lowbrow huabu opera gained ground (or at least became more the subject of literati commentary), the elegant Kun opera continued in the repertoires of the Hui troupes. Hand-copied and printed scripts that survive from this era also reflect a hybridization of genres, with title pages frequently identifying a particular play as in the joint *kun-yi* style.[71] The massive miscellany of popular scenes, *A Cloak of Patchworked White Fur*, published in an expanded edition between 1770 and 1777, also captures the diversity of genres in commercial opera, which included scenes from "contemporary plays" (*shiju*) and bangzi alongside standards from the kunju repertoire.[72]

It is against the backdrop of this stylistic cross-fertilization that scholarly writings on theater begin to evince critical concern about the categories of elegant and popular—yabu and huabu—types of opera. The discourse of yabu and huabu, in other words, emerged in dialogue with the multiplicity of genres in the urban opera marketplace. While purist defenders of Kun opera bemoaned its bastardization in commercial performance, other commentators took up the cause of huabu opera, arguing that it was not morally degraded relative to the yabu style.

Ye Tang's (1736–95) corpus of annotated Kun arias, *Musical Scores from the Last Word Studio* (published in 1794), exemplifies the first of these responses to commercial opera in the late eighteenth century. A native of Changzhou in Suzhou Prefecture, Ye Tang was intimately familiar with the Kun opera tradition. His wealth afforded him the leisure to devote his life to the study of music, although he also performed avocationally in public. Ye was an expert in the "pure-singing" (*qingchang*) style of Kun music, which had been practiced by learned gentlemen from the Jiangnan region since the late Ming. In pure singing, arias from renowned dramas were delivered unencumbered by makeup, costume, dialogue, or stage movement.[73] Li Dou esteemed his contemporary Ye Tang as the best of these recital singers and, by virtue of his *Last Word Studio* publications, as having the most lasting influence.[74] Ye's anthology, the culmination of his fifty years of research on musical prosody, published the arias and musical scores from more than 350 scenes of dramas in the kun musical style.[75] It omitted all dialogue and plot context for the arias, thereby signaling his intention to favor the song-recital version of Kun opera. Pure-singing kunqu was, according to Joseph Lam, a site of ya performance—the highest expression of civilized comportment and attainable only by men of great learning.[76]

As Lam has also noted, "Whenever *ya* was proclaimed, it always referenced the *su*."[77] Recital singing, the ultimate expression of ya, was the antithesis of popular commercial performance, which was characterized as su. Ye Tang's anthology was a direct challenge to earlier drama miscellanies such as *Cloak*, which aimed to capture on the page a faithful facsimile of operas in live performance (featuring full dialogue and some stage directions); Ye Tang's work was thus in direct conversation with the opera performed in the commercial playhouses by vocational actors. In his preface to his *Last Word Studio* collection Ye wrote that he aimed to "rectify the textual mistakes" and "harmonize the pitches" of Kun opera arias to reclaim the tradition from the popular actor who "had no master teacher to instruct him" and thus "perpetuated mistakes."[78] If the title of the anthology—calling it his "last word" on Kun opera—does not alert us to Ye's insistence on the superiority of his own style of Kun singing, his "Opening Guidelines" (*fanli*) certainly should.[79] "My notation for the scores," he wrote, "has undergone thorough consideration and precise editing. If you come across a passage that seems difficult, you must work it through carefully; you may not simply change it."[80] But perhaps Gong Zizhen (1792–1841), remarking some years later on Ye Tang's contributions to kunqu, best captured the attitude of some Jiangnan elites toward the difference between pure singing and acting by commercial troupes. "'Pure singing,'" he claims, "is for elegant gatherings; 'staged singing' is for debauched intimacy [with actors]. The two have absolutely nothing in common."[81]

In their defense of pure singing, these music sophisticates claimed Kun opera as their own based on both geography and class, restoring the purest manifestation of the genre to its native locale and to recital singing by elite amateurs. Recital singing was thus the elegant alternative to commercial kunju's popular (and bastardized) expression. Its rise to prominence in the late eighteenth century was an exercise in social distinction, part of "a desire to keep the uninitiated at arm's length."[82] Protecting the ya essence of Kun music against blended genres required making it less theatrical, less kinetically realized. That conscious effort to isolate the elegant form of Kun opera from all other performance styles would become central to the increasingly rarefied perception of the genre, ultimately contributing to the loss of much of its commercial popularity by the late Qing.[83]

Ye Tang's aria anthology took a bold stance with regard to both commercial opera and court patronage. Not only did the prefaces to the *Last Word Studio* anthology distinguish recital singing by elite amateurs from commercial, staged kunju, but they also both acknowledged and distanced the project from the court-compiled *All Nine Modes*. The court, Ye Tang hinted, would not get the "last word" on defining elegant or canonical music. Wang Wenzhi (1730–1802), fellow Jiangnan native, coeditor of the *Last Word Studio* anthology, and the author of one of its prefaces (dated to 1792), wrote: "In a weaving there must be warp and weft in order to form the patterns and the ornamentation.... In the field of music the nine modes are the warp.... Ever since the publication of *All Nine Modes* . . . composers have had a standard to go by. But *All Nine Modes* is only the warp. Without the harmonizing pitches of the miscellaneous songs to serve as the weft, there would be no infinite variety."[84] In other words, the court-sponsored *All Nine Modes* (the warp) might capture the principles of dramatic composition, but it could not do full justice to the weft of live performance, which might even incorporate hybrid musical forms drawn from commercial performance, here identified as "the miscellaneous songs." Wang, Jiangnan sophisticate though he was, here was setting out a middle ground between an idealized rendering of music as approved by the Qing court and popular practice. Ye Tang's *Last Word Studio* collection, according to Wang, achieved this middle ground by "bringing that which was popular [su] back in concert with elegance [ya]."[85] Thus, as Wang's observations indicate, even within the realm of elegant opera (yabu), there could be both ya and su expressions. The commercial kunju of the metropolitan theater was cast as the popular manifestation of the elegant kunqu.[86]

. . .

Distinguishing ya from su was not only a concern for Suzhou connoisseurs of Kun opera. If they seem preoccupied with ensuring that Kun opera remain sufficiently elegant and exclusive, other educated opera aficionados more enamored of commercial performance turned their attention to characterizing huabu opera. The huabu designation, as we have seen, was not only a marker of aesthetic difference. Very often it revealed assumptions about the sophistication of the music and the librettos—and by extension, the class derivations—of such operas, connoting that the typical audiences for such plays tended to be less literate and of lower socioeconomic status.

Connoisseurs' attitudes toward huabu styles of opera could be quite conflicted. Some—often casting themselves in the role of iconoclast—went out of their way to praise the robust, earthy quality of performance associated with huabu opera. We have seen that the flower-register author Wu Changyuan represented his fascination with huabu opera as an expression of individualistic eccentricity, a kind of "bohemian" identification with the common folk (and thereby authenticity) that distinguished him from the general run of educated theater fans.[87] Wu, however, was by no means unique in his aesthetic preferences. Several other turn-of-the-century flower registers, including *New Odes to While Away the Winter*, *Record of Viewing Flowers in the Precinct of the Throne*, and *New Odes on Listening to Youth* (*Tingchun xinyong*), also record biographies of huabu actors. The early nineteenth-century drama critic Jiao Xun, in the opening passage to his *Country Chats on Flowery Opera* (*Huabu nongtan*), declared his own eccentric taste in theater: "In the realm of theater, all give praise to the music of Wu [kunju]. As for the 'flowery' opera, its tunes and lyrics are rustic; and so everyone calls it 'chaotic strumming' [luantan]. I alone am fond of it."[88] Jiao went on to commend huabu as being easier to understand (even women and children, he said, could comprehend its lyrics), and its stories as more expressive of the values of loyalty, filiality, chastity, and righteousness (*zhong, xiao, jie, yi*). In contrast with these virtues, he contended, the lyrics of kunju were nearly impossible to understand without having read the script first, and with the exception of about a dozen noteworthy dramas, its operas all dwelled on illicit love. In addition, he averred, huabu music was more energizing, causing the blood to stir.

Jiao's statement about the more morally edifying content of the huabu musical genre is problematic, since, as we have seen, other contemporaneous sources describe huabu operas (at least as performed in urban centers such as the capital) as replete with flirtation and illicit assignations. Jiao's comments may thus be an attempt to dress his yeoman's taste in opera in the trappings of morality.

Indeed, the Manchu courtier Zhaolian, writing at approximately the same time, presents a somewhat different picture of huabu opera: "Recent times have seen the emergence of qinqiang, Yihuang, and the various melodies known as 'chaotic strumming.'[89] The lyrics are all lewd and crude, full of the language of street chatter and alleyway gossip, so the words are immediately intelligible to the city people. In addition, the music is most seductive and pleasing to the ear; sometimes it enables one to forget one's troubles, so more and more people flock to it by the day."[90] In his *Record of Viewing Flowers in the Capital* Yang Maojian echoes Zhaolian's impression of opera strains such as erhuang and bangzi as "seductive music" (*mimi zhi yin*).[91] In a guide to actors published in 1878, the opera connoisseur Yi Lansheng opined, "Nowadays, [er]*huang* melody is all the rage. . . . The lyrics are rustic and crude, all the stuff that people of this ilk make up on the spot. Since they have not been touched by the brushes and ink of educated men, [these plays] are not suitable for formal company."[92]

By the mid-1800s, most commentators writing about huabu opera were in fact referring to the amalgamation of singing styles known as pihuang. Continued literati disdain for this genre is probably best captured in Chen Sen's novel *A Precious Mirror for Ranking Boy Actresses*, which includes the following mocking poem about bangzi and pihuang performers:

"Ji-ji, ge-ge," that's bangzi opera song;
"Yi-yi, ya-ya," they're singing erhuang.
You boast: "These actors are as fair as the gossamer clouds are fine";
[And] when you're in the heat of passion, even farts smell divine.[93]

Throughout this novel, which was written circa mid-nineteenth century, pihuang opera is presented as a déclassé counterpart to the elegant kunju, as an art form that takes little skill and that just about anyone can master in two months' time.[94] Granted, this novel presents an overly romanticized depiction of kunju performance in the capital, but it is at one with other sources in claiming that the music and practices associated with pihuang were considered the lowbrow entertainment of common city people. Even those literati who admired huabu/pihuang were aware that their tastes were traversing class aesthetic boundaries. Writing in 1840, one of the earliest-known literati playwrights of pihuang operas, who went by the pseudonym Playwatching Adept (Guanju daoren), defended the genre, claiming that "erhuang plays are crude; and yet, I say that is not because erhuang itself is crude but rather that the writing of such plays has been crude."[95] Playwatching Adept set himself the task of improving the storybooks for such operas. Still, as late as 1880 a sarcastic ditty circulating in the capital expressed the following judgment on the quality of erhuang:

The people of Yuan times best knew how to write good plays;
And opera scores of old would harmonize their *do*s and *re*s.
Like fans of "Bright Spring" and "White Snow," true music mavens are rare;[96]
In the opera halls these days, nothing but erhuang plays there.[97]

This comic verse, although acknowledging widespread appeal, nevertheless voices dismay that the unsophisticated erhuang could now command such overweening popularity.

In mid-nineteenth-century flower registers at least half of the actors listed are kunju singers, and only those players that specialized in pihuang (and many were proficient in both styles) are singled out as having this particular skill. In other words, the unstated expectation was that kunju was still the exemplary metropolitan opera form. Starting in the 1870s or 1880s this pattern was reversed: huapu writers found it unnecessary to mention that a given actor specialized in pihuang, and only made it explicit if he was also skilled in kunju or in some other, regional, opera style.[98] The turn-of-the-century amateur performer-cum-playwright Chen Moxiang (1884–1943) maintained that, into the early twentieth century, educated avocational performers still tended to view pihuang with some disdain, preferring to be associated with the music and performance of Kun opera.[99]

Whether focused on yabu or huabu opera—and whether laudatory or derogatory—discussions about performed drama between 1790 and 1860 were intent on fixing categories that were, in reality, in considerable flux. I understand yabu and huabu not as definitive designations for known entities but as a response by diverse commentators to the variety and mixture of musical genres within the metropolitan opera marketplace. Just as the elegant kunju could, in the eyes of some Kun purists, become sullied by association with commercial performance, so, too, could the lowly huabu opera gain stature when, first, marginalized literati, and then, a patron with real power—the Qing court—began to succumb to its seductive sounds.

Court Patronage and Regulation after 1860

The Qianlong reign (1736–95) and the Tongzhi-Guangxu years, especially under the influence of Empress Dowager Cixi (1862–1908) were the two high points in court patronage of opera during the Qing. The Qianlong court officially promoted yabu and suppressed huabu; during the Tongzhi-Guangxu era pihuang (by then the reigning form of huabu) became the genre of choice of the imperial family. In the intervening years, as we have seen, the court economized, greatly winnowing its staff of actors, releasing all non-eunuch actors (who had been requisitioned via the Imperial Textile Manufactory in Suzhou) from court service back to their native-places, and reorganizing the Nanfu into a new agency, the Bureau of Ascendant Peace (Shengping shu).[100] Over the half-century valley between the peaks of patronage, the imperial family occasionally allowed a huabu opera to slip into its own entertainment roster within the palace. In the second half of the nineteenth century the court rather suddenly embraced huabu opera and, still within the palace, came to prefer viewing plays by commercial performers from the city to the court's own eunuch actors. Through new mechanisms of oversight of actors in the commercial sector, the court further shaped the development of opera and musical taste in the capital and beyond.

Growing interest in huabu (more specifically, pihuang) by the court over the course of the nineteenth century is documented in the archives of the Shengping shu. The earliest record of performance of a huabu play at court dates to 1802.[101] Huabu operas (in court documents referred to as *kuaxi*) were presented at court twice during the Daoguang reign (1821–50), the first on 5 March 1825, and the second on 28 August 1825.[102] The Daoguang emperor deemed this highly inappropriate, and he issued an edict to the effect that thereafter such plays not be shown within the palace before the assembled princes and officials.[103]

A musical generation gap ensued between the Daoguang emperor and his sons. The next sovereign, the Xianfeng emperor (r. 1851–61), was much more kindly disposed toward huabu opera. It was among this generation of the imperial family—including the emperor, his brothers and cousins, and their consorts—that pihuang opera first acquired a loyal following at court. All subsequent Manchu rulers and nobles (under the sway of members of the Xianfeng generation until the century's end) followed suit. According to one source,

> [The Xianfeng emperor] always took delight in music appreciation during his leisure from affairs of state. He often claimed that Kun music was overly languid and indolent, softer than it was steely. Throughout the entire empire, only the music of Huanggang and Huangpi [i.e., erhuang] was high and unwavering, soaring and not cloying. So he summoned the various erhuang players to perform before him in the palace. He tapped out the rhythms and fixed the scores, and he could home in on defects such that all the actors were awed by him. During the chaos of 1860, the capital was thrown into turmoil and all the actors dispersed. After the Tongzhi emperor ascended the throne [1862], the practice of summoning actors to perform within the palace was resumed.[104]

According to the calculations of the late Zhu Jiajin, during the court's temporary retreat to Rehe after the allied British and French forces sacked the Summer Palace in 1860, the imperial entourage viewed approximately one hundred luantan operas, constituting one-third of all the plays watched while the court was in exile.[105]

During the Xianfeng reign, the court once again began to call upon actors from outside the palace to supplement its entertainment needs. In 1855 the chief eunuch in charge of the Shengping shu requested an increase in musicians to flesh out the dwindling numbers within the court performance pool.[106] According to the Shengping shu archive, on 5 July 1860 twenty-four commercial actors were commissioned to participate in a court performance; of those, seventeen opted to remain within the palace for future service.[107] Several weeks later, for the first time, entire commercial troupes were requested to perform before the emperor for his thirtieth birthday, with two of the famous Hui troupes, Sanqing and Sixi, scheduled for 14 July and 19 July, respectively.[108] Mei Qiaoling, troupe leader of the Sixi Troupe (and grandfather of the famous twentieth-century Peking opera dan Mei Lanfang), was among those in attendance on 19 July.[109] This practice was temporarily halted after the sudden death of the Xianfeng emperor in 1861 but resumed with increasing frequency following completion of the period of state mourning in 1863.[110]

By the 1880s the tide had shifted even further, and it had become common practice for the court to send for the best commercial pihuang actors to perform in the palace. A flower register from the late 1800s records: "The Xiaoqin empress [Empress Dowager Cixi] had an extreme passion for opera, which intensified in her later years. . . . She was most fond of the plays starring Tan Xinpei, Hou Junshan, and Yang Xiaolou; during palace performances, if these actors were not featured, she would not be pleased."[111] Pihuang actors regularly summoned to the palace, such as the famous *laosheng* (older male role) actor Tan Xinpei, were given ranked positions under the auspices of the Shengping shu.[112] As the court became an ever more eager patron of huabu opera—especially pihuang—it came to exert greater control over commercial opera in the city. This was accomplished through new court oversight of the Beijing Actors' Guild, or Jingzhong Temple.

The Jingzhong Temple had served as the site for the Actors' Guild within the city of Beijing since Ming times; originally, it had no formal connection with the court.[113] Rather, the Actors' Guild of the Laolang Temple in Suzhou, which was under the administrative supervision of the Suzhou

Imperial Textile Manufactory, supplied actors when requested for Qing palace performance. In the mid-nineteenth century, as the court began to invite local performers and troupes from Beijing to perform within its palaces, it created a new agency known as the Office for the Management of Affairs of the Jingzhong Temple (Jingzhong miao guanli shiwu yamen), which was commissioned to issue orders to acting troupes in the city of Beijing via the Actors' Guild.[114] As the research of Ye Xiaoqing has shown, the head of the Jingzhong Temple guild (chosen from among the actors) was expected to report to the Shengping shu. Henceforth, all commercial opera troupes and their members were to be registered with the guild, and that information forwarded to the Shengping shu. An edict of 1863 records:

> A record is to be kept of all troupes in the capital, who is in them, and who their troupe leaders are. We order that the head of the Jingzhong miao, Cheng Changgeng, bring the troupe leaders to the office of the *yamen* for investigation. A new troupe must immediately report to Cheng Changgeng. It is not permitted to form a troupe without permission. Performers may not join a troupe on their own decision.[115]

This court micromanagement of commercial troupes and actors via the proxy agency of the Jingzhong Temple was unprecedented. It was needed, in part, for security reasons; clear lists needed to be maintained for anyone who might have access inside the palaces, especially actors, who were suspect because of their historically debased status.

Through such directives we can also see that by this time the court was thoroughly at ease with pihuang opera. Cheng Changgeng (1811–80), a performer of laosheng roles, was the leader of the Sanqing Troupe and is considered one of the foundational actors of the pihuang style. He was also the first actor to serve as Jingzhong Temple guild head under this new arrangement with the court. The introduction of this new oversight system brought commercial actors in the city within the ambit of court surveillance. As the figural wall between palace entertainment and commercial opera in the capital broke down, the court no longer needed to issue blanket prohibitions of entire musical genres; it could now keep tabs on troupes, actors, and their operas via the Beijing Actors' Guild.

In addition, an institutional mechanism was now in place for the musically exciting huabu opera to be regulated to court satisfaction. A court edict from the 1860s that was carved onto a stone stele in the Jingzhong Temple, and then copied and pasted onto all doors of the capital playhouses, offers further evidence of the new reach of the court into commercial performance in the capital in the late nineteenth century:

> Drama performances must celebrate our great prosperity and must desist from lewdness and violence in order to preserve propriety. . . . This order is especially issued to the head of the Jingzhong miao . . . to pass it on to all the troupe leaders and theater proprietors in the capital. . . . If any performers should pretend to agree but in actuality disobey or make false allusions, either in a theater or in a private residence, the guild head is authorized to truthfully report the facts to this office, which will dispatch *yamen* runners to arrest them and manacle them immediately and hand them over to the Office of Palace Justice. There will be no leniency.[116]

In theory, at least, by enlisting the heads of commercial troupes into surveillance of their own performers, the state achieved new depths of penetration into individual performances—in playhouses and in private homes; troupes became collaborators in preserving state-sanctioned morality and social order. Through this new approach to regulating commercial opera, the court acquired more direct influence not only over the musical style of opera performed in the capital but also over the content of plays. Greater self-censorship on the part of commercial acting troupes helped sanitize the genre, making it, in the eyes of the court, more suitable for palace viewing. By this time, too, some of the huabu innovations that had seemed so shocking in the late eighteenth century—such as dan actors wearing qiao shoes and long-haired wigs—had become commonplace among practitioners of pihuang opera, more accepted, perhaps, by virtue of established precedent.

As the court valorized this new genre, pihuang took on greater artistic cachet within the capital as a whole and moved up the ladder of opera hierarchy. Manchu aristocrats, too, became avid fans of pihuang in the latter half of the nineteenth century, as both patrons and amateur players. Writing at the end of the century, Luo Ying'an observed that Prince Su (Shanqi, 1863–1921) and his family were all accomplished pihuang performers, concluding his observation with the wry remark that one could find Manchu nobles who were illiterate but none who were not proficient in opera.[117] Han elites, especially in the north, also began to consider pihuang acceptable for high-society gatherings. The same Hui troupe actors (who now specialized mostly in pihuang) circulated between capital playhouses, private salons, and performances at court.

At roughly the same time that the court began to actively regulate the commercial opera troupes of Beijing, the balance of cultural power between the court and Jiangnan, in uneasy equilibrium throughout the eighteenth century, underwent sudden and radical transformation. Suzhou was cut off from the capital by a political and military crisis, the Taiping Rebellion (1850–64). The war and its suppression were devastating for Jiangnan. By some accounts, the bloody fighting to take, defend, and retake Suzhou between 1860 and 1863 wiped out 50 percent of its population.[118] This had major repercussions on opera and on culture in general in the capital. The strong connections between Jiangnan and the capital, which had flourished up through the mid-1800s, were severed by the fighting and never reestablished once the civil war ended. The chaos of the Taiping years compromised Jiangnan supremacy in civil-service examinations.[119] The war interrupted the flow of actors and audiences to the capital for kunju. "Ever since the fighting in Jiangnan," one observer noted, "youths from Suzhou and Yangzhou are no longer sold [into the acting profession] in the capital. For this reason, northerners now take the lead within the Chrysanthemum Quarter."[120] A stele inscription from the Suzhou Laolang Temple dated to 1915 shows that it took more than fifty years to finally refurbish the local Actors' Guild.[121] The Suzhou elite who survived the civil war took shelter in Shanghai, and although some eventually returned to Suzhou, Jiangnan gentry thereafter were oriented not to the capital and political center in Beijing but to the emerging cosmopolitan entrepôt of Shanghai.[122]

Shanghai, thriving as the preeminent treaty port in the late nineteenth century, began to rival Beijing as a center for commercial opera entertainment. Beginning in the 1880s the best pihuang actors of the capital, famous in large part because of active court sponsorship, were able to leverage their court-derived prestige into renewed commercial success in the theaters of Shanghai and other coastal cities.[123] Whereas late Qing court patronage had brought pihuang opera under stricter state oversight, the new opportunities provided by urban centers under partial colonial administration (and so partly sheltered from court meddling) began to fray the ties of actors to the court. The dual pull of late Qing court patronage and commercial opera in the treaty-port cities—one offering prestige, the other economic independence—enabled top-flight pihuang actors to begin to negotiate their own compensation as free agents. Actors' newly advantageous position gave rise to modern stars whose fame and fortune would rival that of the late eighteenth-century qinqiang actor Wei Changsheng. With the Jiangnan elite wounded after more than a decade of civil war, the Qing court in the north now took the lead in setting standards of taste in opera. Court patronage of the once lowbrow pihuang was thus instrumental in raising the genre to elite status, acknowledged empirewide. By the end of the nineteenth century, pihuang—soon to become identified as Peking opera—came to be cast as representative of the high (state) culture of Beijing in contrast to the "crass" economic opportunism of Shanghai and other treaty-port cities.

Conclusion

Three key factors shaped the rise of pihuang opera: court patronage in the second half of the nineteenth century; court oversight and management of commercial troupes via the Jingzhong Temple Actors' Guild, which exerted a disciplining force on the content of performances; and the unintended consequences of war, which weakened the Jiangnan elite (and their favored yabu opera) such that Beijing could thenceforth assume the lead in reordering the hierarchy of opera in the capital and beyond.

As opera history, this narrative of musical genre in the Qing capital relates the rise and fall in popularity of yabu and huabu; as social history, it examines the responses of various social players—the Manchu court, Jiangnan elites, marginalized but educated aficionados, vast but anonymous audiences, and even actors—to the variety of genres staged in the capital; and as political history, it reveals that taste in opera served as a site for cultural contestation.

Situating the artistic features of opera genre within the larger sociocultural and political context of Qing China, I have suggested that the conceptual categories of *yabu* and *huabu* were not simply neutral labels. Rather, these terms were generated in conversation with the myriad, overlapping, and shifting opera genres available in commercial playhouses in metropolitan centers such as the capital. Social prestige and cultural taste did not always align in expected ways. Nor did Manchu rulers always share the cultural proclivities of the Han social elite; even when they did, these two elites sometimes competed over who possessed sufficient cultural capital to set the norms of erudition and good taste. Beginning in the late eighteenth century, some opera connoisseurs took a keen interest in lowbrow genres of opera music. Their out-of-the-ordinary passion for huabu distinguished them—so they claimed—as men of distinction.

Furthermore, although some huabu opera genres were originally viewed as subversive of the social order, they also had the potential to be recouped for normative purposes. By the second half of the nineteenth century, wooed by its musical dynamism and easy intelligibility, the Manchu court threw its support behind huabu opera. In the process, through direct oversight of the opera troupes, the court was instrumental in sanitizing pihuang—one variety of the once suspect huabu style of opera. As a result, the late nineteenth-century court exerted much more influence on the content of commercial opera in the capital than earlier—ostensibly more powerful—rulers who had tried to control urban entertainment by strictly regulating both urban space and opera genre. From circa 1770 through the first half of the nineteenth century, try as it might, the court could neither literally nor figuratively contain commercial opera in the capital. By the end of the dynasty, however, commercial opera had become a stage upon which the court might project its moral and political ideals. To better assess what some of those ideals were, and how and by whom certain opera genres might be appropriated for different purposes, I turn in the next part to specific performance scripts and the ways in which they captured the sympathies and concerns of diverse audiences.

PART THREE

Plays and Performances

FOUR

Social Melodrama and the Sexing of Political Complaint

> When I was making my catalog of the orchids of Yan, I found it a pity that there were not any actors from [my native] Hangzhou. Fu Tingshan told me: "Twenty years ago there was a Kun opera boy actress in a capital troupe who was originally from Hangzhou, but I have forgotten his name. He was outstanding in the role of Zhao Cui'er, and very watchable in other plays, too." And then I recalled a time in the fall of 1766 when I was attending some plays with Master Rang, the abbot of Longxiang Monastery, in Tongxiang [Anhui Province]. An Indian monk in attendance said to me: "The little boy actress in this troupe who plays the part of Zhao Cui'er really makes one's mouth water." Master Rang looked embarrassed. I said: "This teacher's Chan enlightenment exceeds even a cup of tea from the Patriarch of Zhao."[1] We looked at one another and laughed. As for the actor whom Master Fu saw, can I presume that he, too, made one's mouth water?
>
> 余作《燕蘭譜》,惜杭伶乏人。符丈亭山曰:"廿年前京班一崑旦為杭人,忘其姓氏。演趙翠兒一時獨步,其他劇亦可觀。"余憶丙戌秋,在桐鄉與龍翔方丈讓公觀劇,一天竺僧謂余曰:"此班小旦作趙翠兒,真令人發渴。"讓公慚色。余曰:"阿師禪悟勝趙州茶矣!"相與大噱。今符丈所見,想亦發渴者耶?
>
> Wu Changyuan, *A Brief Record of the Orchids of Yan*, 1785[2]

Zhao Cui'er was a creation of elite male fantasy, as Wu Changyuan tells it, capable of ensnaring audiences—both lay and clerical—in the illusionary world of the eighteenth-century stage. She is the central character in the play *The Garden of Turquoise and Jade* (*Feicui yuan*), a title that puns off the given names of its two female ingenues, Ma Feiying and Zhao Cui'er.[3] *Garden*, attributed to the mid-seventeenth-century Suzhou playwright Zhu

Suchen (ca. 1620–1701 or after), is loosely based on historical figures and events of the Ming dynasty.[4] In twenty-six scenes, the drama presents a classic struggle between humble virtue and high-ranking villainy: a poor but righteous scholar, Shu Depu, attempts to save his tiny plot of household land from annexation by a greedy and ruthless official. He is assisted in his struggle by a clever and attractive traveling seamstress, Zhao Cui'er, and by a bumbling but goodhearted and sometimes-employed deputy of the law, Wang Mantou (Wang Steamed-Bun). When the legal system fails Shu Depu, Cui'er and Steamed-Bun take matters into their own hands. This triad of righteousness—the poor scholar, the comely and quick-witted but lowborn young woman, and the trustworthy clown—is held up as the moral antidote to cronyism and the destructive power of masculine privilege.

The themes explored in *Garden* are typical of the plays written by contemporaries among the so-called Suzhou writers' group of early Qing dramatists.[5] Their dramas depict confrontations between goodness and evil and are melodramatic in structure and tone. They explore questions of individual moral virtue, they make free and ready use of historical materials for their plots (drawing especially from the Ming dynasty), and they often pair scholar-and-beauty romances with court-case dramas about social justice; but since typically justice is not served through official channels in these plays, these plots also frequently showcase knights-errant protagonists. As with so many of these early Qing dramas, abridged versions and selected scenes from *Garden* remained popular Kun opera programs well into the nineteenth century.

Garden's popularity suggests that urban audiences identified with the plight of the downtrodden. For all its critique of a social and political order gone awry, though, the complete script offers audiences a happy ending: for their righteous (albeit extralegal) deeds, Steamed-Bun is appointed to a post in the Palace Guard and Zhao Cui'er is wedded to the scholar's son (who has since won top honors in the examinations). Old enmities are forgiven, and Ma Feiying, the kindly daughter of Shu Depu's rich and powerful nemesis, is also married off to Shu's now-eminent son. Her virtue wins pardon for her father's crimes. In the end, the lowly have been elevated in the social hierarchy for their good deeds, the learned have been recognized and accorded a position in the official bureaucracy consonant with the meritocratic ideal, and the corrupt have been reprimanded and punished; the travesty of justice gives way to comedic-romantic order; and one young man gets paired—or triangulated—happily ever after with two beautiful and virtuous women.

The play's gender and class politics are highly conventional, reflecting a retreat from the critical social vision of many late Ming dramatic masterworks. This accords well with our received understanding of the intellectual and literary climate under the Qing. Commercial Kun opera in the eighteenth and nineteenth centuries rarely staged complete plays, however. The selection of scenes staged significantly altered the meanings that might be derived from the performances; and since livelihood dictated that commercial troupes shape their plays to popular demand, the traces of live performance captured in surviving scripts can be read as a gauge of audience likes and dislikes. Performance versions of the *Garden* script frequently dispensed with the supposedly requisite happy ending of the Chinese dramatic tradition; their climactic scenes featured the daring deeds of the heroine but ended, typically, with the protagonists on the run and the seamstress grieving for her mother's murder by the henchman of the corrupt official. Audiences, it turns out, were more attuned to sentimentalized depictions of injustice than to the restoration of social order. Commercial opera, in other words, offered audiences not only a space for escape but also a forum for expression of social complaint. This melodrama of *ressentiment* was inflected with class and gender sympathies: the good tended to be poor, female, or both; the bad, rich, powerful men and their conniving flunkies.

Scenes from *Garden* featuring the seamstress and the clown became the most popular. The clear audience favorite was the scene "Stealing the Tally" (Dao ling) in which Zhao Cui'er filches the official tally authorizing execution of the imprisoned scholar, vigilantism being the only recourse against the corruption of the system.[6] Cui'er, low of status and captivating in looks and personality, embodied underdog resistance; her wit, her pluck, and (in some scenes) her pathos struck a chord in urban playgoers. Furthermore, as the salivating recollections of Wu Changyuan and other opera aficionados of the time reveal, mid-Qing audiences for such melodramas did not have to choose between alternative imaginings of social justice and sensory delights. A skilled actor in the role of Zhao Cui'er stole more than just the insignia of state power; Cui'er also stole men's hearts. This sexing of political complaint—both the gendered face of virtue in action and the sensual allure of the actors—became one of the hallmarks of commercial Kun opera in the Qing capital.

By tracing this play from full manuscript to abridged performance editions and to popular selected scenes, it becomes clear that during the heyday of commercial kunju, from the late eighteenth through the first half of the nineteenth century, the urban playhouse became a social arena in which yearnings—for opera stars and for social justice—could be indulged. Often in this setting gender transgression flirted promiscuously with political sympathies. Contrary to common assumption, sentimentality and sex—so central to late Ming critical reflection on society and politics—did not disappear from public discourse during the Qing, although where and how they were expressed underwent significant transformations. In essence, these tropes moved from the page to the stage, and thereby spread down the social hierarchy to reach a middling stratum of urbanites.[7] The kunju melodramas of the metropolitan commercial playhouses became a key conduit for the expression of these polemics.

The Garden of Turquoise and Jade *and Its Sources*

There is much that we do not know about *Garden* and its author. Almost certainly none of the surviving redactions of the script—including the seemingly complete twenty-six-scene manuscript edition republished in Series Three of *Collected Publications of Rare Editions of Drama* (*Guben xiqu congkan*)—reflect the earliest version.[8] Nor can we be certain that Zhu Suchen is the author of the play. With the exception of two nineteenth-century drama catalogs, which attribute the play to Xue Dan (act. mid-seventeenth century), nearly all other Qing dynasty catalogs of plays list *Garden* as anonymous.[9] The first work to attribute the play to Zhu is the encyclopedic *Abstracts of the Complete Titles of the Sea of Drama* (*Quhai zongmu tiyao*), dated to the Qing but first published in 1928. Most modern editors of drama reference texts accept this attribution.[10] Scanty as the evidence for authorship may be, we know that the playwright, whoever he was, was highly familiar with the works of the most famous and prolific Suzhou dramatist of the mid-seventeenth century, Li Yu; Zhu, who coauthored several plays with Li Yu, surely fits that profile.[11]

Evidence of familiarity with Li Yu's work is also one of the few scraps of information that helps establish a rough date for *Garden*. Li Yu's play *A Reunion of Ten Thousand Leagues* (*Wanli yuan*) features a clown named Wang Zhenglong (Wang Steamer-Rack). The character Wang Steamed-Bun in *Garden* explicitly traces his paternity to Steamer-Rack, explaining, "You may ask, why have I been given this august appellation? My father was the famous Wang Steamer-Rack of Suzhou. My friends say, since I'm the output of a Steamer-Rack, they call me Steamed-Bun. But I tend to do things in a big way, and this Bun here ended up growing bigger than its Rack."[12] This genealogy of clowns likely was an in-joke among contemporary playwrights and actors.[13]

The plot of *Reunion of Ten Thousand Leagues* was inspired by the travel diaries of Huang Xiangjian (1609–73), who journeyed from Suzhou to Yunnan and back again in search of his father during the turbulent years following the fall of the Ming. Given that Huang's travels did not end until 1653, we can be certain that neither play could have been written prior to that date. Presumably Li Yu's play was written shortly after the publication of Huang's account (cashing in on the travelogue's overnight sensation); and in order for Steamed-Bun's account of his ancestry to have retained its immediate comic impact, *Garden* would have to have been created shortly thereafter, likely circa 1660s.[14]

Tracing the influences on the plot of *Garden* is somewhat easier. The play is loosely based on events that befell a handful of historical figures whose lives spanned the turn of the sixteenth century. The first of the plot threads is drawn from the early years of Shu Fen (1484–1527), a native of Jiangxi Province who won first place in the 1517 metropolitan examination and went on to serve in the prestigious Hanlin Academy.[15] In *Garden* Shu Fen's story takes a back seat to that of his less successful but no less illustrious father, Shu Fa (rendered in the play as Shu Depu). On record as having served as a sitting instructor at a private academy in Hubei, Shu Fa is best known for having given away his schoolteacher's meager salary to a couple in desperate need. In the following hundred-plus years, near-hagiographic accounts of his compassion circulated in commonplace books such as *Daily Records from the Cottage of Yesteryear's Mistakes* (*Zuofeian rizuan*) and *A Compendium of Trustworthy Words and Prudent Deeds* (*Yongxing bian*), and by the mid-seventeenth century literati imaginations had attributed the son's examination success to the father's self-sacrificing generosity.[16] The entry as recorded in *Daily Records from the Cottage of Yesteryear's Mistakes* reads:

> After two years as a teacher in Hubei, Master Shu of Jiangxi [Province] was returning home with fellow provincials by boat. [Once,] when he went ashore to stretch his legs, he heard the sound of a woman wailing most pitifully. He asked her why she was crying, and she said, "My husband is thirteen taels behind in his account books, so he is selling me to make up the difference. My infant son will surely die without me around to suckle him, and so I grieve." The man said, "Everyone on the boat is a schoolteacher. If each of us were to contribute one tael of silver, it would be enough to solve

your predicament. He returned and related this to his fellow travelers. Not one of them responded. So Master Shu gave the woman the entire stipend he had received for his two years as an instructor. When he was still over thirty *li* from home, he had already depleted all of his provisions. Most of his companions thought it his own fault, but a few took pity upon him and invited him to eat with them. Master Shu did not presume to eat his fill. On arriving home, he told his wife, "I've been starving for two days. Hurry and cook up a meal of rice." His wife said, "Where am I supposed to get rice?" Master Shu said, "Borrow it from the neighbors." She said, "I've borrowed from them too often. I've been waiting for your return so that I can pay them back." Master Shu then told her the reason why he had given away his money. His wife said, "In that case, I'll go search for a simple meal that will feed us both." Thereupon she picked up a basket and headed to the hills, where she gathered bitter weeds and roots. These she boiled until they were soft, and together they ate their fill. That night as the wife lay sleeping, someone called out to her in her dream: "Though tonight you eat bitter weeds, in the coming year you will give birth to an examination winner." She woke her husband and told him [of her dream]. Master Shu said, "The gods have told this to me, too." That night she conceived, and in the following year gave birth to a son, whom they named Fen. He did indeed win top place in the examinations.[17]

This legend became the kernel around which the plot of *Garden* was elaborated.

The second historical episode woven into the plot of *Garden* is the 1519 rebellion of the Prince of Ning, Zhu Chenhao (d. 1521). Zhu Chenhao's fiefdom was located in Nanchang Prefecture in northern Jiangxi. Even before his open defiance of the throne, the prince had acquired a reputation as a regional bully—often seizing neighboring landholdings for his personal use and intimidating officials posted to the region.[18] In *Garden*, the Prince of Ning remains an offstage presence; but the play casts his chief henchman, the fictional Ma Fengzhi, as its lead villain. The approximate convergence of time and place in early sixteenth-century Jiangxi apparently sufficed to bring the two source stories together in the playwright's imagination.[19]

Garden embellishes upon these historical sources, weaving them into an intricate and powerful melodrama that mixes judicial misprision, scholar-beauty romance, high treason, and military cunning. The play opens with its protagonist, Shu Depu, about to return home to Nanchang for the year-end holidays from a teaching position in Hubei. En route he encounters Wang Steamed-Bun, a down-on-his-luck yamen runner who, finding himself short thirty taels of silver from official coffers, has arranged to sell his wife to make up the difference. Moved by their plight, Shu exhausts his entire teaching stipend to buy the woman back. He then goes on his way without mentioning his name.

Back in Nanchang, Shu's wife, Madam Wei (Wei shi), and grown son, Shu Fen, wait anxiously for him to return home. With the New Year fast approaching, mother and son hike into the nearby hills to scavenge for edible wild plants, where they are discovered by the imperious steward of the neighboring Ma family estate. He warns them that they are trespassing on the designated burial grounds of the household of the Prince of Ning. Cowed by this encounter, mother and son return home, where they find the newly returned Shu Depu. Shu confesses that he has given away his entire earnings to strangers, but Madam Wei is pleased rather than angered by her husband's altruism, and the family resigns itself to a meal of stewed bitter weeds.

The next scene introduces Mama Zhao and her attractive daughter, Cui'er (also called Cuiniang).[20] The two make their living boating from place to place as traveling seamstresses, and Cui'er is renowned especially for her fine jade-studded needlework, a reputation captured in her given name, which translates loosely as Jade Miss. Having found a frequent patron in the wealthy Ma family, Mama Zhao and Cui'er have temporarily moored their boat nearby. On New Year's Day mother and daughter awake to the voice of a god relating Shu Depu's act of charity and foretelling a change in fortune for the Shu family. Since Cui'er has just recently finished a commission, they have money to spare. Cui'er suggests that they offer some silver to Madam Wei to tide her through the hard times. Mama Zhao teases her daughter, saying she has taken a liking to the handsome Shu Fen. Cui'er protests that she is acting solely out of neighborly consideration, and besides, she observes, her status as a traveling seamstress could never make her a suitable match for the budding scholar. Mother and daughter call upon Madam Wei.

Meanwhile, at the Ma family mansion Ma Fengzhi is pondering ways to ingratiate himself with his overlord. He seizes upon the idea of building a garden on the grounds of his family estate—a Garden of Turquoise and Jade—at which to entertain the prince. He is frustrated, however, because the land he has available for such a garden is not a perfect square; the Shu property abuts his land at an angle, disrupting the best aesthetic and geomantic design for his venture. Ma's steward informs him that the neighbors are so poor they were forced to gather weeds for their New Year's "feast." Surely, the steward suggests, they would be willing to sell their property just to make ends meet; and he volunteers to arrange the purchase.

But when Ma's steward offers to buy the land, Shu turns him down. His property may not be much to boast of, he explains, but it has been handed down in his family for generations, so selling it off would constitute a lack of filial respect. Here, Shu Depu holds tenaciously to ideal—if impractical and outdated—Confucian ethics, while Ma's steward, the overreaching servant, urges him to sell the land in accord with the demands of a market economy. His plans foiled, the steward vows revenge.

Back at the Ma residence, Ma Fengzhi flies into a rage upon hearing that his purchase offer has been rejected. Ma and his steward then scheme to trump up charges against Shu Depu as an excuse to confiscate his property. Ma's steward proposes that they accuse Shu and his son of cutting down trees and defiling the graves in the Prince of Ning's familial burial grounds, infractions punishable by death for their malignant geomantic consequences. The steward offers to perjure himself by claiming to have witnessed the crime. Ma's virtuous daughter, Ma Feiying, who has been eavesdropping, rushes in and pleads with her father to forgo this nefarious design, but Ma Fengzhi stubbornly refuses to heed her.

As luck would have it, Steamed-Bun is assigned as yamen runner for the case. He picks up the arrest warrant for Shu Depu and Shu Fen and is told to await instructions from Ma Fengzhi. Ma promises Steamed-Bun ample rewards if he captures the suspects but threatens him with punishment should they manage to escape. Steamed-Bun joyfully heads off to make this lucrative arrest.

Back at the home of Shu Depu, the family is fretting that they have offended their powerful neighbors. Cui'er, who has learned of the warrant while visiting with her patron and friend Feiying, rushes on to warn them of the impending arrest. Steamed-Bun enters and states the crime: cutting down trees and robbing graves on the prince's property. About to haul the father and son off to court, Steamed-Bun suddenly recognizes Shu as his benefactor. He then faces a dilemma: turn them in to reap his financial reward (and fulfill his official duty) or honor his ethical debt to Shu's earlier kindness. Urged by Cui'er to follow his conscience, Steamed-Bun lets the father and son escape.

Shu Depu and Fen take flight, but they get separated while traveling and Fen is kidnapped by bandits. Having lost his son, Shu Depu resolves to turn himself in and face the bogus charges. The judge for the case, Magistrate Hu Shining, turns out to be both honest and wise.[21] He dismisses the charges and releases Shu. But Magistrate Hu's authority is no match for the real powers that be. Shortly thereafter, a messenger arrives announcing that he has been impeached from office by order of the prince.

Ma Fengzhi is appointed as the new judge, and a retrial is called. Ma convicts Shu of grave robbing, has him thrown in jail, and confiscates the Shu property. As Madam Wei and Steamed-Bun despair, Cui'er volunteers to solicit Ma Feiying's help.

At nightfall a deputy from the Prince of Ning's palace arrives at the Ma mansion with an official tally that will authorize the execution of Shu Depu. Ma Fengzhi is out entertaining guests, so the tally is left in his study. Cui'er visits Ma Feiying and implores her to urge her father to reconsider. But Feiying laments that the order has already been issued; it is too late for pleading. Nevertheless, she invites Cui'er to keep her company until her father returns. Ma Fengzhi returns drunk. He insists on taking a nap before attending to the tally. Cui'er bids farewell to Feiying. She then sneaks into the study and steals the tally out from under the nose of the sleeping Ma. Cui'er hands the tally off to Steamed-Bun, who rushes to the prison to save Shu.

Cui'er's theft is soon discovered, and one of Ma's henchmen is dispatched to exact revenge. The henchman tracks down the boat where Madam Wei and Mama Zhao (Cui'er's mother) are anxiously awaiting word from Cui'er. He murders the first person he encounters, who turns out to be Mama Zhao, and then flees, thinking he has killed Cui'er. Cui'er returns. Her joy at having saved the poor scholar turns to woe when she learns that her mother has been murdered. Madam Wei warns Cui'er that Ma's men will no doubt return after they realize their mistake, and the two of them retreat by boat to safer waters.

The plot then veers back to Steamed-Bun, who uses the prince's tally to authorize Shu's release from jail. Back at the Ma household, Ma Fengzhi explains that even though Shu and his son have fled, he has nevertheless managed to seize their land, and the Garden of Turquoise and Jade is even now in process. He further divulges that, at his urging, the Prince of Ning has decided to move against the imperial court. This brings the first half of the drama to a resolution and sets in motion a new conflict for the second half of the play.

Part two of *Garden* depicts the travels and travails of the protagonists on the run and the suppression of the rebellion. The newly appointed magistrate of Nanchang, Lu Dahao, turns out to be Shu Depu's former student. With the help of Steamed-Bun, they strategize to crack the rebel hold on

Nanchang, where Ma Fengzhi is in command. As chance would have it, Shu Depu becomes aide-de-camp to the former magistrate, Hu Shining, who has now been recalled to office as the general in charge of suppressing the rebels. The four of them plot to defeat Ma Fengzhi. They need some token from the Prince of Ning that Ma might interpret as an order to open the city gates, whereupon the imperial troops would rush in. Steamed-Bun comes to the rescue. He makes known that he still has in his possession the tally from the Prince of Ning. This becomes the perfect device to dupe Ma. The rebellion is suppressed.

After the victory Lu Dahao is assigned to confiscate Ma's property and determine the fate of his dependents. Under Ming law capital punishment for treason extended to the entire family, which would have meant death for Ma's daughter. But Steamed-Bun urges the magistrate to take pity on her. Feiying can only be spared, however, is if she is already betrothed and thus a member of another household. Feiying, asked about her marital status, refuses to lie. Realizing that she is both virtuous and filial, Lu Dahao betroths her to his adopted son, a youth whom he had purchased out of captivity and who has just placed as the new top candidate in the metropolitan examination. The youth turns out to be none other than Shu Fen.

Meanwhile, in the capital, Madam Wei is reunited with Shu Fen, who is being paraded through the streets in recognition of his accomplishment in the exams. In gratitude to Cui'er, Madam Wei adopts her as a daughter; she thereby authorizes a sibling (and not a marital) bond between Cui'er and her son.

Word arrives that the emperor has reversed the criminal charges against Shu Depu and Shu Fen, and the match between Feiying and Shu Fen is proposed to the Shu family. When at first they refuse, Cui'er pleads for her friend, claiming that the theft of the tally would not have been possible without Feiying's help, whereupon the Shu family relents. Feiying, in turn, accedes to the match on two conditions: her father's life must be spared, and Cui'er must also be brought into the marriage. Madam Wei confesses that all along she had been eyeing Cui'er as a concubine for her son, and she happily agrees to this request. An edict from the emperor arrives, commanding the double nuptial to go forward; Steamed-Bun is appointed a member of the imperial bodyguard; the repentant Ma Fengzhi is pardoned but stripped of all titles and ranks, and all his former lands—including the Garden of Turquoise and Jade—are awarded in perpetuity to the Shu family. The play comes to a close with Shu Depu marveling at the workings of destiny. How uncanny, he observes, that the name of the garden should combine the names of his son's two marital companions, Fei and Cui.

Garden *and the Ethics of the Early Qing Suzhou Playwrights*

The early Qing Suzhou playwrights excelled at melodrama. Their plays exhibit its classic features: "The world according to melodrama," to borrow the insights of Peter Brooks, "is built on an irreducible manichaeism, the conflict of good and evil as opposites not subject to compromise."[22] Often exulting in the triumph of the poor and downtrodden, these early Qing plays nevertheless advocated the restoration of a fractured social hierarchy. Gone are the late Ming meditations on the transcendent and transformative power of love (*qing*), what the litterateur Feng Menglong (1574–1646) once famously referred to as the "cult of *qing*" (*qingjiao*).[23] In its place a new ardor for social justice dominates the emotional center of these dramas, betraying a hushed politics of resistance, often further colored by local Suzhou or Jiangnan flavor. Less lyrical than many of the late Ming works, these early Qing dramas—precisely because of their melodramatic qualities—made for highly engaging live theater.[24]

The themes explored in *Garden* are manifest in Zhu Suchen's other plays as well. Probably the author is best known for his play *Fifteen Strings of Cash* (*Shiwu guan*), an adaptation of a Song-dynasty vernacular short story; Zhu's drama tells a tale of crossed identity and mistaken criminal allegation against two brothers and their eventual lovers, all of which gets put right in the end by the wise prefect of Suzhou, Kuang Zhong (1384–1442).[25] As in *Garden*, the plot inserts historical figures into a fictional invention in which the prevailing interest is the perversion and then restoration of justice. And as in *Garden*, a touch of romance is thrown in for good measure. A darker court-case drama by Zhu, *Palace of the Dawn Star* (*Weiyang tian*), depicts a travesty of justice so great—adultery, murder, and false incrimination—that the gods refuse to let the sky lighten at the striking of the fifth watch, the dawn hour at which convicts are executed.[26] Following melodramatic convention, justice prevails in the end.

Zhu's concern with social justice was shared by his community of early Qing playwrights, as suggested by the preponderance of plays coauthored within this community.[27] Zhu and Li Yu collaborated, for instance, on one of the most overtly political melodramas of the early Qing, *A Register of the Pure and Loyal* (*Qingzhong pu*). Set in the late Ming at the time of the persecution of the Donglin partisans by the notorious eunuch-dictator Wei Zhongxian (1568–1627), the script centers on the martyrdom of the righteous Suzhou scholar-official Zhou Shunchang (1584–1626) and the local riot that his death inspired.[28] The events upon which *Register of the Pure and Loyal* were based would have been fresh in people's memory (especially in Suzhou) and would have readily lent themselves to stark black-and-white rendering of the characters. This, then, was the literary milieu in which *Garden* can be situated.

The Manichaean quality of *Garden* is clearly drawn—good and evil easily distinguished—so that, with the exception of Cui'er and Steamed-Bun, the characters feel flat. Compared with some of the masterpieces of dramatic literature from the late Ming, the politics of *Garden* feel stridently moralistic. Even alongside pre-1644 works of the Suzhou playwrights, such as Li Yu's *A Handful of Snow* (*Yipengxue*), the characters of *Garden* fall more easily into heroes and villains.[29] *Garden* attacks corruption and treachery in high places, but the cause of official malaise is a few selfish and overweening men, not anything endemic to the system of public office. The good judge, Hu Shining, falls victim to political machinations, but eventually he, along with the other honorable characters, is restored to high rank by an offstage emperor. It is hard to know if this ending would have been read as ironic in the second half of the seventeenth century—a time when no Ming emperor, much less the notoriously cavalier Zhengde emperor (r. 1505–21), could put things right for society anymore.[30]

Zhu Suchen and the other early Qing Suzhou dramatists chose career playwriting, in part, as a conscious rejection of official service under the new regime.[31] Most of the dozen or so Suzhou playwrights active in the second half of the seventeenth century never sat for the exams or took up posts under the Qing.[32] But if preference for cultural over bureaucratic livelihood was in itself a political stance, like so many of the loyalists who survived the dynastic transition, the Suzhou dramatists reserved their harshest criticism for the failures of the Ming (reflected, surely, in the preponderance of plots set during the Ming). It was the breakdown of normative hierarchies and the accompanying loss of a moral rudder, they insinuated, that had led to political corruption and social chaos, and ultimately the humiliation of alien rule. Failings on the personal level had direct implications for the welfare of the larger polity.

This strain of critical self-reflection exemplified larger early Qing trends. Both at the level of high politics and in local philanthropic endeavors, many early Qing men of learning rejected the School of Mind (*xinxue*) and Taizhou School interpretations of neo-Confucian thought that had been so popular in the late Ming.[33] They did so in part because they blamed the corruption of late Ming politics and the ultimate fall of the dynasty on the influence of these philosophies, which in their more extreme articulations had validated selfish desires and questioned social authority. Consistent with that early Qing critique of late Ming extreme subjectivity, we can read the ultimate restoration of ideal hierarchies and the concern with individual integrity in *Garden* as response to a time of perceived moral equivocation.

The social melodrama presented in *Garden* combines this early Qing moralistic bent with late Ming romantic sympathies.[34] Its emphasis on courtroom justice (or lack thereof) harkens back to Yuan variety-play (*zaju*) plots, while it also shares the structural and thematic characteristics of Ming scholar-beauty romance dramas. The play is pro-establishment and pro-hierarchy, so long as rank within the social order is based on Confucian ideals of merit and moral worth. At the same time it exhibits continuity with a critical strain of imaginings about gender and class (influenced by Gong'an School intellectual currents), which had shaped so much of late Ming fiction and drama in which young women and the poor speak truth to power.[35]

Surely, early Qing playwrights' return to the court-case themes so central to Yuan drama was rife with symbolic import. Life under alien rule was a salient aspect of both periods, and this would not have been lost on Han writers from early Qing Jiangnan, the hot spot of greatest resistance to the Manchu conquest. Literary depiction of judicial process (especially when displaced onto times past) was a relatively safe way of registering dissatisfaction with the status quo. But early Qing dramatists, while drawing inspiration from Yuan zaju, also added their own twists to the subgenre of court-case drama. Compared with their Yuan models, the early Qing plays exhibit much more cynicism about the potential for justice to be served through official channels. The typical Yuan court-case play features two trials, the first of which is a travesty of justice by a corrupt judge, and the second in which the mistaken verdict is overturned by an honest official (*qingguan*).[36] In *Garden* this pattern is reversed. The first of the trials in *Garden* is presided over by the upright Hu Shining, only to be followed by a retrial in which the duplicitous Ma Fengzhi acts as both plaintiff and judge. Redress of grievance being impossible within such a system thus necessitates the intervention of heroic figures such as Cui'er and Steamed-Bun, and in ways not entirely lawful. This vindication of vigilante action as a tactic of the weak accentuates a polemical bite to the play, traces of which were retained even as it circulated in truncated form in commercial performance over the next 150-plus years.

The gender and class politics of *Garden* are also a blend of old and new. Cui'er, *Garden*'s central figure, is indebted to late Ming literati fascination with characters who exhibit *bense*, or linguistic and emotional authenticity, which came especially to be mapped onto young, desiring, and desirable women.[37] But what began in the late Ming as a "counterhegemonic discourse of cultural redemption," as the work of Maram Epstein and others has shown, is by Qing times often simply a playful literary trope, stripped of its implied social criticism.[38] Perhaps this same inclination also helps explain the marriage destinies in *Garden*. The late Ming "cult of qing" ideal, which had begun to embrace singular romantic devotion, is passed over for the (playful) fantasy of getting "two-in-one" and thus foreshadows the resolutions (whether comic or tragic) of so much of later Qing fiction and drama.[39] In the character of Cui'er, then, we find the outward trappings of transcendent qing authenticity, but this ideal type is now harnessed to a "restorationist" (*fugu*) sentiment—socially, if not politically.

In this appropriation of the literary topoi of the Ming romantics for a socially conservative agenda, Cui'er prefigures characters such as Thirteenth Sister (Shisan mei) in the late Qing novel *A Chronicle of Lovers and Heroes*. Like Thirteenth Sister, Cui'er has the qualities of a female knight-errant (*xianü*). And the character openly comments in some of her key arias on her place within a long line of intrepid women in literature, first popularized in Tang-dynasty prose tales.[40] In the scene in which Cui'er steals the tally, she sings: "I may lack her vast powers, yet still I imitate Miss Hongxian, who stole the golden charm";[41] and again in a subsequent aria: "This may not compare with the theft of the military tally that saved the kingdom of Zhao, but my deed is still something to crow about."[42]

Like those literary predecessors whose daring acts were typically the preserve of consorts or servile women, Cui'er is lowborn. If, on the one hand, her social origins liberate her from the social etiquette of elite women, such as her alter-ego friend, Feiying, on the other hand, Cui'er is painfully aware of her low status relative to that of the Shu family. Although Cui'er and her mother have more money than the Shu household when the play opens, the character takes as a given that she is not a fitting match for Shu Fen, and she rebukes her mother for even suggesting that attraction or social climbing might be her motive for lending assistance to the Shu family. The play thus presents deference to scholarly potential as natural to the social order.

The clown, Steamed-Bun, exhibits this same deference to the learned and awareness of his low social station. Steamed-Bun takes for granted that his own life is of less value than that of the scholarly Shu Depu, his benefactor. Though not in service to the Shu household, Steamed-Bun takes upon himself the role of the "righteous servant" (*yipu*) willing to risk his life for that of his master. This, too, was a favorite theme of the early Qing Suzhou dramatists, as the works of Li Yu and Zhu Suchen's brother Zhu Zuochao attest.[43] The theme of serving one master unto death surely would have lent itself to political allegory in the early Qing.[44]

In contrast, the villains of *Garden* are all men who usurp authority; they arrogate to themselves positions above their allotted stations, like the steward of the Ma estate who attempts to negotiate the purchase of the Shu property as if he were the owner's equal, or the Prince of Ning, who goes from seizing other people's lands to coveting the imperial throne. Often, too, trouble is instigated not by the master but by the conniving servant. It is Ma Fengzhi's steward who comes up with the plan to eliminate Shu Depu; just so, it is Ma Fengzhi who goads the prince to rebel. Together, these characters fulfill the stereotype of the *haonu*, or vainglorious slave. This caricature may also have resonated with audiences reflecting upon the bondservant uprisings of the late Ming or the shifting allegiances of the generals of the Three Feudatories—from the Ming to the Qing and finally to their own imperial designs.[45] In its critique of the raw pursuit of ambition, the play clings to a romanticized vision in which morality rather than power and market forces determines social relations.[46]

It has been speculated that an earlier, no longer extant version of the complete drama did not subscribe to such nostalgia for the preservation of status hierarchy. Based on a comparison of the existing versions of *Garden* with the plot synopsis in *Abstracts of the Complete Titles of the Sea of Drama*, which is thought to reflect the earliest edition, the late Lu Eting, eminent scholar of Kun opera, has suggested that the drama underwent major revision, probably shortly after its original creation in the second half of the seventeenth century. In that original version Cui'er is betrothed to Shu Fen at the start of the play, an indication that the families were imagined as more nearly equal on account of their approximate economic standing. The *Abstracts* synopsis also indicates that in the original version Cui'er's mother is not murdered. In the present version, in contrast, it is implied that Mama Zhao is somehow less than pure for even suggesting that her daughter might climb the social scale through virtuous deeds. Mama Zhao's death, then, represents the inexorable workings of karmic justice in which those who harbor improper ambitions are in the end duly punished.

More significant still, perhaps, in the originally conceived drama the savior of Shu Depu was not Zhao Cui'er but Ma Feiying, who double-crosses her own father to steal the execution tally and rescue the hapless scholar.[47] When the family discovers Feiying's heroic deed, only then do they agree to bring her into the marriage with Shu Fen and Cui'er, all with the explicit sanction of the emperor. This sequence of events might have afforded the play a more plausible ending, in which both women have equal claim to marriage with the new top graduate: Cui'er because of her prior engagement, and Feiying on account of her brave and righteous act. Some of the changes, clearly, especially in commercial scene-selection performance, were designed to streamline the play for dramatic effect, but we can also detect in the rewriting a retreat from the social vision of the original. In the revision of *Garden* filial devotion must be preserved at all costs, even when that obedience is due a villain, and only women of marginal status and respectability are given the leeway to play the knight-errant.[48] But if the new, class-inflected moralism of the redacted *Garden* trumped the gender and class politics of the original, the virtues of hierarchy again took a back seat to social complaint when scenes of the play moved into production in the commercial marketplace.

Garden *on the Commercial Stage*

"Virtually all theatrical literature," Stephen Orgel has written in regard to the Elizabethan stage, "must be seen as basically collaborative in nature."[49] Authorial intention—even for the likes of Shakespeare—was rescripted by the needs of troupes and performers, ultimately with an eye to pleasing crowds and turning a profit. This observation about the traits of performed literary culture in early modern England holds equally true for commercial theater in mid- to late Qing China. It is thus the performance scripts—with attention to what was left in and what was left out—that can alert us to the various cultural receptions of dramatic literature.

When *Garden* moved from page to stage, typically three variant production formats might be adopted: the play might be presented in truncated form in eight to twelve scenes; it might consist of the solo scene "Stealing the Tally";

or, sometimes, "Stealing the Tally" might be combined with the subsequent "Murder on the Boat" (Sha zhou), or, less commonly, with the concluding "Parading the Top Candidate" (You jie). Examining each of these treatments and audience responses to them in mid- to late Qing Beijing makes clear that in performances Zhao Cui'er was the key attraction, and that sentimentality and sensuality (leavened with plenty of humor) were the overriding entertainment aesthetics of these scenes.

Although it is speculated that *Garden* may have been originally composed for commercial production, the earliest evidence of how it might have been performed on the stage dates from 1770—at least a century after it was written—in the excerpts published in the massive Qing drama anthology *A Cloak of Patchworked White Fur*.[50] The *Cloak* edition features twelve scenes, all drawn from the first half of *Garden*; the dramatic action of the linked scene sequence concludes with Cui'er's theft of the tally, the murder of Cui'er's mother, and Shu Depu's escape from prison. The selected scripts published in *Cloak* were intended to capture a likeness to stage performance.[51] Although the stage directions in the *Cloak* scripts are minimal and musical notation is typically not recorded, the selected scenes included in this miscellany in other ways exhibit traces of live performance, such as expanded dialogue and dialect humor. As evidence of the strong link between *Cloak* scenes and performance scripts, an early nineteenth-century script of *Garden*, which claims provenance from the famous Sanqing Troupe in Beijing, turns out to be copied nearly word for word from the scenes in the *Cloak* anthology (Figure 14).[52] Yet another indication of how *Garden* was rendered in performance comes from an entry in the anonymous diary *Playwatching Journal*, which records a staging on 15 January 1798 at the Tianle Playhouse of all the scenes from the opening "Heavenly Announcement" (Yu bao) to "Stealing the Tally." Since no scenes from any additional play cycles were performed on that day, we can be fairly certain that this notation indicates the truncated performance of the eight to twelve scenes standardized in *Cloak*.[53] In addition, a list of scenes from plays in the repertory of the Jifang Troupe, which was active in the capital in 1828–29, indicates simply that it could perform "the eight scenes" from *Garden*.[54] This, clearly, was the favored abridgment for acting troupes purporting to stage the "complete" version of *Garden*.[55]

These abridgements cut out, with one exception, all scenes from the second half of the play. The battles and military strategizing—not Kun opera's typical strength—were jettisoned in favor of scenes with stronger individ-

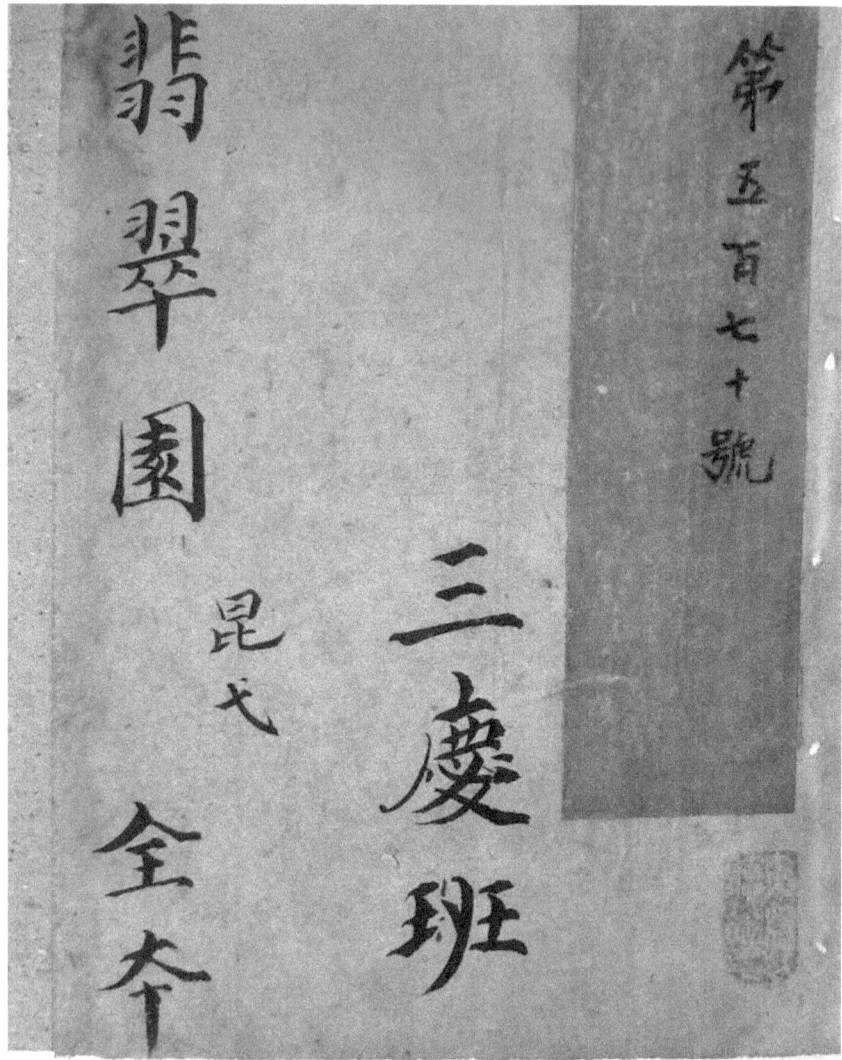

Figure 14. Cover page of the Sanqing Troupe edition of *The Garden of Turquoise and Jade* (*Feicui yuan*). Zhongguo yishu yanjiuyuan Library, Beijing.

ual characterization and greater social drama. This production choice also ensured that the play ended at a climax of emotional intensity. Whereas the *Cloak* selection ends with the escape of Shu Depu, the Sanqing script (which advertises itself as the "Complete Edition") omits his escape and ends with the scene in which Cui'er discovers her mother's death. The Sanqing version, thereby, becomes most markedly a vehicle for display of the virtuosity of the actor playing Cui'er. Cui'er's final aria combines grief with filial remorse. She sings:

> YA, YA, YA! YA, MY HEART IS PIERCED WITH PAIN!
> YA, YA, YA! YA, MY HEART IS PIERCED WITH PAIN!
> LOOK, LOOK, LOOK! LOOK AT THIS BODY SPLAYED OUT IN A POOL OF BLOOD; A MURDER MOST INHUMANE!
> IT MUST, IT MUST, IT MUST! IT MUST BE THAT SHE MET UP WITH AN OLD ENEMY ON A NARROW LANE.
> (Spoken): Oh, I know! It must have been that old bastard Ma Fengzhi. Enraged that I saved Scholar Shu through trickery, he must have sent someone after me to do me harm. But I was a step too slow in returning. My mother on the boat was accidentally murdered in my place. Ah, Mother . . .
> YOU, YOU, YOU! YOU HAD LOOKED ONLY TO ME TO PASS YOUR TWILIGHT YEARS IN A PEACEFUL VEIN.
> AND NOW, NOW, NOW! NOW, ALL BECAUSE OF YOUR DAUGHTER, YOU INSTEAD ARE SLAIN.[56]

In the Sanqing version it becomes clear that performance scripts likely ended with the murder of Mama Zhao for the sake of highlighting the dramatic potential of Cui'er's suffering and for the resulting surge of audience sympathy. The climax of the play wallowed in melodramatic excess. The impact of the words—even the stutter written into the poetic prosody—would have been further accentuated by the tempo of the music, which for this aria is both staccato and fast, underscoring the character's angst.[57] To invoke Brooks, "Nothing is *under*stood, all is *over*stated. Such moments provide us [the audience] with the joy of a full emotional indulgence."[58] Such sentimentalized depiction of injustice, in other words, was the stuff that grabbed at audience heartstrings. And *Garden* was not alone in projecting this aesthetic of emotional hyperbole.[59] Rather, this over-the-top sentimentality was much of the attraction of commercial kunju performance in the capital, whether seen in the character of Cui'er or the character of Hongniang (Crimson) in the scene "Beating Hongniang" (Kao Hong) from the *Story of the Western Chamber* (*Xixiang ji*) drama cycle, or in the reluctant nun in the play "Longing for the Secular Life" (Sifan).[60] The same actors, not surprisingly, tended to play these several roles.[61] These were actors who specialized in the "secondary young female lead" (*tie dan*) role types, typically lower-class characters or individuals with bold and transgressive personalities.

Debates within the scholarly literature on Western melodrama as to whether the genre should be considered conservative or progressive become moot in the Chinese context,[62] for although the playwright's edition of *Garden* concludes with the restoration of normative social hierarchies, the performed versions frequently afforded no such comforting closure. Cui'er's tears of remorse and *ressentiment* served as both climax and denouement. Sentimentality became the mode in which social complaint was voiced.[63] Such complaint was not necessarily directed. The elasticity of opera scenes drawn from historical dramas, especially, was such that their polemical bite was always displaced in time and the signified target just vague enough that it might be appropriated in different ways by any number of different audiences at different times. Might the eight to twelve scenes of *Garden* performed on 15 January and 8 June of 1798 have reminded the author of *Playwatching Journal* of the depredations of the notoriously corrupt Manchu Grand Councilor Heshen (1750–99), whose unprecedented abuses of power—including embezzlement of state funds—were enabled by his intimacy with the recently abdicated but still all-powerful Qianlong emperor?[64] Or did Cui'er's railings against injustice arouse sympathy in operagoers who felt themselves victimized (feminized) by those with power, but who nevertheless aspired in life to play the knight-errant's part? Opera aficionado Zhang Jiliang's maudlin self-positioning comes to mind: "I have observed closely the present state of the world; I can advise about what will benefit it and can cure it of its ills. But since I had no one to provide me with an introduction, I dared not submit suggestions or write them in books; hence, I cried bitterly."[65] Sentimental tears—whether on the opera stage or on the virtual stage of literati self-fashioning—could convey a polemical stance.

Playhouse audiences need not have shared similar gender or class status with Cui'er to empathize with her plight. Rather, as Peter Stallybrass and Allon White have noted in the case of communal spectacle in early modern Europe, "the positioning of the subordinate classes as the object of respectable gaze created the possibility of identification and even a sort of alliance between the . . . object of display" and more elite spectators.[66] This identification worked across gender as well as class among eighteenth- and nineteenth-century Chinese opera audiences. Frequently, within the abridged melodramas of the capital playhouses the sentimentality of complaint was gendered female, suggesting continuities not just with late Ming preoccupations with feminine authenticity but also with a much longer literary tradition of political critique ventriloquized through the trope of the lamenting woman.[67]

The sentimentality worked all the better when it was enacted by the doubly feminized attractive cross-dressing youths. And, in fact, as Wu Changyuan observed in 1785, this was the stuff that could make spectators' mouths—as well as eyes—water. The actor Song Yulin, of the Chuntai Troupe, for instance, captured audience fancy. Yulin, born to a northerner father and a Suzhou mother and raised in Yangzhou, was fluent in the dialects of Suzhou and Yangzhou. He was reportedly especially good in the scene "Stealing the Tally." With "limpid eyes capable of transmitting emotion and a willowy waist able to strike poses, the natural grace of a young lady is born in him."[68] A decade later fans were still infatuated with the actors playing Cui'er, as in a comment about Tianran from the Sixi Troupe, who according to one Master Qixiang, had a fine voice and a pleasingly plump appearance.[69] The erotic allure of the cross-dressing actors who played selfless and brave young women risking all for justice further endeared audiences to the plight of the character. Within the space of the commercial playhouse, then, entertainment value did not cede to but rather enhanced the effectiveness of veiled polemics.

If the emphasis in the production scripts of *Garden* was not on the injustices perpetrated against the female protagonist, then the dramatic interest lay in her clever mischief perpetrated against the rich and mighty in the name of justice. This is evident in the second possible production format of scenes from the *Garden* story cycle. More often than not, by the late eighteenth century urban audiences encountered just one—at most two—scenes from *Garden* in any one viewing. Of the hand-copied scripts from the dramatic cycle that have come down to us, the great majority are for the scene "Stealing the Tally." Clearly, the scene in which Cui'er steals the tally out from under the nose of the sleeping Ma Fengzhi could be performed as a solo piece. According to *Playwatching Journal*, of the thirteen performances based on *Garden* played by the Sanduo Troupe during 1797, eight of them consisted only of "Stealing the Tally."[70] Comments scattered throughout flower registers, too, tend to focus on actors who excelled at "Stealing the Tally." Only occasionally are other scenes, such as "Murder on the Boat" or "Parading the Top Candidate," mentioned, and then only in tandem with "Stealing the Tally."[71]

Performed alone, "Stealing the Tally" would have been a showcase piece for the tie dan role, with plenty of suspense, stage business, and comedy surrounding the theft of the tally, and further leavened by the humor of the clown, Steamed-Bun, who peppers his observations about Cui'er's daring feat with Suzhou colloquialisms. According to detailed stage directions in an actor-copied script dated to 11 December 1861, the moment of the theft required the actor playing Cui'er to display the highly demanding skill of scurrying around the stage *on his knees*. The actor also had to attempt the theft of the tally three times, alternately cowed and spurred on by coughs and snores from the actor playing Ma Fengzhi.[72] These antics were the stuff of commercial entertainment. The anonymous diarist of *Playwatching Journal* liked the Sanduo Troupe's "Stealing the Tally" well enough to give the performances he saw one red circle of commendation (out of a rating scale of zero to five red circles).[73] He further recorded that Qian Qiaoling of the Jinyu Troupe was completely convincing as Cui'er: "The moment he takes a step, he becomes the very likeness of a lady [jade] vendor."[74] Another early nineteenth-century enthusiast heaped praise on the actor Li Lülin in the role of Cui'er: "I've seen him perform 'Stealing the Tally' and 'Murder on the Boat,' and the acting is full of emotion and pleasing to the eye; he masters the very likeness of the character in both movement and voice."[75] Nor was Li Lülin alone in capturing the essence of the role. "Some say Yuling's rendition of 'Stealing the Tally' is overly panicked," claimed another spectator; "but if you think about it, with [the character's] life in the balance, how could [s/he] still mince about the stage?"[76] In other words, time and again, literate audiences in the commercial playhouses registered affective identification with the characters and plots *and* a critical awareness that they were watching actors ply a craft.[77]

On occasion audiences for commercial kunju in eighteenth- and nineteenth-century Beijing also would have had the satisfaction of witnessing a comedic resolution to the *Garden* plot. Sometimes the scene "Parading the Top Candidate" was paired with "Stealing the Tally," although at times it could be performed solo, as in the stagings by the Sanduo Troupe on New Year's Day (28 January) and 23 July 1797.[78] The treatment of the denouement in staged renditions of the scene varied from the playwright's ending, typically favoring a final disposition for Cui'er in which she did not have to share her husband. In the staged rewrite, Madam Wei, instead of first acknowledging Cui'er as a daughter, immediately betroths the seamstress to her son.[79] The episode as rendered in a single-scene version reads:

> ZHAN:[80] Ah, Madam, today you two, mother and son, have been reunited. What joy, indeed! There is nothing more for Cui'er to do here. I may as well take my leave of you.
> ZHENG:[81] Cuiniang, what talk is this? We two have been together through thick and thin for such a long time. How could I bear to part with you? What luck that today my son has tested as top of the class and been named top candidate. I'm of a mind to make a match between the two

of you, to pair you off as husband and wife. (The ZHAN acts out looking embarrassed.)[82]

Audiences responded enthusiastically to this scene, commenting particularly on the special joyous walk the character of Cui'er performs on learning that she will be married to Shu Fen (and after the other characters have exited the stage). Wu Changyuan recorded his friend Old Master Fu's observation that Cui'er's few slow steps in this scene were "most marvelous" (*zui miao*).[83] Yet another enthusiast commented on this revealing gait as well, praising the actor Chen Guilin for his rendition of the "unexpected encounter with young master Shu," in which "those slow steps create a special likeness of Zhao Cui'er."[84] The prevalence of extant scripts of the scene, as well as commentaries on performances, further hints at its popularity with playhouse spectators. Presumably, audiences (literate or not) voted with their feet; if these scenes from the *Garden* story cycle attracted good houses, troupes readily obliged by performing them often.

In all popularly performed versions of "Parading the Top Candidate," the story line ends with the single marriage between Cui'er and Shu Fen. No mention is made of a second, impending marriage between Ma Feiying and Shu Fen. In other words, in the telescoped two-scene commercial performance version of the play, a companionate marriage becomes Cui'er's reward for her compassion and courage. And that further suggests that the late Ming cultural ideal of companionate marriage survived into the High and late Qing.[85]

In contrast, only one extant "complete" production script of *Garden*, which we know was created explicitly for the viewing pleasure of members of the Qing royal household in the 1860s, preserves the two-in-one marriage found in the *Collected Publications of Rare Editions of Drama* version. The script, with complete music and choreography scores, was prepared by Du Shuangshou (1836–?), a native of Suzhou and a Kun opera dan active in commercial troupes in the capital in the 1850s (Figure 15).[86] In 1860 Du was selected to serve in one of the court acting troupes, which performed for the sole pleasure of the imperial family and its invited guests. Du's production script of *Garden* was written during his tenure in the court troupe; thus, we know that it was intended for a very exclusive audience. As if advertising the appropriation of Suzhou culture by the court, the cover page of the script is marked by a large Manchu-language seal in black. To my knowledge, this is the only surviving production script that includes the scene

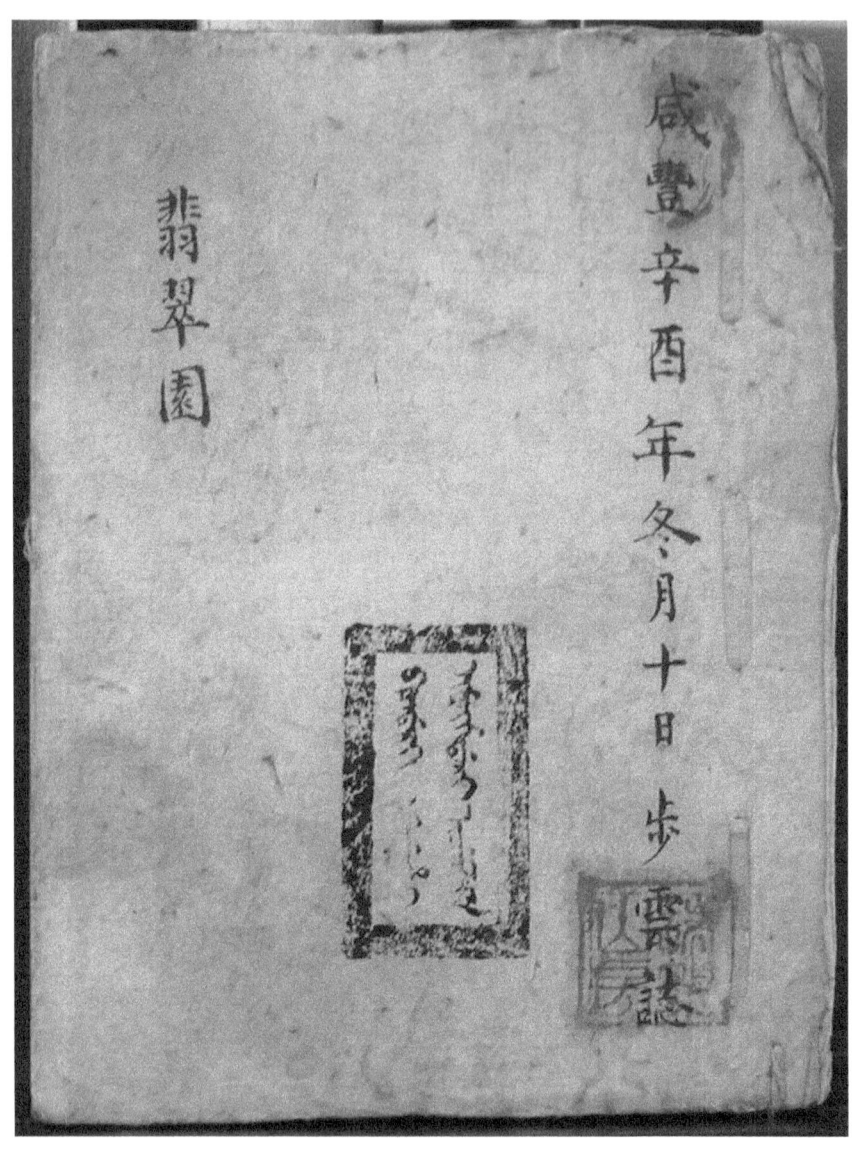

Figure 15. Cover page of Du Buyun copy of *Tale of the Garden of Turquoise and Jade* (*Feicui yuan chuanqi*). Copy dated to 1861. Peking University Rare Books Library.

"Making the Jade Whole" (Cui yuan), in which both Feiying and Cui'er are matched with Shu Fen, and which further suggests that the nineteenth-century court appreciated the conservative social message in the conclusion of the *Collected Publications of Rare Editions of Drama* edition (Figure 16).[87] Its uniqueness underscores the extent to which most performances for the commercial stage dispensed with the comforting restoration of social order and normative gender hierarchies at the conclusion of the play. Instead, audiences for commercial Kun opera preferred to wallow in histrionic railing against injustice or, alternatively, to delight in the victories of underdog vindication and restitution.

Audience response to the characterization of Steamed-Bun is harder to trace, partly because Qing opera aficionados rarely wrote about actors specializing in the clown role until the second half of the nineteenth century (and even then only sporadically). Whereas in the full drama Steamed-Bun functions as an essential plot device, being the catalyst for the various coincidences that drive the narrative action, in selected performance scripts the clown's greatest source of appeal would have been in his humor. This, as well as the clown's use of dialect throughout the scenes, shaped his characterization. In the various production scripts—from the *Cloak* abridgment to the many single copies of "Stealing the Tally"—Steamed-Bun speaks in Suzhou dialect, or Subai. Difficult as it is to adequately capture the flavor of dialect in translation, an exchange between Steamed-Bun and Cui'er in the scene "Stealing the Tally" may suffice to offer a taste of the folksy colloquialisms that the clown scatters throughout his speech. Cui'er has just stolen the tally. As she makes her escape, she encounters Steamed-Bun, who has come to the Ma household to check on her:

> CHOU:[88] Hey, is that Cuiniang up ahead headin' this way?
> ZHAN: Is that Brother Wang coming this way?
> CHOU: Yup, it is.
> ZHAN: Aiya, Brother Wang, things aren't good!
> CHOU: What's up?
> ZHAN: Just now I went to Administrator Ma's place to make some inquiries. (CHOU: Hey, where did this tally come from?)[89]
> ZHAN (continues): Who would have thought that the prince's establishment would have sent down a sentencing tally instructing that Scholar Shu be beheaded, with the done deed to be reported back by no later than the fifth watch tonight.

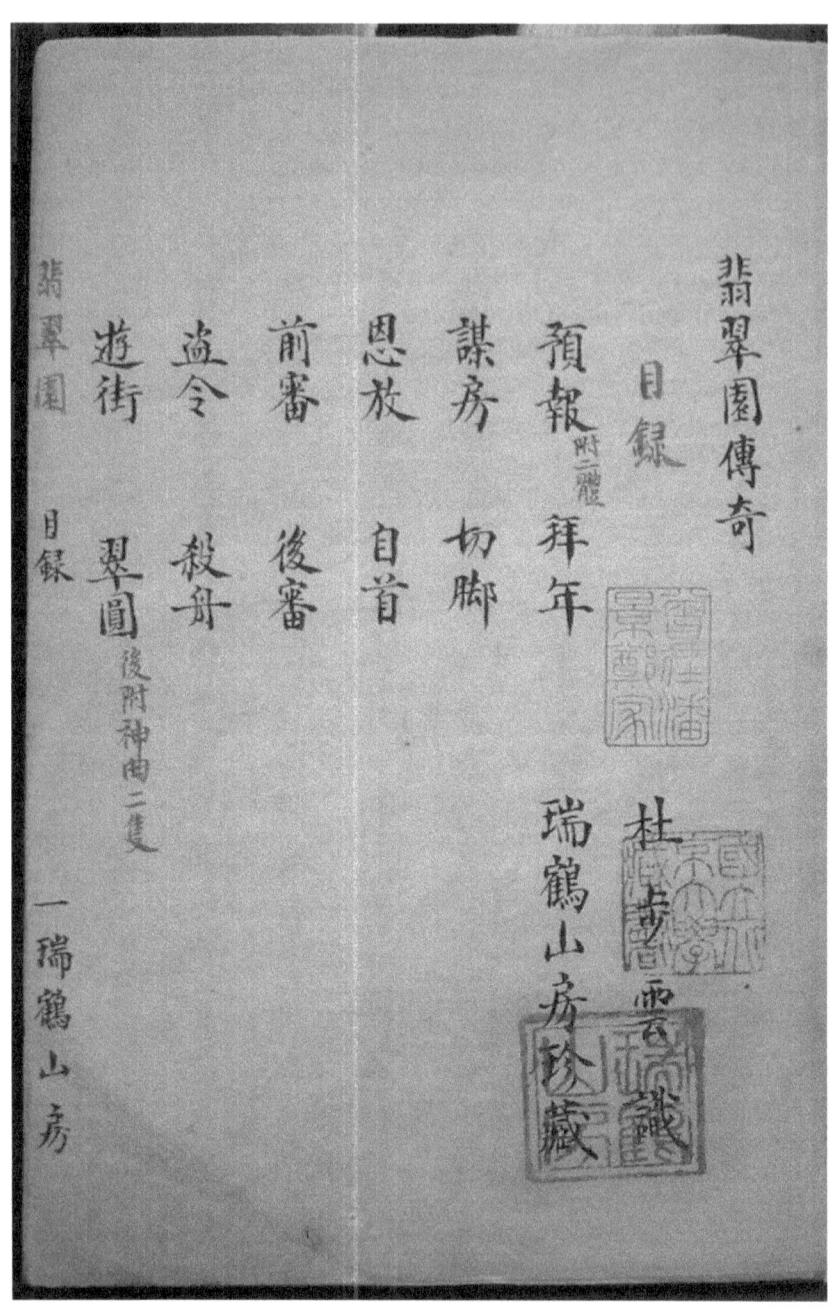

Figure 16. Table of contents page for Du Buyun copy of *Tale of the Garden of Turquoise and Jade*. Peking University Rare Books Library.

CHOU: It's over. He might as well be a perch roasted in the hollow of a writing brush: he's dead—*straight and stiff*! Ain't nothin' we can do.[90]

The clown's riddlelike proverb about the perch in the writing brush—a colorful way of saying that Shu Depu is as good as dead—would have been both amusing and linguistically marked to listeners of the scene.

In the earliest playwright's edition of *Garden*, the clown's use of dialect is not presented in the writing; possibly this feature of the character did not need to be indicated on the page because it was assumed that actors would adopt the registers of speech appropriate to their role types. The clown's speech, being the most colloquial, would naturally be rendered in the local dialect. By the time scenes from the play were chosen for collection in the various eighteenth-century drama anthologies such as *Cloak*, however, the clown's lines appear in Subai inflection. *Garden* was not alone in this regard. As Catherine Swatek has shown, this pattern of writing the clowns' lines in dialect in the selected scenes also appears in the plays of Li Yu, the most prolific of the early Qing Suzhou playwrights.[91] Likely these drama anthologies were attempting to capture on the page the flavor of live performance; and thus, they reflect textually that which was only implicit in the playwright's master-script. As we shall see in the following chapter too, in the eighteenth and nineteenth centuries most kunju production scripts made a point of textually capturing the Subai of the clowns.

While the use of dialect makes sense in the context of the drama's original creation in Suzhou, when kunju was performed in the capital, it is likely that the Subai had a rather different effect on audiences. The use of local brogue marked Steamed-Bun as low class but at the same time as from the most culturally advanced region within the empire. In essence, the use of Suzhou dialect in opera production in the capital would have distinguished sojourning Jiangnan audiences from others within the Beijing commercial playhouses. Dialect insiders (and there were plenty of them in the capital) would have experienced a kind of intimacy and immediacy with Steamed-Bun, and common regional and linguistic identity would have endeared him to them regardless of his marginal class position.[92] Commercial Kun opera in the capital city, then, retained within it (whether consciously or not) certain larger social fault lines between Jiangnan literati and northerners, at times reinscribing the differences between the sophisticated culture of the south and the alien overlords that many of these men of learning now served.

Conclusion

The scenes from *Garden* were but a handful among a much larger repertoire of plays that filled the stages of the capital playhouses. They belonged, however, to an important subset of dramatic works produced by the early Qing Suzhou playwrights. Scenes from all of these dramas shaped the tenor of commercial Kun opera in Qing Beijing (and perhaps in other urban communities too), making up a full fourth of the five hundred-plus plays included in the eighteenth-century drama anthology *A Cloak of Patchworked White Fur*.

Time and again, the commercially performed excerpts from these plays emphasized the sufferings of the wronged heroines and heroes. In these plays, too, young women and the poor both line up on the side of righteousness and authenticity and act to see justice done. The commercial productions taken from the *Garden* plot, then, exemplify the gendered (and classed) face of social complaint. Such complaint typically was not specific, and that made it infinitely malleable, capable of expressing a generalized disaffection. Its overriding expression evinced sympathy for ordinary people and outrage at the abuse of power and privilege. The playhouses of the Qing capital were some of the key venues in which this complaint was voiced. The audiences who indulged in (and wrote about) such public displays of sentimentality and sensuality consisted of marginalized literati and other men with sufficient means to frequent the capital playhouses. And the stories presented by the hybridized, commercial Kun opera that these men patronized catered to the sotto voce grumblings of such audiences.

We can find this gendered polemics of social complaint in other facets of Qing metropolitan theater culture too. We can find it in the guides to the boy actresses, in which the marginalized literati authors deeply identified with the feminized and debased youths of the opera demimonde. We can find similar sentiments in the mid-nineteenth-century novel *Precious Mirror for Ranking Boy Actresses*, whose motto, to quote Keith McMahon, might be "let us all be *dan*"; in other words, willingly playing the feminized part constituted a pointed rejection of the privilege that came with status.[93] We can find it even in the culture of sensuous Jiangnan—epitomized in the Suzhou-derived Kun opera—which was perceived as feminine vis-à-vis the Manchu-identified court in Beijing.[94]

. . .

In her study of the theater of 1940s Italy Mabel Berezin has proposed that it was not the content of the plays that made them fascist but rather the form—by which she means the ways in which they were subsidized and produced—that imbued them with political meaning.[95] Berezin's observations about the centrality of both content and form to understanding the cultural meanings of art mesh with my discoveries in this chapter about the performance scripts of *Garden*. The cumulative effects of the emendations to the playwright's script in commercial Kun opera performance skewed the original message of the play. The abridged eight- to twelve-scene versions of *Garden* and the paired or single-scene selections of popular excerpts turned supporting characters—Cui'er and Steamed-Bun—into leads. The lack of narrative closure in the multiscene productions undercut the restoration of normative social hierarchies that appeared in the playwright's text, substituting spectacle, sentimentality, and sensuality for social order. "Stealing the Tally" valorized Cui'er's "rivers-and-lakes," or *jianghu*-style, justice, sanctioning personal lawbreaking as a means of settling public scores. And the reward for such vigilante heroism, as exemplified in the scripts of "Parading the Top Candidate," was an ideal companionate marriage with an equal exchange of social benefits: he lent her status; she offered him real-world savvy.

Thus, we can see that traces of late Ming romantic imaginings about gender and class—in which young women and common folk were represented as repositories of authenticity—carried over in modified form into the social melodramas of the Qing. During the Qing, however, these plays moved from the playwright's page to the commercial stage, bringing such concepts to a larger, more heterogeneous, and less socially exalted audience. In the process, these romantic imaginings were sometimes transformed by commercial acting troupes from trenchant social critique into sentimental kitsch.[96] But the social melodramas of the eighteenth- and nineteenth-century kunju stage nevertheless embodied a new polemics of sentimentality.

Scholarship on the politics of feeling in late imperial China—often in shorthand referred to as the "cult of qing"—has tended to assume that these ideas waned with the fall of the Ming. The Qing, in contrast, has been characterized as a time of renewed Confucian rigor and authoritarian repression.[97] This analysis of one play cycle in performance context argues that sentimentality was still very much alive in the Qing. We have not noticed it, however, because we have not looked for it in the right places. We find it in the operas presented on the metropolitan commercial stages and in audience responses to them. Undoubtedly, at the level of high intellectual discourse the early Qing saw a rejection of late Ming School of Mind neo-Confucianism in favor of renewed School of Principle (*lixue*) ritualism, or, alternatively, in favor of the seemingly apolitical empiricism of the "investigative learning" (*kaozheng*) movement, both of which were actively endorsed by the Qing state.[98] The surveillance mechanisms of the Qing were formidable, and the state was readily capable of exercising its punitive power to quash public dissent.[99] And yet there were societal interstices that the state could never effectively penetrate, even in Beijing. The commercial playhouses of eighteenth- and nineteenth-century Beijing were such spaces: attempts to regulate them notwithstanding, they eluded the state's full control.[100] The ephemeral quality of live theater (scripts might be left behind, but their performances vanished into memory) further made productions extremely difficult to police. And even if the state could have effectively monitored political innuendo and public morality on the basis of play content, the plasticity of form—in which operas could be staged in full or truncated, as single or paired scenes—meant that efforts at censorship could always be evaded. During the Qing the commercial playhouse was the site in which private emotion was put on public display. By reading the operas from the *Garden* story line as they appear in performance context, we see one example of the public expression of polemically charged sentimentality and sensuality in the Qing capital.

Ironically, perhaps, this polemics of complaint was strongest when the Qing court attempted to contain urban theatricals within the outer section of the capital city, which was dominated by the tastes of Han literati. By the second half of the nineteenth century, as the court began to embrace and patronize commercial opera, it came to have much more influence over the content of performance within the urban space. Concurrently, the feminized polemics of complaint that had been so central to commercial Kun opera (and which voiced literati disaffection) came to be eclipsed by new narratives of male heroics, which were harnessed to the preservation of state-endorsed moral and social hierarchies.

FIVE

Sex versus Violence in "I, Sister-in-Law" Operas

> The various papers of Tianjin have published many pieces under the byline "I, Sister-in-Law." This [name] stems from a special type of dan role in the theater who, upon opening her mouth, calls herself, "I, Sister-in-Law." These reviews focused specifically on this sort of opera, hence the choice of "I, Sister-in-Law" as a pen name. The first of such reviews analyzed the opera *The Cobbler Kills His Wife* [*Pijiang sha qi*]. It described the I, Sister-in-Law character with loosened hair and a [half-]naked body, and as knocking her head to the ground as if pounding a piece of garlic—all creepy to the nth degree; yet the point [of such plays] is to caution against licentiousness, so one need not be overly critical.
>
> 天津各新聞紙，登載許多嫂子我稿件，只因梨園有一種旦角，張嘴自稱嫂子我。這幾篇文字專評這一派的戲，所以署名嫂子我。頭一次的稿就評的是《皮匠殺妻》。說的嫂子我披頭散髮，露體赤身，磕頭如搗蒜，肉麻到一百分，只用意是個戒淫，還可以不加責備。
>
> Chen Moxiang, *Sketches from a Life of Watching Theater*, 1930[1]

"I, Sister-in-Law" operas (*saozi wo*)—so designated because these were the first words uttered by the protagonist as she entered the stage—narrate the woman's estrangement from her husband, her thwarted attempt to seduce her husband's (biological or sworn) brother, her subsequent adultery with a different lover, and the final retribution inflicted upon the woman for her licentiousness—and sometimes worse.[2] Chen Moxiang (1884–1943)—critic, playwright, and amateur performer of dan roles—was so taken with these plays that he adopted "I, Sister-in-Law" as one of his literary pen names. As Chen's remarks show, these plays offered the arousing spectacle of licentiousness, presumably with the downfall of the wanton woman imparting redeeming social value. Yet the didacticism of such operas sometimes was obscured by their entertainment value. In many of the scripts it is clear that the adulterous sex and the violent retribution (and a measure of comedy to leaven both the sex and the violence) were the central attractions of the productions.

The great majority of sister-in-law operas staged in Beijing playhouses during the Qing emanated from the *Water Margin* story cycle. In the early seventeenth century the three narratives of the dangerous women of *Water Margin*—Yan Poxi, Pan Jinlian, and Pan Qiaoyun—were rewritten into individual chuanqi dramas, entitled *The Record of the Water Margin* (*Shuihu ji*), *The Righteous Hero*, and *Cuiping Mountain* (*Cuiping shan*), respectively. Over the course of the next two centuries (and on into the present), the story material further migrated from page to stage as it was adapted and reworked into various opera genres. Operas based on these notorious femmes fatales became popular fare in the playhouses of the Qing capital.

By the mid- to late nineteenth century these sister-in-law plays had generated spin-offs—crude imitation plots with no pretense to literary merit and no actual characters from the *Water Margin* story cycle, such as the copycat scene "The Cobbler Killer" (*Sha pi*)—revealing just how popular this theme of adultery and murderous revenge was among audiences at the time.³

Using multiple redactions of eighteenth- and nineteenth-century performance scripts from the kunju and pihuang opera repertoires, I elucidate the interplay between text, performance, musical genre, and audience reception of gender roles in these operas. Through attention to stage directions in scripts and written responses to performances by opera enthusiasts, I aim to reconstruct live performance during the Qing and analyze what made the "I, Sister-in-Law" plot so compelling for spectators. Comparison of multiple versions of these operas reveals that the greater the literary sophistication of a text, the more it exuded a sense of sympathy for the woman. Crudely cobbled-together scripts directed to less literate audiences tended to stress the revenge and murder.

I further address the "scene-selection" (*zhezi xi*) production practice of commercial playhouses of the eighteenth- and nineteenth-century capital, particularly the way scene-selection productions skewed (or even entirely omitted) the didactic message of "I, Sister-in-Law" operas. In kunju performance practice the focus of the plot was less the husband's humiliation and revenge than the woman's seductive power and subsequent liaison. The husband became a supporting actor; she, the amorous lead. In the most extreme examples of this reframing, Yan Poxi was recast in the role of the neglected woman, essentially explaining away her illicit affair.

Less polemical than the scenes featuring the chivalrous seamstress in *Garden*, these sister-in-law kunju operas nevertheless reflect a similar fascination on the part of urban audiences with sensuality and sentimentality, and a similar excitement generated by the staging of social transgression and inverted gender roles. But whereas in *Garden* sympathy with underdog gender and class positions coalesces in the characters of Cui'er and the clown, in the *Water Margin*–derived plays female transgressors are posited as in conflict with righteous male folk heroes. Commercial kunju "I, Sister-in-Law" plays tended to evoke sympathy for the transgressive woman; later pihuang operas sided with the male bravos.

With the development of pihuang in the mid- to late-nineteenth century, *Water Margin*–derived plays reinstated the aggrieved husband and his brother as the protagonists, which called for playing the story through to the end, where the woman was punished for her sexual license. The climactic scenes in pihuang sister-in-law operas centered on the marital and martial tensions leading to the murder of the unfaithful wife. In part, this reflected the conventions of the pihuang genre, in which the arias were designed more to advance the story and less to explore the singer's internal emotions. But these simpler conventions also catered to less educated audiences—audiences more attuned to plot than poetry.

Opera genre, as we have seen, became an index of audience clientele. In general, kunju appealed to a literati-centered, transregional audience in the Qing capital (although its fans could include everyone from the high cultural and political elite to wealthy tradesmen and disaffected literati), whereas pihuang operas initially attracted more marginally literate, locally based petty urbanites. This, too, changed over time. As discussed earlier, beginning in the mid-nineteenth century, the court made a public show of embracing pihuang and its most accomplished commercial actors. As a result, during the second half of the nineteenth century the pihuang musical genre eclipsed kunju performance in the commercial playhouses of Beijing.

Through close readings of a series of "I, Sister-in-Law" plays, I demonstrate that mid- to late nineteenth-century court patronage of the originally lowbrow pihuang opera genre forged an odd-couple union between action-play violence and state-promulgated orthodoxy regarding gender norms. As court patronage of pihuang opera helped to elevate the genre's cultural status, a more misogynistic and moralistic performance tradition was disseminated to and ultimately embraced by a wider and more elite urban audience. Even within this performance tradition, however, although audiences might take away from a sister-in-law opera a clearer moral message, evidence suggests that what they came to see was not necessarily the moralistic ending. Rather, the dramatic excitement lay in vivid and artful portrayal of vigilante violence directed against a sexually transgressive woman.

The Stories

The early seventeenth-century chuanqi-style written dramas, *Record of the Water Margin*, *Righteous Hero*, and *Cuiping Mountain*, which became the progenitors of subsequent performed sister-in-law operas, had their own textual antecedents, all drawn from embellished Water Margin legends about the exploits of an early twelfth-century band of righteous rebels. We can trace the origins of at least two of the three Water Margin dangerous-women tales—those featuring Yan Poxi and Pan Jinlian—as far back as the Yuan dynasty (1279–1368), although the various sixteenth-century recensions of the novel were the first to combine all three stories in one literary treatment.[4] With each new iteration of these plots—from early legends and plays to the sixteenth-century editions of *Water Margin* and finally to the late Ming written dramas—the female antiheroes in these episodes gradually came to take center stage.

RECORD OF THE WATER MARGIN

From its earliest recorded version, the troubled relationship between the bandit hero Song Jiang and his purchased servant-girl-cum-wife Yan Poxi has been linked to legends about the outlaws of the Liangshan Marshes.[5] The story of Song Jiang and his murder of Yan Poxi emerged from twelfth- and thirteenth-century songs and storytelling traditions and took form in the early fourteenth-century historical romance *Forgotten Events of the Xuanhe Reign* (*Xuanhe yishi*). Simply and briefly, that narrative relates that Song Jiang—a clerk in the Yuncheng County magistrate's office—receives a pair of gold hairpins from the bandit chief Chao Gai in exchange for having helped him escape the clutches of the law. Song gives the gold hairpins to a singing girl by the name of Yan Poxi, who learns their origin. Later, on visiting Yan Poxi, Song Jiang discovers that she has taken a lover. Enraged, Song Jiang kills Yan Poxi and her lover.[6] In this and all later fictionalizations it is this act that turns Song Jiang into a fugitive and sets him on the path to becoming leader of the Liangshan outlaws. In this first recorded narrative of the story no moral valence is placed either on Song's act of murder or on Yan's romantic betrayal.

With the development of full-length editions of the novel *Water Margin* in the late sixteenth century, not only does the conflict between Song Jiang and Yan Poxi receive much fuller treatment but it is reframed as a clash between good and evil, in which Song Jiang is cast as the wronged hero and Yan Poxi as the double-crossing villainess.[7] The basic outline of the episode in the novel is as follows: Yan Poxi, a singing girl, and her parents come to Yuncheng County to work for an official, only to find themselves stranded without work. When the father dies, Madam Yan enlists the help of Mama Wang, a local matchmaker, to borrow some money from Song Jiang, who is reputed for his generosity. Madam Yan then insists on marrying the young and beautiful Yan Poxi to the middle-aged, short, and swarthy Song Jiang in recompense for the loan. Song agrees to the match reluctantly and, more interested in martial arts than in bedroom arts, leaves Yan Poxi unsatisfied.

One day Song Jiang brings Zhang San (more formally named Zhang Wenyuan)—a young fellow clerk in the magistrate's office—home with him for tea. Soon Zhang San entices Yan Poxi into an affair. Song hears rumors but ignores them. Madam Yan then persuades him to come home to her daughter for the night, but Poxi is cold toward Song Jiang. After a long night in which neither Yan Poxi nor Song Jiang disrobes, Song hurriedly leaves the house, only to realize that he has left behind his clerk's document pouch, in which he has stashed a piece of gold and a secret missive sent to him by the Liangshan bandits. By the time he returns to collect the pouch, Yan Poxi has discovered it and uses it to blackmail Song Jiang into granting her a divorce. Not content with simply being allowed to marry her lover, she threatens to expose Song Jiang's communications with the outlaws to the authorities, thereby placing Song's life in jeopardy. Sorely tried, Song Jiang attempts to wrestle the incriminating letter away from Yan Poxi. As they struggle, Yan yells "murder!" and only then—as if cued by her cry—does Song Jiang grab his knife and stab her to death. Forced to flee from his crime, Song Jiang joins the Liangshan bandits.[8]

As much as possible, the *Water Margin* rendering of the tale underscores the cuckolded Song Jiang's long-suffering restraint and the woman's utter perfidy. In the novel this account of malignant treachery and unpremeditated killing becomes the first of a series of increasingly more ruthless murders of adulterous wives—in which male heroism is linked to sexual abstinence and violence against sexually ardent women.[9] Underscoring the moral message of the Song-Yan episode, Jin Shengtan, an early seventeenth-century editor and commentator on the novel, writes that the author "uses this . . . to describe the evil within women's hearts. It illuminates all their darkness and thoroughly exposes them in all their ugliness. When old Lotharios read it, they will wag their tongues in amazement; when young Lotharios read it, they will rein in their emotions. Truly, the words of this story are fabulous needles to prick the consciences of all philanderers."[10]

As numerous literary critics have observed, for all its seemingly negative portrayal of Yan Poxi, this episode is far more developed than the account in the *Forgotten Events* source story. *Forgotten Events* dispenses with the murder in a handful of lines; the novel gives it a full chapter. So vividly characterized is Yan Poxi that in large measure she steals the spotlight from Song, the hero. Clever dialogue and skillful narrative description reveal Yan Poxi's willfulness and chart her desperate missteps as her conflict with Song escalates to the point of no return. The character's treacherous infidelity is compelling, if not endearing. This pattern is also apparent in the figurally linked episodes of Pan Jinlian and Pan Qiaoyun—those other colorful sisters in adultery—in later chapters of the novel.[11]

The various recensions of *Water Margin*, as Andrew Plaks and other scholars have shown, can be read as an expression of a late Ming literati critique of heroic action.[12] The novel's juxtaposition of the passionate, active Yan Poxi with the taciturn, passive Song Jiang may reflect a conscious attempt by sixteenth- and seventeenth-century literary redactors to deflate, at least to some degree, the novel's male heroes. Certainly the seventeenth-century commentator Jin Shengtan, vitriolic regarding the character of Yan Poxi, was hardly more flattering in his comments about the novel's ostensible hero, Song Jiang.[13] The late Ming literati versions of the novel, as many have argued, undermine the righteous image of its male heroes through artful manipulation of character contrasts and figural recurrence, thereby introducing shades of gray into a tale of adultery and vigilante justice that on the surface seems to be drawn in bold black-and-white strokes.[14]

In the early seventeenth century, at roughly the same time that *Water Margin* was becoming fixed in final novelistic form, the Jiangnan scholar and playwright Xu Zichang (1578–1623) reworked the core chapters from the novel featuring Song Jiang's metamorphosis from clerk to outlaw into a thirty-two-scene drama entitled *The Record of the Water Margin*.[15] Alternating scenes of the righteous goodfellows of Liangshan with those of Song Jiang's domestic troubles, the play follows the exploits of Song Jiang from the time he befriends the bandit Chao Gai through his murder of Yan Poxi, his capture following the crime, and his eventual rescue from execution by the Liangshan braves.

The changes that Xu Zichang introduced into the dramatic text bolster a conventionally moralistic reading of the tale. No trace of irony remains. By mirroring scenes and paralleling contrasting character types, he presents Song Jiang and the Liangshan band as more unequivocally good and makes Yan Poxi, her mother, and her lover Zhang San more venal and duplicitous. As if sensing that the extrafamilial status of the Liangshan outlaws in the novel might strike readers as problematic, the playwright turned Song Jiang into a more conventional family man. By inventing a primary wife named Lady Meng (Meng Shi) for Song Jiang, Xu tempered his characterization, making it clear that Song Jiang does not have a problem with all women, only with Yan Poxi. Lady Meng serves as a positive foil for Yan Poxi's moral deficiencies. When confronted by evil bandits (as opposed to the Liangshan principled outlaws), Lady Meng risks her life in defense of her virtue and her husband's honor. Yan Poxi is not only a libertine but a would-be blackmailer whose treacherous threats would have cost Song Jiang's life. The playwright even added a short scene in which the matchmaker, Mama Wang, divulges to Lady Meng that Song Jiang has taken Yan Poxi as a concubine. To the matchmaker's surprise, Lady Meng responds, "What harm is there in that? My husband lives all alone away from home. He really should find someone who can take care of him."[16]

Xu Zichang's treatment also cheapens the romantic relationship between Yan Poxi and Zhang San. In scene 29, Zhang San, knowing full well that Yan Poxi has only just been killed, attempts to seduce Lady Meng. Even the role types assigned to the various characters in Xu Zichang's drama offer clues to their moral stature. As the protagonist, Song Jiang is portrayed by the lead male role (*sheng*). Zhang San is played by a character-actor role (*jing*). Lady Meng is performed by the lead female role (*zheng dan*), Yan Poxi by a secondary female role (*xiao dan*). Xu, in other words, intended Yan Poxi and Zhang San as supporting characters.

Although in many aspects the dramatized version of Song Jiang's ill-fated encounter with Yan Poxi is more moralistic than in the novel, in other ways certain changes introduced by the playwright—perhaps unwittingly, perhaps to please audiences—undermined its didacticism. Whereas in the novel Song Jiang's relationship with Yan Poxi is dispensed with in a single chapter, in the drama nearly a quarter of the scenes are devoted to Yan's triangular entanglements with Song Jiang and Zhang San. Further, the scenes featuring Yan Poxi and Zhang San outshine the exploits of the virtuous protagonists.

In those scenes Yan Poxi may be far from virtuous, but she is not completely evil. Rather, she is presented as the dupe of her venal mother and the lascivious Zhang San. By depicting her thus, the playwright also set the scene for his most significant departure from the source story: in the penultimate scene, "Response from the Grave" (Ming gan), Yan's ghost returns to claim the life not of her murderer, Song Jiang, but of her seducer, Zhang San. These changes, although they deprived Yan Poxi of the feared power of a sexually potent woman (which the novel granted her), transformed her from trollop into avenging victim. Although no renditions of the story fully expunged the stigma of wantonness, later production versions of the script enhanced the character's sympathetic side.

RIGHTEOUS HERO

The second of the adultery and revenge narratives from the *Water Margin* story cycle revolves around the characters Wu Song, his dwarfish brother Wu Da, the brother's wife Pan Jinlian, and Pan's lover Ximen Qing. This story material, too, has a documented textual history long preceding its reworking into the novel. The title of a thirteenth-century variety play (*zaju*), *Sacrificing Two Heads, Wu Song Exacts Vengeance* (*Shuang xiantou Wu Song da baochou*), no longer extant, summarizes a plot that likely corresponds to the contents of chapters 24–26 in *Water Margin*.[17] Other late thirteenth-century literature such as the play by Hongzi Li Er (act. 1295–96) entitled *With Only a Broken Staff, Wu Song Fights a Tiger* (*Zhe daner Wu Song da hu*), and Song vernacular short stories (*huaben*) such as "Pilgrim Wu" (Wu Xingzhe), reveal a well-developed cluster of narratives centering on the exploits of Wu Song. Much of this would be incorporated into the ten chapters in *Water Margin* devoted to Wu Song (chaps. 23–32).

In the novel this sequence of adultery and revenge follows immediately upon Song Jiang's murder of Yan Poxi; it reprises and expands the themes of male martial valor and female sexual ardor. The sequence begins with Wu Song returning to his natal town in Qinghe County to seek out his elder brother. En route he gets drunk and in that state kills a tiger with his bare fists. Hearing of this, the magistrate of Yanggu County appoints Wu militia commander.

In Yanggu County Wu Song finds his brother Wu Da. The luckless Wu Da turns out to be as short, feeble, and ugly as Wu Song is tall, muscular, and handsome. Wu Da is known to the local townspeople by the nickname "Pock-Faced Three-Inch Nail" (Gushupi sancun ding).[18] His wife, Pan Jinlin, is beautiful. This mismatched couple has recently moved to Yanggu County to escape the taunts of Qinghe County wiseacres who had taken to standing outside their door and shouting, "A juicy piece of mutton has fallen into a dog's mouth."[19] Wu Da now makes his living by hawking baked biscuits. When Wu Da invites his brother home to meet Pan Jinlian, she is instantly smitten.

One blustery winter day, in one of the most dramatic scenes in the novel, Pan Jinlian attempts to seduce her brother-in-law.[20] Wu Song has just returned from a day's work, and Wu Da is out selling biscuits. Pan Jinlian gives Wu Song wine and coaxes him to warm himself by the fire. Pan drinks with her brother-in-law, and her tongue and inhibitions loosened by the wine, she gradually circles in for the attack. Pan's burning desire and Wu Song's frosty response are set against the mise-en-scène imagery of fire and snow; the thrusting and parrying with words recalls Wu Song's earlier combat with the tiger. Wu Song swiftly rebukes Pan's advances, dousing her ardor with the threat that, should he hear of any future impropriety on her part, his eyes may still recognize her as sister-in-law, but his fists—those same fists that vanquished the tiger—won't.[21]

Shortly thereafter Wu Song is sent on a mission by the magistrate. Before setting off, he cautions his brother to spend more time at home and to keep the rattan window blinds lowered to avoid unwelcome attention from outsiders. One day, just as Pan Jinlian is lowering the blinds with a bamboo pole, she drops the pole, which hits a passerby in the street below. The passerby is Ximen Qing, a wealthy medicine-shop owner, notorious womanizer, and local bully. The two make eye contact, and from that moment Ximen lusts after Pan. With the help of Pan's neighbor, Mama Wang, Ximen Qing connives to seduce Pan Jinlian. The elaborate plot is successful, and an affair begins but is soon discovered. When Wu Da charges into the trysting room in the rear of Mama Wang's teahouse, Ximen Qing kicks him in the chest and makes his escape.

With the affair now exposed, Mama Wang instructs Pan Jinlian to get rid of her husband by adding arsenic to his medicine. Returning from his mission months later, Wu Song learns of his brother's sudden, and suspicious, death. He gathers evidence of the adultery and the murder and brings it before the local magistrate. But Ximen Qing's bribes get the case dismissed, leaving Wu Song determined to settle accounts on his own. Gathering the neighbors to witness a private trial before his brother's spirit tablet, he coerces confessions out of Pan Jinlian and Mama Wang, kills Pan Jinlian, and then carves out her heart as an offering before his brother's altar. Ximen Qing he hunts down in the Lion Street Tavern, returning with his severed head to Wu Da's altar. Vengeance satisfied, Wu Song turns himself in to the magistrate to await reckoning.

The plot of this second femme fatale story is longer and more complicated. Good and evil are also more sharply contrasted. Of all the vigilantes in the novel, Wu Song is perhaps the most deserving of the accolade of righteous outlaw. In contrast to Song Jiang, who murdered Yan Poxi almost accidentally as he struggled to save his own skin, Wu Song killed not out of self-interest but to avenge the death of his innocent brother. Besides, he resorts to violence only after failing to obtain justice through legal channels. And having attained a blood-soaked "justice," Wu Song makes no attempt to flee the consequences. Even those scholars who read an ironic deflation of the heroic subject into the sixteenth-century editions of the novel agree that in the first half of the Wu Song decicycle the hero pursues his revenge with a measure of restraint. Late Ming readers sprinkled their copies of the novel with marginalia reflecting like opinions: "Wu . . . is truly a man who holds his head to the heavens and his feet to the ground."[22]

In contrast, Pan Jinlian is surely the least sympathetic of the *Water Margin* adulteresses. She murders her utterly innocent husband with barely a flicker of hesitation. As with Yan Poxi, Pan Jinlian's unbridled sexuality makes her impervious to any ethical considerations, and hence dangerous, a force to be controlled and eliminated. This is underscored by her given name—Jinlian, or Golden Lotus—a gloss for her tiny bound feet, and the ultimate symbol of female allure. There is a raw, animal-like quality to her desire—underscoring her figural linkage to the tiger—that is further matched to Wu Song's impetuosity and penchant for violence.[23]

Pan Jinlian's trajectory in the novel—from forlorn wife of a sorry excuse of a husband to seductress and finally to adulteress and murderer—so entranced readers that her villainy gained a literary life of its own, beyond the relatively brief narrative in *Water Margin*. Pan Jinlian's cameo appearance in that novel—and the entire complex of her intrigues with Mama Wang and Ximen Qing—became the kernel of the late sixteenth-century novel *The Plum in the Golden Vase*, which recast her and her lover as the central characters. Jinlian is depicted in *Plum in the Golden Vase* even less sympathetically than in *Water Margin*; and yet, given that this story material was redeployed in other fictional works of the time, it indicates a certain late Ming fascination with this particular cunning enchantress.[24]

Nearly contemporaneous with the publication of *Plum in the Golden Vase*, the playwright Shen Jing (1553–1610) rewrote the Wu Song decicycle into a chuanqi drama entitled *The Righteous Hero*.[25] *Righteous Hero* shifts the focus from the sordid deeds of Pan Jinlian and Ximen Qing to the heroic feats of Wu Song. As with Xu Zichang's dramatic reinterpretation of Song Jiang's adventures in *Record of the Water Margin*, the drama comes across as less subversive of social norms than late Ming literati versions of the source novel. Shen Jing stays quite close to some of the original language and plot of *Water Margin* in his script; nevertheless, he does introduce certain innovations into his narrative, foremost among them his fabrication of the character Miss Jia (Jia Shi), who is cast in the role of Wu Song's fiancée.[26] Miss Jia and her mother (virtuous complements to the treacherous Pan Jinlian and Mama Wang) are woven in and out of the thirty-six-scene drama, at times set upon by robbers, at times threatened by Wu Song's enemies, and in the end reunited with Wu Song through the good offices of the other righteous bandits of Liangshan. This revision serves to blunt Wu Song's rough edges; it turns him from an outlaw whose aggressive martial impulses make him unsuitable for family life into a loyal son-in-law who postpones marriage only until his financial prospects have improved and his legal encumbrances diminished, allowing him to assume the role of responsible husband. *Righteous Hero* concludes with a classic romantic comedy marriage and with all of the Liangshan outlaws pardoned for their crimes against the state.

Shen Jing, the author of seventeen plays and several treatises on musical prosody, was considered one of the founders of the Wujiang School of dramatic craftsmanship. Practitioners of this style advocated making dramatic literature suitable for performance onstage and championed the use of simple dialogue and singable lyrics. Contemporaries praised Shen Jing for his meticulous matching of poetry to music, for "following the regulations to the utmost and insisting that not a single word be incompatible with the prosody."[27] Although Wang Jide (?–1623) criticized Shen's lyrics as "especially clumsy," other seventeenth-century commentators such as Qi Biaojia (1602–45) and Lü Tiancheng (1580–1618) praised *Righteous Hero* for its robust and realistic characterizations of Wu Song and Pan Jinlian.[28]

Another major departure from the novel in *Righteous Hero* was less ideological, perhaps, than practical. In the scene in which Pan attempts to seduce her brother-in-law, the playwright switched the season from winter to summer, forgoing the original contrast of heat and cold in favor of Jinlian flaunting her thinly clad body before Wu Song. Shen Jing may simply have been accommodating to the conventions of an essentially set- and prop-free stage, on which it would have been difficult to simulate the action of huddling around a fireplace. This change of season, however, costs the scene much of its literary sophistication. As will become evident, however, the scene still held sufficient dramatic excitement for audiences.

Shen Jing clearly had no interest in turning Pan Jinlian into a romantic heroine. She appears in the first half of the drama only, dying halfway through the play in scene 18. As in Xu Zichang's *Record of the Water Margin*, the adulterers in *Righteous Hero* are played by supporting actors.[29] Notwithstanding the playwright's original emphasis, when this material moved off the playwright's desk and onto the stage, Pan Jinlian, and her carnal and transgressive actions, came to overshadow most of the other scenes in the play.

CUIPING MOUNTAIN

For early prototypes of the third of the *Water Margin* adultery tales and its dramatic offshoots, documentation is sketchier. Although Yang Xiong and Shi Xiu, the protagonists of this episode, are listed among the ranks of the original thirty-six Liangshan outlaws in *Forgotten Events*, no further mention is made of their exploits in that source.[30] A late thirteenth-century variety play written by Hongzi Li Er (no longer extant) features Yang Xiong as its protagonist, but its title is simply *The Lesser Yang Xiong* (*Bing Yang Xiong*), making it impossible to ascertain the plot.[31]

The first telling of Yang Xiong's domestic strife and blood bond with his sworn brother is thus found in *Water Margin* (chaps. 44–46). In this third account of adultery and murder the wife's transgressions are the least egregious. Pan Qiaoyun does not kill her husband, nor does she attempt to blackmail him. Her culpability lies in her sexual liaison with a monk (breaching both marital fidelity and religious taboo) and, even more heinous in the eyes of her male arbiters, her slanderous accusations against her husband's sworn brother. The reprisal against Pan Qiaoyun for her challenge to patriarchy and fraternity, however, is by far the most extreme of the three episodes.

The tale begins with Shi Xiu coming to the aid of Yang Xiong, the local jailer and executioner, in a fight with local toughs. Yang Xiong and Shi Xiu thereafter swear a bond of brotherhood. Yang Xiong brings Shi Xiu home to meet his wife, Pan Qiaoyun, and his father-in-law, Old Man Pan, who is a butcher by trade, and upon learning that Shi Xiu is also a butcher, Old Man Pan hires him to run the shop.

Pan Qiaoyun, who was a widow prior to her marriage to Yang Xiong, has arranged to have Buddhist prayers recited on the anniversary of her former husband's death. The monk who comes to perform the rite, Abbot Hai (Hai sheli), is a longtime friend of the Pan family, and he plays upon that bond to seduce Pan Qiaoyun. The lovers devise a plan whereby Abbot Hai can sneak into Pan's house through the back door anytime that her husband is serving night duty at the jail. Ying'er, Pan Qiaoyun's maid, is induced to cover for her mistress; Abbot Hai bribes an itinerant Daoist to stand watch in the back alley and to wake the couple at dawn with cries for alms so that the monk can slip away before daylight.

Shi Xiu, who sleeps in the workroom behind the butcher stall every night, soon detects their scheme. He seeks out his sworn brother, tells him all, but cautions Yang Xiong not to let on yet that he knows. Just then, messengers arrive from the prefect, commanding Yang Xiong to appear before him for a performance of his martial skills. After the performance the prefect wines and dines Yang, who returns home drunk. As Pan Qiaoyun and Ying'er attend to Yang Xiong's toilet before bed, he mutters a few drunken threats at his wife. Pan Qiaoyun immediately realizes that he knows of her affair and surmises that it was Shi Xiu who told him. When Yang Xiong wakes at dawn, Pan Qiaoyun, to discredit Shi Xiu, claims that he has on numerous occasions propositioned her and her maid. Ying'er confirms the story. Believing his wife, Yang Xiong, furious, breaks off relations with Shi Xiu, who leaves the Yang household.

But determined to clear his name and have revenge, Shi Xiu surreptitiously stakes out the alleyway behind the house at dawn. As the Daoist and Abbot Hai attempt to sneak away as usual, he murders them both. Armed with this new evidence, Shi Xiu seeks out Yang Xiong, who now realizes that he has been duped by his wife and has wrongly doubted his bosom friend. Shi Xiu suggests that Yang Xiong bring Pan Qiaoyun and Ying'er to a desolate location at the top of Cuiping Mountain the next day to question them and then draft a writ of divorce. Yang Xiong agrees. The next day, on pretext of wanting to repay a vow at a temple, Yang Xiong tricks Pan Qiaoyun and her maid into accompanying him to Cuiping Mountain. At the summit Shi Xiu is waiting. When Shi Xiu confronts them, first Ying'er and then Pan Qiaoyun confess to the affair. Pan Qiaoyun begs her husband's forgiveness, but Shi Xiu stokes Yang Xiong's rage. Goaded by Shi Xiu, Yang Xiong first kills the maid, after which Shi and Yang together strip Pan Qiaoyun naked, strap her to a tree, cut out her tongue, disembowel her, and finally hack her body into pieces. After this gruesome slaughter, unable to return to lawful community, the sworn brothers set off to join the Liangshan band.[32]

As numerous literary scholars have demonstrated, these three cycles of adultery and revenge are all figurally linked.[33] The Cuiping Mountain episode is the most complicated and macabre of the three. If Song Jiang is the accidental desperado (stumbling passively and unthinkingly into murder), and Wu Song the acme of vigilante righteousness (resorting to violence only when all other means have failed), then Shi Xiu and Yang Xiong display a precipitate or preemptive aggression, shedding blood not out of self-defense or to avenge the death of an innocent but to assuage their wounded pride. The punishment exacted upon the transgressive woman in the three episodes is compounded in inverse proportion to the closeness of the injured party to the avenger—from self, to blood brother, to sworn brother. Unlike Yan Poxi and Pan Jinlian, who plot the deaths of husbands, Pan Qiaoyun never threatens the life of Yang Xiong. More so than Song Jiang and Wu Song, Shi Xiu and Yang Xiong are tagged from the beginning as executioners by trade—the one of animals, the other of humans. Even in the seventeenth century some literati readers of the Shi Xiu, Yang Xiong, and Pan Qiaoyun episode seemed discomfited by its excesses of violence and malice. In his opening commentary to the chapter in which Shi Xiu kills Abbot Hai and his Daoist helper, the commentator Jin Shengtan compares the scheming Shi Xiu not to the hero Wu Song but to the conniving panderer from that earlier episode, Mama Wang.[34] The relevant chapters of Jin Shengtan's edition of the novel are dotted with marginalia that repeatedly refer to Shi Xiu as "scary" (*ke wei*) and "cunning" (*guaijue*), the implication being that Shi Xiu is embarked on premeditated murder—a plan he cleverly conceals from his emotional and easily manipulated sworn brother until the moment of execution.[35] Perhaps most damning is Jin Shengtan's short commentary essay at the head of the chapter in which Pan Qiaoyun is murdered, wherein he makes the comparison explicit: "Wu Song's two murders," he writes, "were entirely to avenge the death of his brother; injury to his own person was never at stake in the retribution. Shi Xiu's four murders were committed for no other reason than to vindicate his own reputation and had nothing to do with Yang Xiong."[36] The conclusion: Wu Song's bloodshed is selfless; Shi Xiu's is selfish.

Yet other literary strategies employed in this episode help generate sympathy for the morally compromised woman and mark the male response to her transgressions as excessive. These chapters play with the notion of family—stretching its definitions and stressing its fragility. Pan Qiaoyun is on her second marriage; Yang Xiong lives with his wife and his wife's father, his uxorilocal residence suggesting divergence from the dominant pattern of traditional Chinese marriage practice (and this marks him as weak and perhaps henpecked); Yang Xiong and Shi Xiu unite in a bond of fictive kinship; and the monk, Abbot Hai (supposedly inhabiting a spiritual realm beyond the ties of familial life), recognizes Old Man Pan as his godfather and Pan Qiaoyun as his god-sister. If that makes the adultery incestuous (and so more egregious), their brother-sister bond is counterposed to the oath between the sworn brothers (through parallelism exposing a subtle homoeroticism to Shi Xiu's insistence on undivided brotherly devotion from Yang Xiong). And while the fictive fraternity between Yang Xiong and Shi Xiu is a recent and mercurial friendship, the siblinglike relationship between Pan Qiaoyun and Abbot Hai is long-standing, going back to childhood. Such juxtapositions helped to make Pan Qiaoyun more sympathetic—more victim than vixen—and to make her gory demise unsettling to readers of the novel.

That this ending was unsettling is also evident in the story's reshaping from fiction to drama in the early seventeenth century. Shen Zijin's (1583–1665 or 1580–1660) play, *Cuiping Mountain*, addresses this problem by making Pan Qiaoyun more culpable and Shi Xiu more maligned. Shen Zijin was a distant relative of the playwright Shen Jing, and his play shows indebtedness to his elder kinsman in both style and content. Written sometime prior to 1636, the twenty-seven-scene play follows the typical structure of chuanqi dramas—interlacing parallel and contrasting scenes of the heroes and villains.[37] Quite possibly influenced by the other two *Water Margin* plays, Shen Zijin gave his hero-protagonist, Shi Xiu, a wife, whom he leaves at the start of the play to eke out a better living. His wife is kidnapped by a bandit. A few Liangshan braves rescue her, after which she spends the rest of the play searching for Shi Xiu. They are reunited in the final scene, after the sworn brothers have revenged the adultery and joined the other righteous outlaws at their Liangshan lair. Again, likely influenced by Shen Jing's concluding scene, Shen Zijin's play ends with the issuance of an official pardon for all the Liangshan outlaws. But the core of the play, even more so than the earlier two *Water Margin*–based dramas, focuses on the tensions between the wayward wife and the male heroes.

Whereas in the novel each new enactment of the femme fatale plot is shaded differently, in the drama versions (and, I suspect, in popular imagination) those subtle distinctions were erased. In Shen Zijin's play there is a conscious collapsing of the two women surnamed Pan. Shen Zijin introduced into *Cuiping Mountain* a scene lifted directly from the Pan Jinlian–Wu Song encounter in the novel and in *Righteous Hero*. *Water Margin* contains little suggestion that Pan Qiaoyun makes amorous overtures to her husband's sworn brother. In the play script, however, not only does Shen Zijin imitate *Righteous Hero* by adding a flirtation scene between Pan Qiaoyun and Shi Xiu, but within that scene he has Qiaoyun make explicit reference to Pan Jinlian's unsuccessful seduction of Wu Song. Qiaoyun begins by treating Shi Xiu to wine when they are alone together. She then asks if he has heard the recent news that a certain Wu Song has killed his sister-in-law. When Shi Xiu replies that Wu Song did the right thing, Qiaoyun demurs: "What a pity. That sister-in-law had nothing but the best of intentions," after which she brushes against Shi Xiu. Shi Xiu responds, "Sister-in-law, have a little respect." She sings: "SHUSHU,[38] THOUGH THE SAGES TELL US, 'MAN AND WOMAN SHOULD NOT TOUCH,' still, don't you know [the saying]: 'IF BROTHER'S WIFE IS WEAK, YOU MUST TAKE HER BY THE HAND'?" Shi Xiu replies: "Humph! Sister-in-law, Shi Xiu here is no book-reading kind of man. No need for all this fancy talk."[39] With that, he glares at Qiaoyun and quickly stomps off the stage.[40]

In *Cuiping Mountain* this scene is placed just prior to the one in which Qiaoyun and Abbot Hai strike up their flirtation during the ritual for the woman's former husband. The cumulative effect of these changes is to make Qiaoyun more brazen—more like Jinlian in her unscrupulous pursuit of a husband's brother. It further makes her that much more deceitful when she later accuses Shi Xiu of propositioning her. And, finally, it shows her to be an indiscriminate sexpot. Anyone will do—first Shi Xiu, then, when he rebuffs her advances, a monk—making the affair between Qiaoyun and Abbot Hai that much more tawdry.

For all his efforts to shore up justification for Shi Xiu's revenge—to make him a less equivocal hero—Shen Zijin nevertheless made Pan Qiaoyun extremely colorful and compelling. Unlike the morally tainted women in *Record of the Water Margin* and *Righteous Hero*, in *Cuiping Mountain*, the role of Pan Qiaoyun is played by a lead female, perhaps so that the part of the maid can be played by the supporting female role.[41] The conflation of the sisters-in-law in these *Water Margin*–based plays—a trend first seen in the playwright's version of *Cuiping Mountain*—is something that would be played out more fully when these narratives moved from page to stage. The conflux of scenes featuring these transgressive sisters-in-law in all of these plays made that transition more successfully than any of the other subplots.

. . .

All three chuanqi dramas, written for performance in the kunju genre, had a formative influence on later performance versions of the plots. Once fixed to set tune patterns, the words of the arias changed only minimally over a two hundred–year history of kunju performance. Just as the novel became the originary source for the plots of the dramas, the dramas became the originary sources for all later lyrics in performance scripts, especially for those to be performed in the kunju opera system. Given the conservative force of musical structure on content change, the extent to which the message of these plays could be manipulated in later performance practice becomes all the more striking.

From Page to Stage

Record of the Water Margin, *Righteous Hero*, and *Cuiping Mountain* are playwrights' desk copies (*antou ben*).[42] Almost concurrent with the completion and publication of these plays, scenes from them started appearing in seventeenth-century published collections of popular dramatic works. Increasingly over time the scenes selected for inclusion in these anthologies begin to reflect the plays as they evolved in the performance tradition.[43] Roughly a quarter of the scenes from each of the plays are featured in various late Ming and Qing drama miscellanies. From the thirty-two-scene *Record of the Water Margin*, for instance, seven scenes made their way into seventeenth- and eighteenth-century anthologies. Of those, only one does not feature Yan Poxi and her lover, Zhang San. From *Righteous Hero*, with the exception of "Battling the Tiger" (Da hu) (a vocal and acrobatic exhibition piece for the actor playing Wu Song), and a few mostly comic scenes featuring the dwarf Wu Da, the only scenes chosen for inclusion in the anthologies center on Pan Jinlian, mostly together with her paramour but occasionally with her husband and brother-in-law.[44] All six scattered scenes selected from *Cuiping Mountain* feature Pan Qiaoyun. In each case, all of the scenes focusing on the illicit affairs—and hardly any others—ended up in the drama anthologies, suggesting that those scenes were the ones that readers and audiences found most enticing. These few scenes bridged the transition from page to stage; everything else either fell out of or never made it into the kunju performance tradition. In each of the three plays, these several scenes, when played in sequence, became their own cohesive dramas in which the licentious women emerged as the leads.

As preserved in seventeenth- and eighteenth-century drama miscellanies, these selected scenes plot a gradual progression from scripts designed for reading to scripts reflective of performance practice. One of the earliest Ming miscellanies to include scenes from *Record of the Water Margin* and *Righteous Hero*, for instance, the Chongzhen-era (1628–44) *Dark Snow Catalog* (*Xuanxue pu*), supplements its finely engraved text with illustrations (Figures 17 and 18). The illustrations are reminiscent of those in printed vernacular fiction from the same era and point to a similar circle of elite readership (Figure 19).[45] That the publisher included illustrations suggests that the scripts in his miscellany were intended for readers, as aides to visualization, something not necessary when watching the performances onstage. Moreover, with the exception of a few of the scene titles (which have been rendered into more colloquial language), these seventeenth-century texts match nearly word for word the published full editions of the playwrights' scripts.

A century later the eighteenth-century drama anthology *A Cloak of Patchworked White Fur* was being marketed as containing scripts that were near replicas of performances on the commercial stage. Over time, roughly four major changes can be identified. The scene titles come to be rendered in more colloquial language. Much more spoken dialogue is added into the scenes, which is used both for explanatory and comic effect. Numerous intoned poetic passages are cut, long arias are shortened, and even complete arias are interspersed with dialogue that would have helped explicate their meaning for a listening audience. The character-actor jing roles—usually in these plays the lovers of the femmes fatales—had begun to be assigned to actors specializing in clown role types—the comic male (*fu*) or the clown (*chou*)—and their spoken lines as printed in the anthology all reflect Suzhou dialect.

Xu Zichang's *Record of the Water Margin* offers an apt example of the increasingly more colloquial scene titles employed in performance. In mid-seventeenth-century anthologies the name of the scene in which Yan Poxi returns as a ghost is changed from the author's original "Response from the Grave" to "Hooked by Passion" (Qing gou); in eighteenth- and nineteenth-century performance scripts it has become "Captured Alive" (Huo zhuo).

Figure 17. Illustration for a set of selected scenes from *Record of the Water Margin* (*Shuihu ji*) in *The Dark Snow Catalog* (*Xuanxue pu*). Ca. Ming Chongzhen era (1628–44). Reprinted from *SBXQCK*, 50:289.

Figure 18. Illustration for a set of selected scenes from *Record of the Righteous Hero* (*Yixia ji*) in *Dark Snow Catalog*. Ca. Ming Chongzhen era (1628–44). Reprinted from *SBXQCK*, 51:559.

Figure 19. Illustration for chapter 5 of *The Prosemetric Plum in the Golden Vase* (*Jin Ping Mei cihua*). From *Jin Ping Mei cihua* 1617.

Often the retitling of scenes does more than simplify the language. It also tends to redirect the focus from the male to the female leads: by the time of the 1770 publication of *Cloak* the scene "Shouting Down Evil" (Chi xie), from the playwright's text of *Righteous Hero*, becomes "Flirting with Brother-in-Law" (Xi shu), which makes clear that the real attraction was not Wu Song's chaste rejection of Pan Jinlian but her wanton wooing of him. The episode so influenced by this scene in Shen Zijin's later *Cuiping Mountain* underwent a title change from "Spying a Weakness" (Qu zhan) to (also) "Flirting with Brother-in-Law," which again reflects the conflation of the "I, Sister-in-Law" characters in popular imagination.[46]

Comparing a passage from the scene "Sprouts of Villainy" (Meng jian) in the playwright's original *Righteous Hero* with its corresponding miscellany version should suffice to alert us to some of the changes in performance editions of scripts. "Sprouts of Villainy" is the scene in which Pan Jinlian and Ximen Qing first meet. Their encounter in the original unfolds as follows:

> JING ([Ximen Qing] enters): I'VE NO PRIDE; ONLY JUST ARISEN FROM A MIDDAY SNOOZE, I TAKE A STROLL OUTSIDE. (Acts like he's thinking.) IT DAWNS ON ME, I DO RECALL, THAT MAMA WANG PROMISED TO FIND A MATCH FOR ME. AND SO, I WALK ALONG TO AMETHYST LANE; I WALK ALONG TO AMETHYST LANE.
> XIAO DAN ([Pan Jinlian] enters): I've got the bamboo pole here with which to lower the blinds.
> JING (sneaks a look and sings): WHOSE HOUSE BLINDS ARE THESE, OPEN JUST HALFWAY? (The bamboo pole strikes JING's hat; JING acts out seeing XIAO DAN; he sings as an aside): Ah, THIS KNOCK ON THE HEAD HAS KNOCKED ME SILLY WITH LOVE. (JING stares at her.)
> XIAO DAN: I BESEECH YOU, SIR, (she curtsies; he salutes her) DON'T BE ANGRY WITH ME. I LOST MY GRIP AND THE POLE SLIPPED FROM MY HANDS.
> JING (bows): It's nothing, Madam. No need to be so polite.
> MAMA WANG (enters and watches; she laughs and intones): My, sir, you're MOST SOLICITOUS. YOU'RE NOT EVEN LIVING UNDER HER EAVES AND YET YOU BOW YOUR HEAD. A good knock! THAT KNOCK HAS KNOCKED ALL THE STRAIGHTNESS OUT OF YOU.
> JING (laughs): YOU WERE RIGHT TO HIT ME. Madam, YOU REALLY WERE RIGHT TO HIT ME.
> XIAO DAN (laughs; sings): YOU'LL EMBARRASS ME WITH SUCH TALK.
> JING (salutes her and sings): MY LADY, NO NEED TO BE SO MODEST.[47]

The equivalent sequence in a script published in a 1764 edition of the *Cloak* anthology, here entitled "Lowering the Blinds" (Tiaolian), reads as follows (to better distinguish the changes, all new lyrics and dialogue are presented in italics here and later):

FU [Ximen Qing] (enters): I'VE NO PRIDE; ONLY JUST ARISEN FROM A MID-DAY SNOOZE, I TAKE A STROLL OUTSIDE. *A plan comes to mind. A few days ago someone whispered in my ear that a pretty dame lives in this Amethyst Lane. Could he have meant here?* I RECALL THAT MAMA WANG PROMISED TO FIND A MATCH FOR ME. I WALK ALONG TO AMETHYST LANE; I WALK ALONG TO AMETHYST LANE. WHOSE HOUSE BLINDS ARE THESE OPEN JUST HALFWAY? *(*TIE *enters.*⁴⁸ *The stick for the blinds hits the* FU.*)*⁴⁹ *Who is that knocking me on the head and noggin? Oh, rapture!* THIS KNOCK ON THE HEAD HAS KNOCKED ME SILLY WITH LOVE.

TIE [Pan Jinlian]: I BESEECH YOU, SIR, DON'T BE ANGRY WITH ME.

FU: *Who would dare to be angry?*

TIE: I LOST MY GRIP AND THE POLE SLIPPED FROM MY HANDS.

FU: *Say nothing about losing your grip; what matter even if you had done it on purpose?*

LAO DAN [Mama Wang] (enters): *What a beautiful day! Oh, here's Master Ximen.* YOU'RE MOST SOLICITOUS.

FU: *Who's there? Well, if it isn't godmother!*

LAO DAN: NOT EVEN LIVING UNDER HER EAVES AND YET YOU BOW YOUR HEAD. *A good knock!* THAT KNOCK HAS KNOCKED ALL THE STRAIGHTNESS OUT OF YOU.

TIE: *Godmother, come here.*

FU: *Who's calling you?*

LAO DAN: *It's the young mistress standing at the door.*

TIE: *I was lowering these blinds when I lost my grip and hit this gentleman's head. Go tell him not to be angry with me. Convey my apologies to him most entreatingly.*

LAO DAN: *Ah, Master Ximen, the young mistress says that she accidentally lost her grip, so the pole hit you on your head. Don't be angry with her. She asked me to . . .*

TIE: *Convey my apologies to him most entreatingly.*

FU: *What a thing to say! It's too bad that my head's so dense and not at all suitable for hitting. Still, if the lady would like, I can let her take it home to use as a wooden-fish percussion block and strike it a hundred times; what do you say?*⁵⁰

LAO DAN: *What nonsense!*

FU: *Godmother, go tell this young lady;* SAY: SHE WAS RIGHT TO HIT ME.

LAO DAN: SHE WAS RIGHT TO HIT YOU?

TIE: YOU'LL EMBARRASS ME WITH SUCH TALK.

FU: *WHAT NEED, MY LADY, TO BE SO MODEST?* (*He salutes* [striking a pose].)

LAO DAN: *What's the meaning of that?*

FU: *Well, it's commonly said that it means an aria is about to begin.*

LAO DAN: *Stop being silly!*⁵¹

The dialogue passages in the eighteenth-century *Cloak* scene are much less economical. They reflect intent to explain the language of the arias. And the relationships between the characters are reiterated, perhaps for an audience that is watching this scene in isolation from the larger story. The script adds much more business—shtick, if you will—between the characters. Just in case the audience has not caught the rather erudite joke in Mama Wang's aria about bowing and straightness—her suggestion that the hitting of the pole has had a salutary effect on Ximen Qing—the production script has added its own comic interlude, turning Mama Wang into the literal go-between for the tie and fu's brief verbal flirtation. A lot of plain silliness is also added—Ximen offering his head to be used as a percussion instrument, and his breaking the illusion of the play with his final joke about stage conventions—"it means an aria is about to begin."[52]

Although injecting humor is a major purpose of much of the expanded dialogue in production scripts, in some instances the additional shtick has the effect of altering the characterizations of the central figures. Dialogue and stage directions added to the *Cloak* editions of "Sewing Clothes" (Zuo yi), from *Righteous Hero*, for instance, reveal how the seduction of Pan Jinlian by Ximen Qing would have been played out onstage. In the original playwright's script, the two swear undying love for each other, bow to each other, and then exit.[53] In the *Cloak* script the following acting business is added after they swear their oaths:

> TIE [Pan Jinlian]: I'm going home.
> FU [Ximen Qing]: Ah, you're going to kill me with longing.
> (TIE acts out resistance. FU embraces [TIE] and carries offstage.)[54]

This coquettish resistance makes Pan Jinlian less wanton. Accordingly, the male lover's sexual conquest becomes more of a triumph. Making these transgressive female characters less uninhibitedly lubricious made them that much more appealing to audiences.

Perhaps even more telling of audience preferences and sympathies, nineteenth-century production scripts of scenes from *Cuiping Mountain* treat the scene "Murder on the Mountain" (Sha shan) quite differently than the playwright's text. First, they make it clear that Shi Xiu, the sworn brother, rather than Yang Xiong, the husband, wields the knife that kills Pan Qiaoyun. Then, after Pan has been killed, an extra line is added for Yang Xiong. He cries out her name, and the stage directions read, "He cries, cries, cries."[55] If we can interpolate from later Chinese opera practice, this would have been the cue for the actor to burst into a long, operatic wail. This reworking changes the emotional tenor of the scene, suggesting that audiences found the husband's grisly murder of his wife too extreme. They wanted to see Yang Xiong unable to carry out the revenge—partly, perhaps, because Pan Qiaoyun was such a compelling character (in spite of her flaws), and partly because this cast Yang Xiong, the putative hero, in a more humane light.

Following a practice first adopted in Yuan zaju plays, all Ming desk-copy scripts ended each scene with two rhyming couplets. Perhaps originally a device to demarcate scene divisions, these couplets acted as a coda in the playwright's own voice to the action just presented, summarizing the plot or the key thematic messages of the scene. One of the first signs of emendation for stage production is that these ending couplets have been cut. In the few instances in which the couplets are preserved, instead of standing apart as concluding commentary, they are worked into the dialogue or lyrics of the scene. For instance, in the scene "Lowering the Blinds" from *Righteous Hero*, the original ending pair of couplets reads:

> If you've got money, even ghosts will grind your grain;
> The more you spend, the more you will obtain.
> If you tell lies and if your heart's untrue,
> The wrath of Heaven will be unleashed on you.[56]

These couplets served as the playwright's judgment on the venal Mama Wang, who in the immediately preceding scene, agreed—for a price—to help Ximen Qing seduce Pan Jinlian. The first couplet acknowledges the power of money; the second offers a moralistic truism on what happens to evildoers. When repackaged for stage performance, these lines are reabsorbed into the dialogue in the following manner. The first of the couplets is inserted at the end of the fu's aria thanking Mama Wang for her ten-step plan to seduce Pan Jinlian.[57] He sings: "Let this ten-step plan create an entry in the book of romantic destinies." Mama Wang, concerned about getting paid, reminds Ximen Qing:

> LAO DAN [Mama Wang]: The more you spend, the more you will obtain.
> FU [Ximen Qing]: If you've got money, even ghosts will grind your grain.
> LAO DAN: *Now, don't lie to me.*
> FU: If *I* lie and if *my* heart's untrue . . .
> LAO DAN: *Swear an oath!*
> FU: *Let* the wrath of Heaven be unleashed on *me.*[58]

The scene concludes with the two of them preparing to act on their plot, using language that completely skews the original emphasis of the playwright's couplets. The first couplet is now part of the bargaining between Mama Wang and Ximen Qing. The second couplet, while still perhaps foreshadowing Ximen Qing's death, is no longer presented as a moral truth; it has now become part of the dramatic action of the play. As such, the exhortatory message of the lines, if not altogether obscured, has been significantly muted.

Other cuts introduced into production scripts served to make the scenes more self-contained, easier to understand in isolation from the rest of the story line; for example, the scene "Reverse Accusal" (Fan kuang) from *Cuiping Mountain* in the 1770 edition of *Cloak*. This is the scene in which Pan Qiaoyun convinces her husband that Shi Xiu has propositioned her, thereby deflecting suspicion from her own infidelity. The earliest full edition of the play, possibly emanating from the court and with a copy date equivalent to 1731, begins the scene by explaining why Yang Xiong has returned home drunk.[59] An extra (*wai*) comes onstage and summons Yang Xiong to give an exhibition of his martial skills before the county prefect. After the two exit together, Pan Qiaoyun enters for a solo aria. Yang Xiong then reenters, drunk from the feasting following his exhibition. In the earliest *Cloak* version and in subsequent production scripts the scene begins with Pan Qiaoyun's entrance.[60] In production scripts, then, "Reverse Accusal" becomes a fully contained skit with just three central characters: Pan Qiaoyun, Yang Xiong, and their maid, Ying'er. This trimming turns Qiaoyun into the central figure of the scene, as she gets both the opening and closing speeches.

Thus, a mid-seventeenth-century version of this scene (probably closest to the playwright's original) ends with Yang Xiong shouting offstage to his father-in-law to close down the butcher shop, followed by the requisite paired couplet coda:

> BEFORE OTHERS, WHO IS NOT THE VERY FACE OF DIGNITY?
> YET BEHIND THE BACK, MEN LOSE ALL SENSE OF DECENCY.
> WHEN SOWING FLOWERS, SOW NOT THOSE THAT BEAR NO FRUIT;
> WHEN MAKING FRIENDS, BEFRIEND NOT MEN OF ILL REPUTE.[61]

In contrast, in the *Cloak* recension of "Reverse Accusal" Pan Qiaoyun gets the final say. After her husband exits, the stage directions read: "TIE acts out laughing." She then concludes the scene with: "Aiya, see how, with no more than two or three words, this drunkard has been fooled into believing me? You drunkards, you drunkards (makes a gesture with the hand), know that you, too, will surely tread this path."[62] It may not be far-fetched to imagine this final line (and the accompanying gesture noted in the stage directions) being played directly to the audience. The production-script ending changes the moral of the scene. No longer is the scene an exploration of friendship and marital trust; instead, it has now become a more banal lesson in the evils of drinking, with the trickster woman as instructor. Structural cuts in two commonly performed scenes from *Righteous Hero* result in the lovers Pan Jinlian and Ximen Qing never getting caught, with the effect that audiences saw no retribution exacted for their adultery.

Dialect, too, tells us something about the audience for and appeal of these plays. An entry in Qi Biaojia's early seventeenth-century catalog of plays mentions that in one of Shen Jing's plays, "all the dialogue for the jing actor and the clown parts uses the local language of the people of Suzhou."[63] As noted previously, Shen Jing and his Wujiang School of playwriting were particularly renowned for the simple and authentic language employed in their plays.[64] Yet there is little evidence of dialect in the written language of the playwright's versions. The one exception comes from Xu Zichang's *Record of the Water Margin*. Although Xu was a native of Jiangnan, the full version of his play is written in a standard (southern) Mandarin. All the characters, irrespective of personality, speak in essentially the same register of language. The only explicit use of dialect in Xu's script is also the only obvious joke in the play. That moment comes in scene 21, "An Illicit Union" (Ye he), as Zhang San is making headway in his seduction of Yan Poxi. Using the common parlance to refer to a friend's wife, Zhang repeatedly addresses Yan Poxi as "Honored Sister-in-Law." She responds:

> XIAO DAN [Yan Poxi]: What's with this honored sister-in-law. . . ? If you're going to call me honored sister-in-law, then you should know the saying, "One should not entice a friend's wife."
> JING [Zhang San]: Oh? Then what would you like me to call you?
> XIAO DAN: I'd like you to call me mother.
> JING (laughs): If I did, I'd be just what the people of Suzhou say when they curse me—a "sneaky motherfucker." (XIAO DAN laughs; JING embraces XIAO DAN.)[65]

In later production scripts this bit of local color is excised. Instead, Zhang San replies with a much more benign, "Why didn't you say so earlier? Aiya, my nearest, dearest, hot Mama."[66] The changes to the production script make the language less risqué. Although this might seem to go against the general tendency of production scripts to extract the scenes of flirtation out of the moral packaging of the complete drama, as the illicit lovers of these scenes become central characters, they are also made more sympathetic. This was achieved by eliminating the characters' most outrageous words and actions and by injecting a kind of sweet silliness into the language and comic business of the scenes. Commercial kunju performance, in other words, worked out a compromise between titillation and decorum—accentuating flirtation and romance without letting the performances become downright lurid.[67]

If in production scripts the clowns tend to avoid outright sexual obscenities, their lines nevertheless contain plenty of scatological humor. In the scene "Flirting with Brother-in-Law," when Pan Jinlian complains to Wu Da that Wu Song has propositioned her, Wu Da responds with a long string of expletives. Pan Jinlian sings:

> TIE [Pan Jinlian]: WHO WOULD HAVE THOUGHT HE WOULD BE SO UNKIND AS TO TAKE ADVANTAGE OF ME.
> CHOU [Wu Da]: *Ptui, ptui, ptui.* "Take advantage of me, take advantage of me!" *What a load of horny sow, fake, blubber-nose, super-smelly dog farts!*[68]

This and so many of the clowns' other lines are chock-full of Wu-dialect colloquialisms. Beginning in the mid-eighteenth century, in the kunju scripts collected in anthologies such as *Cloak* and in other production texts extra phonetic characters were inserted in an attempt to capture in writing the sound of the dialect.[69] Dialect-based humor becomes a trademark of kunju performance scripts, whether it is Wu Da rambling on in the local patois about how many biscuits he has sold for the day while Wu Song tries in vain to warn him about Pan Jinlian, or the comic playing Ximen Qing deliberately poking fun at the literary language of the arias.[70] Certain comic "bits," or set pieces, are recycled, with minor variations, among many of the different performance scripts, and these are telltale signs of actor rather than playwright invention. Well into the nineteenth century even those kunju scripts that can be linked to performers and performances in the capital preserved the Subai dialogue of the clowns, as seen in the clown's dialogue in *Garden*. In order for humor to be effective, of course, it has to be immediately intelligible to its audience. This, then, provides further evidence of who was attending such kunju performances in Beijing, confirming that the commercial troupes singing Kun opera in the capital drew their audiences, in large part, from the vast network of Jiangnan officials, literati, and tradesmen sojourning in the north.

The sequential staging of the flirtation scenes alone radically reshaped the sister-in-law plots, especially that of *Record of the Water Margin*. When these selected scenes were strung together without the intervening episodes about Song Jiang and the Liangshan outlaws, the plot of the drama took on the following contours: The sequence began with "Begging a Cup of Tea" (Jie cha), in which Zhang San asks for a cup of tea from Yan Poxi as an excuse to strike up a flirtation. In this first scene Yan Poxi rebuffs his advances, but not before giving Zhang San hope that he may return and try again. Scene 2 becomes "Returning for the Lost Kerchief" (Shi jin), in which Zhang visits Yan Poxi for a second time. Just as he is making headway, his amorous pursuits are interrupted by the sudden return of Yan Poxi's mother. In scene 3, "The First Seduction" (Qian you), Zhang San returns a third time. This time his seduction of Yan Poxi is interrupted by the sudden arrival of Song Jiang. Notably, beginning in the mid-seventeenth century, scripts of this scene began to add some new stage directions. In Xu Zichang's original script, when Song Jiang enters, the stage directions simply read: "the male lead enters" (SHENG shang). The scene excerpts in anthologies and later production scripts add the word *zui*, so as to read, "the male lead enters drunk." What follows then, sandwiched between old arias, is a new bit of dialogue in which Song Jiang demands tea. When Yan Poxi brings his tea, the stage directions are "the male lead takes a drink and spits it out." This is in total contrast to the cleverly flirtatious manner in which audiences have just seen Zhang San ask for tea in the first scene of the sequence. Yan responds to Song Jiang's boorishness with these newly added lines: "Aiya, disgusting. Go in and go to bed." The stage directions indicate that Yan helps steady him as he walks offstage. These changes, subtle as they are, help explain—perhaps even justify—Yan's infidelity. They also add new meaning and motivation to the old lyrics that follow in which Yan Poxi complains: "SEE HOW HE TREATS ME THIS WAY AS A MATTER OF HABIT? WHO IS IT WHO UNDERSTANDS HOW TO BE TENDER IN THE APPRECIATION OF A DELICATE LADY?"[71] Then comes another new spoken line: "Oh, Sanlang, Sanlang, seeing this disgusting thing makes me think of you all the more."[72] These changes help turn Yan into a plaintive ingénue married to a boor.

"The First Seduction" would have been followed by "The Second Seduction" (Hou you), in which Zhang San melts Yan Poxi's resistance. Their dalliance is discovered by Mama Wang, and the scene ends with Mama Wang threatening to reveal the affair to Song Jiang. Scene 5 in the sequence, "Murder of Yan Poxi" (Sha Xi), portrays Yan Poxi's death at the hands of

Song Jiang. The final scene in sequence would have been "Captured Alive" (Huo zhuo).

In this abridgment Yan Poxi clearly becomes the central figure of the drama. The audience observes the gradual softening of her resistance to Zhang San's charms. And lyrical passages, unchanged from the original script, take on new meaning when sung in closer sequence. For instance, in "Second Seduction," the performance texts add the following bit of dialogue between Yan and Zhang. Just before Yan succumbs to Zhang San's charms, she says, "Sanlang, today, though I do this thing with you . . . [then breaking into a phrase of the original aria she sings:] "Do not take me for some wild flower to be plucked and discarded to the elements at whim."[73] Zhang San replies by swearing an oath: "If I were to forget your love for me today, let me be captured alive and killed." And what scene comes next? "Captured Alive."

In the other two sister-in-law-scene sequences, the transformation from evil temptress to sympathetic ingénue is not quite so complete. In the popular performances of linked scenes from both *Righteous Hero* and *Cuiping Mountain*, the concluding scene depicts the retribution visited upon the woman. These sequences of selected scenes still tell the whole story of illicit romance followed by bloody revenge. And yet these selected scenes are scattered throughout the *Cloak* anthology, which also provides clues to how these selections were staged. The earliest extant edition of *Cloak*, with a preface dated to 1764, includes four scenes in sequence from *Righteous Hero*: "Lowering the Blinds"; "Sewing Clothes"; "Manifestation of the Ghost" (Xian hun, in which Wu Da returns as a ghost to reveal his murder to Wu Song); and "Killing Sister-in-Law" (Sha sao). This selection, abbreviated as it is, completely encapsulates the arc of the more complete femme fatale plot, that is, seduction and adultery followed by retributive murder. The next printing of *Cloak* (issued serially between 1770 and 1777) includes eight scenes from *Righteous Hero*, but the eight are divided among three volumes. Volume 4 includes four contiguous scenes—"Flirting with Brother-in-Law," "Taking Leave of Brother" (Bie xiong), "Lowering the Blinds," and "Sewing Clothes"—the first pair of scenes portraying Jinlian's unsuccessful pursuit of Wu Song, and the second depicting Ximen Qing's successful seduction of Jinlian. Volume 6 contains a scene from a different source tradition.[74] Volume 8 includes two scenes featuring Wu Da as the central character, "Capturing the Adulterers" (Zhuo jian) and "Swallowing Poison" (Fu du). Volume 10 features the single scene "Battling the Tiger." The clustering and ordering of scenes in *Cloak* reflected the practice of selected-scenes performance in commercial playhouses in the eighteenth- and nineteenth-century capital. As will become clear, it was certainly possible to present an abridged version of the full story cycle, but it was not common. Rather, a shorter program of linked scenes tended to be performed—sometimes just the flirtation scenes, sometimes just the death or battle scenes.[75] This allowed audiences to thrill to Pan Jinlian's various flirtations without having to be reminded of her gruesome end.

Scenes from *Cuiping Mountain* are similarly scattered in the *Cloak* anthology of 1770–77. In that edition the scenes appear in three clusters. Again, the retribution and revenge scenes are separate from Pan Qiaoyun's flirtation scenes and from what was likely the most popular scene in performance, "Reverse Accusal," in which Pan Qiaoyun tricks her gullible husband.[76] More often than not, performance practice gave audiences the flirtation scenes and spared them the moralistic outcomes of illicit sex for these sisters-in-law.

Kunju *Performances in Context*

Records by connoisseurs of commercial theater in the eighteenth and nineteenth centuries reveal the reason why *Cloak* and other seventeenth- and eighteenth-century drama miscellanies published only linked scene selections: they were trying to replicate as nearly as possible performances in commercial playhouses. Most illustrative, perhaps, is the anonymous *Playwatching Journal*, compiled beginning in the late eighteenth century, which lists all the performances one operagoer viewed in Beijing between 28 January 1797 and 15 July 1798.[77] Although the single scene "Languishing in the Boudoir" (Xu ge), based on Hong Sheng's drama, *Palace of Eternal Youth* (*Changsheng dian*), was the most commonly performed (seventeen performances over those eighteen months), scenes from all of the *Water Margin*–based adultery-and-revenge stories figure prominently in this journal: "Begging a Cup of Tea" from *Record of the Water Margin*, "Flirting with Brother-in-Law" and "Taking Leave of Brother" from *Righteous Hero*, and "Reverse Accusal" from *Cuiping Mountain* were each performed at least twelve times, according to the journal's author.

Seven of the twelve performances of the scene "Begging a Cup of Tea" were performed in isolation, without any conclusion to the story whatsoever. The scene simply became a cute flirtation piece—no outcome, no moral judgment, no retribution. On three other occasions "Begging a Cup of Tea" was performed along with "The First Seduction."[78] Twice "Begging a Cup of Tea" was followed by "Returning for the Lost Kerchief," and one of those performances concluded with "Captured Alive."[79] Once "The Second Seduction" was performed alone.[80] Only one time, in other words, did audiences see any repercussions for Yan Poxi's actions.

Only four scenes from *Righteous Hero* appear in *Playwatching Journal*: "Flirting with Brother-in-Law" and "Taking Leave of Brother," which were always performed together as a set; and "Lowering the Blinds" and "Sewing Clothes " (Cai yi), another pair of scenes performed in tandem on ten different occasions. Neither the murder nor retribution scenes from this story cycle were ever presented; so although audiences did not see Pan Jinlian get away with murder, they did see her get away with adultery.

Although these four scenes seem to have been standard repertory fare for the Sanduo Troupe, they do not appear to have captured the fancy of the anonymous diarist. The author of the journal marked those operas and performances he liked best with red circles, one to five, five circles signaling his highest mark of excellence. None of the four scenes from *Righteous Hero* ever merited a red circle. The author notes that, during a performance of "Lowering the Blinds" on 4 March 1797, the actor playing Pan Jinlian "forgot the bamboo pole."[81] On 25 July 1797 the diarist left the theater after "Lowering the Blinds" and before the following "Sewing Clothes."[82] The marginal comments in the journal are too abbreviated to indicate why.

The author of *Playwatching Journal* was more favorably disposed to "Reverse Accusal" from *Cuiping Mountain*. Each time this scene was staged (thirteen times in all), he gave it one red circle. Not quite as entranced by this opera as he was by sentimental scenes from the dramas *Peony Pavilion* or *Thunder-Wind Pagoda* (*Leifeng ta*), which often merited three to five red circles, he nevertheless seems to have enjoyed the Sanduo Troupe's many enactments of "Reverse Accusal."[83] Altogether, six scenes from *Cuiping Mountain* are listed in *Playwatching Journal*,[84] but the favorite was clearly "Reverse Accusal," which was performed three times without any accompanying scenes from the larger dramatic cycle, paralleling publication practice in the *Cloak* anthology.[85] Nevertheless, sequences of *Cuiping Mountain* scenes seem to be the norm in *Playwatching Journal*. Most commonly, the performed abridgement began with Pan Qiaoyun's flirtations, first with Shi Xiu and then with Abbot Hai, continued with the scene in which Shi Xiu divulges news of the illicit affair to Yang Xiong, and concluded with

"Reverse Accusal." Only once was the murder of Pan Qiaoyun ever included in one of the *Cuiping Mountain* scene sets.[86] This meant that, usually, the performed sequence ended with Pan Qiaoyun covering up her affair and maligning her husband's sworn brother.

Sometimes scenes from at least two of the three *Water Margin* wanton sister-in-law dramas were performed in succession in a single day. The last five of the eight scenes presented, for instance, on 11 October 1797, were from sister-in-law plays, making it a program of all sisters-in-law almost all the time.[87] If *Playwatching Journal* is representative, and records by other contemporary connoisseurs indicate that it is, it helps confirm the popularity of these operas with capital audiences. Audiences were likely to have been aware of the missing moralistic framing of the larger source stories, but what they wanted to see onstage were those highlight dramatic moments of transgression and flirtation.[88]

. . .

As with performed excerpts from *Garden*, the central performance aesthetic of these commercial kunju operas emphasized sensuality and kitschy sentimentality. Comments by literati spectators about the *Water Margin* sister-in-law operas focus on the emotional intensity of the performers, especially those actors playing the dan roles, and the artistry that enabled them to attain such intensity. In general, the roles performed by the dan actors spanned a continuum from qing authenticity to comic burlesque, with the playful eroticism of the transvestite theater underlying to varying degrees all points along that spectrum. If a serious romantic heroine such as Du Liniang from *Peony Pavilion* marked the far qing end of the continuum, then the various sisters-in-law—Yan Poxi, Pan Jinlian, and Pan Qiaoyun— were situated close to the light, irreverent end, teetering just on the cusp between sentimentality, titillation, and camp.[89]

In part, this is reflected in role-type designations. These sister-in-law characters are usually played by tie dan (secondary dan) rather than zheng dan (primary dan), and the tie dan were known to personify characters of more dubious pedigree and moral stature. According to one late eighteenth-century observer, "The *xiao dan* (little dan) are called boudoir dan; and the tie dan are called floozy dan."[90] The distinction made here is between characters who depicted the romance of young women of proper households (Du Liniang types) and those who portrayed the affairs of women of wild or questionable repute. In the words of the flower-register author

Wu Changyuan, actors specializing in the tie dan role "do not rival Gentlewoman Xie of the inner chambers but are of the Zheng household's literate-maid type."[91] Yet another connoisseur considered the actor Shen Siguan, acclaimed by many for his impersonation of the pitiful heroine Peizhi in the scene "Giving Birth in the Shed" (Chan zi), actually better as more flamboyant characters, such as Pan Qiaoyun in "Reverse Accusal."[92] Actors who specialized in the flirtatious sisters-in-law also tended to play the role of the amorous nun in the opera scene "Longing for the Secular Life" (Si fan).[93] The central character in "Longing for the Secular Life," as I have discussed elsewhere, could be played consistent with the "cult of qing" fetishization of feminine authenticity or could be rendered in a broad, clownish way. Both characterizations held dramatic interest for Qing operagoers—the one situated in romance, the other in humor.[94] The lusty sisters-in-law of the *Water Margin* drama material also tapped into this range of performance aesthetics. In evaluating the actor Xu Caiguan in the role of Pan Qiaoyun in "Reverse Accusal," one fan writes:

> Theater is not real and emotions cannot be false. To have [an actor] without real emotions play falseness onstage is challenging. Even if the emotions are real, creating the illusion of false emotions is also challenging. None of the dan actors come close to getting the real and unreal of the scene "Reverse Accusal." Only Caiguan's feigning of anger and laughter captures the very likeness of [Qiaoyun] so long ago; he is unparalleled at this time.[95]

Another enthusiast observed that when the actor Zheng Sanbao performed in "Longing for the Secular Life" and in "Turning Over the Account Books" (Jiao zhang) (the latter from *Cuiping Mountain*), "the cries of 'hao!' rose up from the four corners of the house, thereby giving the lie to the assumption that the finer things in life are appreciated only by the few."[96]

But there was more to appreciating these actors and plays than simply the pleasure derived from watching good actors ply their craft. These operas were popular also for their eroticism, and the actors for their personal beauty and skill in radiating feminine charm. A poem about the same Xu Caiguan in the role of Pan Qiaoyun in "Flirting with Brother-in-Law" claims, "When onstage he calls out Shushu [Brother-in-Law], his captivating smile is enough to topple fortresses."[97] The compiler of *Viewing Flowers in the Precinct of the Throne* describes the fourteen-year-old Yang Jinbao, who excelled at the character of Yan Poxi in the scenes "Begging a Cup of Tea" and "Captured Alive" in the classic clichés of feminine beauty: "a face like an inverted calabash gourd, a roseate underglow infusing a pale white complexion; arched eyebrows like spring willow fronds, and eyes criss-crossed with autumn waves."[98] And then there was Mao Erguan, who captured men's souls with his eyes whenever he played Pan Jinlian in "Lowering the Blinds."[99] An actor originally from the capital mentioned in Li Dou's late eighteenth-century memoir of Yangzhou was so popular in the role of Yan Poxi that audience members vied with each other to help apply his face makeup:

> Xie Ruiqing of the Cuiqing Troupe from the capital: he was known as The Little Rat [*xiao haozi*] to distinguish him from his teacher, whose nickname was The Rat [*haozi*]. He specialized in the role of Yan Poxi from *Record of the Water Margin*. Every time he mounted the stage, audience patrons personally applied his face powder and draped him in fox furs and silks, and they greatly regretted it if they did not end up with the traces of his powder on their hands.[100]

Reading the flower registers might make it easy to assume that the eroticism of the theater was only in the mind's eye of these connoisseurs; a look at the choreography notes of full production scripts of the plays suggests otherwise. In performance, the sexuality of these plays could often be quite explicit, as exemplified in the comic business added to a production script of the scene "Returning for the Lost Kerchief" from *Record of the Water Margin*. In this scene Zhang San, played by a fu, returns to Yan Poxi's home to resume his flirtation. He is served tea by Mama Yan (played by the lao dan, abbreviated in the script as *lao*) and Yan Poxi (played by the tie dan, abbreviated as *zhan*); not wanting to leave without having a word alone with Yan Poxi, Zhang makes up an excuse to stay longer: he claims to have lost his handkerchief. In the ensuing slapstick exchange, Mama Yan helps search for the kerchief while Zhang San tries surreptitiously to paw the actor playing Yan Poxi. The stage directions during the fu's final aria read:

> FU uses his right hand to fondle the ZHAN's right breast; ZHAN uses left hand to grab his hand and stop him. FU uses left hand to fondle the ZHAN's left breast; ZHAN uses right hand to grab his hand and stop him. [ZHAN] pushes him with both hands and he stumbles backward. He bumps into LAO's butt; they then bump heads. The ZHAN laughs.[101]

Besides being overtly lewd, some of these scenes also used slapstick to defuse the erotic tension of the performances. I think it significant that, in all of the flirtation scenes in sister-in-law operas (as opposed to romantic scenes with more chaste and proper heroines), the tie dan plays opposite a comic male role—a fu or a chou—rather than opposite a male lead, a sheng.¹⁰² The more audacious the content, the more nearly it pushed the bounds of respectability, the more humor was introduced to burst the illusions of the stage. Just how fine the line between sensual flirtation and broad comedy could be is illustrated by praise from opera aficionados for actors who "got it just right," as in Wu Changyuan's comments about the dan actor Li Qinguan:

> His pretty eyes have a twinkle to them, and his slender face is not drawn. . . . He often performs the scene "Sewing Clothes"; his sexuality is reserved, his eyes showing a spark of desire without leering.¹⁰³ A line in the *Book of Odes* says: "Having met you, my heart is mastered." I suddenly "got" this opera. With anyone else, the acting would begin with a studied quality and end in excess, and it would all seem sordid.¹⁰⁴

But another connoisseur complains that the actor Shen Sixi had begun to play characters such as Pan Jinlian and Yan Poxi with broader strokes, imitating the popular practices of the day by his racy and exaggerated comic gestures. When performing the character Yan Poxi, the connoisseur writes, this actor now "kicks the back of his skirt with his heels," adding in dismay, "I ask you, what lady or girl of the inner chambers ever does that? The practice of lewd and wild acting by Kun opera dan actors can be traced to him."¹⁰⁵ Clearly, the flower-register writers preferred performances whose eroticism was sentimental rather than comic-lewd, but since they also cast themselves as belonging to the *minority* of those with taste, we can likely assume that burlesque-style renditions of these operas were at least equally prevalent at the time. Whether the productions were sentimental or comedic, the central characters of sister-in-law operas were rendered entertaining, approachable, and sympathetic.

Popular as these *Water Margin* sister-in-law flirtation plays were, they were not considered the stuff of high art, although acting them well required considerable skill. This helps explain, perhaps, their relative position in the rating scheme used in *Playwatching Journal*—being worthy of mention or, at most, of one red circle for their clever, flirtatious dialogue, but lacking the emotional gravitas of opera scenes depicting pathos or serious romantic love, which often received five red circles. A stigma still attached to these operas—and to the transgressive women characters featured in them—precisely on account of their overt depictions of illicit sex.

Other literature of the time attests to the stigma attached to sister-in-law roles. In Chen Sen's idealized re-creation of the Beijing theatrical demimonde in his novel *A Precious Mirror for Ranking Boy Actresses*—in which the actor and scholar protagonists are hyperpure and the predatory lao dou villains superdegenerate—the talented cross-dressing boy actresses would think themselves tainted by association with sister-in-law roles, whereas a scholar of compromised integrity is depicted as ignorant of serious drama but thoroughly versed in the lines and choreography of sister-in-law operas. When put to the test during an amateur recital of operas, the scoundrel scholar is familiar only with the common repertoire of sister-in-law scenes: "First Seduction," "Second Seduction," "Captured Alive," "Reverse Accusal," "Lowering the Blinds," and "Sewing Clothes."[106] And the sniggers and raised eyebrows of his peer onlookers during his ensuing rendition of the philandering clown, Zhang San, in "Captured Alive" point to conflicted attitudes toward these scenes even among passionate opera devotees.

Given that even sensualist champions of opera—flower-register kenners and the novelist Chen Sen—were made somewhat uneasy by the explicit sexuality of sister-in-law plays, the virulent reaction to them by contemporaneous moralist detractors of opera is hardly unexpected. All the *Water Margin* sister-in-law operas are proscribed in several mid-nineteenth-century private- and state-compiled lists of "licentious plays" (*yinxi*).[107] The Jiangnan philanthropist Yu Zhi (1809–74) in particular railed against the perilous effects to society of plays devoted to flirtation and secret assignations.[108] He composed his own cautionary ditties to warn contemporaries against the dangers of the theater, one of which reads:

> Be it Kun opera, Yiyang, flute melody or erhuang,
> Their five notes and six melodies are all perverse.
> The theater truly is a dangerous place;
> Root of evil and promoter of license, Laolang should be cursed.[109]

Most of the opera scenes contained in the *Cloak* collection, and especially the flirtation plays, Yu Zhi claimed, pointed the path to lecherous decline. When young men who had just awakened to feelings of desire saw them, "their souls would be snatched away, and they would fall into a life of dissipation, which would gradually make them consumptive." As if that were not bad enough, he continued, viewing such plays would "cause chaste girls to lose their chastity and virtuous wives to forgo their virtue."[110] Even opera enthusiasts such as Li Dou, the Yangzhou memoirist, collected cautionary tales in a similar vein. A passage in his *Painted Boats of Yangzhou* (*Yangzhou huafang lu*), about an actor who specialized in the role of the dwarfish husband Wu Da in *Righteous Hero*–related operas, demonstrates the degree of audience enthusiasm for these plays and offers an implicit admonition against them:

> Gu Tianyi, the clown of the Huang Troupe, excelled at the role of Wu Da. . . . On account of him the entire troupe performed a complete version of *The Righteous Hero*. . . . Once, during a performance in the City God Temple, the play selected by drawing lots before the gods had been *The Linked Rings Stratagem* [*Lianhuan ji*], but the audience in front of the stage made a huge clamor.[111] They demanded to see a performance of *The Righteous Hero*. The troupe had no choice but to bow to popular demand. When they got to the scene "Swallowing Poison," Tianyi suddenly fell down off the stage. The audience all believed this was a sign from the City God.[112]

Still, however much celestial and earthly opposition there was to such plays, the moralists were hard pressed to enforce their civilizing vision on popular performance practices. As evidence from *Playwatching Journal* reveals, in addition to its running series of flirtation operas in playhouse venues, on at least two occasions the Sanduo Troupe performed *Water Margin* sister-in-law operas on temple stages—once, "Second Seduction" in the Money God Guildhall (Caishen huiguan), and once, "Flirting with Brother-in-Law" and "Taking Leave of Brother" at the City God Temple on Nanheng Street in the southern section of the capital.[113] The lure of the *Water Margin* sisters-in-law was such that they captured the imagination of urban audiences and, extracted from their encompassing dramatic narratives, they emerged—whether sympathetic, sexy, silly (or some combination thereof)—as the central figures of these kunju operas when performed in the urban commercial milieu.

Eighteenth-Century Court Appropriation of "I, Sister-in-Law" Operas

If moralists were troubled by sister-in-law plays because they threatened standards of social propriety, the Qing court had double reason to be wary of *Water-Margin*–derived drama. The *Water Margin* story cycle—whether in novelistic or dramatic form—made Qing rulers particularly uneasy since, in some versions, the righteous outlaws of Liangshan eventually turned their rebellious fervor against the northern enemies of the native Song dynasty—the Liao (907–1125) and the Jin (1115–1234). Since the Qing state proclaimed that its political heritage and legitimacy derived from the Jin dynasty, popular admiration of *Water Margin* heroes and exploits smacked of seditious, anti-Manchu sympathies. Qianlong-era edicts attempted to prohibit the publication, distribution, and performance of *Water Margin*–based narrative and dramatic literature and to ban its translation into the Manchu language.[114] Even while the court deeply distrusted the implications of the *Water Margin* story cycle, during the Qianlong reign the court commissioned an enormous multivolume drama—a so-called grand opera (*da xi*)—based on the various existing kunju-system *Water Margin* dramas, including *Record of the Water Margin*, *Righteous Hero*, and *Cuiping Mountain*, entitled *The Plan of the Stars of Loyalty and Righteousness* (*Zhongyi xuantu*). In refashioning to Qing purposes this politically sensitive and morally damaging story, the court compromised between entertainment value and moral message, ultimately co-opting the material on which it was based.

Sometime during the middle years of the Qianlong reign (ca. 1750s), at roughly the time the emperor was issuing edicts prohibiting the proliferation of *Water Margin* stories then in public circulation, he commissioned the compilation of the ten-volume, 240-scene *Stars of Loyalty and Righteousness*.[115] Practically nothing is known about the principal authors of this script, Zhou Xiangyu and Zou Jinsheng. But the recollections of the Manchu courtier Zhaolian some fifty years later give a sense of the scale of court-sponsored dramatic entertainment in the Qianlong era and of the relative quality of *Stars of Loyalty and Righteousness* within the corpus of court-commissioned drama. In a long passage on court grand operas, Zhaolian writes:

> In the early years of the Qianlong reign, to celebrate the peace of the era, the Qianlong emperor ordered Zhang [Zhao] to write several plays and present them to the throne so that they could be available for performance by the palace musical troupes; they were performed at each and every festival. The legends of the times . . . were all set to musical scores; [these performances] were called "Seasonal Imperial Commissions" [*yueling chengying*]. On the occasion of various joyous celebrations within the court, they would perform auspicious plays, which were called "Dharma Liturgical Performances" [*fagong yazou*]. Before and after an imperial birthday, they would perform plays in which all the worthies and gods offered blessings, and in which cherubic children and white-haired old men sported about in idyll; these were called "Nine by Nine [Longevity] Grand Celebrations" [*jiujiu daqing*]. In addition, they performed the story of the worthy Mulian saving his mother, which filled a total of ten volumes and was called *A Golden Register for the Promotion of Kindness* [*Quanshan jinke*]. This was performed at the year's

end. . . . They performed the story of Xuanzang traveling to the West to obtain the sutras; this was called *The Precious Raft of Exalted Peace* [*Shengping baofa*]. . . .

Later, Prince Zhuang [Yinlu] was commissioned to put to music the stories of Shu-Han and the *Treatise of the Three Kingdoms*, and this was called *Annals of the Tripartite Division* [*Dingzhi chunqiu*]. Also set to music were the stories of the various outlaws of Liangshan during the Zhenghe reign of the Song dynasty, the battles between the Song and the Jin, and the capture of emperors Huizong and Qinzong; and this was called *The Plan of the Stars of Loyalty and Righteousness*. These scripts were written by courtiers temporarily basking in the glory of the emperor. It was as much as they could do just to piece the stories into a whole. Even though they copied the songs and lyrics from Yuan- and Ming-dynasty dramas such as *The Record of the Water Margin* and *The Righteous Hero* . . . , their corpus was not nearly as great as that of Zhang [Zhao].[116]

Stars of Loyalty and Righteousness, as Zhaolian relates, was stitched together out of all available *Water Margin* literature to create a court-sanctioned version. This becomes apparent from examining the relevant sister-in-law scenes in *Stars of Loyalty and Righteousness*, which reveal traces of the novel *Water Margin*, the three late Ming chuanqi dramas, selected scenes from seventeenth- and eighteenth-century drama miscellanies, and possibly other pre–*Water Margin* plays (no longer extant, but which may have still been accessible in the eighteenth century).[117]

Mastery of the whole seems to have been integral to court appropriation of this potentially sensitive story material. An encyclopedic impulse—seen in so many eighteenth-century court-sponsored literary projects—seems to have shaped the preferred process by which the Qing court arrogated to itself the vast corpus of Han-produced culture, a process first of prodigious collecting and then of thorough winnowing out of anything deemed subversive. Court treatment of the *Water Margin* materials, while clearly conducted on a relatively minor scale, seems to have shared this all-or-nothing approach to cultural acquisition.

One result of this court emphasis on mastering the entire story is that, in *Stars of Loyalty and Righteousness*, the various exploits of the wanton women are re-relegated to subplot status within the larger story. This contrasts directly with the trend in commercial performances, in which the sisters-in-law are the central focus of dramatic interest. For *Stars of Loyalty and Righteousness*, for instance, the court playwrights restored much of Xu Zichang's original story line in *Record of the Water Margin* and trimmed the number of seduction scenes to the minimum necessary to the plot, eliminating "Returning for the Kerchief" and "The First Seduction." More telling still, the Qianlong emperor's authors ended Yan Poxi's tryst with Zhang San with her murder, titling the scene "Miss Yan Acts Wickedly and Becomes an Aggrieved Ghost" (Yan shi fang diao cheng yuangui). Deviating from both the original playwright's version and popular performance practice, *Stars of Loyalty and Righteousness* entirely omitted "Captured Alive," in which Yan Poxi's ghost exacts vengeance for her untimely death. In contrast with commercial performance practice, the character of Yan Poxi is buried under the very volume of dramatic material, denied even the satisfaction of pulling her partner in adultery with her into the underworld.[118]

In the four scenes featuring Pan Jinlian, *Stars of Loyalty and Righteousness* contains a patchwork of arias from the Ming playwright's original drama and expanded dialogue from performance scripts preserved in Qing drama miscellanies such as *Cloak*.[119] Emendations introduced into these scenes by the court playwrights are mostly evident in spoken passages. Although their changes were minor, to the extent that they inflect the message of these scenes, they tend to make Wu Da less henpecked. For example, the *Cloak* script of "Flirting with Brother-in-Law" ends with the couple calling each other names, followed by Pan Jinlian beginning to hit Wu Da, Wu Da threatening to hit back but, unable to reach her due to his short stature, trying to kick her instead.[120] When Pan Jinlian runs offstage, Wu Da exits with the line: "See, one kick and I kicked her all the way into the green room!"[121] The clown's joke—bursting the theatrical illusion—helps diffuse the violence of the scene. The *Stars of Loyalty and Righteousness* redaction of this moment eliminates the humor, replacing it with more moralistic overtones. In the court version Wu Da is given an extra line:

> WU DALANG: You're my wife and I'm your husband. Since time immemorial, the man has been the woman's Heaven. Here you are hitting me for no reason. Don't think that I won't hit back.
> PAN JINLIAN: Would you dare to hit me?
> WU DALANG: Hit you? I'm also going to kick you.

The scene closes with Wu Da's added threat: "Hit, hit, hit; I'll kick you to death, you stinking harlot."[122] Lacking the physical and verbal slapstick of the commercial-production scripts, Wu Da's reassertion of male dominance in the court version comes off as much more strident. None of this ending dialogue was in Shen Jing's original script. All but Wu Da's parting shot was in the various performance scripts, which tells us that the court playwrights knew the commercial versions of these scenes from *Righteous Hero*. Wu Da's added line provided the restoration of male mastery that the imperial audience wanted to experience.

The six scenes from *Cuiping Mountain* incorporated into the court grand opera form a nearly contiguous subplot in the opening scenes of volume 6 of *Stars of Loyalty and Righteousness* (scenes 2, 4–8). These six scenes correspond to those most commonly performed in commercial playhouse productions. Here, too, however, the court script shows a retreat from the changes introduced into *Cuiping Mountain* commercial-production scripts of the same era. The ending scene of the sequence is illustrative. Here entitled "Revelations of Illicit Schemes on Cuiping Mountain" (Cuiping shan dui ming xinji), it retains Yang Xiong as the killer of Pan Qiaoyun and her maid.[123] To ensure that the proper message of the scene comes through, the court script follows the two murders with a new concluding aria. Yang Xiong and Shi Xiu sing in unison:

> Hurriedly, we go together, hero matched to hero;
> Hurriedly, we go together, hero matched to hero. We're off to find refuge in the faraway watery marshes;
> Drawn by the fame of Chao [Gai] and Song [Jiang], whom we've admired for so long . . .
> Today, we've washed away this stain to manly pride;
> We've finished off the trollop and her evil designs.
> On that desolate mountain, there's clamoring in the pines;
> Atop an old grave mound, the crows fight for the remains.
> Our guts, oh, are sucked clean, our vengeance now spent;
> We mustn't, ah, be pulled or bound by ties, but hence with haste.[124]

The triumph of brotherhood and masculine vengeance in this aria is a far cry indeed from the weeping Yang Xiong of commercial-production scripts of "Murder on the Mountain." This new aria is reminiscent in tone of early redactions of *Water Margin*, emphasizing the gruesome blood-bonding ritual of the sworn brothers.

Although in its "Illicit Schemes on Cuiping Mountain" ending *Stars of Loyalty and Righteousness* seems to exult in machismo violence, the Qianlong court was clearly conflicted over how much to endorse vigilante action. In an ironic twist, after a full dramatization of the male heroism in the 120-chapter version of *Water Margin*, *Stars of Loyalty and Righteousness*, in its last sixteen scenes condemns all 108 of the outlaws as false heroes. These final scenes of the grand opera trace the fates of the various dramatis personae in the underworld, where they are judged by King Yama. Song Jiang's crimes, however, being violations of political more than social order, are so great that he is condemned to Hell for eternity and denied any form of rebirth.

This displays the relative value judgment of the Qing court: as harshly as sexual profligacy, marital infidelity, and the associated blackmail and murder may have been condemned, political insubordination was deemed even more disruptive of the public weal. The more moralistic treatment of the "crimes of passion" in the court versions of the sister-in-law scenes are to a certain extent undermined by this ending. Of course, late imperial Chinese fiction and drama are replete with examples of prurience sandwiched between moralistic bookends, a practice that allowed writers and their audiences to have it both ways, that is, to be entertained by salacious stories under the guise of hortatory instruction.[125] The court script of *Stars of Loyalty and Righteousness* seems to have been similar in this regard. The moralistic framing of the grand opera, coupled with court appropriation of the complete saga, neutralized any challenge to social and political order within the script, thereby allowing the imperial audience for the performance to safely enjoy both the sex and the violence of the *Water Margin* story.

If the mid-eighteenth-century Qing court was somewhat ambivalent as to which transgression—sex or violence—represented the greater social threat, by the mid-nineteenth century no ambivalence remained. In patronizing pihuang opera, the nineteenth-century court chose violence over sex as the lesser of two evils.[126]

Violence and the Reinstantiation of Moral Order in the Pihuang *Tradition*

An entertainment ethos of mixed violence and comedy infuses the *Water Margin* sister-in-law plays in the pihuang performance tradition. In these scripts the flirtation and illicit sex are not excised; rather (somewhat akin to what happened to these tales when appropriated by the Qianlong court), pihuang versions of sister-in-law operas restored the full narrative of female transgression followed by male retribution. This new ethos can be traced to the relatively lowbrow origins of the pihuang genre—both in its compositional structure and in the kinds of audiences it initially attracted within urban centers. Predominantly fast paced, these operas told complete stories in simple song, dialogue, and stage combat; and, according to elite observers circa 1790 to 1900, they tended to appeal more to commoners than to the urban elite.[127]

As we have seen, about mid-nineteenth century a cohort of very powerful people at the Qing court—including the Xianfeng emperor, Empress Dowager Cixi, Prince Gong, and Prince Chun—took a liking to pihuang opera. They began commissioning commercial actors into court for command performances before the imperial family and its guests. This patronage raised the prestige of pihuang actors and their art form. By the last decades of the nineteenth century the court had become so enamored of pihuang that, at the behest of Empress Dowager Cixi, it initiated a massive effort to "translate" many of the kunju and Yiyang melody scripts in its holdings into the pihuang style.[128]

This, then, is the backdrop to the various pihuang scripts of sister-in-law operas I next examine. Some of these scripts can be identified as Shengping shu editions (and thus are likely to have been performed at court). The provenance of others is harder to trace, but many have been culled from collections formerly belonging to career actors and may well reflect commercial performance. Circulation between a less literate commercial performance practice and the court's aesthetic and ideological predilections shaped the revitalized machismo of the sister-in-law scripts in the pihuang tradition. As actors circulated between the court and the commercial milieu, so did their scripts and story material. The ruling family's wholesale appropriation of pihuang opera reflected and further forged an aesthetic and moral consonance between the court and the values transmitted via the plays of that emerging musical genre. In the case of the sister-in-law operas the nineteenth-century court preferred the gender story of the pihuang to that of the kunju commercial performance tradition. In other words, it chose vigilante violence over illicit sex, so long as that violence was marshaled in support of orthodox morality.

PIHUANG SISTER-IN-LAW OPERAS

When the *Water Margin*–based chuanqi scripts were adapted for stage performance over the seventeenth and eighteenth centuries, the structural features of the Kun musical system ensured that large passages of original text (especially the arias) would be preserved. Performers might cut or add (jokes, explanatory dialogue, dialect, etc.), but they still had to work with or around a good measure of the playwrights' original words. No such stricture operated when adapting the stories of these operas to pihuang, whose musical structure was entirely different and much simpler. As a result, pihuang versions of the sister-in-law operas retain little of the original language of performance scripts in the kunju genre. In general, this opened up the pihuang scripts to greater individual variation; it also makes it harder to trace direct textual filiations across scripts and over time. Still, certain trends can be discerned, and whether in the realm of language, stage action, or moral message, for the most part these reinventions of the narratives redirect sympathy away from the femmes fatales to the male vigilantes.

In the pihuang scripts all dialogue is rendered in a crisp capital dialect (*jingbai*). Clowns' lines end in Beijing colloquialisms instead of Wu-dialect vocables, suggesting that the target audiences for these operas were now primarily capital natives or northerners, whether of Han ethnicity or the long since naturalized Beijing Manchu nobility and their Banner troops and dependents. Certainly this capital dialect would have been intelligible to southern mandarins temporarily residing in the capital (since all officials needed basic proficiency in Mandarin), but—unlike kunju scripts—pihuang operas did not cater to the patois preferences of Jiangnan sojourners.

To an even greater extent than in the Kun opera scripts anthologized in *Cloak* and in other production scripts, the dialogue of the pihuang sister-in-law scripts is pieced together with set bits, or modules—a sign of actor rather than playwright invention. These set passages or phrases were reused at opportune moments in multiple scripts. One example of such set pieces, the "guessing game," as I call it, is deployed with only minor variations in the pihuang operas featuring two of the *Water Margin* sister-in-law characters. In "Black Dragon Courtyard" (Wulong yuan) the guessing game sets up the dramatic tension between Yan Poxi and Song Jiang.[129] This pihuang version of the story begins with Zhang San visiting Yan Poxi. Their tryst is interrupted by the sudden arrival of Song Jiang. Yan Poxi orders Zhang to hide in her mother's room until she can get rid of Song Jiang. To encourage Song Jiang to leave quickly, she treats him rudely. But Song Jiang is not so easily put off. This launches them into the set piece:

> SONG: Whenever I came to the courtyard in the past, you were always as happy as could be. Today upon my entering, you treat me this way; you must have something weighing on your heart.
> YAN: Ah, I've got a bellyful of things weighing on my heart.

SONG: As for whatever's weighing on your heart, I reckon if I didn't take a guess, then that would be an end to it.
YAN: If you were to guess?
SONG: I'd be right eight or nine times out of ten.
YAN: You won't be able to guess what's in my heart.
SONG: I'll be able to guess it.
YAN: You won't.
SONG: Say nothing about what's weighing on your heart, even when it comes to what's weighing on my master the magistrate's heart. If I don't try to guess, then there's an end to it; but if I try to guess, then I'm right eight or nine times out of ten.
YAN: It's easy to guess what's weighing on the magistrate's heart. What's weighing on mine is going to be a little bit harder to guess.
SONG: I'll be able to guess it.
YAN: You won't.

Song Jiang then breaks into song as he attempts to guess what is wrong: perhaps she is not happy with the food he provides her? No, she responds; her basic needs are being met. Perhaps, he ventures, she does not like her clothes? Yan has no complaints about her wardrobe either, and she taunts him, "See, I told you, you wouldn't be able to guess it." He tries again: "COULD IT BE THAT SECOND AUNTIE MA HAS BEATEN OR SCOLDED YOU?" Yan: "Second Auntie Ma is my own mother. If I do something wrong, it's only right that she beats or scolds me." Song then asks if the yamen runners have been bullying her. They would not dare, she replies, do anything to offend Song Jiang, who clerks in the same office. On the fifth try, Song Jiang thinks he has finally hit on the right answer. He sings:

SONG: COULD IT BE THAT YOU'VE BEEN MISSING ME?
YAN: Aiya, Master Song, this time you've guessed it.
SONG: What can't be guessed? Tell me how you've been missing me.
YAN: The day before yesterday, I . . .
SONG: I had work at the office.
YAN: Yesterday . . .
SONG: I couldn't get away.
YAN: Only today was I really thinking about you.
SONG: Today, I've come, I've come. How have you been thinking about me?
YAN: Early in the morning I arose; I brushed my hair and washed my face. I thought as I walked from the front hall all the way to the back courtyard, and from the back courtyard all the way to the kitchen. In my left hand I held a cup of cold water, and in my right a clove of garlic. I'd drink a sip of water and take a bite of garlic. I thought of you so much that a cold stink settled on my heart.

SONG: Missy, early in the morning you arose; you brushed your hair and washed your face. You thought as you walked from the front hall all the way to the back courtyard, and from the back courtyard all the way to the kitchen. In your left hand you held a cup of cold water, and in your right a clove of garlic. You'd drink a sip of water and take a bite of garlic. She thought so much that a cold stink settled on her heart. Aiya! You weren't missing me![130]

As it dawns on Song Jiang that Yan Poxi has no warm feelings for him, the tension mounts until Yan inadvertently reveals that Song has been cuckolded. The first half of the play ends with Song Jiang exiting their Black Dragon Courtyard in a rage.

Before demonstrating how this bit is reused again in other sister-in-law operas, I offer a few comments about the passage. First, it includes more dialogue than song, and the repartee is both simple and repetitious, ensuring that any audience member would have been able to catch the meaning—if not at first, then at least after the second or third repetition of a phrase. In addition, the dialogue makes use of local proverbs or colloquialisms; the quip about "a sip of cold water and a bite of garlic" (raw garlic being a quintessentially northern condiment) is reminiscent of the droll "leave-off-the-ending" (*xiehouyu*) proverbs still in use in modern-day Beijing. Further, this passage, as well as others within the script, gives Song Jiang a much more substantial role within the play. The audience gets to see the adversaries here (and elsewhere) match wits, and they are an equal match. Yan Poxi comes off as far more shrewish than in performed kunju versions of the story line, and Song Jiang is shown (for the first time) to have a somewhat playful side. The directness and simplicity of the language surely mark it as less literary than the kunju performance scripts. Yet this particular script belonged to the palace Shengping shu collection. It is one example of an imperial repository copy, intended for court review.[131] When Empress Dowager Cixi watched performances of "Black Dragon Courtyard" in the 1880s and 1890s, it is highly likely that she was viewing the staging of this very script.

A similar dialogue module is embedded in a pihuang script of "Cuiping Mountain."[132] The pihuang version of this play very quickly summarizes the plot up through Pan Qiaoyun's commencement of the affair with the monk. By page 2 of the script we are already into the content of "Reverse Accusal." Yang Xiong comes home drunk and curses his wife; she realizes that her affair has been discovered and sets about to discredit her husband's sworn brother. The next morning Yang Xiong finds his wife looking unhappy. The scene continues:

> YANG: You can't hide it from me. I can see from your face that something is weighing on your heart.
> DAN[133] [Pan Qiaoyun]: There is something weighing on my heart, but you won't be able to guess it.
> YANG: Say nothing of what's weighing on your heart, even when my master the magistrate has something weighing on his heart. If I don't guess, then there's an end to it.
> DAN: And if you guess?
> YANG: Eight or nine times out of ten, I'm right.[134]

The guessing game then begins in earnest. Again, the husband makes five guesses: the neighbors, her father, the maid, himself, and finally the sworn brother. Even though the exchanges are not identical with those between Yan Poxi and Song Jiang, the structure of the dialogue is entirely parallel. This is just one example of some of the recurring linguistic and structural patterns of pihuang operas. There were clearly repertoires of such modules available to the actors and "scriptwriters" of such plays, who pieced them together in a kind of bricolage to produce the desired plot sequences. One of the effects of this practice is that it makes the characters nearly interchangeable from one play to another. The dan actors for such characters are all playing a variation on the generic "wanton shrew." With very little internal emotional exposition in the arias, the sister-in-law characters are flattened into the sum of their actions. As further evidence that the pihuang tradition conflates the *Water Margin* femmes fatales into one generic scheming sister-in-law, an early twentieth-century script of "Cuiping Mountain" turns Pan Qiaoyun into the younger sister of Pan Jinlian.[135] Although there is no basis for this anywhere within the *Water Margin* story material, clearly the characters had become so similar in popular imagination that it seemed natural to turn them into sisters on the pihuang stage.

Aside from these linguistic and structural characteristics, the primary shift in emphasis in the pihuang sister-in-law plays is the restoration of the full story, or perhaps more important, the final resolution of the story. This is most obvious in the case of "Cuiping Mountain," which, in pihuang mode, focuses on two highlights—Pan Qiaoyun's attempted deception of her husband and her eventual murder on the mountain. The conclusion of the opera is essentially the same whether in palace scripts, in an anonymous late nineteenth-century "capital melody" version, or in two actors' part scripts for the role of Shi Xiu.[136] The final scene in a court performance script, featuring the commercial actors Tan Xinpei in the role of Shi Xiu and Yu Yuqin as Pan Qiaoyun, is presented as follows:[137]

> SHI: Brother Yang, kill, kill, kill her![138]
> YUN: Aiya! (Sings in the "flowing water" rhythm) MY SOUL FLIES AWAY TO THE NINTH LEVEL OF HEAVEN. I ADVANCE FORWARD AND PLEAD WITH BROTHER-IN-LAW SHI. SHI SHUSHU! THIS WAS MY WRONGDOING, A CALAMITY I BROUGHT UPON MYSELF. I TURN TO FACE MY HUSBAND, DALANG, AND PLEAD WITH HIM. DALANG, THINK UPON OUR FEELINGS FOR EACH OTHER AS MAN AND WIFE AND SPARE ME.
> YANG: I can't kill her.
> SHI: BROTHER YANG, WHY DO YOU STAY YOUR HAND?
> YANG: WE'VE BEEN MAN AND WIFE, AND SO IT'S HARD TO DO THE DEED. HONORED BROTHER, DO IT FOR ME.
> SHI: I fear that you, Brother, will hate me for this.
> YANG: I'm willing to swear an oath to Heaven. HURRIEDLY, I KNEEL UPON THE LEVEL GROUND. YOU GODS AND SPIRITS THAT PASS ON BY, BE MY WITNESS: SHOULD I HARBOR HATRED AGAINST HIM FOR KILLING MY WIFE, TAKE A SWORD TO ME AND CUT MY BODY TO BITS.
> (SHI performs killing YUN.)
> YANG: Honored Brother, tell me about it.
> SHI: The slut's heart was as pink as the profligate peach flower.
> TOGETHER: Throw her down in the ravine.
> YANG: We've killed the two of them. Where should the two of us go for shelter?
> SHI: The two of us should head for Liang . . .
> YANG: Hush! (He performs the action of looking around.) Honored Brother, what "Liang"?
> SHI: You and I should take refuge at Liangshan, where we will find shelter.
> YANG: What you say makes sense. After you!
> SHI: After you![139]

This denouement charts a middle ground between the exultant sworn brothers of the court's *Stars of Loyalty and Righteousness* and the weeping Yang Xiong of kunju production scripts of "Murder on the Mountain." It certainly plays with the idea—probably familiar to audiences already—that Yang Xiong finds it hard to slaughter his wife, but that is balanced against the friendship between the sworn brothers. And in this and all other pihuang versions, Yang invokes the gods to cement the bond of fraternity. According to the early twentieth-century opera connoisseur Chen Moxiang (a.k.a. "I, Sister-in-Law"), some opera fans at the time advocated performing just the first half of "Cuiping Mountain." But that, Chen opined, missed the point. "If you don't sing the two scenes in which the lascivious monk and the dissolute woman are killed, it's like doing alchemy to turn gold into iron." "Besides," he went on, "if you want to assess the real skills of the flower dan, you have to watch the last scene."[140]

The story of *Righteous Hero* was also "translated" into pihuang style in the late nineteenth century, although according to Chen Moxiang, of the operas based on the three *Water Margin* femmes fatales, those featuring Pan Jinlian were the least popular. Chen writes: "When luantan troupes performed 'The Murder of Sister-in-Law,' the role of Wu Song was played by the lead male. As for that disgraceful sister-in-law, most famous dan actors did not play the part very often, so she became a supporting role. Prior to 1900 [this opera] was not very popular."[141] A complete pihuang rendition of *Righteous Hero* in twenty-two scenes was produced (perhaps influenced by the court), however, by the early twentieth century.[142] The twenty-two-scene script restored much of the story material from the novel, beginning with Wu Song's battle with the tiger and ending with his double revenge on Pan Jinlian and Ximen Qing, again redirecting attention toward the exploits of the male hero. Probably more often, even at court, only the last third of the narrative was performed, which came to be identified by the title "Lion Street Tavern" (Shizi lou), the site at which Wu Song hunts down and kills Ximen Qing.[143] An anonymous script bearing this title, possibly of court provenance, is virtually identical with the last four scenes of full "Righteous Hero" scripts in the pihuang genre.[144] In addition, records of viewings of "Lion Street Tavern" at the imperial palace on 24 April 1908 and 15 June 1908 confirm that the court received this pihuang opera with approval.[145]

Although the emphasis of *Righteous Hero* in the pihuang tradition was on the vigilante retribution, this did not entirely supplant the older kunju interest in flirtation. A parallel thread much more closely related to the kunju scripts and focusing on Pan Jinlian's attempted seduction of Wu Song continued alongside the renewed masculine heroic ethos of the pihuang operas. Usually retaining the kunju title "Flirting with Brother-in-Law," these scripts, too, were adapted for pihuang performance. Although the arias of these operas were rewritten into strings of parallel couplets (and simplified in the process), the scripts still bear traces of their kunju origins—most notably, preserving some of the Wu-dialect phrasing of the earlier performance texts.[146] Remarks of educated observers in the late 1800s indicate that in general Pan Jinlian had once again become a secondary role; the most famous dan actors of the time far more often played her alter ego sisters, Pan Qiaoyun and Yan Poxi.

Three titles of the Song Jiang–Yan Poxi story remained in the pihuang performance repertoire: "Black Dragon Courtyard," "Sitting in the Loft and Murdering Yan Poxi," and "Captured Alive."[147] The first two of these titles came to represent the first and second halves of the plot, respectively, with "Black Dragon Courtyard" designating the first half (through the argument and falling out between Yan and Song), and "Sitting in the Loft" the second, in which the quarrel reignites and Song kills her.[148] When performed together, the final climax of the play was the murder scene. The repartee between the spouses served as an earlier and lesser climax.

A variant of "Captured Alive" also made the transition from kunju to pihuang performance. As did "Flirting with Brother-in-Law" from the *Righteous Hero* story line, "Captured Alive" retained certain of its kunju roots even after its dialogue and lyrics had been reworked for pihuang format.[149] A "Captured Alive" script preserved in the Shengping shu reveals how the scene was presented before an imperial audience. First, much of the language and plot of the original novel—even material not included in Xu Zichang's late Ming long dramatic version—was restored.[150] This restored the misogyny of the novel as well. Whereas all the kunju versions of this scene end with Yan Poxi returning from the grave to drag her lover Zhang San to the underworld with her, the court pihuang edition shapes the ending in even more explicitly moralistic terms and gives full reign to Poxi's feelings of anger and resentment:

> JIAO[151] [Yan Poxi]: You cursed-love, you've been so heartless to me. You've forgotten those vows exchanged beneath the stars and the moon. Your inconstancy angers me. ([JIAO] chases him. ZHANG and JIAO grab opposite ends of the table.)
> ZHANG [San]: My heart's all a-flutter and I've no place to run. (ZHANG drops to his knees. JIAO chases him.)
> JIAO: Today, I come at the behest of King Yama of the Underworld to bring you with me. (JIAO circles the table and chases ZHANG. She pulls on a colored ghost-face mask. ZHANG acts out being afraid. JIAO grabs him.)
> ZHANG: My dear, spare me.
> JIAO: IF KING YAMA ORDERS IT, THEN YOUR FATE IS SEALED. HOW CAN I LET YOU REMAIN IN THIS WORLD? IF YOU ARE LASCIVIOUS AND YOUR ACTIONS IMPROPER, YOUR RETRIBUTION WILL BE CLEAR INDEED. (JIAO uses a kerchief to strangle ZHANG; sparks fly from her mouth. JIAO circles the stage with ZHANG in tow; sparks fly from her mouth and she exits.)[152]

226   PLAYS AND PERFORMANCES

This marriage of court and popular taste created a new sister-in-law opera tradition in which normative world orders were restored through violence, and the violence was seen to be as entertaining as the romantic flirtation.

AUDIENCE RESPONSES TO
PIHUANG SISTER-IN-LAW OPERAS

Just how popular these plays were within the pihuang repertoire is hard to tell. Although these titles do not necessarily stand out from others, the sister-in-law operas continue to receive scattered mention in late nineteenth-century flower registers. One such guide written in the 1870s suggests that, for the most part, these plays were associated with troupes that appealed to commoners. Still, a really superb performance could also attract the urban elite:

> The theater troupes of the capital are named Sixi, Chuntai, Sanqing, and Hechun. All four are equally famous, but the Hechun troupe is the only one that is not liked by the elite. When officials hold banquets, they do not call upon the services of Hechun. But the petty urbanites of the city love to watch that troupe. I have a friend who would call for the supporting cast from the other troupes, but then specially request the Hechun actor Songling to perform [Pan Qiaoyun] in "Cuiping Mountain." I had a chance to see him with my own eyes, and he was truly bewitching beyond compare.[153]

Elite patronage of such plays seems to have increased over time, possibly influenced by the aesthetic standards adopted by the court, although influence between court and city traveled both ways.[154] That the court chose to watch performances of pihuang sister-in-law operas by commercial actors indicates that the operas had considerable appeal. The court, presumably, wanted the best commercial operas and performers—seeking a quality that was better than the eunuch actors serving in the palace.

That sister-in-law plays retained an audience following is even more strongly indicated by the spin-offs they generated—such as the pihuang play "The Cobbler Killer," a simple narrative of adultery and retribution. The principal characters are Yang Hu the cobbler; his wife, Lin Yulan; the husband's younger brother Yang Shenggong; and Yue Ziqi, a clerk in the Zhaoyi County magistrate's office. This play is a patchwork of bits and pieces from all the plots of the *Water Margin* sister-in-law operas: the clown/magistrate's clerk, Yue Ziqi, is a double for Zhang San (they even share certain stock lines);[155] Lin Yulan's propositioning her brother-in-law comes from the Pan Jinlian story; and the ending parallels that of "Cuiping Mountain." According to Chen Moxiang, who saw many renditions of these operas at the turn of the century, the same actors who performed Shi Xiu also played Yang Shenggong; even their costuming was identical;[156] and dan actors renowned for their portrayals of the *Water Margin* sisters-in-law (particularly Yan Poxi and Pan Qiaoyun) took the role of "the cobbler's wife."[157] By the 1880s the pihuang "Cobbler Killer" was on the roster of the most famous troupes in the capital.[158]

From the script alone, it is hard to see the attraction of "Cobbler Killer."[159] The language feels formulaic and not particularly clever, despite the humor and sexual innuendo in some of the clown's lines. So what did audiences see in these operas? According to one late nineteenth-century commentator, although plays such as "Sitting in the Loft" and "Cuiping Mountain" fell into the category of "dirty plays," their main appeal was their clever dialogue, and so long as that was "cleaned up" a bit, they were not so bad.[160] A contemporary echoed this sentiment: "Comic dan must have an air of shrewishness about them; the best were Yang Guiyun and Wujiu. Martial dan must have an air of panache to them . . . the best were Yang Xiaoduo and Huifang. Powder dan must have an air of seductiveness about them; the best were Yiwangshui and Guifeng. All these roles rely heavily on dialogue . . . so those actors with a sharp tongue are the best."[161] Gossip-laden anecdotes about the famous patrons of many of the actors mentioned in this passage reveal that the young dan actors of pihuang (as well as kunju) performance still appealed sensually to audiences:

> Wujiu was a pretty capital actor during the Guangxu years. Zhang Yinhuan [1837–1900], vice-minister [in the Zongli Yamen], was extremely partial to him. Yinhuan often summoned him to his house, where he had him wear women's attire and serve as an attendant at his side. For each day he did this, he paid Wujiu fifty taels of silver, and he had his family servants address him as "young mistress."[162]

But talented actors did not need a pretty face to succeed at sister-in-law pihuang plays, as the following passage about the dan actor Yang Guiyun makes clear:

> Yang Guiyun . . . excelled at the tie dan role. His face was wide and fleshy, looking as if he had consumed plenty of wine and meat. His voice had a northern screechy quality to it, being half hoarse, like the cry of a jackal, so he was good at playing shrew operas. . . . In plays such as "The Cobbler Killer" . . . he was effective at impersonating lascivious women—women

who tried to murder their husbands. . . . He was good at crying and good at laughing, and his face captured the two seasons of spring and autumn. When he saw someone he liked, his face was wreathed in smiles, but when he saw someone he hated, his face could barely contain his wrath. He was especially adept at portraying the emotions of decadent women.[163]

These plays were also what were known as stagecraft plays (*zuogong xi*) (as opposed to singing plays [*changgong xi*]). In the case of "Cuiping Mountain," one of the most entertaining moments was likely the silent "face-washing scene," alluded to with the stage directions, "Ying['er] carries on a washbasin. Yang [Xiong] and the dan fight over washing. The water is spilled."[164] Interpolating from visual sources and later performances of this opera, these simple stage directions are the cue for a comic pantomime in which all three characters must share the same basin to wash their faces. This action takes place on the morning after Yang Xiong returns home drunk. Yang Xiong calls for a basin of water, but Pan Qiaoyun insists on washing up first—and uses the water to perform all imaginable ablutions. When she finishes, it is the maid's turn. Finally, the same now cold-and-dirty basin of water is made available to the man of the household. The inversions of normative gender and status orders in this scene were a source of comedy and dramatic tension.

As a painting of this scene commissioned by the Qing court in the late nineteenth century attests, this moment of stage business captured the imagination of audiences (Figure 20). The painting depicts a coquettish Pan Qiaoyun lingering over the washbasin, while the maid stands in attendance at her side. The maid's face wears an expression of alarm, as if she spies the trouble brewing between her mistress and master. A disgruntled Yang Xiong sits in the background, hands on hips, sullenly waiting his turn. In the late nineteenth century the court commissioned many such finely wrought paintings of pihuang operas—recording the central essence of each play. That this particular episode came to be identified with the opera "Cuiping Mountain" indicates that this had become one of the play's iconic moments; it was one of the entertainment highlights of the opera. Other published lithograph editions of the opera script also chose this image as their signature visual representation (Figure 21).[165]

The humor in such scenes leavened the emphasis on martial action in pihuang sister-in-law operas. If the humor stemmed from depiction of gender and social inversion—the woman ruling the roost or the maid outwitting the master—then the violence at the conclusion of such operas restored

Figure 20. Painting of a scene from the *pihuang* version of the drama "Cuiping Mountain." The Palace Museum Collection, Beijing. Courtesy of the Palace Museum.

normative hierarchies. And artful violence against transgressive women became one of the central fascinations of these plays in the pihuang genre. Chen Moxiang claimed that to truly gauge the skills of a flowery dan actor, one had to see the performer negotiate the acrobatic demands of the ending scenes of such plays, particularly on the qiao shoes they wore.[166] What he was looking for in performance is revealed, perhaps, by his lovingly detailed description of the murder of the sister-in-law character in "Cobbler Killer"—a description that also echoes the finale of "Cuiping Mountain."

> Sister-in-Law runs onstage from upstage right and leaps toward the downstage left corner; she swings a long, fallen lock of hair to the side and takes

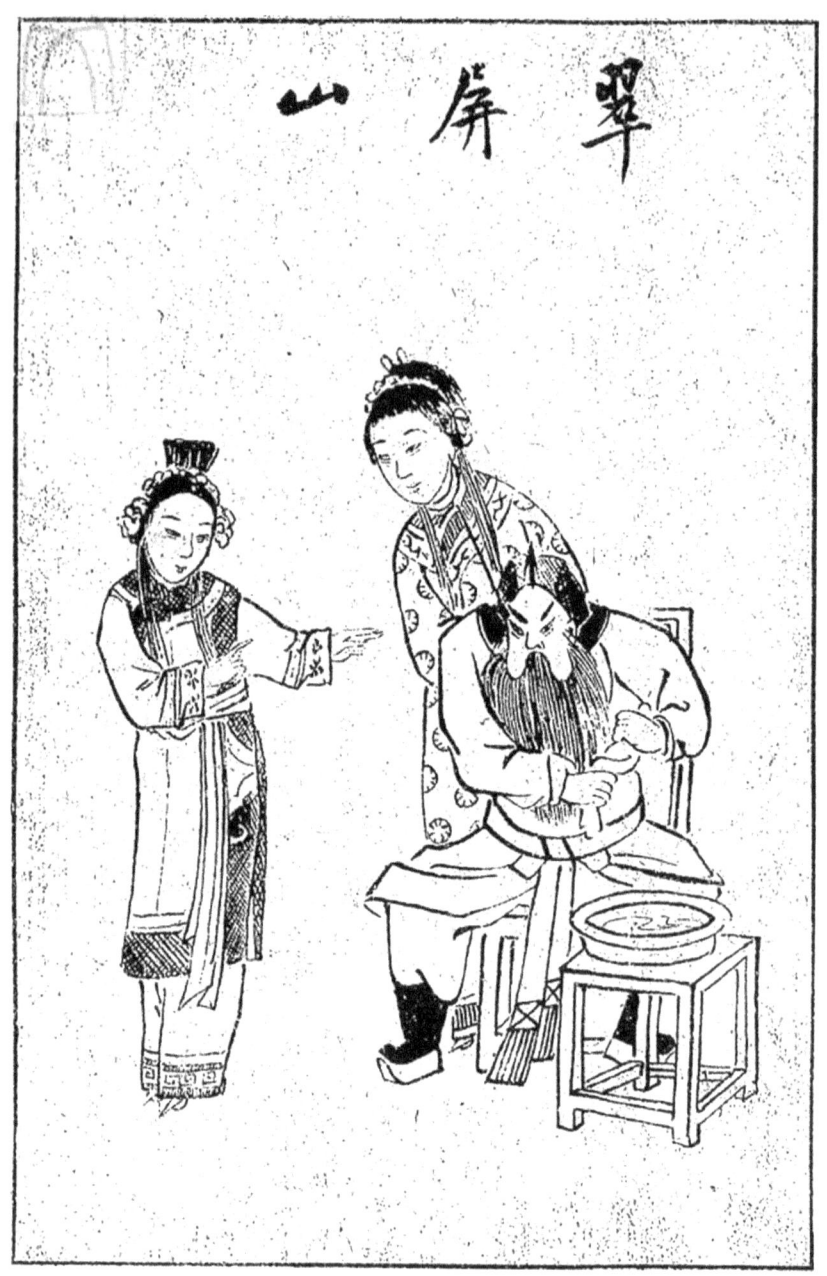

Figure 21. Lithograph print of a scene from the *pihuang* version of the drama "Cuiping Mountain." From *Illustrated Scripts in the Capital Melody from the Capital Sanqing Troupe, in Ten Volumes* (*Huitu jingdu sanqing ban jingdiao jiaoben shiji*), 1912, vol. 10, frontispiece. Sokodo Collection, Toyo Bunka, Tokyo University. Courtesy of Tokyo University.

a step backward. . . . Yang Shenggong rushes on in pursuit, claps her on the shoulder with his hand, and kicks her. Sister-in-Law swings her hair again and does a twisting side shoulder roll toward downstage left. Yang Shenggong thrusts his dagger at her head. Sister-in-Law flees offstage upstage right; Brother-in-Law pursues. . . . Sister-in-Law reenters from upstage left; Yang Shenggong rushes on from behind and kicks her as before. Sister-in-Law swings her hair and does another shoulder roll . . . only this time in the opposite direction. . . . The Cobbler enters, and the three of them chase each other around the stage in a figure-eight pattern. Sister-in-Law crosses in front of Brother-in-Law and stops; the husband crosses behind his brother and stops. Sister-in-Law sinks to her knees. Yang Shenggong grabs her wrists with his left hand and holds up his dagger in the right. The men walk [backward], dragging Sister-in-Law, who follows forward on her knees. . . . When Brother-in-Law reaches center stage, he stops abruptly. The husband falls down stage left. Sister-in-Law falls down stage right. Sister-in-Law climbs into a kneeling position and, while spinning her long ponytail, begins knocking her head to the stage floor, begging for her life. The cuckolded husband's heart begins to soften, but Yang Shenggong will not let up. *This part is played more or less the same as in "Murder on the Mountain"* [from "Cuiping Mountain"].[167] Sister-in-Law throws herself at her husband, and they embrace. Yang Shenggong comes between them from the left and shoves them apart. Husband and wife leap away from Brother-in-Law to stage left and again fall into an embrace. Yang Shenggong comes between them from the right and shoves them apart. . . . Yang Shenggong . . . raises his dagger and slices it down toward the female character's head. Sister-in-Law ducks with a somersault and grabs her dangling lock of hair between her teeth as she flips into a standing position; she grabs the knife, and the two of them circle the stage together. Then, with one horizontal stroke, Yang Shenggong draws his dagger across Sister-in-Law's powdered throat, and she follows her lover to the grave.

Chen ends his narration of the final stage fight with an editorializing apology: "Although one can say that the plot dwells on indecency, still it can serve as a warning to philanderers."[168] The combination of witty dialogue, stagecraft, and violence in these plays is defended in much the same terms by one Wu Tao, who praised the talents of mid- to late nineteenth-century actors specializing in flowery dan roles:

> Only a few actors such as Songling, Changgui, and Yang Guiyun specialized in these plays ["Black Dragon Courtyard" and "Cuiping Mountain"], and they gained quite a reputation. . . . In the past when I watched famous actors such as Songling in flowery dan plays, the emphasis was on action techniques and there were no lewd passages. What is more, they publicized the

punishment coming to those who engaged in indecency. [Watching them,] the wild would know fear, so they might even have had a salutary effect on public morals.[169]

Contemporary observations on the moralizing message of such operas in no way contradict the sense that audience sympathies were meant to be torn in the final sequences of these plays. On the one hand, restoration of the full arc of these stories reminded audiences of the retribution that would be visited upon the femmes fatales—a moral brought home through both narrative message and performance medium. The degradation of the sister-in-law was aestheticized through acrobatic technique—the bulk of which rested upon the skills of the dan actor (the flips and tumbling, the knee scooting, the head tossing, and ponytail twirling), which enhanced audience delight in watching her torment. Thus, the reassertion of male power on the narrative level was buttressed by the pleasure-inducing spectacle of the stage violence perpetrated against the transgressive woman. On the other hand, the drawn-out killing of the woman—the repeated embraces between husband and wife that are furiously broken up by the maligned brother—worked precisely because it played on conflicting audience sympathies. Chen admits as much himself when in a further discussion of sister-in-law plays, he maintains that death is too harsh a punishment for Pan Qiaoyun in "Cuiping Mountain" and for Lin Yulan in "Cobbler Killer," neither of whom has committed (or even threatened) the murder of her husband.[170] The longer the central conflict of the opera—brotherly love versus conjugal devotion—was held in balance, the greater the audience's enjoyment. And this meant that audiences had a certain emotional investment in keeping the woman alive. Holding off the final swish of the knife—that concluding moment of dispatch—prolonged audience pleasure.

This was especially so when audiences could read gossip about actor rivalries into the staging of the fights, as a long description of a performance of "Sitting in the Loft" reveals. "In my whole life of watching plays," aficionado Luo Ying'an recalls, "the one that left me most satisfied was a rendition of 'Sitting in the Loft' by Old Tan and Tian Guifeng." He continues:

> When Guifeng was at his height of popularity, Old Tan often was upstaged by him. Often when Old Tan starred in the second-to-last play and Guifeng starred in the last play [in a day's lineup], no one in the audience would get up to leave. But if Guifeng's play came before Old Tan's, when Guifeng's performance was over, the audience would start to struggle out; so Old Tan would fly into a jealous rage. . . . Every time Guifeng was matched in a play

with Old Tan, Old Tan would be [already] in costume and he would have to wait for Guifeng to scrub his fingernails.... For these reasons, the two of them developed deep differences. Guifeng got on in age and had retired from the stage for some time; the two of them had not acted together for a long time. It was then that I saw them in a performance of "Sitting in the Loft" at the Huguang Lodge. Neither actor would give an inch. During the "Sitting in the Loft" half of the performance, when Yan Poxi [Guifeng] makes fun of Song Jiang [Old Tan], [Guifeng] really pulled out all the stops and Old Tan could not bear it. Old Tan said, "On the basis of our twenty years of friendship, you should leave me with a little face." Guifeng replied, "Who doesn't know what our friendship has been like? What face is there to leave?" When they got to the "Murdering Yan Poxi" part of the play, Old Tan's frustration had been building up for a long time. So he gathered his strength and threw all his energy into it, doing every imaginable movement stunt and prolonging the murder of Poxi. Guifeng was extremely tired and he pleaded with him, saying: "Hurry up and finish me off, will you?" The whole house roared with laughter. This play lasted half an hour longer than the typical production.[171]

As this passage suggests, performances could be altered to meet audience demands or actor idiosyncrasies—in this instance drawing out the death of Yan Poxi because the actors were trying to outperform each other, which made the production that much more entertaining for the spectators. It is certainly possible that such unscripted elements of performance—distractions by the humor and/or the sensuality of the dan performer or audience investment in backstage gossip—undercut the new morality of pihuang sister-in-law operas. Resisted readings of the gender politics of these plays were still possible. On the whole, however, the growing popularity of pihuang opera—transformed into "high art" via court patronage—helped disseminate and popularize a new aesthetic and moral machismo.[172]

Conclusion

The sister-in-law operas were the "B movies" of their times, whether rendered in the kunju or the pihuang musical genres.[173] Kunju performance of these plots made the illicit sex their central theme; the late nineteenth-century pihuang counterparts emphasized vigilante violence against women as their chosen form of titillation. Accordingly, these "B operas" reveal much about the imaginings of gender and class among urban playhouse audiences, especially among the classically educated, disaffected literati of the mid- to late Qing. The trajectory of sister-in-law narratives from the late

Ming through the late Qing posits two at times competing discourses of authenticity—one rooted in the "natural" desires of transgressive but alluring women, and the other in the heroic passions of righteous but violent male outlaws. Both narratives can be traced to the wave of literary production—and especially the outpouring of interest in vernacular literature and drama—in the late Ming. The intellectual currents of the late Ming validated both qing authenticity (figured in the desiring and desirous woman) and interest in all things folk (embodied in the *Water Margin* martial goodfellows). In elite discourses of late Ming politics and culture, both the nubile transgressive woman and the spontaneous male brigand served as regenerative "others," articulating through contrast critiques of degenerate male privilege, careerism, and cronyism. This study of the transformation of the sister-in-law episodes from the *Water Margin* story cycle shows that these themes, brought to the fore most forcefully in the late Ming, retained currency in public entertainment genres through the end of the imperial era. The urban playhouse therefore served as a site in which these ideas could be explored and these representations of gender and class transgression could be projected. If kunju performance gave preference to the gender story, pihuang suppressed that transgression narrative in favor of an equally quixotic class story. By the end of the nineteenth century, representation of the ruffian heroes of the *Water Margin* cycle had come full circle: the machismo vigilantism of sister-in-law plays had become the supernarrative and one that was successfully rendered only through violence against sexually potent women.

This transformation in cultural production accords with a shift in elite discourses surrounding gender and sexuality, in which the late Ming courtesan ideal was rejected in favor of wifely virtue. Susan Mann and others have located this turning point in the late eighteenth century; based on my reading of Qing opera scripts and performances, I have shown that the ebbing away of the qing ideal comes even later—after the Taiping Rebellion.[174] However much diluted, however bowdlerized by the camp and comedy of the urban playhouse stage, an ideal that romanticized feminine sexuality and that imagined female agency as a form of "speaking truth to power" was still alive in the eighteenth-century kunju performance tradition, in both *Garden* and the sister-in-law plays. One reason, I posit, that the gender story receded from view on the stage in the late nineteenth century has to do with the relative disappearance of the marginalized literati who patronized and wrote about opera performance in the capital city. Whether literally wiped out by the class warfare in Jiangnan and southern China or now too impoverished by the economic and military crises of the mid-nineteenth century to lead the same "bohemian" lifestyle of genteel poverty in the capital, the intellectual and emotional heirs to the late Ming romantic discourses on gender inversion and the diehard commercial kunju fans were considerably fewer in the post-Taiping period. They were literally missing from the seats in the playhouses. Perhaps, too, the concerns of the late Ming–inspired gender-transgression narratives paled in the face of new threats—both internal and external—to state power and gentry privilege.

At roughly the same time that the marginalized literati audience was decreasing, the Qing court for the most part succeeded in defusing the inflammatory potential of the urban commercial playhouses. The late nineteenth-century court patronage of pihuang opera helped elevate and further popularize an originally lowbrow performance tradition that gave preference to violence over sex. So long as vigilante justice was marshaled in support of sanctioned social and political norms, the court embraced the message of such plays. Their romanticized projection of male heroic action was a kind of energy that the court felt could be harnessed to its own civilizing mission. I attribute this, in part, to what some scholars have called the "peasantization" agenda of the Qing state. As Matthew Sommer has argued in regard to the state's enforcement of normative gender roles via legal statutes, a "new attention to gender performance . . . went hand in hand with the project of status leveling" whereby the state's own authority was bolstered and secured by establishing gender norms for all subjects that transcended class distinctions.[175] The regulation of sexuality was an arena in which the state could project its power and publicize its claim to moral authority, perhaps the one arena in which the court could still claim unquestioned authority at the end of the nineteenth century.

This parallel development—diminished attendance at commercial theater by the marginalized but learned kunju-loving crowd, coupled with court appropriation of the aesthetics and moralities of the pihuang performance tradition—reshaped the dynamics of the urban commercial playhouse. As court resistance to commercial opera gave way to sponsorship, and, ironically, as playhouses penetrated into more central locations within the capital city, their role as spaces for articulating less than orthodox—even subversive—values contracted.

Coda

Xu Daling, professor of Qing history at Peking University, once challenged his students: "How can you do Qing history if you don't understand Peking opera?"[1] The late Professor Xu's insight captures the spirit of this study of opera in Qing-dynasty Beijing. Commercial opera in the Qing capital from circa 1770 to 1900 was situated at the intersection of state power and commercial interests; it refracted literati discontent and ethnic tensions; it blurred the lines between public and private life (enabling display of private desires in public); and it offered a stage (literally and figuratively) upon which to act out gender and class transgressions.

This narrative has presented opera in the capital as a site of resistance—some imagined, some real—to normative ideologies and practices of gender order, class hierarchy, and state authority. Expressions of that resistance are found in the multiple kinds of inversions of power that played out both in the plays that were staged and in the social world of playhouse dynamics. Urban commercial opera of the Qing staged risqué and subversive comedies replete with sex and outlawry; its elite male fans delighted in the gender-bending eroticism of the transvestite stage; its spectacle and emotional appeal induced officials—both Han and Banner—to violate laws prohibiting their patronage of commercial playhouses; and the attendant demimonde culture that it generated recognized money and power above all else, often to the dismay of those who possessed (or claimed to possess) the merely symbolic capital of learning and good taste. These inversions of power were part of its attraction but also part of what made urban opera potentially seditious—or at least disruptive—especially for the Qing court and other guardians of the dominant social and moral order, although the metaphors of power inversion on display in the theater never manifested themselves as an overt challenge to the state.

Each part of this study has approached opera from a different perspective: Part 1 looked at opera in discourse; Part 2, at opera in social practice; and Part 3, at opera as performance. When these three levels of analysis are examined together, it becomes clear that although the playhouse served as a critical public space, it never coalesced into an oppositional force that might qualify it as a "public sphere." Here, in summary, I begin with the narrowest focus, opera as performance, thence to the discourses surrounding opera, and finally to the social role of opera in the Qing metropolis, in each case assessing the various manifestations of gender and class inversions and the extent to which they constituted a threat to the existing social order.

The disruption of gender and class order is of central concern to many of the dramas played out on the urban commercial stage. Performed renditions of *Garden* delighted audiences by showing Cui'er, the pretty young seamstress, and Steamed-Bun, the lowly yamen runner, outwitting Ma Fengzhi, the powerful political crony. Audience sympathies were directed toward the poor and downtrodden, sometimes male, but typically female. The cautionary morals of the *Water Margin* sister-in-law plays fell away when only the flirtation scenes were chosen for performance in the playhouses, thereby transforming the female antiheroes—Yan Poxi, Pan Jinlian, and Pan Qiaoyun—into sexually desirable leads, at least within the kunju repertoire. Such excerpts turned the commercial playhouses into public sites for male indulgence in romantic fantasy—fantasy further sustained by the possibility of purchasing the beauties on the stage for companionship and dalliance. Here, perhaps more fully than in the home, men of some means (although not just the high elite) could lighten the yoke of social prescript and give rein to private desires.

But the desiring and desirable woman trope that was invoked in *Garden* and the *Water Margin*–based operas was also tinged with greater significance, at least in the minds of the literati aficionados of drama. Tapping into the late Ming discourse of the beautiful woman as emblem of spontaneity and authenticity, operas that featured gender transgression were also obliquely about social transformation. The cohort of learned men who cataloged the late eighteenth- and early nineteenth-century urban opera theater envisioned themselves as participating in a trans-dynastic conversation about authenticity and self-worth. In *Garden*, inversions of gender and class order, represented by the figures of the heroine, Cui'er, and the clown, Steamed-Bun, who together fight corruption and restore justice with their own wit and courage, restore equilibrium to the social realm. Commercial Kun opera performance offered audiences stories in which clever women saved the day, romantic couples entered into extramarital liaisons, attractive youths (costumed as attractive women) initiated sexual encounters, and moralizing commentary about such deviations from the prescriptive ideal was temporarily put on hold. That audiences would sit through scene after scene of such plays (sometimes even on the same day) suggests just how popular this theme was. Whether playgoers simply indulged in the fantasy or read something personally or socially meaningful into these plays, the commercial opera theater carved out a legitimate space for sentimental inclination and sensational license within a quasi-public (all-male) setting.[2]

There were limits, however, to just how transgressive these flirtation plays could be. The romantic comedies of the playhouse worked out a balance between titillation and transgression. The ribald humor of these plays, while an affront to neo-Confucian propriety and decorum, nonetheless probably made the gender inversions of the plots less socially threatening. As comedy devolved into camp and parody, instead of offering audiences another world of social possibilities, the exaggerated performances of the clowns (and even of some dan actors) exploded the potential realism of that imaginary world.[3] Even so, the playhouse afforded all its constituents—actors as well as audiences—opportunities for self-fashioning.[4] Whether it was a dan actor choosing to accentuate the eroticism of a scene, a merchant posing as magnanimous patron, or a down-and-out literatus playing the culture aesthete, the literal and figurative role-playing of the commercial opera venue enabled participants to transcend themselves, and that potential for self-projection empowered all playhouse constituents with a liberating modicum of social agency. Surely, this too was one of the attractions and delights of the opera theater.

Perhaps the best examples of this social role-playing come from the avid opera fans who captured both the fantasies and realities of metropolitan opera in their flower registers. The flower register was a text that imagined the boy actresses as courtesan-like beauties. The dan actors—doubly stigmatized by career and cross-dressed feminine identity—were championed by their literati admirers. If the feminized victimization of their lives made them ripe material for allegories of unjustly subjugated talent and virtue, their physical charms and performative gifts gave them an affective sway over their far more powerful fans. Beauty, talent, even vulnerability, gave them the potential to transcend their lowly status (even if only fleetingly), to disrupt the social hierarchy, and to bring down men of real wealth and stature. Huapu writers exulted precisely in these stories of inversion, dishing up gossip about such-and-such an official moved to suicide by rejection or the upstart merchant so-and-so driven to financial ruin by his passions.

However much marginalized literati connoisseurs took satisfaction (even solace) in examples of social and gender inversion drawn from the world of performance, their guides to the opera theater were not simply self-serving morality tales. Actors—at least those talented enough to make it into the registers—probably got something out of them, too. The publicity engendered by such writings brought them fame, more fans, and better economic prospects. Hence, the stories in flower registers about actors such as Wei Changsheng and Chen Yinguan, whose rise to stardom reportedly brought them wealth that far outstripped their place in the status hierarchy. For the great majority of actors who did not strike it rich, the publicity generated through such guides to the acting demimonde at least won them fame for skill and virtue—a reputation that would have, if nothing else, made it more likely that they could make their living by selling their acting skills rather than sex.

Turning from the transgressions in flower-register discourse to those in social practice, we can see that some were more threatening than others. Of the various "boundary crossings" fostered by the metropolitan playhouse, the cross-dressing of the commercial stage (and its sideline market in male prostitution) was not regarded as a particularly alarming form of gender transgression. Although the playing out of sexual fantasies in public gave pause to the state and other upholders of social norms, it was, after all, simply long-accepted convention for young boys to play female roles. The blurring of ethnic and class distinctions within the audiences, however, became causes of great concern to the Qing court and, in some instances, to learned elites. Fear of dilution of the Manchu Way informed court regulation of commercial opera from the late Qianlong years into the first half of the nineteenth century. The social "transvestism" within the playhouse, in which wealthy merchants mimicked the cultural habits of the literati elite and played patron to the actors, provoked far more anxiety among the socially marginalized connoisseurs than any crossings-over of gender boundaries. By reading the discourses of social inversion side by side with social practice, we begin to see the limitations to resistance within the playhouse venue. In their preferred dramas and in their writings about actors and opera, these marginalized elites may have dreamed of finding common cause with women and others of low status, but at the same time they shunned identification (much less solidarity) with the mercantile clientele of the commercial theaters. Though cultural elites may have shared the romantic fantasies of the stage with merchants and other patrons, common sociability in the playhouses bred contempt for rather than common cause with fellow members of the audience.

The flower registers reveal that the disaffected literati who patronized the theater did identify to a certain extent with the actors about whom they wrote. This gesture of recognition on the part of the educated connoisseurs, however, was for the most part predicated on the literati's deep-seated awareness of the enormous status gulf that actually existed between actors and their educated aficionados. Perhaps even more daunting to any thoughts of the theater as a site of social resistance to court-supported social norms (or to alternative imaginings of social power), commercial actors, I suggest, were unreliable partners in resistance to those norms.[5] To maintain their marketability, actors had to cater to audience demands, but they also had to modify their performance to circumnavigate the many court regulations on opera genre in the capital. When court edicts excoriated qinqiang opera as being too racy and banned its performance in the environs of Beijing, commercial troupes responded both by altering the name of their performance style (a purely formalistic change) and by curbing the genre's most egregious excesses of wanton display (a substantive change). Preservation of their livelihood demanded that troupes be equally attentive to audience taste and court interdiction, so actors modified their own performances—simultaneously evading proscriptions and censoring themselves. And this tendency toward caution and self-censorship made the acting troupes less than ideal partners in offering an alternative vision of the social order. For all its potential to disrupt gender and social hierarchies, then, the commercial playhouse never was sufficiently secure from state intervention; political suasion and economic coercion always impinged upon the dynamics of the playhouse such that it never coalesced into a site for oppositional politics.

. . .

This study of opera in the city also has presented a narrative about the eventual co-optation of metropolitan theater by the court toward the end of the Qing dynasty. At the beginning of the period under evaluation, in the last quarter of the eighteenth century, commercial opera—albeit always subject to the twin pincers of court surveillance and market demand—retained some autonomy from the state. By 1900, through patronage of commercial performance, the court had for the most part succeeded in taming the inflammatory potential of the urban theatrical marketplace, and opera had become to a large extent the last bastion of the beleaguered court's expression of cultural power. Up to the mid-nineteenth century, the farther one got from Beijing, the more the court's edicts were up to local officials to enforce (or not). Toward the end of the dynasty, court taste and popular taste were so in tune that edicts and enforcement hardly mattered anywhere (or at least mattered less and less).

This transformation is seen most dramatically in the court's purposeful patronage of the once lowbrow pihuang opera; as the late nineteenth-century sister-in-law scripts show, court and city versions of these operas were nearly indistinguishable, and circulation of both operas and actors between court and commercial performance became the norm. Manifestation of the Qing court's less hostile and more engaged attitude toward the opera marketplace is also evident in the reduced number of edicts and regulations concerning location and genre of opera. Still further reflections of this transformation appear in the newly forged aesthetics of entertainment violence and masculine vigor. The transformation is likewise evident even in the flower registers, for it is in the third quarter of the nineteenth century when opera connoisseurs begin to compose biographies for actors specializing in the older male role types.

Thus, we can isolate a real sea change about the middle of the nineteenth century: in the court's relationship to urban commercial theater, in elite preferences in opera, and in shifting sympathies toward gender and class transgression as they were played out onstage. As the pihuang sister-in-law scripts reveal, the female-centered narrative of sex, romance, and agency (so prominent in commercial kunju performance) was suppressed in favor of a male-centered narrative of vigilante violence. This represented a shifting class aesthetic as well, since the pihuang operas were lowbrow in origin. Spearheaded by the court, but also embraced by a wider audience (including elites) in commercial venues, the elevation and dissemination of the narrative dominant in lowbrow opera were in large part a response to the cataclysmic crisis of the mid-nineteenth century: the Taiping Rebellion.

Opera in the capital before the Taiping Rebellion looks quite different from opera after it. I suspect that this was not just a matter of which genres gained popularity; nor was it simply the expression of a newly imposed cultural parochialism in the capital as supply routes from the south were suspended by the war, with dire consequences for both audiences and actors of the Jiangnan-identified kunju. Rather, opera became an important public site for performing patriotism and, for the Qing court, for "performing" ethnicity. The new configuration of ethnic identity the court wished to project was refracted through the class and gender narratives played out upon the metropolitan stage.

Recent scholarship on Qing ethnicity has identified the eighteenth century as a critical moment in the (re)construction of Manchu identity. In the eighteenth century, faced with increasing Manchu acculturation to Han practices, the Qing state insisted on maintaining (or, by some accounts, inventing) cultural difference.[6] We see this preoccupation in the sphere of urban opera through the many court regulations regarding Manchu and Banner participation in playhouse and demimonde culture—an anxiety typically expressed as a concern over ethnic pollution. Opera in the early Qing was a Han-identified cultural form; for Manchus and bannermen to be seduced by it risked erosion of ethno-dynastic particularity, and, by implication, the logic of Manchu apartheid.

The eighteenth-century court also had class biases in regard to opera. When the Qing court decreed which genres of opera would be allowed within the commercial marketplace of the capital, this veiled a subtle judgment about social class. Commercial kunju performance (despite its sometimes bawdy story content) was permissible because the court trusted the more literate crowds that it attracted to control themselves; the rowdy huabu opera, however, with its earthy origins and populist audiences, was cause for concern. And thus, while edicts concerning opera genre often spoke in terms of morality, the concern at their heart was the maintenance of social order in the capital.

The crisis of the mid-nineteenth century changed all that. In the face of the Taiping attack on Qing sovereignty, which was waged as both class and ethnic warfare, the court chose to identify with and promote the values and messages of the lowbrow pihuang plays—outlawry (and, more particularly, violence against sexually transgressive women) performed in the service of moral order. This aesthetic preference presumably was not entirely cynical; the central power players of the Xianfeng, Tongzhi, and Guangxu reigns seem to have genuinely enjoyed pihuang. But the lowbrow sympathies of pihuang, I suggest, made it especially appealing to the ruling clique in part because the court identified this aesthetic with what it meant to be culturally Chinese. Threatened by reason of its ethnic difference, the Manchu court closed ranks politically with the Han elite but culturally with Han commoners; in so doing, it helped construct a new cultural identity for both the state and society.[7] In other words, the Qing court waged a rather effective propaganda counterwar against the Taipings in which it championed a socially conservative commoner aesthetic over a more permissive literati one, then erased from it the markers of class and ethnicity, and promoted this new social vision as something quintessentially "Chinese." In this process the more indulgent, even forgiving, attitudes toward women's sexuality and gender transgression (which had been so integral to Qing playhouse performance) were sacrificed to moral rectitude and the reassertion of patriarchal authority. As defenders of this ideal cultural order, the Manchu court also finessed ethnic difference, reinventing itself, once again, as the legitimate ruler of the empire. Metropolitan opera, then, became a key stage upon which the court renegotiated ethnic identity (via gender and class) in the face of racially charged overt political resistance.

There is a double irony here. Through choosing the glorification of vigilante violence in the pihuang plays over the sexual license of the kunju repertoire, the court was ostensibly opting for the more disruptive social vision, and this precisely at a time when the regime was fighting for its life against an insurrection led by violent, *Water Margin*–type toughs. But perhaps the pihuang message appealed to the court as a way to project solidarity with the social classes most likely to be wooed by the Taiping movement. The court, ostensibly taking the lead in reshaping aesthetic taste, was perhaps also engaged in a desperate game of catch-up, responding to the preferences of the majority of petty urbanites within the capital playhouses (silent only in that they have left fewer traces in the textual record), who "voted with their feet" for operas that exulted in vigilante justice and the new masculinist ethos.[8] To the extent that the Qing state's anti-Taiping and post-Taiping cultural agenda was effective, it won over the hearts and minds of commoners by appealing to popular moral values rather than to elite sensibilities. And, I suggest, the crisis was of such magnitude that elites of all ethnicities were also forced to make a "you're-with-us-or-against-us" choice in cultural preferences. The romanticized gender- and class-transgression discourse that had held such currency in literati cultural production since the late Ming paled in the face of the mid-nineteenth-century threats to elite status and privilege; and the (less Jiangnan-centered) elites who withstood the crisis tended to take their cue from the court when it came to cultural patronage. In opera, this meant a newly acquired taste for the lowbrow-inflected stories and messages of pihuang plays, now reinvented as high culture.

One of the consequences of this realignment of cultural authority was the rise of a new moralism. Shrill proponents of a kind of Confucian "fundamentalism," whether moralizing philanthropists like Yu Zhi in Jiangnan or the revitalized Tongzhi Court in Beijing, captured the cultural mainstream. This was happening at the same time that the social and institutional power of the Qing state was devolving to local control. Perhaps, then, we can think of this power play by the court in the realm of culture as turning to cultural gestures when social and political power was all but lost. Clearly, it was not enough to preserve the threatened dynasty; its most enduring impact was the reshaping of the tenor of the last stage of late imperial Confucianism, or what we might call, a "first stand" of Confucian conservatism.[9]

By the end of the nineteenth century, through its preferences in and patronage of opera, the court had largely won the battle over moral values within the commercial playhouses. The state's co-optation of the opera marketplace was never complete; the nature of theatrical performance—those inevitable gaps between page and stage and between performance and audience reception—meant that there was always room for competing interpretations. Late nineteenth-century audiences still enthusiastically patronized the playhouses and reveled in the imaginary world they put on display. Many of the interpersonal dynamics of the playhouse continued unabated; the demimonde culture, with its attendant market in actor-catamites, did not fall into abeyance until the early years of the twentieth century (at which time these practices were then targeted for attack by modern reformers and altered by the reintroduction of women onto the stage and into audiences). Nevertheless, compared with the commercial opera theater circa 1770–1860, the urban playhouse had lost much of its independence from state interference in ideological content, and consequently, much of its potential as a site for expression of heterodox aspirations, desires, and fantasies. As a result, the playhouse also became less central as a site for public discourse within the urban setting.

I emphasize this mid- to late nineteenth-century turning point because I think it signals the closure of an era of potential and possibility for metropolitan opera; through contrast, it also underscores the vibrancy and variety of urban public discourse in the eighteenth- and early nineteenth-century capital. It is important, too, I think, to mark the sharp rift between pre- and post-Taiping urban culture because so much of our understanding of Qing China has been shaped by the contours of culture—and, in particular, the socially restrictive blend of neo-Confucian moralities—that emerged in the later half of the nineteenth century. The foregoing study of opera in the city helps undermine certain stereotypes that have come down to us as the monolithic "Chinese tradition." We are often presented with a picture of the "straitjacket-like" effect of late neo-Confucian thought on social values and practice. No one would deny the very real effect that elite moral injunction and state inculcation exerted upon this "civilizing project" and social practice. Many had little power to resist such pressure. But the example of classically trained men participating in the fantasies of the Qing urban theater shows that the moralistic pietism that we often take for *de*scription was in large part *pre*scription.

Reference Matter

APPENDIX ONE

Glossary of Drama Terms, Opera Genres, and Performance Role Types

Dramatic Terms

chuanqi 傳奇: Romance dramas; a form of dramatic composition popularized by literati playwrights during the Ming dynasty (and continuing through the Qing); typically made up of thirty to fifty scenes. Chuanqi became the basis for most operas and scene selections during Ming-Qing times.

zaju 雜劇: Variety plays; a form of dramatic composition begun during the Yuan dynasty (1279–1368); typically composed of four acts and, sometimes, an introductory "wedge" (*xiezi* 楔子) scene. Although plays in this structure continued to be written into the Qing, their popularity in performance waned relative to the chuanqi style of drama by the mid-Ming.

Opera Genres

bangzi 梆子: Rhythmic wooden-block opera; the name comes from the percussive blocks used to keep the beat of the music; especially associated with the musical and dialectal characteristics of northern and northwestern China; arias in this musical system are made up of simple parallel couplets; many regional styles of opera fall within the larger bangzi music system; operas in the bangzi musical system were considered far simpler and less sophisticated than Kun opera.

huabu 花部: Flowery opera; a generic designation for various regional styles of opera music other than kunju; generally considered lowbrow in comparison with yabu; the term was coined in the late eighteenth century.

Huiban 徽班: Hui troupes; often talked about as the "four great Hui troupes" (*sida huiban* 四大徽班), although there were in actuality more than four. The Hui troupes entered Beijing in the 1790s as part of the citywide performance festivities associated with the celebrations for the Qianlong emperor's eightieth birthday. The troupes stayed on in the city, establishing permanent performance runs through the playhouse circuits. Hui troupe actors also performed operas in the kunju style. The four most famous of the Hui troupes—Sanqing 三慶, Sixi 四喜, Chuntai 春臺, and Hechun 和春—were known for their skills, especially in pihuang opera, by the second half of the nineteenth century.

huidiao 徽調: Hui tunes; a style of music originally local to the region of Huizhou in what is present-day Anhui Province. This genre of opera was introduced into Beijing in the 1790s. Hui tunes are considered one of the important musical influences on the emergence of pihuang opera.

jingdiao 京調: Capital tunes; a variant term for the hybrid pihuang in circulation in the capital in the late nineteenth century.

jingqiang 京腔: Capital melody; a variant of Yiyang melody popular in the capital in the eighteenth century; becomes mixed with qinqiang by the end of the eighteenth century.

kunju 崑劇 (*kunqu* 崑曲, Kunshan *qiang* 崑山腔, *kunqiang* 崑腔): One of the four major musical systems of the mid-Ming; the genre developed in the mid-sixteenth century. The popularity of this genre, based on tunes and the dialect of the Kunshan (Suzhou) region, quickly spread throughout China. By the seventeenth century the genre had become the favored style of the elite, gaining recognition as the classical, or elegant, opera.

luantan 亂彈: Chaotic strumming; another term for huabu opera (originally conveying a derogatory attitude).

pihuang 皮簧: Designates the musical traditions that form the basis of what is now referred to as Peking opera (*jingju* 京劇). The two major musical styles of this genre include *xipi* 西皮 and *erhuang* 二簧. The neologism *pihuang* is a contraction of *xipi* and *erhuang*.

qinqiang 秦腔: A genre of opera associated with the musical and dialectal characteristics of the Shaanxi-Shanxi-Sichuan region; thought to have migrated along merchant trade routes to the capital in the late eighteenth century. The musical structure of qinqiang is within the bangzi musical system, in which the music is underscored by strong percussive beats and arias are composed of simple couplets of even line length.

yabu 雅部: Elegant opera; a generic designation for kunju, or Kun opera; the term was in circulation by the late seventeenth century.

Yiyang *qiang* 弋陽腔: Yiyang melody; one of the four major musical systems of the mid-Ming; the genre had spread throughout the empire by the late Ming; it acquired regional flavor and dialect characteristics in the various host locales; in Beijing this musical style was known as *yiqiang* 弋腔, or, alternatively, *jingqiang* 京腔 or *gaoqiang* 高腔. One of the two genres of opera music sanctioned by the Qing court, this style was popular in Beijing throughout much of the eighteenth century. By the late eighteenth century, the genre mixed with qinqiang.

Performance Role Types

dan 旦: The female role type.

> *daoma dan* 刀馬旦: Literally, the sword-and-horse dan; this role type specializes in plays with significant martial action; a common designation in pihuang-style operas.
>
> *fengyue dan* 風月旦: Romantic dan; typically this role type portrays romantic heroines of questionable moral repute.
>
> *guimen dan* 閨門旦: Boudoir dan; typically this role type portrays young romantic heroines in the kunju style.
>
> *hua dan* 花旦: Flower dan; typically this role type portrays young romantic or flirtatious women in pihuang-style opera.
>
> *lao dan* 老旦: Older female role; in production scripts, often abbreviated as *lao* 老.
>
> *liu dan* 六旦: An alternative designation for the guimen dan.
>
> *qingyi* 青衣: Literally, the blue-robed dan; young female lead in pihuang-style opera.
>
> *tie dan* 貼旦: Secondary young female role; in the scribal shorthand of production scripts this role type is often abbreviated as *zhan* 占.
>
> *wu dan* 武旦: A female role type that stresses martial skills.
>
> *xiao dan* 小旦: Secondary young female role; alternatively, can indicate a younger female romantic lead.
>
> *zheng dan* 正旦: Lead young female role.

sheng 生: Lead male role type.

> *lao sheng* 老生: Mature male lead; in production scripts often abbreviated as *sheng*.
>
> *wu sheng* 武生: A male role type that stresses martial skills.
>
> *xiao sheng* 小生: Younger male lead; often plays romantic characters.

chou 丑: Clown role type.

fu 付: Comic male; a designation used in chuanqi dramas and their kunju production-script variants; tended to play comic villains rather than likable clowns; the term fell out of use in pihuang scripts.

jing 淨: Character-actor male role; in pihuang opera often designated as the *hualian* 花臉, or painted-face role; typically these role types play larger-than-life characters—military generals, gods, villains, etc.

wai 外: An "extra," walk-on male role.

APPENDIX TWO

Scripts of *Feicui yuan* 翡翠園
(arranged by approximate production/copy date)

Multiscene Scripts

1. *Feicui yuan* 翡翠園. 1957 rpt. In *Guben xiqu congkan san ji* 古本戲曲叢刊三集, comp. Guben xiqu congkan bianji weiyuanhui. Beijing: Wenxue guji kanxingshe.

2. *Feicui yuan* (including: "Bainian" 拜年, "Shuofang" 說房, "Qiejiao" 切腳, "Zhuona" 捉拿, "Toudao" 投到, "Fushen" 覆審, "Daoling" 盜令, "Fangzou" 放走). Copy dated to 1749. Hand-copied by the Cao Family Weiyatang 維雅堂曹記. Name stamps on the cover page indicate that this script was once in the possession of a certain He Yongyan 何永言. Later this script became part of the private collection of Cheng Yanqiu 程硯秋. Held in the Traditional Drama Archive of the Zhongguo yishu yanjiuyuan 中國藝術研究院, Beijing.

3. *Feicui yuan chuanqi* 翡翠園傳奇. 2 vols. (Vol. 1 includes "Yubao" 預報, "Bainian" 拜年, "Shuofang" 說房, "Qiejiao" 切腳, "Shifang" 釋放, "Toudao" 投到, "Qianshen" 前審, "Houshen" 後審, "Daoling" 盜令, "Wusha" 誤殺. Vol. 2 includes versions of scenes 2, 3, 6, 17, 18, 19, 20, 21, and 24 [or "Youjie" 遊街] of the Guben edition.) Qing copy. Undated, but indicates awareness of the Guben version. Part of the Fu Xihua 傅惜華 Collection. Held in the Traditional Drama Archive of the Zhongguo yishu yanjiuyuan, Beijing.

4. *Feicui yuan* 翡翠園 (including "Yubao" 預報, "Bainian" 拜年, "Shuofang" 說房, "Qiejiao" 切腳, "Fangtao" 放逃, "Toudao" 投到, "Qianshen" 前審, "Houshen" 後審, "Youjie" 遊街.) Copy date of *bingxu* 丙戌 (1766? 1826? 1886?). Hand-copied by Han Yunshan 韓筠山. Later this script became part of the private collection of Cheng Yanqiu. Held in the Traditional Drama Archive of the Zhongguo yishu yanjiuyuan, Beijing.

5. *Feicui yuan* (including "Yubao" 預報, "Bainian" 拜年, "Moufang" 謀房, "Jianfu" 諫父, "Qiejiao" 切腳, "Enfang" 恩放, "Zishou" 自首, "Fushen" 副審, "Fengfang" 封房, "Daopai" 盜牌, "Shazhou" 殺舟, "Tuotao" 脫逃). In *Zhuibaiqiu* 綴白裘, comp. Wanhua zhuren 玩花主人 and Qian Decang 錢德蒼. In *Shanben xiqu congkan*, ed. Wang Qiugui 王秋桂, 65:2685–2770. 1770. Facsimile edition, Taipei: Taiwan xuesheng shuju, 1987.

6. *Feicui yuan ba chu shenduan pu* 翡翠園八出身段譜 (including "Yubao" 預報, "Bainian" 拜年, "Moufang" 謀房, "Qiejiao" 切腳, "Enfang" 恩放, "Zishou" 自首, "Fushen" 副審, "Houshen" 後審). Copy date of 11th month of Jiaqing 2 (1797). Hand-copied by Songzhai shi 松齋氏 for the Gengxintang 耕心堂. Gengxintang was a commercial publishing outlet for hand-copied drama and narrative performance scripts.[1] Recollated by Cao Xiling 曹錫齡. This script is now part of the Fu Xihua collection. Held in the Traditional Drama Archive of the Zhongguo yishu yanjiuyuan, Beijing.

7. *Feicui yuan kunyi quanben* 翡翠園昆弋全本. Early to mid-nineteenth century. The "kun-yi" designation—meaning a musical mix of kunqu and Yiyang-style arias—on the cover page suggests that the script dates to the first half of the nineteenth century. Cover page claims the script to be from the Sanqing Troupe 三慶班. Underneath a red strip of paper with a later cataloging number are written the characters Chen Changgeng 陳常賡. The script is copied word for word from the *Zhubaiqiu* edition. Later this script became part of the private collection of Mei Lanfang 梅蘭芳. Held in the Traditional Drama Archive of the Zhongguo yishu yanjiuyuan, Beijing.

8. *Feicui yuan* (including "Yubao" 預報, "Bainian" 拜年, "Moufang" 謀房, "Qiejiao" 切腳, "Enfang" 恩放, "Zishou" 自首, "Qianshen" 前審, "Houshen" 後審, "Daoling" 盜令, "Shazhou" 殺舟, "Youjie" 遊街, "Cuiyuan" 翠圓). Copy dated to 11 December 1861. Hand-copied by Du Shuangshou 杜雙壽 (style, Buyun 步雲). Du was an actor in the service of the court. The cover page has a stamp with Manchu writing, which reads "ineggidari ichemleme biyadari iundehei." This translates into Chinese as a four-character auspicious phrase meaning *rixin yuesheng* 日新月盛 or "May your days be many and your months plentiful." Held in the Rare Books Library, Peking University, Beijing.

9. *Feicui yuan* (including "Daoling" 盜令, "Shazhou" 殺舟, "Diaojian" 吊監, "Youjie" 遊街). In *Liuye qupu heng ji* 六也曲譜亨集, comp. Zhang Fen 張芬 (Yian zhuren 怡庵主人). Shanghai: Chaoji shuzhuang, 1908.

10. *Feicui yuan* (including "Yubao" 預報, "Bainian" 拜年, "Moufang" 謀房, "Jianfu" 諫父). In *Huitu jingxuan kunqu daquan* 繪圖精選崑曲大全, collection 2, comp. Zhang Fen. Shanghai: Shijie shuju, 1925.

Single or Two-Scene Scripts

11. "Dao lingpai zonggang" 盜令牌總綱 (one scene in a collection with three other scenes from other drama cycles). Copy dated to 2 May 1840. Hand-copied by the Cao Family Jinyutang 金玉堂曹記. Stamp on cover page reads "whistling rain and flowing clouds" (*xiaoyu xingyun* 嘯雨行雲). A strip of red

---

1. On Gengxintang, see Guo Jingrui 郭精銳, *Che wangfu quben yu jingju de xingcheng* 車王府曲本與京劇的形成, p. 22.

paper on the cover has the characters Chunshan 春山, an indication that Cao Chunshan 曹春山 (ca. mid- to late nineteenth century) once owned this script. Cao Chunshan worked as an actor in the court, which suggests that this script may have some relation to court (Shengping shu 昇平署) provenance. Sloppy handwriting; likely an actor's edition. Later this script became part of the private collection of Cheng Yanqiu. Held in the Traditional Drama Archive of the Zhongguo yishu yanjiuyuan, Beijing.

12. "Daoling" 盜令 (one scene in a two-volume collection of single-scene scripts from eight drama cycles entitled *Shengping shu chaoben dan zhe bazhong* 昇平署鈔本單折八種). Includes percussive beat notation (*guban* 鼓板). Qing Shengping shu hand-copied edition. Undated but post-1827, likely ca. mid- to late nineteenth century. Later this script became part of the private collection of Qi Rushan 齊如山. Held in the Traditional Drama Archive of the Zhongguo yishu yanjiuyuan, Beijing.

13. "Daoling" 盜令 and "Shazhou" 殺舟 (two scenes in a collection of four scenes from various drama cycles). Undated, but an extraneous note written on the back cover of the booklet mentions an unrelated incident on 8 November 1861; hence this copy had to be in circulation prior to that date. Hand-copied by Xin 鑫記. Sokodo 雙紅堂 Collection, Tokyo University.

14. "Daoling" 盜令 and "Shazhou" 殺舟 (two scenes in a collection of eight scenes from various drama cycles). Dated *guisi* 癸巳 (1833? 1893?). Hand-copied by Wang for Luquantang 祿泉堂王記. Part scripts for the role of Zhao Cuiniang 趙翠娘. Academia Sinica Popular Culture Collection. Also included in *Su wenxue congkan* 俗文學叢刊, ed. Huang Kuanzhong 黃寬重 et al., ser. 1, 84:379–95. Taipei: Xin wenfeng chuban youxian gongsi, 2001. Note that the order of the scenes has been reversed in *Su wenxue congkan*.

15. "Shazhou" 殺舟. Undated. Ca. late-nineteenth century. Part script for Ma Rong 麻容. Included in *Su wenxue congkan*, ser. 1, 84:65–78.

16. "Daopai" 盜牌 (in a collection of eight scenes from various drama cycles). Ca. nineteenth century. Includes arias only, with cue lines and musical notation. Hand-copied by Sheng 盛記. Held in the Traditional Drama Archive of the Zhongguo yishu yanjiuyuan, Beijing.

17. "Daoling" 盜令 and "Diaojian" 吊監. Ca. late nineteenth century (Guangxu era). Hand-copied. Includes musical score. Cover page indicates that this comes from the collection of Xu Nongbo 徐穠伯. Beijing.

18. "Youjie" 遊街. Ca. late nineteenth century (Guangxu era). Hand-copied. Includes musical score. Cover page indicates that this comes from the collection of Xu Nongbo. Beijing.

19. "Youjie" 遊街 (in a collection of five scenes from various drama cycles). Ca. nineteenth century. Part script for the character Zhao Cuiniang. Hand-copied by Qian Lanxiang 錢蘭香記. Held in the Traditional Drama Archive of the Zhongguo yishu yanjiuyuan, Beijing.

APPENDIX THREE

Mostly Rare, Hand-Copied Scripts of *Saozo Wo* 嫂子我 Plays

(arranged by title and approximate production/copy date)

Cuiping shan chuanqi quanjuan 翠屏山傳奇全卷. In 27 scenes. Copy dated to 1731 by Duanyi tang Wan Shi 端宜堂萬氏. This script is an exact replica of the version included in *Guben xiqu congkan*, ser. 2, vol. 76. Recollated by the Cao Family Jinyutang studio 金玉堂曹記 in 1855. Part of the Cheng Yanqiu 程彥秋 Collection. Held in the Traditional Drama Archive of the Zhongguo yishu yanjiuyuan, Beijing.

Cuiping shan zongmu 翠屏山總目. Copy dated to September 1841. Recorded by Cao 曹 (Chunshan 春山?) (act. mid-nineteenth century). Held in the Traditional Drama Archive of the Zhongguo yishu yanjiuyuan, Beijing.

Cuiping shan 翠屏山 (including "Bainian" 拜年, "Qianghua" 搶花, "Jieyi" 結義, "Zengchuan" 贈串, "Jiaozhang" 交賬, "Songli" 送禮, "Foya" 佛牙, "Zhiqing" 知情, "Jiulou" 酒樓, "Fankuang" 反誆, "Zhutuo" 誅陀, "Sheji" 設計, "Baoxin" 報信, "Shashan" 殺山). Copy dated to November 1861. Hand-copied by Du Shuangshou 杜雙壽 (style name, Buyun 步雲). Du was a commercial actor taken into court service in 1861. The cover page has a stamp with Manchu writing, which reads "ineggidari ichemleme biyadari iundehei." This translates into Chinese as a four-character auspicious phrase meaning *rixin yuesheng* 日新月盛 or "May your days be many and your months plentiful." Held in the Rare Books Library, Beijing University.

"Cuiping shan zongben" 翠屏山總本. Qing Shengping shu script, ca. 1891–93. Version performed at court by Tan Xinpei 譚鑫培 (1847–1917) and Yu Yuqin 余玉琴 (1868–1939). In *Cheng cang Qing Nanfu Shengping shu juben erji* 程藏清南府昇平署劇本二集, no. 174. Part of the Cheng Yanqiu Collection. Held in the Traditional Drama Archive of the Zhongguo yishu yanjiuyuan, Beijing.

"Cuiping shan" 翠屏山. Ca. late nineteenth, early twentieth century. In *Jingdiao ximu* 京調戲目, no. 17. Held in the Traditional Drama Archive of the Zhongguo yishu yanjiuyuan, Beijing.

"Cuiping shan" 翠屏山. Ca. twentieth century. Held in the Beijing yishu yanjiusuo archives, Beijing.

"Cuiping shan" 翠屏山. Copy of a Wang Lianping 王連平 (1898–?) performance script. Held in the Beijing yishu yanjiusuo archives, Beijing.

"Cuiping shan" 翠屏山 (with "Sha yinseng" 殺淫僧 and "Shuang toushan" 雙投山). 1912. In *Huitu jingdu sanqing ban jingdiao jiaoben shiji* 繪圖京都三慶班京調腳本十集, vol. 10. Sokodo Collection, Tokyo University.

"Cuiping shan, Shixiu" 翠屏山、石秀. Copy dated to 15 April 1896 by Li Shouchen 李壽臣 (1882–1918) of Wenxingtang 文杏堂. Held in the Capital Library, Beijing.

"Cuiping shan, Shixiu" 翠屏山、石秀. Qing manuscript. Held in the Capital Library, Beijing.

"Hou you zongmu" 後誘總目. Qing manuscript. Copy dated to 1853 by the Qinghe Cao Family Jinyutang studio 清和金玉堂曹; recopy dated to 1855. Held in the Traditional Drama Archive of the Zhongguo yishu yanjiuyuan, Beijing.

"Hou you zongmu" 後誘總目. Qing manuscript. Recopied by the Cao Family Weiyatang studio 維雅堂曹記, dated to 1855. Held in the Traditional Drama Archive of the Zhongguo yishu yanjiuyuan, Beijing.

"Huo zhuo" 活捉. In *Huaining Cao shi cangqu jingju ji* 懷寧曹氏藏曲京劇集. Copy dated to 15 January 1909 by the Cao Family Jinyutang studio 清和金玉堂曹. Held in the Traditional Drama Archive of the Zhongguo yishu yanjiuyuan, Beijing.

"Huo zhuo" 活捉. Ca. late nineteenth century. Qing Shengping shu script. Held in the Beijing yishu yanjiusuo archives, Beijing.

"Jiaozheng 'Zuolou sha Xi' jingdiao quanben" 校正坐樓殺媳京調全本. Ca. late nineteenth, early twentieth century. In *Jingdiao ximu* 京調戲目, no. 11. Held in the Traditional Drama Archive of the Zhongguo yishu yanjiuyuan, Beijing.

"Jie cha" 借茶 and "Huo zhuo" 活捉. Qing manuscript, n.d. In *Kunqu qi chu* 崑曲七齣. Held in the Capital Library, Beijing.

"Jie cha" 借茶 and "Huo zhuo" 活捉. Ca. late nineteenth century. Likely Qing Shengping shu script. Held in the Beijing yishu yanjiusuo archives, Beijing.

"Jie cha" 借茶. Cyclical date of *renchen* 壬辰 (1832 or 1892?). Recopied by Jingqing shi 靜清氏. Held in the Capital Library, Beijing.

"Sha pi zongmu" 殺皮總目. Copy dated to 20 January 1853. Hand-copied by the Cao Family Jinyutang 金玉堂曹記. Stamp on cover page reads "Whistling rain and flowing clouds" (*xiaoyu xingyun* 嘯雨行雲). Sloppy handwriting; likely an actor's edition. Held in the Traditional Drama Archive of the Zhongguo yishu yanjiuyuan, Beijing.

"Sha pi zongjiang" 殺皮總講. Qing. Bieye tang 別埜堂 edition. Bieye tang was a commercial copy house for drama and narrative arts performance. It operated stalls at the various temple fairs in Beijing. Academia Sinica Popular Culture Collection, microfilm reel 209. Microfilm held in the University of California, Berkeley Library.

"Shizi lou zongben" 獅子樓總本. Ca. late nineteenth, early twentieth century. Likely Qing Shengping shu script. Held in the Beijing yishu yanjiusuo archives, Beijing.

Shuihu ji 水滸記 (including "Shijin" 拾巾, "Qian you" 前誘, "Hou you" 後誘, "Huo zhuo" 活捉). Qing manuscript, n.d. Held in the Traditional Drama Archive of the Zhongguo yishu yanjiuyuan, Beijing.

"Tiaolian caiyi" 挑簾裁衣. Copy of a Li Wanchun 李萬春 (1911–85) performance script. Held in the Beijing yishu yanjiusuo archives, Beijing.

"Wulong yuan" 烏龍院. Ca. 1880–90? Qing Shengping shu script. Held in the Traditional Drama Archive of the Zhongguo yishu yanjiuyuan, Beijing.

"Wulong yuan" 烏龍院. Guangxu lithograph edition. In *Huitu jingdiao shiqiji* 繪圖京調十七集, vol. 5. Cover page indicates that this is the script of the "first-rate star of the capital, Wanzhandeng" 京都頭等名角萬盞燈曲本 and "the original edition of the Xiang'e xingyunlou of the capital" 京都響遏行雲樓原稿. Sokodo Collection, Tokyo University.

"Wulong yuan" 烏龍院. Collation dated to 29 September 1912. Copied by the Zhenglü xingwenshe 正律興文社. Held in the Traditional Drama Archive of the Zhongguo yishu yanjiuyuan, Beijing.

"Wulong yuan" 烏龍院. Ca. early twentieth century. Manuscript. In *Jingju shisan ji* 京劇十三集. 6 vols. Part of Mei Lanfang's 梅蘭芳 collection. Held in the Traditional Drama Archive of the Zhongguo yishu yanjiuyuan, Beijing.

"Wulong yuan" 烏龍院. Shanghai lithograph edition, Jicheng tushu gongsi 集成圖書公司, n.d. In *Huitu jingdu sanqing ban jingdiao shierji* 繪圖京都三慶班京調十二集, vol. 1. Inner frontispiece indicates that these scripts are from the "Sanqing Troupe" and "in the capital melody and Shan-Shaan bangzi styles" (Sanqing ban jingdiao Shan-Shaan bangzi qiang 三慶班京調山陝梆子腔). Sokodo Collection, Tokyo University.

"Xi shu" 戲叔 and "Bie xiong" 別兄. Qing manuscript, n.d. In *Kunyi quxuan* 崑弋曲選. Part of the Fu Xihua 傅惜華 Collection. Held in the Traditional Drama Archive of the Zhongguo yishu yanjiuyuan, Beijing.

Yixia ji 義俠記 (including "Da hu" 打虎, "Mai bing" 賣餅, "Ying hu" 迎虎, "She fu" 設伏, "Xi shu" 戲叔, "Bie xiong" 別兄, "Tiao lian" 挑簾, "Cai yi" 裁衣, "Zhuo jian" 捉奸, "Fu du" 服毒, "Xian hun" 顯魂, "Sha sao" 殺嫂, "Chou fa" 籌罰, "Wu hai" 誣害, "Feiyun pu" 飛雲浦, "Yuanyang lou" 鴛鴦樓). Copy dated to December 1861. Hand-copied by Du Shuangshou. The cover page has a stamp with Manchu writing, which reads "ineggidari ichemleme biyadari iundehei." Held in the Rare Books Library, Beijing University.

Yixia ji 義俠記. Ca. late nineteenth, early twentieth century. Performance version formerly in the collection of Yu Lianquan 于連泉 (1900–1967) [stage name, Xiao Cuihua 小翠花, also 筱翠花]. Held in the Beijing yishu yanjiusuo archives, Beijing.

Yixia ji zong ben 義俠記總本. Copy dated to 4 September 1931. Based on a Qing Shengping shu script. Held in the Beijing yishu yanjiusuo archives, Beijing.

"Zhuojian fudu" 捉奸服毒, "Jinlian xi shu" 金蓮戲叔, and "Wu Er bie xiong" 武二別兄. Ca. late nineteenth-, early twentieth-century manuscript. In *Jingdiao ximu* 京調戲目. Held in the Traditional Drama Archive of the Zhongguo yishu yanjiuyuan, Beijing.

Character List

a-ge 阿哥
andian ben 安殿本
antou ben 案頭本
"Bai xiang" 拜香
Baiben Zhang 百本張
Baishe zhuan 白蛇傳
Baitasi 白塔寺
baixue 白雪
"Banchang guaiqi" 搬場拐妻
Banqiao zaji 板橋雜記
baojuan 寶卷
baotou 包頭
baqi zidi 八旗子弟
Bazi 八姊
Beici guangzheng pu 北詞廣正譜
Beili zhi 北里志
beiqu qupai 北曲曲牌
bense 本色
Bi Wei 畢魏
"Biao dasao beiwa" 表大嫂背娃
Bing Yang Xiong 病楊雄
Bukong Heshang 不空和尚
"Cai yiliao Jinlian ye he" 裁衣料金蓮野合
Caizi-Jiaren Mudan ting 才子佳人牡丹亭
"Cangzhou" 藏舟
Canhua xiaoshi 餐花小史
Caozhu yichuan 草珠一串
ce 冊
Cemao yutan 側帽餘譚
"Chan zi" 產子
Chang'an kanhua ji 長安看花記
changgong xi 唱工戲

Changshen dian	長生殿
Changyin ge	暢音閣
Chao Gai	晁蓋
chayuan	茶園
Chen Miaochang	陳妙常
Chen Yanheng	陳彥衡
Chen Yinguan	陳銀官
Cheng Changgeng	程長庚
Cheng Qiong	程瓊
"Chi xie"	叱邪
chizi	池子
chou jie	愁結
"Chu xiong"	除凶
Chuanqi huikao biaomu	傳奇匯考標目
chuiqiang	吹腔
Chunming mengyu lu	春明夢餘錄
Chunxiang	春香
"Cifu"	賜福
Congshen	從諗
"Cuiping shan dui ming xinji"	翠屏山對明心跡
Cuiqing ban	翠慶班
da chawei	打茶圍
"Da hu"	打虎
da xi	大戲
Dajuesi	大覺寺
dao guanxiang	倒官廂
Dashalar	大柵欄
daye	大爺
De Shuoting	得碩亭
Deng Jiugong	鄧九公
Deshengyuan	德勝園
Deyi lu	得一錄
di	笛
Diehua yinguan shichao	蝶花吟館詩鈔
Dingzhi chunqiu	鼎峙春秋
Ditan	地壇
Dongjing menghua lu	東京夢華錄
Du Fu	杜甫
Du Liniang	杜麗娘
Du Mu	杜牧
"Duan qiao"	斷橋
"Dui hua"	堆花
Dumen zayong	都門雜詠
Dumen zhuiyu	都門贅語

Dumen zhuzhici	都門竹枝詞
fagong yazou	法宮雅奏
"Fang shu cezi"	訪鼠測字
Fangcaoyuan	芳草園
fanli	凡例
fanzhuang	飯莊
feiniao yiren	飛鳥依人
fen bao	分包
"Fen su"	憤訴
Feng Menglong	馮夢龍
Fengcheng huashi	鳳城花史
Fengshen zhuan	封神傳
Fengyacun	風雅存
fu gu	富賈
Fu Tingshan	符亭山
Fuchengyuan	阜成園
fugu	復古
Funu	富奴
Gao Langting	高朗亭
geguan	歌館
gong	宮
Gong Zizhen	龔自珍
Gong'an pai	公安派
goulan	勾欄
Gu Gongxie	顧公燮
Gu meijiu dai taiping ling	沽美酒帶太平令
gu shuixian zi	古水仙子
guaijue	乖覺
guan zuo	官座
Guangdelou	廣德樓
Guanghelou	廣和樓
Guangzhen	廣真
Guanju daoren	觀劇道人
Guanju riji	觀劇日記
Guben xiqu congkan	古本戲曲叢刊
guci	鼓詞
"Guishu"	閨塾
"Gunlou"	滾樓
guoju	國劇
Guoju huabao	國劇畫報
Guozi jian	國子監
gushu pi sancun ding	谷樹皮三寸丁
Hai sheli	海闍黎
Haiou xiaopu	海漚小譜

Han diao	漢調
Han Youli	韓又黎
Hanjiang xiaoren youxianke	邗江小人遊仙客
hanren xiqi	漢人習氣
Hanxiang	寒香
hanxu	含蓄
hao	好
hao ke	豪客
haonu	豪奴
Haotian ta	昊天塔
haozi	耗子
He Liangjun	何良俊
Helü shi	鶴侶氏
Heshen	和珅
Hexun	和順
Hong Sheng	洪昇
Honglou meng	紅樓夢
Hongniang	紅娘
Hongxian	紅線
Hongzi Li Er	紅字李二
Hou Junshan	侯俊山
Hu Shining	胡世寧
huaben	話本
Huabu nongtan	花部農譚
Huaifang ji	懷芳記
Huang Xiangjian	黃向堅
huapu	花譜
Huaxu dafu yue	華胥大夫曰
huaya zhi zheng	花雅之爭
Huguosi	護國寺
hui xi	回戲
Huitu jingdu sanqing ban jingdiao jiaoben	繪圖京都三慶班京調腳本
Huoshenmiao	火神廟
Ji Liangxuan	姬亮軒
"Jia lao dou tan"	假老斗嘆
Jia Shi	賈氏
Jia Yi	賈宜
"Jian du"	見都
"Jianbie"	餞別
jianghu	江湖
Jiao Xun	焦循
Jiaofang si	教坊司
jiaren	佳人
"Jiayuan le"	家園樂

Jile shijie	極樂世界
Jin Dehui	金德輝
Jin Ping Mei cihua	金瓶梅詞話
Jin Shengtan	金聖歎
jingbai	京白
Jingchai ji	荊釵記
Jingcheng neiwai shoushan quantu	京城內外首善全圖
Jingshan	景山
Jingtai chayuan	景太茶園
Jingzhong miao guanli shiwu yamen	精忠廟管理事物衙門
Jingzhongmiao	精忠廟
jinshi (js)	進士
Jintai canlei ji	金臺殘淚記
Jinyu ban	金玉班
Jinyue kaozheng	今樂考證
Jiqing ban	集慶班
Jiugong dacheng nanbeici gongpu	九宮大成南北詞宮譜
jiujiu daqing	九九大慶
Jiuju congtan	舊劇叢談
Jiuliandeng	九蓮燈
jiulou	酒樓
juan	卷
Juanqinzhai	倦勤齋
Jubu congtan	菊部叢談
Jubu qunying	菊部群英
jue	角
juren	舉人
Jushuo	劇說
Jutai jixiu lu	鞠臺集秀錄
"Kao Hong"	拷紅
"Kao huo"	烤火
kaozheng	考證
ke wei	可畏
Kuang Zhong	況鍾
kuaxi	侉戲
kuben	庫本
Kun-du-le	坤都勒
"Kuoda nainai ting shanhui xi"	闊大奶奶聽善會戲
Laiqingge zhuren	來青閣主人
"Lan wen"	蘭問
lao dou	老斗
Laolang	老郎
Leifeng ta	雷風塔
"Li hun jing meng"	離魂驚夢

Li Kaixian	李開先
Li Xu	李煦
Li Yú	李漁
Li Yù	李玉
Lianhuan ji	連環記
Lianxiang ban	憐香伴
Liaodu geng	療妒羹
Lige piping jiu ximu	笠閣批評舊戲目
Lin Yulan	林玉蘭
"Lingguanmiao"	靈官廟
Lingtai xiaobu	靈臺小補
"Lingzhuo shuangfeng xian bingtou"	靈桌霜鋒獻並頭
liu da ban	六大班
Liu Mengmei	柳夢梅
liu pin	六品
Liuchunge xiaoshi	留春閣小史
lixue	理學
Liyuan jiuhua	梨園舊話
Longfusi	隆福寺
Lu Dahao	盧大浩
Lü Tiancheng	呂天成
Luo Ying'an	羅癭庵
Luomoan laoren	蘿摩庵老人
Ma Feiying	麻翡英
Ma Fengzhi	麻逢之
Ma Yi	馬義
"Mai cuihua"	賣翠花
Mao Xiang	冒襄
Mei Lanfang	梅蘭芳
Mei Qiaoling	梅巧玲
"Meng jian"	萌奸
Meng Shi	孟氏
Meng Yuanlao	孟元老
Menghua suobu	夢華瑣簿
Menghua wailu	夢華外錄
Miaofeng shan jinxiang tu	妙峰山進香圖
Miaoguan	妙觀
mimi zhi yin	靡靡之音
"Ming gan"	冥感
Mingtong helu	明僮合錄
Mo Cheng	莫成
Mo Huaigu	莫懷古
mouer	某兒
mouguan	某官

Mudan ting	牡丹亭
Nan Xixiang ji	南西廂記
Nanbu yanhua lu	南部煙花錄
Nanci dinglü	南詞定律
Nanfu	南府
Nashuying qupu	納書楹曲譜
nayin	納音
Neiwufu	內務府
Ni Zan	倪瓚
Pan Bizheng	潘必正
Pan Jinlian	潘金蓮
"Pan Jinlian chiqing you shu"	潘金蓮痴情誘叔
Pan Qiaoyun	潘巧雲
Pan Qiguan	潘其觀
"Pan zhan"	判暫
Panhua oulu	判花偶錄
Peizhi	佩芝
Pianyu ji	片羽集
pin	品
Pingding Annan tu	平定安南圖
pinwei	品味
Pu Songling	蒲松齡
Qi Biaojia	祁彪佳
Qian Decang	錢德蒼
qiao	蹺
"Qiao zan"	巧讚
qing	情
Qing gong zhen bao Bi mei tu	清宮珍寶皕美圖
"Qing gou"	情勾
qingchang	清唱
qingcheng	傾城
qingguan	清官
qingjiao	情教
Qingle yuan	慶樂園
qinglou	情樓
Qinglou ji	青樓集
"Qingyan"	請宴
Qingyin ge	清音閣
Qingzhong pu	清忠譜
qiu dan	求淡
Qiu Yuan	丘園
Qu Yuan	屈原
"Qu zhan"	覷綻
quan bao	全包

quanben xi	全本戲
Quanshan jinke	勸善金科
Quhaimu	曲海目
quhui	曲會
Qulü	曲律
Qumu xinbian	曲目新編
Qupin	曲品
Rixia jiuwen kao	日下舊聞考
Rixia kanhua ji	日下看花記
Ruan Dacheng	阮大鋮
Ruan Ji	阮籍
Ruan Yuan	阮元
Rulin waishi	儒林外史
"San yuan jidi"	三元及第
San yuan zheng bei	三元徵北
san zuo	散座
Sanduo bu	三多部
Sanqing yuan	三慶園
se	色
shang	商
shangchang men	上場門
shanhui	善會
Shanqi	善耆
Shen Defu	沈德符
Shen Jing	沈璟
Shen Shixing	申時行
Shen Taimou	沈太侔
Shen Zijin	沈自晉
Sheng Jishi	盛際時
Shengping baofa	昇平寶筏
Shengping shu	昇平署
Shi Xiu	石秀
Shier hong	十二紅
shiju	時劇
Shisan mei	十三妹
Shiwu guan	十五貫
Shizhuo ji	拾鐲記
Shu Depu	舒德溥
Shu Fa	舒法
Shu Fen	舒芬
Shuang xiantou Wu Song da baochou	雙獻頭武松大報仇
Shuangqing ban	雙慶班
Shufangzhai	漱芳齋
Shuihu zhuan	水滸傳

shuimo qiang	水磨腔
"Shuotijie"	說題解
shushu	叔叔
Si da qing	四大慶
Sibu toutuo	四不頭陀
"Sifan"	思凡
Siku quanshu	四庫全書
"Silang tanmu"	四郎探母
So Hosu	徐浩修
Song Jiang	宋江
Song Yu	宋玉
su	俗
Su Shi	蘇軾
Subai	蘇白
Suijin cipu	碎金詞譜
Sun Chengze	孫承澤
Sun Danwu	孫丹五
Sun Qi	孫棨
Suzhou Laolang miao minguo buqi beiwen	蘇州老郎神廟民國補契碑文
"Ta kan"	踏勘
Taihua chaxuan	太華茶軒
Tan Shaowen	譚紹聞
Tanbo	曇波
tanci	彈詞
Tang Qin	唐勤
Tang Xianzu	湯顯祖
Tang Xuanzang	唐玄奘
tanghui yanchu	堂會演出
Tian Chengsi	田成嗣
Tian Guifeng	田桂鳳
Tianle yuan	天樂園
Tianlingsi	天靈寺
Tianningsi	天寧寺
Tiantan	天壇
Tieqiao shanren	鐵橋山人
Tingchun xinyong	聽春新詠
Tongle yuan	同樂園
"Tou shi"	偷詩
Tu Long	屠隆
Wang Da	王大
Wang Jide	王驥德
Wang Mantou	王饅頭
"Wang Mingfang liansheng sanji"	王名芳連升三級
Wang Wenzhi	王文治

Wang Xizhi 王羲之
Wang Yangming 王陽明
Wang Zhenglong 王蒸籠
Wanli yuan 萬里緣
Wanshou shengdian chuji 萬壽盛典初集
Wei Changsheng 魏長生
Wei Liangfu 魏良輔
Wei Shi 衛氏
"Wei tiaolian wuyi chuanqing" 為挑簾無意傳情
"Wei zhong huai zhu xiaoshi" 闈中懷諸小史
Wei Zhongxian 魏忠賢
Weiyang tian 未央天
Wen Zhengming 文徵明
wo bei 我輩
Wu Changyuan 吳長元
Wu Da 武大
"Wu Erlang chulu bie xiong" 武二郎出路別兄
Wu Song 武松
Wu Song shi hui 武松十回
Wu Tao 吳燾
Wu Xingzhe 武行者
Wu Zhensheng 吳震生
"Wutai" 五臺
Xi Shiyi 奚十一
Xia Tingshi 夏庭芝
xiachang men 下場門
"Xiang hui" 相會
xianggong 相公
xiansheng 先生
xianü 俠女
xiao haozi 小耗子
Xiao Taihou 蕭太后
Xiao tiedi daoren 小鐵笛道人
Xiaohan xinyong 消寒新詠
Xiaoqin 孝欽
Xiaoqing 小青
Xiaoxia xianji zhaichao 消夏閑記摘鈔
Xicheng waishi 西塍外史
xiehouyu 歇後語
xiguan 戲館
Ximen Qing 西門慶
xinxue 心學
Xiqu kao 戲曲考
xiuse ke can 秀色可餐

Xixiang ji	西廂記
Xiyou ji	西遊記
xiyuan	戲園
Xu Daling	許大齡
"Xu ge"	絮閣
"Xu Lingguanmiao"	續靈官廟
Xu Wei	徐渭
Xu Zichang	許自昌
Xuanhe yishi	宣和遺事
Xuannan lingmeng lu	宣南零夢錄
Xuanxue pu	玄雪譜
Xue Dan	薛旦
Xueyan	雪艷
Xun Huisheng	荀慧生
ya	雅
Yan Poxi	閻婆惜
"Yan shi fangdiao cheng yuangui"	閻氏放刁成怨鬼
Yan Shifan	嚴世番
Yan Song	嚴嵩
Yang Cuiyan (Suhaian jushi)	楊翠巖（粟海庵居士）
Yang Hu	楊虎
Yang Jingting	楊靜亭
Yang Maojian	楊懋建
Yang Miren	楊米人
Yang Shenggong	楊盛恭
Yang Xiaolou	楊小樓
Yang Xiong	楊雄
yangchun	陽春
Yangzhou meng ji	揚州夢記
Yanlan xiaopu	燕蘭小譜
Yantai hongzhua ji	燕臺鴻爪集
Yantai jiaohua lu	燕臺校花錄
Yantai kouhao yibai shou	燕臺口號一百首
Yao Ying	姚瑩
Yaowangmiao	藥王廟
ye	爺
"Ye he"	野合
Ye Shizhang	葉時章
Ye Tang	葉堂
yi	藝
Yi Lansheng	藝蘭聲
Yigeng	奕賡
Yihuan	奕譞
Yihuang	宜黃

Ying'er	迎兒
Yinghua xiaopu	鶯花小譜
yingshu	楹書
Yinlu	胤祿
yinxi	淫戲
Yipengxue	一捧雪
yipu	義僕
Yiqing ban	宜慶班
Yixiang jushi	藝香居士
Yixin	奕訢
Yongqing ban	永慶班
yongwu	詠物
youwu	尤物
Yu Ji	余集
Yu Zhi	余治
Yuan Haowen	元好問
Yuan Hongdao	袁宏道
Yuan Wenzheng huanhun ji	袁文正還魂記
Yuan Zhen	元稹
Yuan Zhongdao	袁中道
Yuan Zongdao	袁宗道
Yuanshan tang jupin	遠山堂劇品
Yuanshan tang qupin	遠山堂曲品
Yuchai ji	玉釵記
Yue Ziqi	岳子奇
yueling chengying	月令承應
Yuji-an	玉極庵
Yundu shi	韞匵氏
Yuzan ji	玉簪記
zashua guan	雜耍館
Zha Kui	查揆
zhanchun ji	湛春集
Zhang Dafu	張大復
Zhang Dai	張岱
Zhang Jiliang	張際亮
Zhang San (Wenyuan)	張三（文遠）
Zhang Yinhuan	張蔭桓
Zhang Yixuan	張彝宣
Zhang Zhao	張照
Zhao Cui'er (Cuiniang)	趙翠兒（翠娘）
Zhao Qiugu	趙秋谷
Zhaodai xiaoshao	昭代簫韶
Zhe daner Wu Song da hu	折擔兒武松打虎
zhezi xi	折子戲

Zhi Fengyi	支豐宜
zhong, xiao, jie, yi	忠孝節義
Zhongxiang guo	眾香國
Zhongxiang zhuren	眾香主人
Zhongyi xuantu	忠義璇圖
Zhou Shunchang	周順昌
Zhou Xiangyu	周祥玉
Zhu Chenhao	朱宸濠
Zhu Jiu Pangzi	朱九胖子
Zhu Suchen (Hao)	朱素臣（鶴）
Zhu Zuochao	朱佐朝
Zhuhan jushi	竹酣居士
Zhuibaiqiu	綴白裘
zhuzhici	竹枝詞
zidi shu	子弟書
Ziyixuan yuepu	自怡軒樂譜
zongben	總本
Zongli Yamen	總理衙門
Zou Jinsheng	鄒金生
zui	醉
zui miao	最妙
zuogong xi	做工戲
Zuo zhuan	左傳

Notes

Abbreviations

PERIODICALS CITED MORE THAN ONCE

HJAS *Harvard Journal of Asiatic Studies*
JAS   *Journal of Asian Studies*
JOS   *Journal of Oriental Studies*
LIC   *Late Imperial China*
TP   *T'oung-Pao*
XQYJ *Xiqu yanjiu* 戲曲研究

SOURCES CITED BY ABBREVIATION

Asterisked items appear in full in Appendix 3.
Cui A*   *Cuiping shan chuanqi quanjuan* 翠屏山傳奇全卷
Cui B*   *Cuiping shan zongmu* 翠屏山總目
Cui Bb*   *Cuiping shan* 翠屏山 (November 1861)
"Cui" C*   "Cuiping shan zongben" 翠屏山總本
"Cui" D*   "Cuiping shan" 翠屏山 (ca. late nineteenth, early twentieth century)
"Cui" E*   "Cuiping shan" 翠屏山 (ca. twentieth century)
"Cui" F*   "Cuiping shan" 翠屏山 (1898–?)
"Cui" G*   "Cuiping shan" 翠屏山 (1912)
DQLCSL   *Da Qing lichao shilu* 大清歷朝實錄
GBXQCK   *Guben xiqu congkan* 古本戲曲叢刊
"Hou" A*   "Hou you zongmu" 後誘總目 (1853)
"Hou" B*   "Hou you zongmu" 後誘總目 (1855)
"Huo" A*   "Huo zhuo" 活捉 (1909)

"Huo" B*   "Huo zhuo" 活捉 (ca. late nineteenth century)

"Jie/Huo" A*   "Jie cha" 借茶 and "Huo zhuo" 活捉 (n.d.)

"Jie/Huo" B*   "Jie cha" 借茶 and "Huo zhuo" 活捉 (ca. late nineteenth century)

"Jie"*   "Jie cha" 借茶 (1832 or 1892?)

Jingdiao Yi scenes*   "Zhuojian, fudu" 捉奸服毒, "Jinlian xi shu" 金蓮戲叔, and "Wu Er bie xiong" 武二別兄

Liushi   Mao Jin 毛晉, Liushizhong qu 六十種曲

PHBJ   Chen Sen 陳森, Pinhua baojian 品花寶鑒

QBLC   Xu Ke 徐珂, Qing bai leichao 清稗類鈔

QCWF zidi shu ji   Liu Liemao 劉烈茂 and Guo Jingrui 郭精銳, Qing Che wangfu chaocang quben: zidi shu ji 清車王府鈔藏曲本—子弟書集

QRSQ J   Qi Rushan 齊如山, Qi Rushan quanji 齊如山全集

QYLS   Zhang Cixi 張次溪, Qingdai Yandu liyuan shiliao: zhengxu bian 清代燕都梨園史料—正續編

SBXQCK   Wang Qiugui 王秋桂, Shanben xiqu congkan 善本戲曲叢刊

"Sha" A*   "Sha pi zongmu" 殺皮總目 (20 January 1853)

"Sha" B*   "Sha pi zongjiang" 殺皮總講

"Shi part script" A*   "Cuiping shan, Shixiu" 翠屏山、石秀 (15 April 1896)

"Shi part script" B*   "Cuiping shan, Shixiu" 翠屏山、石秀 (Qing manuscript)

"Shizi lou"*   "Shizi lou zongben" 獅子樓總本

Shui A*   Shuihu ji 水滸記

Shuofu   Tao Zongyi 陶宗儀, Shuofu 說郛

SHXQ J   Fu Xihua 傅惜華, Shuihu xiqu ji 水滸戲曲集

"Tiao/Cai" pihuang A*   "Tiaolian caiyi" 挑簾裁衣

"Wulong" A*   "Wulong yuan" 烏龍院 (ca. 1880–90?)

"Wulong" B*   "Wulong yuan" 烏龍院 (Guangxu lithograph ed.)

"Wulong" C*   "Wulong yuan" 烏龍院 (29 September 1912)

"Wulong" D*   "Wulong yuan" 烏龍院 (ca. early twentieth century)

"Wulong" E*   "Wulong yuan" 烏龍院 (Shanghai lithograph ed.)

"Xi/Bie" A*   "Xi shu" 戲叔 and "Bie xiong" 別兄

Xiangyan congshu   Chong Tianzi 蟲天子 (Zhang Tinghua 張廷華), Xiangyan congshu 香豔叢書

Xikao   Xikao daquan 戲考大全

Yi A*   Yixia ji 義俠記 (ca. late nineteenth, early twentieth century)

Yi Aa*   Yixia ji 義俠記 (December 1861)

Yi B*   Yixia ji zong ben 義俠記總本

YMQ jinhui xiaoshuo xiqu   Wang Liqi 王利器, *Yuan Ming Qing sandai jinhui xiaoshuo xiqu shiliao* 元明清三代禁毁小說戲曲史料

ZBQ   *Shixing yadiao Zhuibaiqiu xinji hebian* 時興雅調綴白裘新集合編

ZGXLJ   *Zhongguo gudian xiqu lunzhu jicheng* 中國古典戲曲論著集成

Zuiyiqing   *Xinke chuxiang dianban shishang kunqiang zaqu Zuiyiqing* 新刻出像點板時尚崑腔雜曲醉怡情

"Zuolou"*   "Jiaozheng 'Zuolou sha Xi' jingdiao quanben" 校正坐樓殺媳京調全本

Overture

1. From the opening passage of the face-and-voice (*xiangsheng*) routine, "Guan Gong Does Battle with Qin Qiong" (Guan Gong zhan Qin Qiong), in *Chuantong xiangsheng huiji* 1:318–21. A version of this routine can be found in the 1970s recording performed by master xiangsheng artists Hou Baolin and Guo Qiru, "Guan Gong zhan Qin Qiong."

2. On the practice of supplying theatergoers with hot washcloths, see Qi Rushan, "Xiguan," pp. 63a–64b; manuscript in the private collection of Mr. Lu Qing, Beijing. I am grateful to Mr. Lu for providing me with access to this text.

3. This "middlebrow urban sensibility" is difficult to define as an isolated term. Educated observers at the time, however, recognized the opera (and its sensibilities) associated with urban culture of the mid- to late Qing as different from, on the high end, literati drama, and on the low end, rural performance, by virtue of both style and content. Disdained by some literati for its crass commercialism, urban opera nevertheless incorporated elements from both ends of the sociocultural spectrum into a new and distinctive urban form. On the highbrow/lowbrow distinction in theatrical performance in nineteenth-century America, see Levine, *Highbrow/Lowbrow*. Catherine Swatek has adopted Levine's highbrow/lowbrow distinction in her study of the transformation of performance of *The Peony Pavilion* over time. See Swatek, Peony Pavilion *Onstage*.

4. Some of the pioneering popular culture studies on opera include Barbara E. Ward, "Regional Operas and Their Audiences: Evidence from Hong Kong," and Tanaka Issei, "The Social and Historical Context of Ming-Ch'ing Local Drama," both in Johnson, Nathan, and Rawski, *Popular Culture in Late Imperial China*; Johnson, *Ritual Opera*; Tanaka, *Chugokū saishi engeki kenkyū*; and, recently, Qitao Guo, *Ritual Opera and Mercantile Lineage*; Johnson, *Spectacle and Sacrifice*.

5. See, for instance, Johnson, *Ritual Opera*; Qitao Guo, *Ritual Opera and Mercantile Lineage*.

6. See Tanaka, "The Social and Historical Context of Ming-Ch'ing Local Drama," in Johnson et al., *Popular Culture in Late Imperial China*, pp. 143–60.

7. On eighteenth-century population figures, see Rozman, *Urban Networks*; see also Elliott, *The Manchu Way*.

8. On guildhalls and the development of opera stages in Beijing and other urban centers, see Wang Qiang, *Huiguan xitai yu xiju*.

9. Elman, *Cultural History of Civil Examinations*, p. 226.

10. On bannermen and leisure in Beijing, see Naquin, *Peking*, p. 377. See also Elliott, *The Manchu Way*, pp. 284–90 passim.

11. On eighteenth-century demographic pressures, see Kuhn, *Soulstealers*, esp. chap. 2.

12. Most histories of Peking opera begin with this event. See, among others, Ma Shaobo et al., *Zhongguo jingju shi*; Su Yi, *Jingju erbainian gaiguan*.

13. On public theatrical spectacle and early modern states see, for instance, Orgel, *The Illusion of Power*; Ravel, *The Contested Parterre*; Terzioğlu, "The Imperial Circumcision Festival of 1582," pp. 84–100; Berry, "Public Life in Authoritarian Japan," pp. 133–65.

14. On opera in eighteenth-century Yangzhou, see Colin Mackerras, "Yangzhou Local Theatre in the Second Half of the Qing," and Lindy Li Mark, "*Kunqu* in Yangzhou Then and Now," both in Olivová and Børdahl, *Lifestyle and Entertainment in Yangzhou*, pp. 207–24, 225–44; see also Meng Yue, *Shanghai and the Edges of Empire*, chap. 3 passim.

15. For the origins of the concept of "gender as a category of analysis," see Scott, "Gender," pp. 1053–75.

16. See, for instance, Su Yi, *Jingju erbainian gaiguan*; Ma Shaobo et al., *Zhongguo jingju shi*; Dolby, *History of Chinese Drama*; Mackerras, *Rise of the Peking Opera*.

17. Exceptions include Swatek, Peony Pavilion *Onstage*; and a forthcoming history of opera at the Qing court by the late Ye Xiaoqing.

18. Representative works in this tradition include Zhang Geng and Guo Hancheng, *Zhongguo xiqu tongshi*; Zhou Miaozhong, *Qingdai xiqu shi*.

19. For a study that deconstructs the inevitability of the transformation of Peking opera into *guoju*, see Goldstein, *Drama Kings*.

20. Habermas, *Structural Transformation of the Public Sphere*.

21. The most influential of these studies have been Rowe, *Hankow: Commerce and Society*, and *Hankow: Conflict and Community*; Strand, *Rickshaw Beijing*. Slightly later studies of urban institutions distanced themselves from the Habermasian model; see, for instance, Goodman, *Native Place, City, and Nation*; Judge, *Print and Politics*.

22. See, for instance, R. Bin Wong, "Great Expectations," pp. 7–50; Wakeman, "The Civil Society and Public Sphere Debate," pp. 108–38, and "Boundaries of the Public Sphere," pp. 167–89. Defenders of the usefulness of the public-sphere concept in China have included Rowe, "The Public Sphere in Modern China," pp. 309–29, and "The Problem of 'Civil Society,'" pp. 139–57; Rankin, "Some Observations on a Chinese Public Sphere," pp. 158–92.

23. Berry, "Public Life in Authoritarian Japan," pp. 154–55.

24. Naquin, *Peking*.

25. Si-yen Fei, *Negotiating Urban Space*.

26. On theaters as not-so-rational public spheres in pre-Revolutionary France, see Ravel, *The Contested Parterre*; on the place of theater in public culture in early nineteenth-century France, see Kroen, *Politics and Theater*.

27. See, for instance, the essays in Crossley and Roberts, *After Habermas*.

28. Lean, *Public Passions*; Haiyan Lee, *Revolution of the Heart*; see also the essays in *Modern China* 27.3 (2001).
29. For exceptions, see Swatek, Peony Pavilion *Onstage*; Qitao Guo, *Ritual Opera and Mercantile Lineage*; and my "The Nun Who Wouldn't Be," pp. 71–138.
30. Sommer, *Sex, Law, and Society*; Theiss, *Disgraceful Matters*.
31. See my "Boy Heroines."

Chapter One

1. *Dumen zhuzhici*, in Lu Gong, *Qingdai Beijing zhuzhici*, p. 39.
2. De Shuoting, *Caozhu yichuan*, in Lu Gong, *Qingdai Beijing zhuzhici*, p. 50.
3. The term *lao dou* designates a wealthy patron of courtesans or actors. Legend has it that the term was a holdover from the patois of official entertainment culture during the Tang dynasty, in which the emperor was called *yaigong* and his pleasure was referred to as *xiandou*. See Cui Lingqin, *Jiaofang ji*, in Wang Yunwu, *Jiaofang ji ji qita jiu zhong*.
4. Yang Maojian, *Menghua suobu* (1842), in *QYLS*, p. 353. In Qing-era playhouses it was considered desirable to sit far away from the din of the orchestra (stage right) and the sounds and smells of the crowds in the "pond" (center front).
5. For Western-language histories of Qing opera that make use of huapu, see Mackerras, *Rise of the Peking Opera*; and Darrobers, *Opéra de Pékin*.
6. Wu Cuncun, *Homoerotic Sensibilities*, esp. chap. 5; Wu Cuncun, *Ming Qing shehui xing'ai fengqi*, esp. pp. 179–97; see also Siu Leung Li, *Cross-Dressing in Chinese Opera*.
7. Wu Cuncun, *Homoerotic Sensibilities*, pp. 134–35; and Wu Cuncun and Stevenson, "Speaking of Flowers," pp. 100–129. For one recent critique of the elision of the sex industry in histories of Qing theater, see Yao Shuyi, "Xiqu shi xushuzhong de Beijing 'tangzi,'" pp. 47–60.
8. For the claim that the theater was "nowhere better than in the capital," see Xiao tiedi daoren, *Rixia kanhua ji* (1803), in *QYLS*, p. 55. See also Lu Eting, *Kunju yanchu shigao*, p. 223. The notable exceptions are the two juan on the theater of Yangzhou and its performers (many of whom also performed in the capital) in Li Dou, *Yangzhou huafang lu*, esp. juan 5, 9.
9. Wu Changyuan, *Yanlan xiaopu* (1785), in *QYLS*, p. 3.
10. Sikong Tu's *Ershisi shipin*, with its categories of poetic description rendered in verse, is particularly influential in setting styles and contributing critical vocabulary to latter-day exercises in literary and other types of connoisseurship. On the poetic form of Sikong Tu's aesthetics, see, for instance, Robertson, ". . . 'To Convey What Is Precious,'" p. 332; Yu, "Ssu-k'ung T'u's *Shih-P'in*," 1:97–98; Zu Baoquan, *Sikong Tu Shipin zhushi ji yiwen*, p. 68.
11. The opening sentence, for instance, of Fan Chengda's Song-dynasty catalog of flowering plum trees begins: "The plum flower is a thing of ultimate beauty under Heaven." Fan Chengda, *Meipu*, in Chong Tianzi, *Xiangyan congshu*, 3:2863. Fan uses the term *youwu* again to describe the "Mandarin Duck Plum" (*yuanyang mei*); see ibid., 3:2866.

12. On the late Ming connoisseurship discourse on boy actresses as luxury goods, see Volpp, "Classifying Lust," pp. 109–16, and "The Literary Circulation of Actors," pp. 963–72. See also Wu Cuncun, *Homoerotic Sensibilities*; Darrobers, *Opéra de Pékin*, pp. 333–74 passim.
13. Clunas, *Superfluous Things*, p. 8. See also Wai-yee Li, "The Collector," pp. 269–302; and Zeitlin, "The Petrified Heart," pp. 1–26.
14. Clunas, *Superfluous Things*, pp. 86–87; Wai-yee Li, "The Collector," p. 280.
15. Wai-yee Li, "The Collector."
16. Clunas, *Superfluous Things*, pp. 13, 86–87.
17. Wu Changyuan, *Yanlan xiaopu*, in *QYLS*, p. 3.
18. Authorship of *Nanbu yanhua lu*, formerly attributed to Yan Shigu (581–645), is most likely a later composition ascribed to Yan so as to increase the prestige of the text. It is reprinted under the title *Daye shiyi ji* in Chong Tianzi, *Xiangyan congshu*, 1: 649–56.
19. The final couplet in Du Mu's quatrain "Qian huai" reads: "Awaking suddenly from a ten-year dream of Yangzhou / I had earned but a reputation as a fickle cad among the women of the Blue Towers." The romantic aura surrounding Du Mu is also memorialized in Yu Ye's (act. 867) embellished account of Du Mu's life, *Yangzhou meng ji*, which was published shortly after the poet's death; see Yu Ye, *Yangzhou meng ji*, reprinted in Wang Yunwu, *Jiaofang ji ji qita jiu zhong*.
20. Sun Qi's *Beili zhi* (ca. 888) is a record of the pleasure quarters of late Tang Chang'an; *Gujin shuohai* edition, reprinted in Wang Yunwu, *Jiaofang ji ji qita jiu zhong*. Yu Huai's *Banqiao zaji* (1697) is a nostalgic account of the courtesans of the famous Qinhuai pleasure quarters of Ming-era Nanjing; reprinted in Chong Tianzi, *Xiangyan congshu*, 4:3637–71. Zhao's *Haiou xiaopu* (1704) relates the author's encounters with renowned courtesans in the Tianjin region during the early Qing; also reprinted in *Xiangyan congshu*, 1:477–89.
21. See Xicheng waishi, "Tici," in *Yanlan xiaopu*, in *QYLS*, p. 5.
22. See Sun Chongtao and Xu Hongtu, *Qinglou ji*; see also Idema and West, *Chinese Theater*, pp. 104–72.
23. Zhou Yude, *Xiaohan xinyong*, p. 3.
24. Yixiang jushi, in *Yinghua xiaopu* (1819), in *QYLS*, p. 218.
25. Qixiang shi, *Pinghua*, p. 3a.
26. Yang Maojian, *Chang'an kanhua ji* (1837), in *QYLS*, p. 316.
27. From Canhua xiaoshi, "Houxu," in Xiao tiedi daoren, *Rixia kanhua ji*, in *QYLS*, p. 108.
28. A pun may be at work in this pen name since *xiao shi* is also a literary term for actors.
29. On the trope of obsession in early modern literary texts, see Zeitlin, *Historian of the Strange*, pp. 61–97. On the obsessive personality of the seventeenth-century connoisseur, with particular reference to passion for actors, see also Volpp, "Classifying Lust."
30. Xiao tiedi daoren, *Rixia kanhua ji*, in *QYLS*, pp. 75, 92, 93, 89.
31. Wu Changyuan, *Yanlan xiaopu*, in *QYLS*, p. 21.

32. Xiao tiedi daoren, *Rixia kanhua ji*, in *QYLS*, p. 69.
33. Zhang Jiliang, *Jintai canlei ji* (1829), in *QYLS*, p. 232.
34. Xiao tiedi daoren, *Rixia kanhua ji*, in *QYLS*, p. 168.
35. Ibid.
36. Luomoan laoren, *Huaifang ji* (1876), in *QYLS*, p. 583.
37. Wu Changyuan, *Yanlan xiaopu*, in *QYLS*, p. 23. Emphasis mine.
38. Xiao tiedi daoren, *Rixia kanhua ji*, in *QYLS*, p. 103.
39. Ibid., p. 40.
40. For arguments about late Ming courtesans and literacy, see esp. Paul S. Ropp, "Ambiguous Images of Courtesan Culture in Late Imperial China"; Wai-yee Li, "The Late Ming Courtesan: Invention of a Cultural Ideal"; and Dorothy Ko, "The Written Word and the Bound Foot." All in Widmer and Kang-I Sun Chang, *Writing Women in Late Imperial China*.
41. For discussion of these questions in seventeenth-century writings about actors and the theater, see Volpp, "The Literary Circulation of Actors."
42. On homoerotic ideals in the Ming and Qing literary tradition, see Vitiello, "Exemplary Sodomites," pp. 207–57; Volpp, "Classifying Lust"; Wu Cuncun, *Homoerotic Sensibilities*. The huapu *Xiaohan xinyong* includes biographies and poems for actors who specialize in the young male (*xiao sheng*) roles as well as for dan roles. This text records a total of eighteen actors, half of whom specialized in dan and half in xiao sheng. This is the earliest huapu (1795) regularly to comment on actors playing male roles, and it compares the nine xiao sheng performers to flowers.
43. On male and female prostitution, see, for instance, Wang Shunu, *Zhongguo changji shi*, pp. 317–27; Wu Cuncun, *Ming Qing shehui xing'ai fengqi*, pp. 78–81, 179–97. For boy actresses doubling as male prostitutes, see Mackerras, *Rise of the Peking Opera*, p. 150; Wu Cuncun, *Homoerotic Sensibilities*, esp. pp. 116–58; Darrobers, *Opéra de Pékin*, pp. 333–74.
44. Mackerras also has observed, "Boy-actors can be best compared not to ordinary prostitutes but to high-grade courtesans"; *Rise of the Peking Opera*, p. 152.
45. For a discussion of the stigma associated with male-male sexual penetration during the Qing, see Sommer, *Sex, Law, and Society*, chap. 4.
46. Wang Shunu, *Zhongguo changji shi*, pp. 317–27; see also Yeh, *Shanghai Love*, pp. 96–135.
47. Yang Maojian, *Menghua suobu*, in *QYLS*, p. 365.
48. Zhang Jiliang, *Jintai canlei ji*, in *QYLS*, p. 246. Another (most likely apocryphal) explanation of *xianggong* as an appellation for dan actors claims that the term is a corruption of the compound *xianggu* (one who resembles a girl). See Yi Lansheng, *Cemao yutan* (1878), in *QYLS*, p. 603. Even if that etymologically is false, it underscores awareness of the mapping of feminine qualities onto boy actresses. For a strong refutation of the *xianggu/xianggong* phonological association, see Qi Rushan, *Xiban*, in *QRSQJ*, 1:42b. See also the discussion in Wu Cuncun, *Ming Qing shehui xing'ai fengqi*, pp. 179–81.
49. See esp. Ropp, "Ambiguous Images of Courtesan Culture"; Wai-yee Li, "The Late Ming Courtesan"; and Ko, "The Written Word and the Bound Foot." Many

of the scholar-participants in the cult of qing discourse and courtesan culture were also patrons of actors. On actors as signifiers in seventeenth-century literati discussions of romance, authenticity, and the self, see Volpp, "Classifying Lust." Wu Cuncun, *Homoerotic Sensibilities*, traces the fascination of Qing literati with boy actresses into the eighteenth and nineteenth centuries. See also Hinsch, *Passions of the Cut Sleeve*, pp. 139–61.

50. In this voice, too, however, they were still connoisseurs, collectors of the lore and beauty of the theatrical world. Protestations to the contrary, some of them were buyers in the sexual market for boy actresses. On the sexual dimension of liaisons between actors and their connoisseur patrons, see Wu Cuncun, *Homoerotic Sensibilities*, pp. 116–58.

51. Volpp, "Classifying Lust," pp. 94–97.

52. Yi Lansheng, *Cemao yutan*, in *QYLS*, p. 608.

53. This same sensibility is reflected in Chen Sen's mid-nineteenth-century novel set in the Beijing demimonde, *Pinhua baojian*. Keith McMahon has eloquently discussed the novel's aesthetics of chaste same-sex male desire, in which "tumescence is enough," in "Sublime Love," pp. 70–109.

54. See, for instance, Zhang Jiliang, *Jintai canlei ji*, in *QYLS*, p. 252.

55. Zhou Yude, *Xiaohan xinyong*, p. 3.

56. Wai-yee Li, "The Late Ming Courtesan," p. 47.

57. West, "Playing with Food," p. 69.

58. *Rixia jiuwen kao* was published in 1785. It was based on the 1688 guide to Ming Beijing, *Rixia jiuwen*, which had been compiled by the early Qing scholar Zhu Yizun. On the compilation of the latter guide, see Naquin, *Peking*, pp. 453–59. On official versus private historiography, see Kahn, *Monarchy in the Emperor's Eyes*, pp. 47–64.

59. Yang Maojian, *Menghua suobu*, in *QYLS*, p. 347.

60. Ibid.

61. Zhou Yude, *Xiaohan xinyong*, p. 3.

62. Xiao tiedi daoren, *Rixia kanhua ji*, in *QYLS*, p. 55.

63. Zhang Jiliang, *Jintai canlei ji*, in *QYLS*, pp. 228–53.

64. Wu Changyuan is one of the few huapu authors who did not openly acknowledge the influence of the urban guidebook on his record of theater. Yet he was well acquainted with this tradition: three years after the publication of his *Yanlan xiaopu*, he also published a more comprehensive guide to the city of Beijing, *Chenyuan shilüe*, which was essentially intended as a privately issued "pocket edition" of the imperially commissioned *Rixia jiuwen kao*.

65. Wu Changyuan, *Yanlan xiaopu*, in *QYLS*, p. 46.

66. Zhang Jiliang, *Jintai canlei ji*, in *QYLS*, p. 246. Here Zhang is bothered that the older-style suffixes—lexical diminutives that appended to actors' names (and that denoted servile status)—have gone out of fashion and that actors' sobriquets now imitate those of men of letters.

67. Yang Maojian, *Menghua suobu*, in *QYLS*, p. 347.

68. James Clifford, "On Ethnographic Allegory," in Clifford and Marcus, *Writing Culture*, p. 112.

69. Dames, *Amnesiac Selves*, p. 4. See also Desai, "Old World Orders," pp. 140–42.

70. According to legend, Confucius was responsible for compiling the *Chunqiu*; he stopped his record at the "capture of the unicorn." As a result, the *Chunqiu* is often referred to as the Classic of the Unicorn (*Lin jing*) or History of the Unicorn (*Lin shi*).

71. Zhang Jiliang, *Jintai canlei ji*, in *QYLS*, p. 225.

72. Xiao tiedi daoren, *Rixia kanhua ji*, in *QYLS*, p. 55.

73. Paul Rabinow, "Representations are Social Facts," in Clifford and Marcus, *Writing Culture*, pp. 23–66.

74. Xiao tiedi daoren, *Rixia kanhua ji*, in *QYLS*, p. 103. *Yanlan xiaopu* is also explicitly referred to in Zhou Yude, *Xiaohan xinyong*, pp. 70–71.

75. See, for instance, Zhang Jiliang, *Jintai canlei ji*, in *QYLS*, pp. 249, 250; Yang Maojian, *Menghua suobu*, in *QYLS*, pp. 367, 379.

76. This essay is appended to the 1803 huapu *Viewing Flowers in the Precinct of the Throne*; Canhua xiaoshi, "Lan wen," in Xiao tiedi daoren, *Rixia kanhua ji*, in *QYLS*, pp. 112–15.

77. Zhongxiang zhuren, *Zhongxiang guo* (1806), in *QYLS*, p. 1011. The phrase "actors as comely as Song Yu" is also responding to the last line of the preface to *Yanlan xiaopu*: "But why should I fear tossing out [this piece] of Yan Stone [*Yan shi*] so long as it calls forth Song Jade [*Song yu*] from others." Wu Changyuan, *Yanlan xiaopu*, in *QYLS*, p. 3.

78. Laiqingge zhuren, *Pianyu ji*, in *QYLS*, p. 145.

79. Canhua xiaoshi, "Houxu," in Xiao tiedi daoren, *Rixia kanhua ji*, in *QYLS*, p. 109. The last three of the texts mentioned here are no longer extant.

80. Xiao tiedi daoren, *Rixia kanhua ji*, in *QYLS*, p. 55.

81. Zhuhan jushi, "Ba," in Wu Changyuan, *Yanlan xiaopu*, in *QYLS*, p. 52.

82. Liuchunge xiaoshi, *Tingchun xinyong*, in *QYLS*, pp. 149–207.

83. Tianyai fangcao ciren, "Bianyan," in Liuchunge xiaoshi, *Tingchun xinyong*, in *QYLS*, p. 152.

84. See the numerous descriptions of literati poetry parties (with actors in attendance) in Chen Sen, *PHBJ* (1849), chaps. 7, 15, 17, 20, 24, esp. 60.

85. Wu Changyuan, *Yanlan xiaopu*, in *QYLS*, p. 3.

86. The identifiable authors are Wu Changyuan, *Yanlan xiaopu* (1785); Zhang Jiliang, *Jintai canlei ji* (1829); Yang Cuiyan, *Yantai hongzhuaji* (ca. 1832); and Yang Maojian, *Xin ren gui jia lu* (1834), *Chang'an kanhua ji* (1837), *Dingnian yusun zhi* (1837), and *Menghua suobu* (1842). My determination that Yang Cuiyan composed *Yantai hongzhua ji* is a new finding. All of the Chinese-language scholarship on these texts follows the original editor of *QYLS* in assuming that the identity of the author, who goes by the pseudonym Suhaian jushi, cannot be recovered.

87. For analysis of the authorship of *Xiaohan xinyong*, see Zhou Yude, "*Xiaohan xinyong* zhaji," appended to Zhou Yude, *Xiaohan xinyong*, p. 137. For *Rixia kanhua ji*, an internal textual note, coupled with analysis of the author's chosen sobriquet, suggests the possibility that the author was surnamed Yang. See Xiao tiedi daoren, *Rixia kanhua ji*, in *QYLS*, pp. 88, 109.

88. From the "Houxu" by Canhua xiaoshi, in Xiao tiedi daoren, *Rixia kanhua ji*, in *QYLS*, p. 109.

89. Yang Maojian writes that, having stayed in the capital for seven to eight years, he was witness to three generations of actors. Yang, *Dingnian yusun zhi*, in *QYLS*, p. 330.

90. Laiqingge zhuren, *Pianyu ji* (1805), in *QYLS*, pp. 119–23. The author of this text likely was surnamed Yuan; he calls himself a latter-day Yuan Haowen (p. 122), and his poems and prefaces are all cobbled together with phrases from the poetry of either Yuan Zhen or Yuan Haowen. This style of creating text from a patchwork of lines from Tang- and Song-dynasty poetry is also exhibited in Bohua jushi, *Yantai jiyan* (1823), in *QYLS*, pp. 1037–55.

91. As a social-cultural type, these authors essentially correspond to what David Johnson has termed the "classically educated/self-sufficient" group—a group that "played a very important role in the integration of Chinese culture"; see Johnson, "Communication, Class, and Consciousness in Late Imperial China," in Johnson, Nathan, and Rawski, *Popular Culture in Late Imperial China*, pp. 58–61.

92. See Yu Ji's preface to Wu Changyuan's *Chenyuan shilüe*. For additional biographical sketches of Wu Changyuan, see the huapu author biographies by Zhang Cixi in *QYLS*, p. 24, and also Mackerras, *Rise of the Peking Opera*, pp. 237–39.

93. The birth of this genre of theatrical connoisseurship and the roughly contemporary development of a full-fledged commercial theater in Beijing may also have been facilitated by the influx of scholars into the capital for imperially sponsored projects during the later Qianlong years. On the lure of eighteenth-century Beijing to the scholarly elite and on Yu Ji's role in the Siku project during the 1770s and 1780s, see Guy, *Emperor's Four Treasuries*, pp. 47–49, 126. On the imperial sponsorship of the *Rixia jiuwen kao*, see Naquin, *Peking*, pp. 457–59.

94. Laiqingge zhuren, *Pianyu ji*, in *QYLS*, pp. 136, 142; Zhou Yude, *Xiaohan xinyong*, p. 3.

95. For biographical information on Zhang Jiliang, see the biography by Yao Ying in *Zhang Hengfu shixuan* (1882), 1.1b–4a, in Xu Gan, *Shaowu Xu shi congshu*, vols. 29–34. See also the huapu author biographies by Zhang Cixi in *QYLS*, p. 25; and Mackerras, *Rise of the Peking Opera*, pp. 240–41. Zhang Jiliang is also discussed in Polachek, *Inner Opium War*, pp. 70, 81, 218–24.

96. Polachek, *Inner Opium War*, pp. 87–94.

97. See, for instance, Zhang Jiliang, *Jintai canlei ji*, in *QYLS*, pp. 231, 244.

98. Cuiyan is likely Yang's style name (*zi*). I have not been able to learn his given name (*ming*). Zhang and Yang were *tongnian*—that is, they both passed the provincial-level examination in Fujian during the same session. That Zhang Jiliang contributed several dedicatory poems to Yang's *Yantai hongzhua ji* further attests to the close personal ties of participants in flower-register creation.

99. Yang Cuiyan (pseud. Suhaian jushi), *Yantai hongzhua ji* (1832), in *QYLS*, p. 266.

100. Yang Cuiyan's teasing mock jealousy of the actor in this poem suggests that literati peer bonds, too, were cemented through participation in the theatri-

cal demimonde. For more on the way in which poems written in praise of actors forged homosocial bonds among seventeenth-century literati, see Volpp, "The Literary Circulation of Actors," pp. 963–72.

101. Yang Cuiyan, *Yantai hongzhua ji*, in *QYLS*, pp. 269–70, 263.

102. Zhang Jiliang, *Zhang Hengfu shixuan*, in Xu Gan, *Shaowu Xu shi congshu*, 32:6.39a.

103. For scholarship on Ruan Yuan (1764–1849) and his Xuehai Academy (est. 1820), see Elman, "The Hsüeh-hai T'ang," pp. 105–13, and *From Philosophy to Philology*, pp. 125–26. See also Miles, "Celebrating the Yu Fan Shrine," pp. 33–73.

104. For additional biographical sketches of Yang Maojian, see the huapu author biographies by Zhang Cixi in *QYLS*, pp. 25–26; Mackerras, *Rise of the Peking Opera*, pp. 241–42.

105. Yang Maojian, *Menghua suobu*, in *QYLS*, p. 348. I suspect that those authors we can trace—Wu Changyuan, Zhang Jiliang, and Yang Maojian—are likely to have been the most successful and prominent on the politico-literary scene. Often, because individuals have left behind other literary compilations, we can trace their literary sobriquets. Moreover, this trio of identified authors tended to be more innovative huapu writers; the nameless authors seem more derivative.

106. It is hard to tell how much this statement reflects the writer's actual circumstances and how much it is rhetorical posturing to distance him from the stigma of participation in the sex market. Zhongxiang zhuren, *Zhongxiang guo*, in *QYLS*, p. 1011.

107. The Dream of Nanke is an allusion to a Buddhist-inspired fable about a man who falls asleep beneath a tree. In a dream, he embarks on the scholar's career path, passes the examinations, and becomes embroiled in the domain of high politics. He awakes to discover that what he thought was an entire lifetime has been nothing more than an afternoon nap. Zhongxiang zhuren, *Zhongxiang guo*, in *QYLS*, p. 1011.

108. Opening passage of the dedicatory remarks by Xicheng waishi in *Yanlan xiaopu*, in *QYLS*, p. 4.

109. Xiao tiedi daoren, *Rixia kanhua ji*, in *QYLS*, p. 55.

110. The symbolic imagery of certain flowers in huapu—the preference, say, for orchids—can also be linked to the self-image of the connoisseur; the orchid was associated with both Qu Yuan and Wang Xizhi, and the flower came to stand for literati integrity. See Schneider, *A Madman of Ch'u*, pp. 52–59. See also Zhou, *Androgyny in Late Ming and Early Qing Literature*, p. 205.

111. Wang Xizhi, acknowledged as one of China's canonical calligraphers, was most noted for his poems written at the Orchid Pavilion Gathering (Lanting hui), and especially for his preface to the collection of these poems.

112. This is an allusion to Du Fu's poem "Yonghuai guji," the second stanza of which elegizes the poet Song Yu (ca. 290–ca. 223 BCE), lamenting that Song Yu's poem "Gaotang fu" had not been understood. "Gaotang fu" tells the legend of the meeting between King Xiang of Chu and the Fairy of Wu Mountain. This tale became the *locus classicus* for "clouds and rain" as meaning sexual congress; perhaps

the allusion—safe from allegations of bawdiness because of its ancient date—is invoked here to deflect potential accusations that huapu were prurient.

113. Xicheng waishi, in *Yanlan xiaopu*, in *QYLS*, p. 5. Notice how embedded the language is: to make the meaning intelligible in translation, I must add explicit mention of the implied allusions, the *Orchid Pavilion Collection* and Song Yu's rhapsody; to the expected audience of literary insiders, such explication would have been unnecessary.

114. Polachek, *Inner Opium War*, pp. 83–87. The allure of eccentrics and outcast officials to nineteenth-century literati is also discussed in Miles, "Celebrating the Yu Fan Shrine," esp. pp. 56–58.

115. Huapu authors also had models from the more recent past, some of whom pointed the way for the literati taste in opera and male dan. One such model was the scholar Chen Weisong (1626–82), whose literary influence on early nineteenth-century scholar elites is discussed in Polachek, *Inner Opium War*, p. 27. On Chen's anthology of poems about the young actor Yunlang, see Volpp, "The Literary Circulation of Actors," pp. 963–72. In one poem in *Yanlan xiaopu*, Wu Changyuan explicitly compares his admiration for the late eighteenth-century actor Wang Xiangyun with the story of Chen Weisong and Yunlang; see Wu Changyuan, *Yanlan xiaopu*, in *QYLS*, p. 11.

116. On this trend in seventeenth-century writings, see Struve, "Ambivalence and Action," p. 331; Wakeman, "Romantics, Stoics, and Martyrs," pp. 631–65.

117. The "late Grand Mentor" refers to Zhu Gui (1731–1807), who served as chief tutor of the princes during 1799–1805; see Hummel, *Eminent Chinese of the Ch'ing Period*, pp. 185–87.

118. Yang Maojian, *Menghua suobu*, in *QYLS*, p. 368.

119. Ibid., pp. 376–77.

120. For scholarship on the spread of qinqiang—and more generally bangzi qiang—throughout northwest China and into Beijing, see Liu Wenfeng, *Shan-shan shangren yu bangzi xi*. See also Mackerras, "Growth of Chinese Regional Drama," pp. 58–91.

121. Only at about this time did other texts—texts more strictly in the tradition of music and drama scholarship—begin to be written about huabu plays and performance. See, for instance, Li Diaoyuan, *Ju hua*, in *ZGXLJ*, 8: 30–72; Jiao Xun, *Huabu nongtan*, in ibid., 8: 221–31. These texts are more in the tradition of "talks on poetry" connoisseurship. Some of the huapu created shortly after the publication of *Yanlan xiaopu* are not quite so eclectic in musical taste. *Xiaohan xinyong* (1795), for instance, focuses primarily on kunju actors and performance.

122. Wu Changyuan, *Yanlan xiaopu*, in *QYLS*, p. 6.

123. Ibid.

124. Ibid., p. 18.

125. Xicheng waishi, "Tici," in ibid., p. 4.

126. See also Pan Lizhu, *Qingdai zhongqi Yandu liyuan shiliao pingyi sanlun yanjiu*; Chen Fang, *Qianlong shiqi Beijing jutan yanjiu*, pp. 304–36.

127. Xiao tiedi daoren, *Rixia kanhua ji*, in *QYLS*, p. 107.

128. The "downgraded expectations" for actors and courtesans as honorary literati are also noted in Starr, "Shifting Boundaries," p. 292.

129. Luomoan laoren, *Huaifang ji*, in *QYLS*, p. 585.

130. Some actor biographies even comment on the actor's capacity to hold liquor. See, for instance, Yang Maojian, *Menghua suobu*, in *QYLS*, pp. 377–78.

131. Liuchunge xiaoshi, *Tingchun xinyong*, in *QYLS*, p. 167.

132. Yi Lansheng, *Cemao yutan*, in *QYLS*, p. 605. The iconoclast Zhang Jiliang is the only huapu author to have explicitly acknowledged a sexual liaison with an actor companion. Zhang explains: "After failing . . . in the summer of 1826, I stayed on in the capital. [Other] sojourners were wont to invite me to watch operas, but my interest was not keen. Only upon meeting Xiao Xi was my passion aroused. That winter on the fifteenth of the tenth month [24 November 1826], a Buddhist ceremony was held on behalf of the actor Wu at the Longquan Monastery. XX invited XXX and myself to go, and Xiao Xi was among those present. After that, we gradually became intimate. I wrote for him 'A Song for Xulang' [Xulang qu], which came to be rather widely circulated"; Zhang Jiliang, *Jintai canlei ji*, in *QYLS*, p. 229.

133. Yang Maojian, *Chang'an kanhua ji*, in *QYLS*, p. 310.

134. For *hanxu*, see, for instance, Liuchunge xiaoshi, *Tingchun xinyong*, in *QYLS*, p. 204; for the concept of *qiu dan*, see also Zhou Yude, "Xiaohan xinyong zhaji," appended to Zhou Yude, *Xiaohan xinyong*, p. 144.

135. Wu Changyuan, *Yanlan xiaopu*, in *QYLS*, p. 27.

136. Ibid.; see also ibid., p. 47, for similar comments.

137. Xiao tiedi daoren, *Rixia kanhua ji*, in *QYLS*, p. 69.

138. For the entries on Wei Changsheng and Chen Yinguan, see Wu Changyuan, *Yanlan xiaopu*, in *QYLS*, pp. 32–33, 17–18; 44–47, respectively. Wei Changsheng is also mentioned in *Rixia kanhua ji*, in *QYLS*, pp. 104–5; *Tingchun xinyong*, in *QYLS*, p. 204; Li Dou, *Yangzhou huafang lu*, p. 132.

139. On situating performance along a *qing/qi* (authenticity/strange) continuum in the portrayal of the heroine of the romantic comedy "Si fan," see my "The Nun Who Wouldn't Be," pp. 113, 113n131.

140. The heyday of female impersonators playing ingénue roles well into middle age and beyond lay far in the twentieth-century future.

141. Yang Maojian, *Xin ren gui jia lu*, in *QYLS*, p. 282. Qixiang shi, in contrast, writing in 1816, praises an eighteen-*sui* (seventeen-year-old) dan for not having lost his charm even though he was "getting on in years"; Qixiang shi, *Pinghua*, 8b.

142. Luomoan laoren, *Huaifang ji*, in *QYLS*, p. 588. See also the comment in *Yanjing zaji*: "The period of fame for boy actresses is no more than a few years; it starts when they are about thirteen or fourteen *sui* and lasts until they are seventeen or eighteen *sui*; by the time they reach twenty, they have already gone into retirement and the traffic outside their doors has grown scarce"; *Yanjing zaji*, cited in Zhang Cixi, *Beijing liyuan zhanggu changbian*, in *QYLS*, p. 898.

143. From Yang Jingting, *Dumen zayong*, cited in *QYLS*, p. 1174.

144. Wu Changyuan, *Yanlan xiaopu*, in *QYLS*, p. 47. The Alum-Paper Winehouse, or Fanlou, was a famous tavern in Song-era Kaifeng. Recorded in *Dongjing*

menghua lu, the Alum-Paper Winehouse (so named because it was located near the shop of alum-paper merchants) is described as a place frequented by wealthy merchants. From the description, it is clear that among its main attractions were the prostitutes who worked out of it. Wu's invocation of the Fanlou is surely his oblique way of commenting on the parallel role of the dan in his own times.

145. From *Yanjing zaji*, cited in Zhang Cixi, *Beijing liyuan zhanggu changbian*, in *QYLS*, p. 897.

146. That is, after he reached capping age (nineteen years old, or twenty sui). Zhang, *Jintai canlei ji*, in *QYLS*, pp. 246–47.

147. Ibid., p. 243. The XX in this passage corresponds to two blank spaces in the original text. Throughout Zhang's huapu, blank spaces—either two or three—substitute for the names of people in official positions. As far as I can tell, these blank spaces were the doing of the author and not later emendations by the editor of *QYLS*. If so, then these omissions are most revealing. Zhang, gossiping about contemporaries in office, did not wish to invite trouble by naming them, knowing that contemporary readers (and certainly political insiders) could easily guess the identities. If anything, the blank spaces, introducing a not-too-difficult guessing game into the text, would have enhanced the readers' fun. It was also a way of distinguishing readers in the know (the insiders) from the wannabes (the outsiders), thus neatly tagging the author as someone in the know.

148. Ibid.

149. Yang Maojian, *Menghua suobu*, in *QYLS*, p. 376.

150. Wu Changyuan, *Yanlan xiaopu*, in *QYLS*, p. 19.

151. Zhang Jiliang, *Jintai canlei ji*, in *QYLS*, p. 234.

152. Wu Changyuan, *Yanlan xiaopu*, in *QYLS*, pp. 42–43.

153. Ibid., pp. 48–49.

154. Written in a simple classical style, some of these anecdotes remind me of the stories one might find in Pu Songling's (1640–1715) *Liaozhai zhi yi* [*Strange Tales from the Liao Studio*]. Wu makes a point of specifying his source, as if he were aware that without such attribution this anecdote would read like a fable.

155. Yang Maojian, *Menghua suobu*, in *QYLS*, p. 353.

156. Yang's definition of "the actors" here is clearly limited to those at the top of their field; it is easy to imagine that the less popular actors—those who never made it into huapu collections—would have been less choosy about where they entertained their clientele. Just this sort of differentiation and distinction among actors is revealed in *Pinhua baojian*, which presents a hierarchy within the acting world: the best kunju actors lay claim to the highest rank; less attractive and less skilled kunju actors and pihuang actors fill the middle rungs; and, occupying the lowest rung of the ladder of entertainment and sex work are the barber-boy apprentices who double as singers of popular tunes.

157. Yang Maojian, *Menghua suobu*, in *QYLS*, p. 357.

158. See, for instance, Wu Changyuan, *Yanlan xiaopu*, in *QYLS*, p. 21; and Xiao tiedi daoren, *Rixia kanhua ji*, in *QYLS*, pp. 69, 71, 78.

159. Zhou Yude, *Xiaohan xinyong*, p. 23.

160. Xiao tiedi daoren, *Rixia kanhua ji*, in *QYLS*, p. 78.
161. Zhang Jiliang, *Jintai canlei ji*, in *QYLS*, p. 234.
162. Yang Maojian, *Chang'an kanhua ji*, in *QYLS*, p. 311.
163. Chen Yanheng, *Jiuju congtan*, in *QYLS*, p. 859.
164. Scholarship on theaters in eighteenth-century Beijing speculates that regular commercial playhouses developed out of opera patronage at winehouses and scholar-official lodges and trade guilds. See, for instance, Liao Ben, *Zhongguo gudai juchang shi*, pp. 86–88; Wang Qiang, *Huiguan xitai yu xiju*, pp. 239–312.
165. Chen Sen, *PHBJ*, 1.7b.
166. From *Yanjing zaji*, cited in Zhang Cixi, *Beijing liyuan zhanggu changbian*, in *QYLS*, p. 898.

Chapter Two

1. From Zha Kui, *Yantai kouhao yibai shou* (ca. 1800), in Lu Gong, *Qingdai Beijing zhuzhici*, p. 31.
2. From Anon., "Dumen zhuzhici" (1814), in Lu Gong, *Qingdai Beijing zhuzhici*, p. 42.
3. Lu Eting, *Kunju yanchu shigao*, p. 233. See also the comments put into the mouth of the character Wei Pincai in the novel *Pinhua baojian*; Chen Sen, *PHBJ*, chap. 2, p. 5b.
4. Zhang Jiliang, *Jintai canlei ji*, in *QYLS*, p. 248.
5. For use of these other terms for the playhouse, see, for instance, Wu Changyuan, *Yanlan xiaopu*, in *QYLS*, pp. 45, 46.
6. In his excellent study of Peking opera in Republican China, Joshua Goldstein posits a shift from "teahouse" to "playhouse" that transpired in the Republican era. Goldstein's project articulates a Foucauldian-style break at the onset of modernity in China and demonstrates the various ways in which Peking opera became party to the construction of a modern nation. For his purposes, he tends to emphasize the rift between the formation of a modern opera theater and all that preceded it. This has the unwitting effect, however, of reifying the "teahouse" as a long-standing and unchanging institution; see Goldstein, *Drama Kings*, esp. chap. 2. In fact, however, the tea garden was a new urban entity in the eighteenth century. I find the term "teahouse" misleading; it blurs the distinction between teahouses devoted to presentation of opera and other, smaller teahouses that featured storytelling and other narrative performance arts. It also sounds too quaint.
7. Liao Ben, *Zhongguo gudai juchang shi*. See also Zhao Shanlin, *Zhongguo xiqu guanzhong xue*; Idema and West, *Chinese Theater*.
8. Wang Qiang, *Huiguan xitai yu xiju*, pp. 9–10. See also Belsky, *Localities at the Center*, esp. pp. 41–50.
9. Liao Ben has identified four transitional playhouse/culinary establishments (*jiuguan*) in the capital in the early Qing: Baiyunlou, Zhajialou, Siyiyuan, and Yueminglou; Liao, *Zhongguo gudai juchang shi*, pp. 77–88.
10. An edict promulgated on 31 January 1725 forbade provincial officials to raise private acting troupes; cited in Wang Liqi, *YMQ jinhui xiaoshuo xiqu*, p. 31. A simi-

lar prohibition was reissued in 1769; see *Gaozong xian huangdi shilu*, juan 845, pp. 19–20, in *DQLCSL*, 33:12072.

11. See Zhang Faying, *Zhongguo jiayue xiban*, pp. 56–58.

12. Ibid., pp. 58–72. For descriptions of the private troupes of the great eighteenth-century Yangzhou salt merchants, see Li Dou, *Yangzhou huafang lu*, juan 5; see also the observations by Yangzhou native Lin Sumen, who maintains that only in the early nineteenth century did Yangzhou establish playhouses in imitation of those in Beijing; Lin, *Hanjiang sanbai yin*, juan 8, pp. 2a–2b.

13. On the lure of Beijing and the *Four Treasuries* project to men of literary talent in the late eighteenth century, see Guy, *Emperor's Four Treasuries*, pp. 47–49.

14. Most writings about performance in the seventeenth century come from commonplace book jottings and usually describe performance by household troupes in private settings. Alternatively, they describe outdoor, occasional performances. For casual jottings of this sort, see, for instance, the various entries on performance in Zhang Dai's *Tao'an mengyi*.

15. On the term "Manchu apartheid" to describe Qing theories and policies of governance, see Wakeman, *The Great Enterprise*, p. 476. For use of this term with particular reference to the spatial segregation of Banner and Han populations, see Elliott, *The Manchu Way*, pp. 98–105 passim.

16. Elliott, *The Manchu Way*, pp. 98–105 passim. For more on the significance and symbolism of the walls of Ming and Qing Beijing, see also Liu Xiaomeng, *Manzu de shehui yu shenghuo*, pp. 322–46 passim; Naquin, *Peking*, pp. 4–11; Dray-Novey, "Spatial Order and Police in Imperial Beijing," pp. 890–94.

17. The walls "marked the 'presence of government' to all who saw them," as Alison Dray-Novey has aptly observed; Dray-Novey, "Spatial Order and Police in Imperial Beijing," p. 890. On the cosmological and ritual significance of walls in premodern Chinese cities, see, among others, Arthur F. Wright, "The Cosmology of the Chinese City," in Skinner, *The City in Late Imperial China*, pp. 33–75; Sen-dou Chang, "The Morphology of Walled Capitals," in Skinner, *The City in Late Imperial China*, pp. 75–100. For the significance of the walls of Beijing, see Naquin, *Peking*, pp. 4–18.

18. On the stationing of the Eight Banner garrisons in the capital see, among others, Elliott, *The Manchu Way*, pp. 101–5; and Liu Xiaomeng, *Manzu de shehui yu shenghuo*, pp. 322–44 passim.

19. For the virtual equation of Banner and Manchu identity, in spite of the heterogeneous ethnic mix within the banner population, see Elliott, who writes: "Just as Manchus became people of the banners, so the different people of the banners gradually became, for practical purposes, Manchus"; Elliott, *The Manchu Way*, p. 8. In 1648, four years after the Qing rulers had made Beijing their capital, all non-Banner Han residents of the Inner City were required to relocate to the Outer City; see ibid., p. 100.

20. Population figures for eighteenth-century Beijing range from about one to three million, with most contemporary studies suggesting a figure closer to the conservative end of this spectrum. See Dray-Novey, "Spatial Order and Police in Impe-

rial Beijing," p. 889n2; Rozman, *Urban Networks*, pp. 277–84; Elliott, *The Manchu Way*, pp. 117–19.

21. See "Chongxiu xishen zushi miao beizhi" (1792), and "Chongxiu xishen dian bei xu" (1827), cited in Liao Ben, *Zhongguo gudai juchang shi*, pp. 88–89. See also *Guanju riji*, manuscript, ca. 1773–1816, Zhongguo yishu yanjiuyuan Library, Beijing. For a typeset version of this text, see Yan Changke, "Zhengui de xiqu shiliao: du 'jiaqing dingsi wuwu guanju riji' shougao," pp. 250–80.

22. Zhang Jiliang, *Jintai canlei ji*, in *QYLS*, p. 250.

23. Ibid. For more on the location of playhouses, see Yang Maojian, *Menghua suobu*, in *QYLS*, pp. 348–51. See also Dray-Novey, "Spatial Order and Police in Imperial Beijing," p. 892.

24. Yan Xu et al., *Qinding taigui*, juan 25, p. 1b. The prohibition on bannermen entering commercial playhouses and winehouses was also written into the Qing penal code under the category "miscellaneous criminal violations" (*xing zafan*); *Qinding libu chufen zeli*, juan 45, "Xing zafan," as cited in Wang Liqi, *YMQ jinhui xiaoshuo xiqu*, p. 20.

25. Yan Xu et al., *Qinding taigui*, juan 25, pp. 17a–b, 25a–b, 35b–36a. See also *Qinding Da Qing huidian shi li*, as cited in Zhang Cixi, *Beijing liyuan zhanggu changbian*, in *QYLS*, pp. 883–85.

26. *Renzong rui huangdi shilu*, juan 169, pp. 11–13, 16–17, in *DQLCSL*, 50:2444–47. Also cited in Wang Liqi, *YMQ jinhui xiaoshuo xiqu*, pp. 57–59.

27. Yang Maojian, *Menghua suobu*, in *QYLS*, p. 350.

28. Ibid.

29. Yan Xu et al., *Qinding taigui*, juan 25, p. 46b.

30. Ibid; for additional mention of night performances and women's seating sections in playhouses, see also the edict of 1852, in ibid., pp. 41a–b; also cited in Zhang Cixi, *Beijing liyuan zhanggu changbian*, in *QYLS*, pp. 885–86.

31. Zhang Jiliang, *Jintai canlei ji*, in *QYLS*, p. 248. Egor F. Timovsky, a member of the Russian Mission in residence in Beijing 1820–21, also observed: "The Mantchoo officers could not go to the theatre, without taking from their caps the distinguishing badges of their rank"; see Timovsky, *Travels of the Russian Mission*, 2:179.

32. Yang Maojian, *Menghua suobu*, in *QYLS*, pp. 353–54.

33. *Shizong xian huangdi shilu*, juan 18, pp. 4a–5a, in *DQLCSL*, 14:280–81.

34. Yan Xu et al., *Qinding taigui*, juan 25, p. 13b.

35. Ibid., p. 35b.

36. I am grateful to Mark Elliott for suggesting the romanization for the Manchu pronunciation of this name.

37. The full edict recounting this incident is in *Renzong rui huangdi shilu*, juan 169, pp. 11–13, 16–17, in *DQLCSL*, 50:2444–47. The edict is dated to 30 November 1806.

38. Ibid., pp. 16–17, in *DQLCSL*, 50:2446–47. This incident is also mentioned in Zhao Shanlin, *Zhongguo xiqu guanzhong xue*, p. 91.

39. For his elaboration of the "Manchu Way," see Elliott, *The Manchu Way*, pp. 8–13 passim.

40. From an edict of 1799; in Yan Xu et al., *Qinding taigui*, juan 25, pp. 17a–b.

41. Ibid., p. 56a.
42. *Renzong rui huangdi shilu*, juan 169, p. 17, in *DQLCSL*, 50:2447.
43. Ibid.
44. Qing suspicion of commercial playhouses as sites of political and social unrest was not unfounded. Several of the participants in the Eight Trigrams Uprising of 1813 had used one of the playhouses in the Outer City as a meeting site on the day before they broke into the imperial palace. This theater is mentioned in Timovsky, *Travels of the Russian Mission*, 2:173–74. For an in-depth analysis of this rebellion, see Naquin, *Millenarian Rebellion in China*.
45. Kuhn, *Soulstealers*.
46. From Yang Jingting, *Dumen zayong* (1845), in Lu Gong, *Qingdai Beijing zhuzhici*, p. 78.
47. For more on citywide curfews and enforcement procedures in Qing Beijing, see Dray-Novey, "Spatial Order and Police in Imperial Beijing," pp. 885–922.
48. The loophole that allowed sons and nephews of sitting officials to take the provincial-level examination in Shuntian Prefecture ensured the arrival of an especially large cohort of exam takers in the Qing capital. This loophole remained in effect until 1807; see Elman, *A Cultural History of Civil Examinations*, p. 226.
49. Zhang Jiliang, *Jintai canlei ji*, in *QYLS*, p. 248.
50. Yang Cuiyan (pseud. Suhaian jushi), *Yantai hongzhua ji*, in *QYLS*, pp. 269–70.
51. Li Lüyuan, *Qilu deng*, p. 957.
52. The Zhalou is a reference to one of the earliest recorded commercial playhouses in Beijing. It is one of the playhouses that transitioned from a jiulou to a chayuan and is thought to have been in operation during the late seventeenth century. Wu Changyuan, in his guide to the city of Beijing, remarks: "The Zhalou was located in the Pork Market [Roushi] neighborhood; the theater was built by the eminent Zha family in the Ming dynasty. During our dynasty it was turned into the Guanghe Playhouse"; Wu, *Chenhuan shilüe*, juan 5, p. 2b. In the passage by the Raconteur cited here, the compound *zhalou* should be taken not as the specific playhouse but as a term for playhouses in general; a parallel construction to the phrase *jubu* (Chrysanthemum Quarter) in the following line. If Wu Changyuan's information is correct, the Raconteur could not possibly have gone to the Zha Playhouse, since by the 1780s it was no longer called by that name. For more on the Zhalou, see also Liao Ben, *Zhongguo gudai juchang shi*, p. 80.
53. "Chrysanthemum Quarter" is a flowery euphemism for the theatrical demimonde.
54. From the "Tici" by Xicheng waishi in Wu Changyuan, *Yanlan xiaopu*, in *QYLS*, p. 4.
55. "Wang Mingfang Ascends Three Ranks" is a farce about an impoverished scholar who travels to the capital to take the exams.
56. Yang Maojian, *Menghua suobu*, in *QYLS*, p. 361. Du Liniang's line is a bastardization of two phrases from the *Analects*. The first phrase is a misreading of a passage in which Confucius is talking to his disciple Zixia about filiality—a comment

that children should "supply their elders with wine and food." The second phrase is a bungled reading of Confucius's instructions to Zixia to "be a scholar in the style of the gentleman." For the correct passages, see Legge, *Confucius*, pp. 148, 189.

57. For descriptions of these characters, see Chen Sen, *PHBJ*, chaps. 3, 13, 18, 19, 23, 27, 34, 35, 40, 47, and 58.

58. Yu Jiao, *Meng'an zazhu*, p. 13. Yang Maojian characterizes the audiences in the pond area as "marketplace horse-trading agents and servile sedan-chair carriers"; Yang, *Menghua suobu*, in *QYLS*, p. 353.

59. Wu Changyuan, *Yanlan xiaopu*, in *QYLS*, p. 18.

60. The figure of crowds of as many as a thousand for performances by the Jifang Troupe in the 1820s comes from Yang Maojian, *Menghua suobu*, in *QYLS*, p. 373. The more modest figure for the late nineteenth century comes from Shen Taimou, *Xuannan lingmeng lu* (ca. 1875–1910), in *QYLS*, p. 805. Qi Rushan estimates that most playhouses could hold from eight hundred to fourteen hundred people; Qi, "Xiguan," p. 21b. A survey completed in 1906 by the city police records that on average each of the seven theaters of the Outer City attracted more than five hundred people per performance; *Jingshi Waicheng xunjing zongting diyici tongji shi* (Beijing, 1907), cited in Naquin, *Peking*, p. 635n35. Comparable numbers filled the "parterre," or the pit section, of theaters in seventeenth- and eighteenth-century France; see Ravel, *The Contested Parterre*.

61. Yang Maojian, *Menghua suobu*, in *QYLS*, p. 353. Soldiers on nighttime surprise maneuvers gripped stalks between their teeth to keep themselves quiet. Here the huapu author is wishing that the uninhibited shouts of the crowds in the pond could be kept quiet by such tactics.

62. Zhang Jiliang, *Jintai canlei ji*, in *QYLS*, p. 249; Yang Maojian, *Menghua suobu*, in *QYLS*, p. 353.

63. Yang Maojian, *Menghua suobu*, in *QYLS*, p. 353.

64. Ibid.

65. Ibid. An excellent overview of the layout of commercial theaters is provided in Liao Ben, *Zhongguo gudai juchang shi*, pp. 92–97; see also Qi Rushan, "Xiguan," pp. 26a–33a.

66. The Shengping shu was the office in charge of performances within the imperial palace. It succeeded the former Nanfu, or Southern Bureau, in 1827.

67. Qi Rushan, "Xiguan," p. 31a. For more on these seats, see the comments in Mei Lanfang's autobiography; Mei Lanfang and Xu Jichuan, *Wutai shenghuo sishinian*, 1:52; Liao Ben, *Zhongguo gudai juchang shi*, p. 94.

68. Zhang Jiliang, *Jintai canlei ji*, in *QYLS*, p. 249. This figure is confirmed by two other sources of the time. In *Pinhua baojian* two tickets in the scattered-seats area are said to cost 300 copper coins; Chen Sen, *PHBJ*, chap. 8, pp. 1b–2a. The Russian envoy Egor Timovsky states the admission price for playhouses in 1820–21 as 150 copper coins; see Timovsky, *Travels of the Russian Mission*, 2:175–76. Another source, dated to 1842, gives the cost of scattered seats as 192 copper coins; see Yang Maojian, *Menghua suobu*, in *QYLS*, p. 349. By the 1870s the price of a seat in the pond had risen to 600 to 800 copper coins; see Shen Taimou, *Xuannan lingmeng lu*,

in *QYLS*, p. 804. A concise overview of playhouse prices can be found in Liao Ben, *Zhongguo gudai juchang shi*, pp. 98–100.

69. In the nineteenth century a catty was equivalent to 1⅓ pounds. These price equivalents are provided in Timovsky, *Travels of the Russian Mission*, 2:199–206, and seem to accord with price information in novels and huapu of the time. They also seem to accord with the information on prices in Peng Xinwei, *Zhongguo huobi shi*, pp. 485–546 passim.

70. From a passage in Chen Sen, *PHBJ*, chap. 3, p. 11b.

71. This estimate of monthly wages, probably on the generous side, comes from Timovsky, *Travels of the Russian Mission*, 2:199–206. According to *PHBJ*, the monthly cost of food and salary for a serving boy came to eight hundred copper coins; Chen Sen, *PHBJ*, chap. 23, p. 13b.

72. The typical monthly salary for a capital bannerman was four taels of silver, usually plus grain stipends and extra bonuses; see Elliott, *The Manchu Way*, p. 192. Conversion rates of silver to copper coinage varied widely over the Qing. One source gives the exchange rate in the capital in 1779 as 1 tael of silver to 880 copper coins; by 1828 the exchange rate was 1:2,550; Timovsky records an exchange rate of 1:1,100 for 1820–21. See also Peng Xinwei, *Zhongguo huobi shi*, pp. 529–38.

73. From Anon., "Dumen zhuzhici," in Lu Gong, *Qingdai Beijing zhuzhici*, p. 42. The playhouses routinely hired bouncers, whose job it was to turn away people attempting to watch for free. Playhouses, it seems, did not collect money from patrons until after they had been seated and had watched a show; see Qi Rushan, "Xiguan," pp. 32b–33a. Much of Qi Rushan's information about the bouncers corresponds to the entry on playhouses in Xu Yusheng, *Yanshi jibi*, pp. 74–77.

74. Qi Rushan, "Xiguan," p. 26b.

75. Wen Kang, *Ernü yingxiong zhuan*, p. 712.

76. For more on the ban on women in commercial theaters, see Mackerras, *Rise of the Peking Opera*, pp. 214–15; Zhou Yibai, *Zhongguo xiqu shi*, p. 737; Qi Rushan, *Jingju zhi bianqian*, in *QRSQJ*, 2:7a. Mackerras claims the ban was suggested to the emperor by the scholar Lang Baochen (1763–1839) and was readily adopted by the Qianlong court. See also Zhao Shanlin, *Zhongguo xiqu guanzhong xue*, pp. 98–101.

77. The first edict regarding playhouses establishing seating sections for women dates from 1852; from *Da Qing Wenzong xian huangdi shilu*, juan 51, as cited in Zhang Cixi, *Beijing liyuan zhanggu changbian*, in *QYLS*, pp. 885–86; also cited in Wang Liqi, *YMQ jinhui xiaoshuo xiqu*, p. 77. See also the account of women and men mixing in playhouses within the Inner City, as recorded by Li Ciming in *Xunxuezhai riji, bingji shang*, in Li Ciming, *Yuemantang riji*, 36:44a. There are also late nineteenth-century accounts of Han women attending operas (in segregated seating sections) in guildhalls located in the Outer City. Probably the most famous instance is linked to the destruction of the Huguang huiguan, a version of which is related in Chen Moxiang, *Guanju shenghuo sumiao*, appended to Chen Moxiang and Pan Jingfu, *Liyuan waishi*, pp. 376–78.

Considerable remigration of Han families and shop proprietors into the Inner City by the late nineteenth century meant that the strict ethnic segregation of space had begun to break down; see Elliott, *The Manchu Way*, p. 286; Rhoads, *Manchus and Han*, p. 263.

78. On the controversy in Beijing after 1908 about admitting women to playhouses, see Goldstein, *Drama Kings*, pp. 83–85.

79. Dray-Novey explains, "The gates closed soon after sundown with a guard ceremony that allowed a short time (about ten minutes) during which stragglers could pass through"; Dray-Novey, "Spatial Order and Police in Imperial Beijing," p. 895.

80. According to Qi Rushan, regulations against lamps in theaters meant that during the winter months the actors were performing the final scene in the dark; Qi, "Xiguan," pp. 47a–b. On the timing of performances, see also Yang Maojian, *Menghua suobu*, in *QYLS*, pp. 354–55.

81. Yang Maojian, *Menghua suobu*, in *QYLS*, pp. 349–50. See also Zhang Jiliang, *Jintai canlei ji*, in *QYLS*, p. 250; Qi Rushan, "Xiguan," pp. 40–41; Liao Ben, *Zhongguo gudai juchang shi*, pp. 97–105; Zhao Shanlin, *Zhongguo xiqu guanzhong xue*, pp. 90–94.

82. Yang Maojian, *Menghua suobu*, in *QYLS*, p. 349.

83. Ibid., pp. 349–50 passim.

84. Zhang Jiliang, *Jintai canlei ji*, in *QYLS*, p. 250. According to Mei Lanfang, this pattern of scene arrangement persisted into the early twentieth century. See Mei Lanfang and Xu Jichuan, *Wutai shenghuo sishinian*, 2:133.

85. Connoisseurs of the theater disdained the acrobatic scenes, preferring the love stories and social dramas. One aficionado writing in the early nineteenth century remarked, "Recently, when the musical troupes mount the stage, they always perform one acrobatic scene. The Songzhu Troupe always does two. . . . It stirs up the dust on the stage and is especially annoying"; Zhang, *Jintai canlei ji*, in *QYLS*, p. 241.

86. Camp was the flip side of the eroticism of the theater. Playing cross-dressing in an extreme, clownish way mocked and defused some of the erotic tension of the transvestite theater. Chinese playwrights were highly conscious of the ironic potential of cross-dressing and put this to great theatrical effect in performance; see my "The Nun Who Wouldn't Be," pp. 71–138.

87. According to Qing legal statutes, career actors were an inferior class. Actors and their descendants to three generations were forbidden to sit for the civil-service examinations; see Mackerras, *Rise of the Peking Opera*, pp. 43, 219; Wang Liqi, *YMQ jinhui xiaoshuo xiqu*, pp. 6, 12. Although the legal category of "mean" people was expunged from the law code under the Yongzheng emperor, in practice the stigma associated with actors remained; see Sommer, *Sex, Law, and Society*, esp. chap. 4. See also Yao Shuyi, *Wan Qing xiqu de bianqe*, pp. 148–240 passim.

88. See Wang Shunu, *Zhongguo changji shi*, pp. 317–27; Mackerras, *Rise of the Peking Opera*, p. 150; Hinsch, *Passions of the Cut Sleeve*, p. 154; and Sommer, *Sex, Law, and Society*.

89. Zhang Jiliang, *Jintai canlei ji*, in *QYLS*, p. 246.

90. Timovsky, *Travels of the Russian Mission*, 2:175.

91. From De Shuoting, *Caozhu yichuan*, as cited in Zhang Cixi, *Beiping liyuan zhuzhici huibian*, in *QYLS*, p. 1172.

92. Chen Sen, *PHBJ*, chap. 1, pp. 20a–21b. A passage in Wen Kang's *Ernü yingxiong zhuan* explicitly satirizes the frequently idealized representation of the commercial theater in *Pinhua baojian*—with even the beautiful boy actresses described as having dirty fingernails and their refined scholarly patrons as lecherous buffoons (pp. 711–15).

93. On this topic, see Elliott, *The Manchu Way*, p. 288; and Crossley, *Orphan Warriors*, pp. 77, 84–85, 176–77; Rhoads, *Manchus and Han*, p. 58.

94. The first commercial playhouse in Beijing that was open to both men and women, the Civilization Playhouse (Wenming chayuan), was constructed in 1907. For more on the influence of Shanghai practices on theaters in Beijing, see Yeh, "Where Is the Center of Cultural Production?," pp. 74–118; Luo Suwen, "Lun jindai xiqu yu dushi jumin," pp. 207–30.

95. Several prominent actors, including the famous dan Tian Jiyun, were instrumental in petitioning the new Republican government to outlaw this practice in 1912. See Yao Shuyi, *Wan Qing xiqu de bianqe*, pp. 190–91; Goldstein, *Drama Kings*, pp. 106–15.

96. On playhouses and the development of a "lower-class enlightenment," see Li Xiaoti, *Qingmo de xiaceng shehui qimeng yundong, 1901–1911*. On actors in new-style, politically themed plays at the end of the Qing, see Goldstein, *Drama Kings*, pp. 90–105; Karl, *Staging the World*, pp. 27–49 passim.

97. On the development of theatrical performance and temple stages during the Song, Jin, and Yuan, see among others, Liao Ben, *Song Yuan xiqu wenwu yu minus*; Idema and West, *Chinese Theater*, pp. 185–201; Tanaka Issei, *Chūgoku engeki-shi*, esp. chaps. 1–4.

98. Rural opera could be well funded, too. On well-funded lineage-sponsored ritual opera in Huizhou, Anhui, see Qitao Guo, *Ritual Opera and Mercantile Lineage*; on ritual opera in village Shanxi, see Johnson, *Spectacle and Sacrifice*.

99. On court patronage of Beijing temples, see Naquin, *Peking*. For her discussion of temple stages and temple performance, see ibid., pp. 84–85, 612–21, 632–38.

100. Ibid., p. 84, and n.109. See also Chang Renchun, *Lao Beijing de fengsu*.

101. For the temple-fair schedules of the Huguosi and Longfusi, see Dun Lichen, *Yanjing suishi ji*, pp. 53–54. See also Chang Renchun, *Lao Beijing de fengsu*, pp. 6, 19–30. For the Baiben Zhang bookstall rotations through the various temple fairs in the city, see Fu Xihua, "Baiben Zhang xiqu shuji kaolüe," pp. 317–29.

102. Chang Renchun, *Lao Beijing de fengsu*, pp. 42–43, 16. On the Yaowangmiao and Huoshenmiao, see also Naquin, *Peking*, pp. 26–29, 628, respectively.

103. For an eighteenth-century account of annual festivals, see Pan Rongbi, *Dijing suishi jisheng*; this is translated in Naquin, *Peking*, pp. 442–43. For a late nineteenth-century version of the annual festival calendar, see also Dun Lichen, *Yanjing suishi ji*.

104. *Guanju riji*, p. 20b.

105. See the entry for 1 December 1797 in ibid., p. 20a. Qingchun Playhouse was

one of the smaller houses; it was located on Poplar-Plum-Bamboo Diagonal Street (Yangmeizhu xie jie) in the Outer City.

106. Ibid., p. 20b. Wealthy temple patrons often sponsored plays as requital for supernatural assistance from the gods of an efficacious temple. It is unclear whether the performances on 18 December 1797 at the Jiangnan City God Temple on Nanheng Street were sponsored by the temple for a festival or by an individual or group of patrons as requital plays. According to Chang Renchun, the regularly scheduled festivals at this temple occurred on the Qingming Festival, on 7/15, and on 10/1 of the lunar calendar; thus, it is likely that the performances on 11/1 were not part of the regularly scheduled ritual calendar; see Chang Renchun, *Lao Beijing de fengsu*, pp. 11, 92–94.

107. From De Shuoting, *Caozhu yichuan*, in Lu Gong, *Qingdai Beijing zhuzhici*, p. 52.

108. Sun Danwu, *Diehua yinguan shichao* (1861), as cited in Zhang Cixi, *Beiping liyuan zhuzhici huibian*, in *QYLS*, p. 1175. Although the poem mentions Tianlingsi, this has to be a corruption of Tianningsi, which was famous for its chrysanthemums. A comment about the Tianningsi appended to an early twentieth-century collection of poems about Beijing notes: "The Tianning Monastery is located to the west of the capital city; mounted couriers traveling west make this [temple] their first stop. The monks of the monastery make jasmine-scented snuff and cultivate exquisite varieties of chrysanthemums to support themselves." From He Gangde, *Huameng ji* (1925), p. 12. See also Dun Lichen, *Yanjing suishi ji*, pp. 79–80, on Tianningsi as famous for its chrysanthemums. The term that I have translated as "ladies," literally, "jade ones" (*yuren*), might also refer to the boy actresses. The Tianning Monastery was a popular spot to which the elites took actors for drinking and feasting during the late nineteenth century; see Chong Yi, *Dao Xian yilai chaoye zaji*, p. 26. Either way, additional sources confirm that women frequented temple fairs in the environs of Beijing.

109. Chong Yi, *Dao Xian yilai chaoye zaji*, p. 95.

110. See Liao Ben, *Zhongguo gudai juchang shi*, p. 128; Zhao Shanlin, *Zhongguo xiqu guanzhong xue*, p. 99.

111. Yan Xu et al., *Qinding taigui*, juan 25, pp. 13a–b.

112. Ibid., pp. 41b–42a.

113. Ibid., pp. 46a–b. The edict is dated to 21 December 1869. It is not clear from the edict whether the commotion was caused by the women or by male spectators watching the women.

114. Ibid., p. 42a.

115. *Xuanzong cheng huangdi shilu*, juan 314, pp. 6–7, 16–18, in *DQLCSL*, 63:5611–17. This incident, in which Yimai (Prince Zhuang), a prince of the first degree, was caught smoking opium, occurred on the eve of the Opium War and against the backdrop of debates at court on legalization versus prohibition of the narcotic; see Polachek, *Inner Opium War*, pp. 113–36. See also the account in Liu Liemao and Guo Jingrui, *Che wangfu quben yanjiu*, pp. 471–73.

116. Yimai's brother Yigeng was a noted author of *zidi shu*, under the pseudonym

Helü shi. Nothing indicates that Yigeng was involved in the creation of the "Lingguanmiao" pieces.

117. Chong Yi, *Dao Xian yilai chaoye zaji*, pp. 19–20.

118. Yundu shi, "Xu Lingguanmiao," in *QCWF zidi shu ji*, p. 266.

119. Yundu shi, "Lingguanmiao," in *QCWF zidi shu ji*, p. 264, top column. The approximate date given in the *zidi shu* corresponds to the date of the edict. The Middle Primordial, or *zhongyuan* (7/15), fell on 3 September in 1838, just over six weeks before the date of the edict.

120. I expect that it would have been far too sensitive to name names in the storytelling pieces. Even if those arrested had fallen out of favor, they still were related to some of the most powerful people at court. Besides, the capital rumor mill would have made it unnecessary to name names, since surely audiences for the *zidi shu* ballads—other Beijing bannermen—would have known who had been caught during the temple raid.

121. Yundu shi, "Lingguanmiao," in *QCWF zidi shu ji*, p. 264.

122. Ibid., p. 265.

123. Ibid.

124. For literary depictions of women at temple performances in locations other than Beijing, see the descriptions in Li Lüyuan, *Qilu deng*, pp. 449, 455–56.

125. These were troupes active in Beijing in the early nineteenth century. Scattered references to actors from these troupes can be found in three early nineteenth-century flower registers: *Rixia kanhua ji* (1803), *Pianyu ji* (1805–6), and *Tingchun xinyong* (1810), all in *QYLS*, pp. 53–116, 117–48, 149–207, respectively. This helps date the *zidi shu* piece to the early nineteenth century; the troupes mentioned here fell out of the historical record by circa 1830.

126. This is a scene from the longer drama cycle *Yuzan ji*. The full chuanqi drama tells the story of the romance between Chen Miaochang (a Daoist nun) and Pan Bizheng. "Stealing the Secret Poem" (Tou shi) is the episode in which the mutual love of the protagonists is revealed.

127. The references are to "Shizhuo ji" and "Shier hong." These are titillating plays, with lots of flirtation, and, in the latter, violence. They could be performed in either kunju or luantan opera style. They have now fallen out of the kunju repertory and have become part of the *jingju* repertoire. The first was radically "cleaned up" in the twentieth century; the latter has not been performed since the 1950s. See the entries for these play titles in Tao Junqi, *Jingju jumu chutan*, pp. 321, 406–7, respectively.

128. Wen Xiyuan, "Kuoda nainai ting shanhui xi," in *QCWF zidi shu ji*, pp. 260–61.

129. The earliest reference to salon performance held in private family homes comes from the "San bu zu" section of Huan Kuan's (act. 73 BCE) *Yantie lun*, which states: "When commoner families have guests, they often entertain them with the acrobatics of singers and actors"; cited in Liao Ben, *Zhongguo gudai juchang shi*, p. 61.

130. Zhao Shanlin, *Zhongguo xiqu guanzhong xue*, p. 58. Lu Eting has calculated that thirty-eight prominent families supported family troupes in the late Ming; Lu, *Kunju yanchu shigao*, pp. 116–32.

131. For scholarship on Ming-period salon performance, see, among others, Birch, *Scenes for Mandarins*; Wang Anqi, *Mingdai chuanqi zhi juchang ji qi yishu*; Qi Senhua, "Shi lun Mingdai jiayue," in Hua Wei and Wang Ayling, *Ming Qing xiqu guoji yantaohui lunwenji*, 1:305–26; Zhang Faying, *Zhongguo jiayue xiban*.

132. Qi Rushan distinguishes between tanghui performances sponsored by native-place (scholar-official) associations and those sponsored by trade guilds, designating the latter as *hang xi*. For his description of hang xi, see Qi Rushan, *Xiban*, in *QRSQ J*, 1:25a–b. See also Mei Lanfang's recollections of hang xi in Mei Lanfang and Xu Jichuan, *Wutai shenghuo sishinian*, 1:60–61.

133. Even within the salon the audience was not necessarily homogeneous. The invited guests tended to be social peers, but the familial sponsorship and setting of performance meant that any member of the familial economy, including servants and retainers, had the potential to view plays in this setting. Nevertheless, because this setting simply replicated the social hierarchies of the familial economy, the mix of social class in the salon venue was less fraught than in the commercial playhouse.

134. Specific edicts forbidding officials and Manchus to raise their own acting troupes were issued in 1725, 1769, 1799, 1808, and 1838. See Wang Liqi, *YMQ jinhui xiaoshuo xiqu*, pp. 31, 46–47, 53–54, 62–63, 74. By 1872 the proscription was no longer directed toward officials but toward eunuchs; see Wang Liqi, *YMQ jinhui xiqu xiaoshuo*, pp. 83–84.

135. The Qianlong emperor's brother Hongchou also had a passion for opera and the means to be entertained by his own private opera troupe; see Kahn, *Monarchy in the Emperor's Eyes*, pp. 113–14.

136. Chen Moxiang and Pan Jingfu, *Liyuan waishi*, p. 146; also mentioned in Chen Moxiang, *Guanju shenghuo sumiao*, p. 378. See also Mei Lanfang's recollections of the private troupes and stages in the mansions of Prince Chun and Prince Gong, in the 1981 edition (Beijing: Zhongguo xiqu) of *Wutai shenghuo sishinian*, 3:224–29 passim; cited in Liao Ben, *Zhongguo gudai juchang shi*, p. 65.

137. *A-ge* was an unofficial Manchu designation for the son of the emperor or a prince.

138. The ethnicity of the tutor is not explicit; he is referred to by the honorific title *xiansheng*.

139. "Jiayuan le," in *QCWF zidi shu ji*, p. 256.

140. The play "The Three Top Candidates Make the Grade" (San yuan jidi) is picked for its auspicious-sounding title, that is, its suggestion that three young men will pass the exams. Its selection is intended to bring good luck in the exams to the host's own three sons. In this description the host picks the opera, but often troupes performed such auspicious operas on ceremonial occasions without being prompted as a way of flattering their patrons. This particular play could be a scene or scene-set from the longer play, *San yuan zheng bei*. That opera is in the qinqiang musical style, possibly an indication that the music performed at the occasion was a form of qinqiang and not kunju. A very similar story (plot essentially identical but set in a different dynasty) is also told in the Ming-era chuanqi drama *Yuan Wenzheng huanhun ji*, perhaps a sign that selections from the chuanqi had moved into

the kunju or *gaoqiang* repertoire. Synopses of these plays can be found in Shaanxi sheng yishu yanjiusuo, *Qinqiang jumu chukao*, p. 434; Tao Junqi, *Jingju jumu chutan*, p. 235. The title of the first scene mentioned in the tale does not permit identifying which style of opera is being performed; the second title is definitely kunju.

141. "Departure of the Soul" / "Awakening from the Dream" (Lihun/jingmeng) is a rendition of two scenes from *Mudan ting*. From the mention of the lanterns and, later in the text, of "flower spirits" dancing with the lanterns, the scene selection quite likely includes a rendition of "Heaped Blossoms" (Dui hua). "Dui hua" was a dance scene that became appended to the famous *Mudan ting* dream scene in the eighteenth- and nineteenth-century-production repertory. It was full of spectacle and seems to have had the effect of watering down the eroticism of the dream sequence in the original script. On the evolution and significance of the "Dui hua" scene, see Swatek, Peony Pavilion *Onstage*, chaps. 4, 5.

142. "Jiayuan le," in *QCWF zidi shu ji*, p. 256.

143. Ibid., p. 257.

144. According to several nineteenth-century sources, the main difference between Manchu/Banner and Han tanghui parties had to do with the style of entertainment selected for the occasion. Han families selected just operas, whereas salons in Manchu and Banner households often featured other narrative performance arts in addition to opera—including zidi shu and other styles of storytelling and ballad singing, and sometimes even magic shows and vocal-impersonation skits; see Zhi Chaozi, *Jiujing suoji*, p. 97; see also the description of birthday salon performances in Lowe, *The Adventures of Wu*, pp. 216–20; Chang Renchun, *Lao Beijing de fengsu*, pp. 238–45; Zhongguo renmin zhengzhi xieshang huiyi Beijingshi weiyuanhui wenshi ziliao yanjiu weiyuanhui, *Beijing wangshi tan*, pp. 129–40 passim. It is strongly implied that the extremely wealthy family of the character Hua Xingbei in the novel *Pinhua baojian* is affiliated with one of the Banners (perhaps a Han Banner family). At some of his lavish tanghui parties in his garden, he arranges for storytelling, xiangsheng, and magic shows, in addition to opera; see Chen Sen, *PHBJ*, chap. 30, p. 12a. This practice is contrasted to the salon parties in the home of Xu Ziyun, the son of a high-ranking non-Banner Han official.

145. This refers to the practice of troupes reopening the costume and prop trunks at the start of each year. Prior to the New Year holiday all troupes sealed the trunks as a sign that the performance season had come to an end. After the New Year the seals were broken and performances resumed; Qi Rushan, *Xiban*, in *QRSQJ*, 1:29a.

146. Wu Tao, *Liyuan jiuhua* (ca. 1870–1900), in *QYLS*, p. 827.

147. "Invitation to the Banquet" (Qingyan) and "The Farewell Feast" (Jianbie) are both scenes from *Southern Story of the Western Wing* (*Nan Xixiang ji*). The first scene depicts the banquet thrown by Madame Cui to thank Student Zhang for having saved the temple in which they are lodged from bandits; the second depicts the parting between the lovers Oriole Cui and Student Zhang. The play selections are kunju.

148. "Meeting at Wutai Mountain" (Wutai) is a scene from the drama *Vast-Sky Pagoda* (*Haotian ta*).

149. Wu Jingzi, *Rulin waishi*, chap. 49, p. 577.

150. Li Lüyuan, *Qilu deng*, p. 194.

151. See, for instance, the salon party depicted in Chen Sen, *PHBJ*, chap. 17, p. 9b.

152. Zhang Chen, *Pingpu zaji*, as cited in Liao Ben, *Zhongguo gudai juchang shi*, p. 73.

153. Chen Sen, *PHBJ*, chap. 2, p. 6a.

154. Ibid., chap. 9, p. 1a.

155. Wu Tao, *Liyuan jiuhua*, in *QYLS*, p. 827.

156. The practice of theaters closing temporarily because their scheduled troupe of actors had abandoned them for a salon arrangement was called "turning away [audiences for] operas" (*hui xi*). For more on this practice, see Qi Rushan, "Xiguan," pp. 44b–47a.

157. From Yang Jingting, *Dumen zayong*, cited in *QYLS*, p. 1174.

158. If passage between the Inner and Outer City was necessary, guests who stayed past the locking of the gates could always spend the night and return the next day. Chapter 30 in *Pinhua baojian* depicts a salon party that lasts all night. Because the host lives in the Inner City, the guests and actors are all invited to spend the night in his home; see Chen Sen, *PHBJ*, chap. 30, p. 2b. (Technically it was illegal for people of Han ethnicity to remain in the Inner City overnight, but I have not come across any cases of people actually being prosecuted for infraction of this regulation.) Salon parties that lasted a full day and night were termed a "full engagement" (*quan bao*), and on such occasions the host was allowed to dictate what was performed. Partial-day salon shows were referred to as "partial engagements" (*fen bao*), and on those occasions the troupe decided the bulk of the scenes to be performed; see Chang Renchun, *Lao Beijing de fengsu*, p. 237.

159. *Qi Rushan huiyi lu*, in *QRSQJ*, 8:343–44. Qi Rushan may be basing this observation, in part, on a short entry in *QBLC* entitled "full-length plays" (*quanben xi*), which also makes the claim that women were especially fond of such plays; see *QBLC*, 11:5022.

160. Women, however, were not entirely divorced from theatrical connoisseurship. The mid-eighteenth-century husband-wife team of Wu Zhensheng and Cheng Qiong, for instance, who annotated *Scholars-and-Beauties Peony Pavilion* (*Caizi-Jiaren Mudan ting*) and who coauthored a critical ranking of dramatic works in *The Master's Evaluation of Old Plays* (*Lige piping jiu ximu*), were surely engaged in connoisseurship; and their collaboration suggests that drama criticism was one of the shared pastimes of couples in companionate marriages. For more on this collaboration, see Hua Wei, *Ming Qing funu zhi xiqu chuangzuo yu piping*. Nevertheless, such mixed-gender connoisseurship still primarily focused on evaluation of the literary merits of drama rather than performance.

161. Qian Decang, *Dangyanji*, vol. 8, cited in Wang Liqi, *YMQ jinhui xiaoshuo xiqu*, p. 257.

162. Wanhua zhuren and Qian Decang, *Zhuibaiqiu xinji hebian*. Cut and distributed by the Hongwen tang in Hangzhou (1770–1777), in *SBXQCK*, vols. 58–72.

163. Wang Zhizhang, *Qing Shengping shu zhilüe*, p. 10. See also Zhao Shanlin, *Zhongguo xiqu guanzhong xue*, pp. 122, 120–29 passim; Ding Ruqin, "Qing gong

yanxi shishi," pp. 209–32; Liao Ben, *Zhongguo gudai juchang shi*, pp. 131–49 passim; Fan Limin, *Qingdai Beijing xiqu yanchu yanjiu*, pp. 47–57 passim.

164. Zhaolian, *Xiaoting xulu*, p. 377. The Garden of Communal Joy (Tongle yuan) was located on the grounds of the Yuanming yuan Summer Palace; see Liao Ben, *Zhongguo gudai juchang shi,* p. 140.

165. Ibid., pp. 377–78.

166. Naquin, *Peking*, p. 322. See also the discussion in Idema, "Performances on a Three-Tiered Stage," pp. 201–20; Zhu Jiajin, "'Wan shou tu' zhong de xiqu biaoyan xieshi," pp. 635–45.

167. Zhao Yi, *Yanpu zaji*, pp. 9–10.

168. According to the Western calendar, this fell on 3 October 1789. The occasion was also political, for the emperor was playing host to an emissary from the new king of Annam. The Qing had just suffered a humiliating rout of its army intervening on behalf of the failing Lê Dynasty. The succeeding Nguyên dynasty sent the new king's nephew as diplomatic appeasement, and the Qianlong emperor spun the event to display the wealth and might of the Qing. On the Qing defeat in Annam in 1789, see Dutton, *The Tây Son Uprising*, pp. 49–50. I am grateful to John Finlay for pointing me to information on the production of the album leaf depicted in Figure 9.

169. The two other three-tiered stages—one located in the Ningshou Palace within the Forbidden City and the other in the Yile Hall within the Yiheyuan Summer Palace—were referred to colloquially as "second master" (*erye*) and "third master" (*sanye*). See the recollections by the late Qing actor Cao Xinquan in his "Qian Qing neiting yanxi huiyi lu," *Juxue yuekan* 2, no. 4 (April 1933); cited in Liao Ben, *Zhongguo gudai juchang shi*, p. 146.

170. Zhao Yi, *Yanpu zaji*, p. 11; also cited in Idema, "Performances on a Three-Tiered Stage," pp. 208–9.

171. So Hosu, *Yonhaengki*, trans. Wilt L. Idema, in Idema, "Performances on a Three-Tiered Stage," p. 211. Additional excerpts from observations of Korean ambassadors to the Qing court are translated in ibid. See also So Hosu, *Yonhaengki*, in Im Ki-jung, *Yŏnhaengnok chônjip*, 51:19. For comments by other Koreans at the Qing court, see also Zhu Jiajin and Ding Ruqin, *Qingdai neiting yanju shimo kao*, pp. 37–38.

172. Cranmer-Byng, *An Embassy to China*, pp. 136–40 passim, esp. p. 140.

173. On the Jacobean and Stuart court masques, see Orgel, *The Illusion of Power*; Bevington and Holbrook, *Politics of the Stuart Court Masque*; Walkling, "The Apotheosis of Absolutism and the Interrupted Masque," pp. 193–231.

174. On Qing intra-Asian diplomacy and guest ritual, see Hevia, *Cherishing Men from Afar*, pp. 29–56. For additional scholarship on the political ideology of court performance under Qianlong, see also Qiu Huiying, *Qianlong shiqi xiqu huodong yanjiu*, pp. 221–25.

175. Liao Ben, *Zhongguo gudai juchang shi*, pp. 137–38.

176. Ibid., pp. 138–39.

177. Ibid., p. 138.

178. Ding Ruqin, *Qingdai neiting yanxi shihua*, p. 71.

179. The lists of plays performed at the court for the various reigns have been tabulated in Fan Limin, *Qingdai Beijing xiqu yanchu yanjiu*, pp. 57–89, 107–22, 129–38.

180. Ye Xiaoqing, "Imperial Institutions and Drama in the Qing Court," pp. 358–59.

181. Fan Limin, *Qingdai Beijing xiqu yanchu yanjiu*, pp. 48–56; see also Ye Xiaoqing, "Imperial Institutions and Drama in the Qing Court." These newer histories of Qing court theatricals all build upon the seminal work of Wang Zhizhang, *Qing Shengping shu zhilüe*.

Chapter Three

1. From an edict dated 1785 and recorded in *Qinding Da Qing huidian shili* (*The Collected Statutes of the Qing, with Sub-statutes Based on Precedent*), p. 425.

2. The eighteenth-century Qing court also patronized variants of Yiyang melody, even though that genre was considered less refined than kunju.

3. Opera genres are defined by their musical structure and the dialect used in their spoken dialogue.

4. Beyond the capital city, the court did not interfere in what opera genres were or were not permissible, but local officials often proscribed certain genres within their districts.

5. On the *Siku quanshu*, see Guy, *Emperor's Four Treasuries*; on the *Rixia jiuwen kao*, see Naquin, *Peking*, pp. 452–59 passim; on mapmaking and state-published ethnographies of border peoples, see Hostetler, *Qing Colonial Enterprise*.

6. On the emergence of the discourse of *ya* in the eighteenth century, see Lam, "Kunqu."

7. Chinese scholarship has characterized this transformation as the outcome of a class-based battle between yabu and huabu, known in the scholarship as *huaya zhi zheng*. This approach predates the demise of Kun opera and thereby downplays the importance of the hybridized commercial kunju in the first half of the 1800s. I see this transformation as more nuanced—the argument as not neatly corresponding to class fault lines—and the outcome a product of mutual accommodation rather than competition; see Guo Anrui (Andrea S. Goldman), "Kunju de ouran xiaowang," pp. 354–66.

8. I am aware of the work of Pierre Bourdieu, but I do not use the term "cultural field" to invoke the same dynamics as in modern Western Europe. If anything, the contested cultural field of opera in the Qing was more complicated than the field of culture described by Bourdieu. Under the Qing, political power was not necessarily synonymous with cultural capital; thus, the vector of ethnicity must be added to those of class and taste.

9. Throughout, I will refer to this genre of opera as *kunju* when discussing its performance in the commercial milieu. When emphasizing the music or singing per se, I will use the term *kunqu*.

10. On *yabu* as an identifying term for Kun opera, see Hu Ji and Liu Zhizhong, *Kunju fazhan shi*, p. 512. For more on the music of kunqu, see Lu Eting, *Kunju yanchu shigao*; Hu and Liu, *Kunju fazhan shi*.

11. The first use of the term *huabu* to refer to opera styles other than kunju occurs in Li Dou's late eighteenth-century *Yangzhou huafang lu*; see esp. juan 5 passim.

12. See Anon., "Jia lao dou tan," in *QCWF zidi shu ji*, p. 299.

13. This agency was further divided into the Nanfu, which housed several companies of eunuch actors, and the Jingshan, which was home to the external actors (mostly selected from Jiangnan) called upon to serve at court; see Fan Limin, *Qingdai Beijing xiqu yanchu yanjiu*, pp. 26–42; Ye Xiaoqing, "Imperial Institutions and Drama," pp. 329–64; Wang Zhizhang, *Qing Shengping shu zhilüe*.

14. On the structure and evolution of the Qing court entertainment bureau, see Fan Limin, *Qingdai Beijing xiqu yanchu yanjiu*; Zhu Jiajin and Ding Ruqin, *Qingdai neiting yanju shimo kao*; Ye Xiaoqing, "Imperial Institutions and Drama."

15. Wang Zhizhang, *Qing Shengping shu zhilüe*, p. 1; Dolby, *History of Chinese Drama*, p. 131.

16. On the court commemorative painting of this event (which displays the forty-nine stages), see Zhu Jiajin, *Gugong tuishi lu*, pp. 635–45.

17. Cited in Jiao Xun, *Jushuo*, in *ZGXLJ*, 8:201. On the role of the Imperial Textile Manufactory in recruiting actor talent into the palace, see Wu Xinlei, "Suzhou zhizaofu gongfeng nanfu yanjiu kao," in Wu Xinlei, *Zhongguo xiqu shilun*, pp. 309–15. See also Fan Limin, *Qingdai Beijing xiqu yanchu yanjiu*, pp. 48–53.

18. Ye Xiaoqing, "Imperial Institutions and Drama," p. 337n24; Wu Xinlei, "Suzhou zhizaofu gongfeng nanfu yanjiu kao," p. 311.

19. Gu Lu, *Qingjialu*, p. 122.

20. On the southern tours and concomitant Qing display of cultural power, see Chang, *A Court on Horseback*. Under the Qianlong emperor, too, the imperial manufactories were made responsible for reporting to the throne on opera-related matters. A comprehensive list of plays and plot summaries from Yuan times into the Qianlong emperor's reign, known as the *Study of Drama* (*Xiqu kao*), was prepared at imperial behest and submitted to the court via the Suzhou Textile Manufactory; see the entry on the *Xiqu kao* in Li Dou, *Yangzhou huafang lu*, pp.107–11. See also Yuan Xingyun, "Qing Qianlong jian Yangzhou guan xiu xiqukao," pp. 225–44; Wu Shuyin, "Shu 'Qing Qianlong jian Yangzhou guan xiu xiqukao' hou," pp. 245–48.

21. See, among others, Crossley, *A Translucent Mirror*, pp. 290–96 passim; Guy, *Emperor's Four Treasuries*. On official historiography in the early to mid-Qing, see also Kahn, *Monarchy in the Emperor's Eyes*, pp. 12–46.

22. Crossley, *A Translucent Mirror*, p. 308.

23. The term "nine modes" designates the various rubrics under which song suites were arranged. According to Rulan Chao Pien, "A basic scale of seven notes can be constructed on any one of the twelve pitches within the octave. . . . In this seven-note scale theoretically each note can be used as the cadencing note of a melody. A mode is thus defined by the pitch on which the basic scale is constructed and by the choice of the cadencing note"; Rulan Chao Pien, *Sonq Dynasty Music Sources*, p. 43. Originally developed for use with lyric poetry, these modes were later adapted to drama. A scene would be written in a set mode or key, which would determine the order of the tune titles for its arias. The tune titles remained constant,

though of course the words differed from one poem or aria to another. The lyrics (or poems) were always matched to the rhythmic properties of the tune.

24. *Beici guangzheng pu*, an anthology of drama song suites (including words and musical notation) in the northern musical system, was compiled by Xu Qingqing in the late Ming; in the early Qing it was revised by Li Yü and Zhu Suchen, two prolific playwrights from Suzhou. *Nanci dinglü*, compiled by Lü Shixiong, Yang Xu, Liu Heng, and Tang Shangxin, preface dated to 1702, was an anthology of musical scores of southern-style lyrics.

25. Yinlu's name is also rendered Yunlu, thereby avoiding use of the generational character in the Yongzheng emperor's personal name.

26. See also Zhou Weipei, *Qupu yanjiu*, pp. 211–23; and Wong, "The Printed Collections," pp. 103–6.

27. On the political import of ritual music during the Ming, see Lam, *State Sacrifices and Music in Ming China*.

28. Yinlu, "Xin Jiugong dacheng xu," in *Jiugong dacheng nanbeici gongpu*, in *SBXQCK*, 87:5–6.

29. Yu Zhen, "Preface," in ibid., pp. 10–12, 21; Wu Yuhua, *Zhongguo gudai xiqu xu ba ji*, pp. 481–82.

30. Including an intercalary month, thirteen months were designated, corresponding to thirteen modes in all in both the southern and northern systems.

31. Yinlu, "Xin Jiugong dacheng xu," in *Jiugong dacheng nanbeici gongpu*, in *SBXQCK*, 87:7–8.

32. Feng Guangyu, "*Jiugong dacheng* de chuanbo yu 'jiugong dacheng xue' de xueke jiangou," p. 20.

33. Liu Wenfeng, *Shan-Shan shangren yu bangzi xi*.

34. For huapu with information about actors from the Western Troupes, see, among others, *Yanlan xiaopu*, *Rixia kanhua ji*, and *Tingchun xinyong*, all in *QYLS*.

35. *Gunlou* is a comic play in which a newlywed couple plot together to seduce yet another woman to become the man's sexual companion. That second woman was originally the man's mortal enemy, and she is martially skilled.

36. Wu Changyuan, *Yanlan xiaopu*, in *QYLS*, pp. 44–45.

37. Xiao tiedi daoren, *Rixia kanhua ji*, in *QYLS*, p. 104. A brief description of Wei's acting innovations can also be found in Dolby, *History of Chinese Drama*, pp. 147–50.

38. Dan actors had previously wrapped their heads in a cloth (*baotou*) to hide the masculine identifying trait of the tonsure, which the Qing required of all men. On Wei Changsheng's innovations, see Yang Maojian, *Menghua suobu*, in *QYLS*, p. 356; Zhang Jiliang, *Jintai canlei ji*, in *QYLS*, p. 244. On the sexual implications of qiao shoes, see also Huang Yufu, *Jingju, qiao he zhongguo de xingbie guanxi*. These innovations quickly became standard costuming for other opera genres. Wearing qiao shoes onstage was eliminated in post-1949 mainland China because of its association with bound feet and female oppression. Recently, however, the practice has reemerged there as a novelty.

39. Yu Jiao, *Meng'an zazhu*, p. 13.

40. From Yang Miren, *Dumen zhuzhici* (1796), in Lu Gong, *Qingdai Beijing zhuzhici*, p. 21.

41. Zhaolian, *Xiaoting zalu*, pp. 237–38.

42. Zhang Jiliang, *Jintai canlei ji*, in *QYLS*, p. 250.

43. On parallel blurring of boundaries of aesthetic taste and the similar anxieties this provoked for French authorities in the second half of the nineteenth century, see Rancière, "Good Times or Pleasure at the Barriers," pp. 45–94.

44. Wu Changyuan, *Yanlan xiaopu*, in *QYLS*, p. 32.

45. Zhao Yi, *Yanpu zaji*, p. 37.

46. Zhaolian, *Xiaoting zalu*, p. 238.

47. Li Dou, *Yangzhou huafang lu*, p. 131. On kunju actors copying Wei's techniques, see also Shen Tongwei, *Xieduo*, as cited in Wang Zhengyao, *Qingdai xiju wenhua shilun*, p. 228.

48. Li Dou, *Yangzhou huafang lu*, p. 131.

49. On the six great troupes, "half of which were under the auspices of the princely households," see Li Guangting, *Xiangyan jieyi*, p. 54. How many of the capital melody troupes were actually sponsored by princely households is not yet clear in the historical record. According to Dai Lu (js 1763), in the years just prior to Wei Changsheng's arrival in the capital, one troupe known as the New Princely Household Troupe became especially popular. Whether that troupe was one of the "six great troupes" is unclear. According to Dai, following an altercation during a performance between an audience member of official standing and one of the actors of the troupe, the official was dismissed from his post (presumably at the behest of the prince). After that, no other elite patrons dared to call upon the service of the princely troupe. That incident, coupled with the popularity of the qinqiang actors, was credited with causing the downfall of the princely/capital melody troupe(s); see Dai, *Tengyin zaji*, p. 51. This incident is also recorded in Dolby, *History of Chinese Drama*, p. 147. See also Liao Ben, "Guanyu jingqiang liuda mingban."

50. Wu Changyuan, *Yanlan xiaopu*, in *QYLS*, p. 32.

51. Li Dou, *Yangzhou huafang lu*, p. 131; Zhao Yi, *Yanpu zaji*, pp. 37–38.

52. Wu Changyuan, *Yanlan xiaopu*, in *QYLS*, p. 32; for other records of actors who excelled at qinqiang, see also the entries in Zhou Yude, *Xiaohan xinyong*.

53. Wei returned to the capital in 1800, only to encounter the moratorium on all entertainment in observance of the mourning ceremonies for the Qianlong emperor. With no work to be had, according to one account, "He set up a stall beyond the Shuncheng Gate where he told stories to make a living"; see Huang Tongsun, "Weilang shuoshu ge," 3:1993. After the moratorium on entertainment was lifted, Wei performed again in Beijing. He died in his temporary lodgings in Beijing shortly after a performance of another of his signature plays, *Cousin's Wife Saves the Child* (*Biao dasao beiwa*). For fuller biographies of Wei, see Wang Zhengyao, "Qinqiang zongshi Wei Changsheng," in *Qingdai xiju wenhua shilun*, pp. 211–37; Zhou Chuanjia, "Wei Changsheng lun," pp. 172–92; Jin Dengcai, *Qingdai huabu xi yanjiu*, pp. 36–38.

54. Zhaolian, *Xiaoting zalu*, p. 238.

55. Zhang Xingmin, "Yong yu chuangxin de ren," *Shanxi xiqu*, no. 2 (1980), as cited in Wang Zhengyao, *Qingdai xiju wenhua shilun*, p. 230n1.

56. The only other mention of official court regulation of qinqiang comes from the writings of Zhang Jiliang, which claim that in 1823 the city censor again petitioned the throne to prohibit qinqiang. By that time the actors performing qinqiang were affiliated with the so-called Hui troupes; Zhang, *Jintai canlei ji*, in *QYLS*, p. 250.

57. Wang Zhengyao, *Qingdai xiju wenhua shilun*, p. 226.

58. *Guanju riji*, p. 11a. *Rixia kanhua ji* identifies the Sanduo Troupe as featuring actors of dan roles in the range of eleven to fourteen years. Its repertoire of plays, however, was similar to that of the Hui troupes; see Xiao tiedi daoren, *Rixia kanhua ji*, in *QYLS*, pp. 90–95.

59. Li Dou, *Yangzhou huafang lu*, p. 131.

60. According to Li Dou, the Huizhou salt merchants in Yangzhou were instrumental in preparing the acting troupes for the Qing emperors' many southern expeditions and for sending the troupes that they sponsored on to the capital in Beijing; see Li Dou, *Yangzhou huafang lu*, pp. 107–8. Not all historians of Chinese opera agree that the Yangzhou Hui troupes were the same troupes that later became famous in Beijing. For a skeptical perspective, see Mackerras, "Yangzhou Local Theatre in the Second Half of the Qing," in Olivová and Børdahl, *Lifestyle and Entertainment in Yangzhou*, pp. 213–14.

61. Xiao tiedi daoren, *Rixia kanhua ji*, in *QYLS*, p. 57.

62. Ibid., p. 105.

63. Chinese music scholars trace the xipi melody to the Han tunes (Han *diao*) of the Hubei region and also stress its strong likeness to bangzi melodies from Shaanxi, positing that it derived from qinqiang or the same sources; see Ma Shaobo et al., *Zhongguo jingju shi*, 1:56–60; Mackerras, *Rise of the Peking Opera*, pp. 9–11, 131; Darrobers, *Opéra de Pékin*, pp. 39–76 passim. For additional research on Shaan-Shan bangzi and its transmission to the capital over the course of the eighteenth century, see Liu Wenfeng, *Shan-shaan shangren yu bangzi xi*.

64. On the blending of musical genres, see also Wang Shipei, *Qian Jia shiqi kunju yiren zai biaoyan yishu shang yinying zhi*, p. 172–78.

65. Xiao tiedi daoren, *Rixia kanhua ji*, in *QYLS*, p. 55.

66. Zhaolian, *Xiaoting zalu*, p. 236.

67. On the development of pihuang opera, see Yu Zhibin, *Nanbei pihuang xi shishu*; Zhuang Yongping and Pan Fangsheng, *Jingju changqiang yinyue yanjiu*; and Zhang Zhengzhi, *Jingju chuantong xi pihuang changqiang jiegou fenxi*.

68. The various explanations (as many as ten different theories) for the emergence of the erhuang musical melody are summarized in Ma Shaobo et al., *Zhongguo jingju shi*, 1:43–47. For Western-language scholarship on this, see Mackerras, *Rise of the Peking Opera*, pp. 9–10, 124–31; Darrobers, *Opéra de Pékin*, pp. 39–76 passim. Yu Zhibin argues that the two basic musical styles that make up pihuang were fully synthesized only after the Hui troupes had become popular in Yangzhou; see Yu, *Nanbei pihuang xi shishu*, pp. 34–45.

69. Wu Changyuan, notwithstanding his praise for qinqiang performers, claimed

that Wei Changsheng was nowhere near as good as the Suzhou actor Tianbaoer in certain kunju plays; Wu Changyuan, *Yanlan xiaopu*, in *QYLS*, p. 43.

70. Hu Ji and Liu Zhizhong have suggested that the Hui troupes specialized in luantan and that luantan was essentially Kun opera lyrics sung to simplified melodic structure—maybe akin to what is later called *chuiqiang*, or flute melody; see Hu and Liu, *Kunju fazhan shi*, pp. 517–32.

71. In such scripts some arias are in the kun melody and others in the yi melody.

72. On the history of the *Zhuibaiqiu*, see Swatek, Peony Pavilion *Onstage*, pp. 105–13 passim, 151–53; Wu Xinlei, "*Zhuibaiqiu* de lailong qumai," pp. 36–43.

73. On Ye Tang and the "pure-singing" tradition, see Lu Eting, *Kunju yanchu shigao*, pp. 249–54; Hu Ji and Liu Zhizhong, *Kunju fazhan shi*, pp. 433–34; Swatek, Peony Pavilion *Onstage*, pp. 134–35; Lam, "Notational Representation and Contextual Constraints," pp. 31–44; Zhou Weipei, *Qupu yanjiu*, pp. 242–49; Wong, "Printed Collections," pp. 108–10. On avocational performers, see also Mark, "The Role of Avocational Performers," pp. 95–114.

74. Li Dou, *Yangzhou huafang lu*, p. 254.

75. In 1792 Ye Tang published the arias and scores from the four famous dream plays by Tang Xianzu under the title *Nashuying "Si meng" quanpu*. This has since become the authoritative guide to Tang Xianzu's plays in the kun musical system. Also in 1795 Ye Tang published the complete arias, arranged for kun singing, from the Yuan drama *Xixiang ji* under the title *Nashuying chongding "Xixiang ji" pu*.

76. Lam, "Kunqu."

77. Ibid, p. 8.

78. Ye Tang, "*Nashuying qupu* zixu," in *SBXQCK*, 82:5.

79. Often the title for Ye Tang's anthology is translated as *Musical Scores from the Bookshelf*. That translation leaves out the allusion hidden in the term *yingshu*, which means a last will or testament (on all the collected sounds, or *nayin*). Given that the anthology represents Ye Tang's life work, and was published shortly before his death, I have translated the title so as to underscore the allusion.

80. Ye Tang, "Fanli," in *SBXQCK*, 82:12–13.

81. Gong Zizhen, "Shu Jinling," juan 4, pp. 7b–8a. Gong Zizhen goes on to tell about Jin Dehui, a commercial actor who tried to learn the essence of Ye's kunqu. Lacking the innate capacity to appreciate the esoteric art of Ye's kunqu, Jin fails utterly.

82. Bourdieu, *Distinction*, p. 33.

83. Ye Tang's strain of Kun opera would ultimately win out in popular imagination by the early twentieth century. On the influence of *Nashuying* scores on later kunqu singing, see Strassberg, "The Singing Techniques of K'un-ch'ü," pp. 45–81, esp. p. 52.

84. Wang Wenzhi, "*Nashuying qupu* xu," in *SBXQCK*, 82:1. Wang, a native of Dantu near present-day Zhenjiang, Jiangsu Province, placed third in the jinshi exam of 1748. For more on Wang, see also Wong, "Printed Collections," p. 108.

85. Wang Wenzhi, "*Nashuying qupu* xu," in *SBXQCK*, 82:3.

86. On actor-centered kunju, see also Swatek, Peony Pavilion *Onstage*, esp. chaps. 4, 5.

87. In Wu's *Yanlan xiaopu* he places the biographies of huabu actors first, but not without an apparently self-conscious defense of his decision to give pride of place to non-kunju performers; Wu Changyuan, *Yanlan xiaopu*, in *QYLS*, 1:6.

88. Jiao Xun, *Huabu nongtan*, in *ZGXLJ*, 8:221.

89. Scholars of Chinese opera music speculate that the term *erhuang* may be a corruption of Yihuang, a reference to the region in Jiangxi where erhuang melody is thought to have developed. For a summary of this argument, see Ma Shaobo et al., *Zhongguo jingju shi*, 1:43–47; Mackerras, "Growth of Chinese Regional Drama," pp. 81–91.

90. Zhaolian, *Xiaoting zalu*, p. 236.

91. Yang Maojian, *Chang'an kanhua ji*, in *QYLS*, p. 310.

92. Yi Lansheng, *Cemao yutan*, in *QYLS*, p. 602.

93. Chen Sen, *PHBJ*, chap. 12, p. 9a.

94. In chapter 34 of *Pinhua baojian*, for instance, young boys apprenticing as street barbers are shown making some money on the side by singing pihuang as well as providing sexual services (Chen Sen, *PHBJ*, chap. 34, p. 16b); in a conversation with a tailor who wants a more lucrative career for his son, one of the accomplished actor characters in the novel recommends that the boy take up luantan opera. Kunju, according to the actor, takes too long to learn well, whereas after just two months' study of luantan, the boy can be ready for the stage; ibid., chap. 32, p. 5a.

95. Guanju Daoren, cited in Zhou Mingtai, *Dao Xian yilai liyuan xinian xiaolu*. For a brief biographical sketch of Guanju Daoren, see Ma Shaobo et al., *Zhongguo jingju shi*, 1:570–72. Guanju Daoren was the author of the volume of pihuang plays *Jile shijie*, which was adapted from several Pu Songling stories.

96. "Bright Spring" (*yangchun*) and "White Snow" (*baixue*) allude to two Warring States–era songs. Only those with excellent taste in music could hum along with these tunes. The compound *yangchun baixue* from then on came to mean rarefied music that most people could not understand.

97. From Han Youli, *Dumen zhuiyu* (1880), cited in Zhang Cixi, "Beiping liyuan zhuzhici huibian," in *QYLS*, p. 1176. In the second line of this verse *gong* and *shang* refer to the first two notes of the Chinese pentatonic scale. I have taken the liberty of translating those notes into near-Western equivalents (*do* and *re*), which allows the rhyme to work in English.

98. For examples of midcentury huapu in which kunju is still the norm, see *Tanbo* (1852) and *Mingtong helu* (1867); transitional texts listing approximately equal numbers of kunju and pihuang actors include *Huaifang ji* (1879) and *Cemao yutan* (1881); the earliest text in which most of the actors are presumed to be proficient in pihuang is *Jutai jixiu lu* (1886); all in QYLS.

99. Chen Moxiang, *Guanju shenghuo sumiao*, p. 421.

100. See Fan Limin, *Qingdai Beijing xiqu yanchu yanjiu*, pp. 34–47; Ding Ruqin, *Qingdai neiting yanju shihua*, pp. 161–206 passim; Ye Xiaoqing, "Imperial Institutions and Drama," pp. 348–49; and Zhu Jiajin and Ding Ruqin, *Qingdai neiting yanju shimo kao*, pp. 68–245 passim.

101. The incident is recorded in Zhu Jiajin and Ding Ruqin, *Qingdai neiting yanju shimo kao*, p. 79.

102. The following discussion relies considerably on Zhu Jiajin's important essay "Qingdai luantan xi zai gongzhong fazhan de youguan shiliao," reprinted in Ma Shaobo et al., *Zhongguo jingju shi*, 1:605–54.

103. Cited in Zhu Jiajin, "Qingdai luantan xi," reprinted in ibid., p. 607.

104. Xu Ke, *QBLC*, 11:5017.

105. Cited in Zhu Jiajin, "Qingdai luantan xi," in Ma Shaobo et al., *Zhongguo jingju shi*, 1:605.

106. Ye Xiaoqing, "Imperial Institutions and Drama," p. 352.

107. Zhu Jiajin and Ding Ruqin, *Qingdai neiting yanju shimo kao*, p. 300; Fan Limin, *Qingdai Beijing xiqu yanchu yanjiu*, pp. 97–101.

108. Zhu Jiajin and Ding Ruqin, *Qingdai neiting yanju shimo kao*, p. 301.

109. Ibid.

110. Ye Xiaoqing, "Imperial Institutions and Drama," p. 353.

111. From Luo Ying'an, *Jubu congtan*, cited in Ma Shaobo et al., *Zhongguo jingju shi*, 1:222.

112. Tan was given a grade-six appointment (*liu pin*); see Chen Yanheng, *Jiuju congtan* (ca. 1930), in *QYLS*, pp. 868–69. County magistrates typically began at the slightly lower grade-seven appointment.

113. See "Chongxiu Tianxi gong zushi xiang bei," in *QYLS*, p. 922; see also Ye Xiaoqing, "Imperial Institutions and Drama," p. 353.

114. Ye Xiaoqing, "Imperial Institutions and Drama," p. 353.

115. Cited in Ye Xiaoqing, "Imperial Institutions and Drama," p. 354. Translation by Ye Xiaoqing; also in Qi Rushan, *Zhongguo ju zhi zushi*, in *QRSQJ*, 1:261.

116. Cited in Ye Xiaoqing, "Imperial Institutions and Drama," p. 355. Translation by Ye Xiaoqing.

117. Luo Ying'an, *Jubu congtan*, in *QYLS*, p. 792.

118. Dong Caishi, *Taiping tianguo zai Suzhou*. See also Polachek, "Gentry Hegemony," pp. 221–56. Depopulation of adjacent Zhejiang Province is also discussed in Rankin, *Elite Activism*, p. 55.

119. Elman, *Cultural History of Civil Examinations*, pp. 573–74.

120. Luomoan laoren, *Huaifang ji*, in *QYLS*, p. 591. See also Gu Duhuang, *Kunju shi bulun*, pp. 95–104.

121. The stele inscription reads:

> In the beginning, those of our profession—Kun and Yi opera commercial actors and pure-singing [amateur] performers—have had a Guild of the Pear Garden, the original name for which was Temple to the Lord of the Yisu (27th) Constellation, alternatively called the Laolang Temple. This was founded in the early years of the former Qing dynasty as a place for members of our common profession—Kun and Yi opera commercial actors and pure-singing [amateur] performers—to gather and discuss our affairs. But ever since the deed to the buildings and land of our guild was lost during the time of Hong [Xiuquan] and Yang [Xiuqing], we have never requested and received a new deed. Now, Xu Jingyang . . . and eleven others of our profession have made diagrams and explana-

tions of the buildings of the guild, which we present to the judge of the Wu County Office of Public Affairs for a new replacement letter of deed, with an accompanying blueprint as a means of protecting [our interests]. In addition to selection of a yearly overseer of the new deed, we have also had carved on the left of this stele a copy of the contents of the new deed as a record for posterity. ("Suzhou Laolang miao minguo buqi beiwen," 1915; from a rubbing of the stele held in the Zhongguo yishu yanjiuyuan, Xiqu yanjiusuo Library, document 133770)

122. On the impact of the Taiping War on Jiangnan and the resulting rise of Shanghai, see also Meng Yue, *Shanghai and the Edges of Empires*, pp. xvii–xix.

123. See Goldstein, *Drama Kings*, esp. chap. 1; Yeh, "Where Is the Center of Cultural Production?," pp. 74–118; Meng Yue, *Shanghai and the Edges of Empires*, chap. 3 passim.

Chapter Four

1. This is an allusion to the Tang monk Congshen (778–897), also known as the Patriarch of Zhaozhou, who was renowned for providing tea to visitors seeking his instruction. He is credited with spreading the art of tea among Buddhist establishments. Here, the allusion calls attention both to the comment about thirst and to the surname of the character Cui'er.

2. Wu Changyuan, *Yanlan xiaopu*, in *QYLS*, p. 44.

3. A homophonic variant of *yuan* (garden) is often used in the title, which can then be translated as *The Destinies of Fei and Cui*.

4. Suchen is the playwright's style name (*zi*). He is also known by his *ming*, Hao. Li Mei notes that the Wu County Gazetteer cites the name by which he was known in public as Zhu Suchen; see Li, *Ming Qing zhi ji Suzhou zuojiaqun yanjiu*, p. 5n3.

5. In addition to Zhu Suchen, the major playwrights associated with the Suzhou writers' group include Li Yu, Zhu Zuochao, Bi Wei, Ye Shizhang, Qiu Yuan, Sheng Jishi, and Zhang Dafu. All were natives of Suzhou, and most were friends or acquaintances, some even collaborating on long chuanqi dramas. I borrow the phrase "Suzhou writers' group" from Li Mei, *Suzhou zuojiaqun*. For additional scholarship on this cohort of dramatists, see Wu Xinlei, "Lun Suzhoupai xiqu dajia Li Yu," in his *Zhongguo xiqu shilun*, pp. 175–86; Kang Baocheng, *Suzhou jupai yanjiu*; Wang Yongkuan, "Mingmo Qingchu Suzhou diqu xiqu chuangzuo fanrong de shehui yuanyin," pp. 165–86; Lu Eting, *Kunju yanchu shigao*, pp. 95–98.

6. This scene is also entitled "Dao pai" or "Dao lingpai."

7. The sexing of political complaint among this middlebrow urban clientele may not have been entirely new in the Qing. But it is eighteenth- and nineteenth-century sources from the capital that allow us our first glimpse of this *ressentiment* among this cohort of spectators.

8. Lu Eting argues persuasively that there must have been a version of *Feicui yuan* predating the *Guben* edition; Lu Eting, *Qingdai xiqu yu kunqu*, pp. 355–59.

9. Yao Xie's attribution of *Garden* to Xue Dan in *Jinyue kaozheng* follows that in Zhi Fengyi's early nineteenth-century catalog *Qumu xinbian*. Other Qing-era drama catalogs such as *Quhaimu* and *Chuanqi huikao biaomu* list the play as anony-

mous. The *Guben* edition follows *Quhai zongmu tiyao* in attributing *Feicui yuan* to Zhu Suchen.

10. See, for instance, the attributions in Qi Senhua et al., *Zhongguo quxue dacidian*; Li Xiusheng et al., *Guben xiqu jumu tiyao*; Guo Yingde, *Ming Qing chuanqi zonglu*.

11. Zhu Suchen is credited with authoring nineteen chuanqi dramas and three zaju-style plays. Only ten of his chuanqi dramas are extant. He authored four additional chuanqi dramas in collaboration with other Suzhou playwrights and coauthored two manuals on dramatic prosody.

12. *Feicui yuan*, *Guben* edition, p. 33a.

13. The character of Wang Zhenglong is based on a real-life yamen clerk who bribed Li Yu with one hundred steamed buns (*mantou*) to be written into his play; see Gu Gongxie, *Xiaoxia xianji zhaichao*, vol. 1, in Huang Wei, *Hanfenlou miji erji*, 1:15b–16a; Swatek, "Beating the Officers and Cursing the Manchus," p. 18n31. The clowns in both plays were likely conceived for particular actors, Steamer-Rack being played by a slight actor and Steamed-Bun by a portly one.

14. For more on the dating of *Wanli yuan*, see Swatek, "Onstage Life." A translation of Huang's travelogue can be found in Struve, *Voices from the Ming-Qing Cataclysm*, pp. 162–78. A record from 1661 indicates the performance of a version of *Wanli yuan*; see Wu Renshu, "Ming Qing zhi ji Jiangnan shishiju de fazhan ji qi suo fanying de shehui xintai," p. 36.

15. Shu Fen, renowned for expertise in classical exegesis, also became embroiled in the vicious court factionalism of the Zhengde (1506–21) and Jiajing (1522–66) reigns, twice being imprisoned and whipped for remonstrating with those emperors; his death at age forty-four is thought to have been hastened by injuries suffered during his second internment. Biographies of Shu Fen can be found in the *Mingshi*, pp. 4759–62; and in Huang Zongxi, *Ming ru xuean*, pp. 1280–85.

16. An early sixteenth-century biography of Shu Fa can be found in Tang Long, *Yushi ji*, juan 3, p. 104; it does not contain the account of his generosity. Records from the mid-seventeenth century begin to describe the iconic deed that became the basis for the plot of *Feicui yuan*. For these later accounts, see Zheng Xuan (js 1631), *Zuofeian rizuan*, vol. 1, juan 20, pp. 10a–b (207); Shi Dian, *Yongxing bian*.

17. Zheng Xuan, *Zuofeian rizuan*, vol. 1, juan 20, pp. 10a–b (207).

18. See *Mingshi*, juan 117, pp. 3591–98. The Prince of Ning's rebellion also is described in Geiss, "The Cheng-te Reign, " pp. 423–30; Israel, "The Prince and the Sage," pp. 62–128.

19. A third possible source for the plot of *Feicui yuan* may be the sixteenth-century drama *The Jade Hairpin* (*Yuchai ji*), which also features a protagonist whose land is stolen, here by a wealthy neighbor desiring to build a luxury garden; since only a handful of scenes from *Jade Hairpin* are currently extant, the extent of borrowing is difficult to determine. For more on this textual influence on *Feicui yuan*, see Guo Yingde, *Ming Qing chuanqi zonglu*, pp. 656–59.

20. Cui'er is the character's familiar name, which she calls herself and her mother calls her. Other characters in the play address her with the more formal Cuiniang.

Opera connoisseurs chose to adopt the more familiar form of address, thereby projecting a degree of intimacy with the character/actor. For consistency, I use Cui'er throughout, unless translating other characters speaking to her as Cuiniang.

21. Hu Shining (1469–1530) is a historical figure. His official biography can be found in the *Mingshi*, juan 199, pp. 5258–63. He, along with Wang Yangming, was responsible for suppressing Zhu Chenhao's rebellion.

22. Brooks, *Melodramatic Imagination*, p. 36. Brooks argues that melodrama is intrinsically modern, the hyperbolic mode of ethical contest between the forces of good and evil being a response to the desacralization of the post-Enlightenment age. While the problem of the fall of the sacred is particular to Europe, I suggest that the fall of Ming had an equally shattering effect on the Chinese seventeenth-century world order. Thus, it is not surprising to see the preoccupation with virtue in both early Qing and nineteenth-century European drama.

23. Feng Menglong, preface to *Qingshi lei lüe*, p. 1.

24. Brooks suggests that melodrama is the ultimate dramatic form. All interiority or character psychology is rendered visible onstage. Brooks, *Melodramatic Imagination*, p. 12.

25. The plot of the play migrated to other Qing-era opera genres and was adapted for other vernacular narrative forms, such as drum ballads (*guci*), strummed ballads (*tanci*), and precious scrolls (*baojuan*). Zhu's script was also chosen as the vehicle for launching a revival of Kun opera in the 1950s and after further adaptation was mounted for the stage and then film under the title *Shiwu guan*. A synopsis of the plot can be found in Li Xiusheng et al., *Guben xiqu jumu tiyao*, pp. 435–36. See also Li Mei, *Ming Qing zhi ji Suzhou zuojiaqun yanjiu*, pp. 54–60. The commonly performed scenes from *Shiwu guan* include "Jian du," "Fang shu cezi," "Pan zhan," "Ta kan," and "Bai xiang." All of these scenes are included in *Zhuibaiqiu*.

26. See Li Xiusheng et al., *Guben xiqu jumu tiyao*, pp. 437–38.

27. In addition to collaborating with Li Yu, Zhu Suchen jointly wrote a series of four plays with Zhu Zuochao (his brother), Qiu Yuan, and Ye Shizhang under the collective title *Four Great Celebrations* (*Si da qing*). See Li Xiusheng et al., *Guben xiqu jumu tiyao*, pp. 444–45.

28. See ibid., pp. 396–97. For the historical background upon which the play was based, see the biography of Zhou Shunchang in the *Mingshi*, juan 245, pp. 6353–55. See also Wakeman, *The Great Enterprise*, pp. 105–10. On the politics of *Qingzhong pu*, see Kang Baocheng, *Suzhou jupai yanjiu*, pp. 64–68.

29. *Yipengxue* relates the tragedy that ensues from the political and personal struggle to gain possession of a jade cup so rare as to have been named "A Handful of Snow." The jade cup belongs to Mo Huaigu, a Ming official. This information is leaked to Yan Shifan, son of the notoriously corrupt Yan Song (1480–1567), perhaps the most powerful official of the dynasty. Yan Shifan covets the cup and will stop at nothing to get it. Tang Qin, a once-starving scroll mounter, who had been taken in by Mo Huaigu, acts as go-between, trying to get Mo to make a gift of the cup to Yan. Unwilling to part with his treasure, Mo supplies Yan with a fake, but Tang

exposes the substitution. Mo Huaigu is forced to flee for his life, but his servant Mo Cheng and concubine Xueyan forfeit their lives to save their lord—but not before Xueyan wreaks vengeance on Tang. The characterization of Mo Huaigu is decidedly ambiguous. Although the victim of machinations by evil men, his hanging on to a *thing* at the expense of human lives calls in question his own integrity. Even as other characters in the play make sacrifices for Mo, it is clear that they are puzzled by his attachment to "A Handful of Snow." On the greater ambiguity of characters in Li Yu's four late Ming plays (as opposed to his Qing plays), see also Kang Baocheng, *Suzhou jupai yanjiu*, pp. 16–18.

30. The Zhengde emperor was infamous for surreptitiously trawling the empire, reputedly to gather women for his pleasure within the palace; see Geiss, "The Cheng-te Reign," pp. 403–39.

31. Many of the late seventeenth-century Suzhou playwrights seem to have written for local troupes, rather than following a slightly earlier Ming model of expressive literati playwriting, which was not necessarily intended for commercial performance. For more on the commercial troupes of Suzhou in the seventeenth century, see Lu Eting, *Kunju yanchu shigao*, pp. 145–55. Many of these Suzhou playwrights were extremely prolific, again suggesting a commercial impetus. Li Yu is credited with writing thirty-three plays, Zhu Suchen nineteen, his brother Zhu Zuochao twenty-five, Zhang Yixuan twenty-nine. They also wrote for local "music associations" (*quhui*), which may or may not have performed commercially. For more on Jiangnan quhui in Ming-Qing times, see Ren Xiaowen, "Ming Qing Jiangnan quhui yu kunqu yanchang lilun de fazhan," pp. 17–20.

32. Kang Baocheng, *Suzhou jupai yanjiu*, pp. 34–42; Wu Xinlei, "Li Yu shengping, jiaoyou, zuopin kao," pp. 131–45; Li Mei, *Ming Qing zhi ji Suzhou zuojiaqun yanjiu*, pp. 16–37.

33. Late Ming xinxue discourses, at least the more radical of them, often attacked the notion of hierarchy. Xinxue extremism was discredited before the Manchu conquest and seemed to have died away soon after it; see Wakeman, "The Price of Autonomy," pp. 35–70. For a discussion of this same intellectual shift and the renewed interest in preserving social hierarchy in the second half of the seventeenth century, see also Brokaw, *Ledgers of Merit and Demerit*, pp. 157–75.

34. Here I use the term "romantic," as does Frederic Wakeman Jr., to refer to the late Ming predilection for the life of the senses, which was triggered in particular by School of the Mind neo-Confucianism; see Wakeman, "Romantics, Stoics, and Martyrs," pp. 631–65.

35. *Story of the Western Chamber* (*Xixiang ji*) begins the tradition of young women standing up for love against the tyranny of parental authority; this trope is seen particularly in the figure of the maid, Hongniang, who defies age and status niceties to rebuke Old Madam Cui for reneging on her promise to betroth Yingying and Student Zhang. See introduction, in West and Idema, *The Moon and the Zither*. By late Ming times, especially as exemplified in Tang Xianzu's *Mudan ting*, the trope of the woman emboldened by desire as emblem of authenticity was well entrenched; see, for instance, discussions of *Mudan ting* in Wai-Yee Li, *Enchant-*

ment and Disenchantment, pp. 50–64; Wang Ayling, *Ming Qing chuanqi mingzuo renwu kehua zhi yishuxing*, pp. 186–201; Zeitlin, "Shared Dreams," pp. 127–79; Ko, *Teachers of the Inner Chambers*, pp. 68–112.

36. See, for instance, the discussion of the structural features of Yuan court-case drama in Hayden, *Crime and Punishment in Medieval Chinese Drama*, pp. 1–15; Perng, *Double Jeopardy*. One scholar has suggested that 10 percent of all Yuan dramas contained court-case or "honest official" themes; Wu Yuhua, "Shi lun qingguan xi de sixiang yiyi," p. 245.

37. Various late Ming playwrights and drama theorists, including Xu Wei (1521–93), Shen Jing (1553–1610), and Wang Jide (?–1623), were particularly concerned with showing bense in dramatic characterizations, by which they meant characters speaking as they would in real life; see, for example, Wang Chang'an, *Xu Wei sanbian*, pp. 1–30 passim; Ye Changhai, *Wang Jide* Qulü *yanjiu*, pp. 48–56; Zhu Wanshu, *Shen Jing pingzhuan*, pp. 64–70. In particular, Shen Jing, a native of Suzhou, had a major influence on the early Qing Suzhou dramatists; Zhu Wanshu, *Shen Jing pingzhuan*, pp. 160–72 passim.

38. See, for example, the discussion of the Yuan brothers—Yuan Hongdao, Yuan Zongdao, and Yuan Zhongdao—and their championing of spontaneity, sensuality, and authenticity, in Epstein, *Competing Discourses*, pp. 107–11.

39. Li Yu's *Lianxiang ban*, Cao Xueqin's *Honglou meng*, and Wen Kang's *Ernü yingxiong zhuan* come to mind as examples. Of course, as many others have shown, the late Ming qing ideal was in itself far from singular in expression. It could valorize the love between Du Liniang and Liu Mengmei in *Mudan ting*, as well as the lovesick pining of the neglected and abused concubine, Xiao Qing. For the ways in which men and women understood the "cult of qing" differently, see Ko, *Teachers of the Inner Chambers*, pp. 68–112.

40. Lin Baochun, "Zhongguo gudai xiaoshuo zhong 'nüxia' xingxiang," p. 44; Wang Yongen, "Shi lun Mingmo Qingchu xiqu zhong de nüjie xingxiang," pp. 45–51.

41. This is an allusion to the Tang-dynasty chuanqi story of Hongxian, who steals a golden box from the tent of the enemy commander, Tian Chengsi, while he (and apparently all his troops) is sleeping. The box is then sent back to Tian as a warning of the capabilities of the opposing army.

42. From the *Zhuibaiqiu* edition of the script, pp. 2757–59. For full citation, see Appendix 2, entry 5. Cui'er's arias are all delivered in the *beiqu* (northern tune) modes, which also highlights her *xia* (heroic) qualities.

43. See, for instance, the character Mo Cheng in Li Yu's *Yipengxue*; the character Ma Yi in Zhu's *Weiyang tian*; or the character Funu in Zhu Zuochao's *Nine-Lotus Lamp* (*Jiuliandeng*). For more on the figure of the righteous servant in these plays, see also Li Mei, *Ming Qing zhi ji Suzhou zuojiaqun yanjiu*, pp. 142–63.

44. Some scholars have suggested that widow chastity became more popular in the Qing partly as an allegory for political fidelity; see Elvin, "Female Virtue and the State in China," pp. 111–52; Mann, "Widows in the Kinship, Class, and Community Structures," pp. 43–45.

45. On late Ming bondservant uprisings and the figure of the haonu, see Zurndorfer, *Change and Continuity in Chinese Local History*, pp. 195–218; Ye Xian'en, *Ming Qing Huizhou nongcun shehui yu dianpu zhi*, pp. 284–89.

46. The fraying of the social fabric in late Ming times, and refracted elite anxiety about this, is discussed in Brook, *The Confusions of Pleasure*, pp. 124–38.

47. Certain scenes in the *Guben* edition, Lu points out, still retain traces of the cut-and-paste job that was done to the scene "Dao Ling," which edited Ma Feiying out of the action and gave her arias to Zhao Cui'er; see Lu Eting, "Du *Quhai zongmu tiyao* zha ji," in his *Qingdai xiqu yu kunju*, pp. 355–58. See also Tianjin shi guji shudian, *Quhai zongmu tiyao*, pp. 917–19.

48. See also Lu Eting, "Du *Quhai zongmu tiyao* zha ji," in his *Qingdai xiqu yu kunju*, pp. 355–58. Lu speculates that the confusion surrounding the play's authorship may have something to do with its revision. Zhu Suchen may have been the author of one of the versions; Xue Dan, perhaps, of the other. These two versions would have been written within a decade of each other.

49. Orgel, "What Is a Text?," p. 87.

50. Most of the Chinese-language scholarship on the early Qing Suzhou playwrights assumes that they were writing for commercial troupes; see, for instance, Kang Baocheng, *Suzhou jupai yanjiu*, p. 23. For the full citation of the *Zhuibaiqiu* script, see Appendix 2, entry 5. An earlier script with a copy date of 1749, marked as once belonging to the collection of He Yongyan, comprises eight scenes, concluding with the scene depicting the murder of Cui'er's mother; see Appendix 2, entry 2. That script was recorded by the Cao Family copyists, which suggests it was closely connected to performance. For more on the Cao Family copyists and the relation of their scripts to performance, see Sun Chongtao, "Zhongguo xiqu xieben shulue," pp. 62–73.

51. Wu Xinlei, "*Zhuibaiqiu* de lailong qumai," pp. 36–42; Zhu Chongzhi, *Zhongguo gudai xiqu xuanben yanjiu*; Swatek, *Peony Pavilion Onstage*, pp. 105–13 passim.

52. See Appendix 2, entry 7. The Sanqing Troupe script includes only eleven of the scenes originally published in *Zhuibaiqiu*, but within those scenes, the language (with the exception of a few mistaken characters) is identical.

53. *Guanju riji*, p. 22b. The typical number of scenes performed on any one day in this style of repertory production ranged from about eight to twelve, although often the scenes were culled from multiple story lines rather than from a single drama.

54. This list of plays was recorded by the Jifang Troupe manager, Wu Jinfeng, in preparation for a midautumn festival celebration in 1829; see "Jifang ban ximu," p. 4a, ms. held in the Zhongguo yishu yanjiuyuan Library. For additional accounts of the Jifang Troupe, active in the early Daoguang years, see Yang Maojian, *Chang'an kanhua ji*, in *QYLS*, pp. 310–11; Yang Maojian, *Menghua suobu*, in *QYLS*, p. 373. See also Wang Zhizhang, *Zhongguo jingju biannian shi*, pp. 101–2; Zhang Faying, *Zhongguo xiban shi*, pp. 145–46.

55. All of the eight full production scripts of *Feicui yuan* that I have collected comprise eight to twelve scenes. The earliest script, dated to 1749, is made up of eight scenes and, like the *Zhuibaiqiu* edition, ends with the release of Shu Depu

from prison (see Appendix 2, entry 2). Another script, dated to 1797, which includes full choreography notes, comprises eight scenes (see Appendix 2, entry 6). An early twentieth-century published anthology of kunju scripts—part of an effort to preserve Kun opera texts—published eight scenes from the *Feicui yuan* cycle in two installments of four scenes each, in 1908 and 1925, respectively (see Appendix 2, entries 9, 10). Only four of those eight scripts include any scenes from the second half of *Feicui yuan*.

56. *Feicui yuan kunyi quanben*, p. 37a; see Appendix 2, entry 7, for full citation.

57. This aria is sung to the "old narcissus flower" (*gu shuixian zi*) tune pattern. The tune suite used in this scene is made up of arias considered to be in the "northern tune" mode, which on the whole were faster and more clamorous than "southern tune" mode arias.

58. Brooks, *Melodramatic Imagination*, p. 41.

59. The reigning aesthetic of the eighteenth-century commercial stage, as Catherine Swatek has observed regarding selected scenes from *The Peony Pavilion*, encompassed a dialectic of elegant and vulgar (*ya* and *su*) characteristics. Sentimentality and comedy, in other words—much to the chagrin of some original playwrights—shaped commercial kunju performance. Some literati playwrights frowned on the license taken by commercial troupes with their scripts. Tang Xianzu, for instance, is claimed to have insisted that actors perform *Mudan ting* exactly as he had written it; see Swatek, Peony Pavilion *Onstage*, pp. 1, 177–83; see also Lu Eting, *Kunju yanchu shigao*, pp. 183–90.

60. For the performance aesthetics of "Sifan," see my "The Nun Who Wouldn't Be," pp. 112–13.

61. See, for instance, comments about the actor Li Yuling, who is noted for his portrayal of the characters of Cui'er in "Dao lingpai" and the little nun in "Sifan," in Zhou Yude, *Xiaohan xinyong*, pp. 87–88. See also the description of the actor Chen Guilin, who played, among other roles, Cui'er from *Feicui yuan*, Chunxiang from *Mudan ting*, the nun from "Sifan," and Hongniang in the scene "Kao Hong" from the *Xixiang ji* cycle; in Xiao tiedi daoren, *Rixia kanhua ji*, in *QYLS*, p. 59. According to *Guanju riji*, the same actor who played Zhao Cui'er also performed in the scene "Broken Bridge" (Duan qiao) from the *White Snake* (*Baishe zhuan*) story cycle; *Guanju riji*, pp. 30a–30b.

62. Peter Brooks posits a Jacobinian impulse to nineteenth-century French melodrama. In the American context, David Grimsted has argued that melodrama had a democratizing effect on audiences. See Brooks, *Melodramatic Imagination*; and Grimsted, *Melodrama Unveiled*. More recent scholarship on the cultural work of melodrama has complicated the picture, showing melodrama to favor the restoration of the status quo ante, and thus, conservative embrace of familial and social hierarchies. See, for example, the essays in Hays and Nikolopoulou, *Melodrama*; and Hadley, *Melodramatic Tactics*. A lucid synthesis of these debates can be found in Poole and Saal, "Passionate Politics," pp. 1–26. The melodramatic tearjerker seems to have been a particularly nineteenth-century phenomenon in many places around the world, including Europe, the United States, and Japan, as well as China. For the

melodramatic mode in Japan's long nineteenth century, see Zwicker, *Practices of the Sentimental Imagination*.

63. Eugenia Lean's study of public sentiment in Republican China has shown that urban audiences were hungry for such soap-opera-type scenarios, whether played out in real life or on the stage; Lean, *Public Passions*.

64. In reference to the performances on 15 January and 8 June, see *Guanju riji*, pp. 22b, 26b. These performances were staged in the year before Heshen's death; presumably in 1798 Heshen was at the height of his power. The day after the Qianlong emperor died, on 7 February 1799, Heshen was stripped of all authority and soon thereafter was executed. For a brief account of Heshen, see his biography in Hummel, *Eminent Chinese of the Ch'ing Period*, pp. 288–90.

65. Zhang Jiliang, *Jintai canlei ji*, in *QYLS*, p. 225.

66. Stallybrass and White, *Politics and Poetics of Transgression*, p. 42.

67. See, for instance, Robertson, "Voicing the Feminine," pp. 63–110; Huang, *Literati and Self-Re/Presentation*, pp. 76–88 passim.

68. Xiao tiedi daoren, *Rixia kanhua ji*, in *QYLS*, p. 68.

69. Qixiang shi, *Pinghua* (1816), p. 11a. One source also suggests that men may not have been the only audiences for this play. A cryptic note scribbled on the back of one hand-copied booklet that includes the two scenes "Dao ling" and "Sha zhou" records a legal altercation that transpired in 1861. The written complaint seems to be crafted in the voice of a woman, suggesting that the booklet was in the possession of a woman, although we do not know whether it came into her possession through her own volition or was brought into her household by someone else. The fact that the back of the script booklet was used as scratch paper also underscores the ephemeral nature of such texts; see Appendix 2, entry 13.

70. See the entries for 14 June, 30 June, 18 July, 4 August, 17 August, 9 October, 24 November, and 4 December in *Guanju riji*, pp. 9a, 10a, 11b, 13a, 14b, 15b, 19a, 20a.

71. See, for example, the comments about actors in *Feicui yuan* scenes in Xiao tiedi daoren, *Rixia kanhua ji*, in *QYLS*, pp. 59, 68, 73; Zhongxiang zhuren, *Zhongxiang guo*, in *QYLS*, p. 1030; Zhou Yude, *Xiaohan xinyong*, pp. 69, 88. I have come across just one mention of the scene "Remonstrating with Father" (Jian fu), which featured the character Ma Feiying, although we know from several multiscene scripts that this scene might be included in the eight- to twelve-scene version. For the mention of "Jian fu" by an opera aficionado, see Xiao tiedi daoren, *Rixia kanhua ji*, in *QYLS*, p. 83. For multiscene scripts that include this episode, see Appendix 2, entries 3, 5, 7, 10.

72. Du Shuangshou edition, pp. 48b–49a; see Appendix 2, entry 8, for full citation.

73. *Guanju riji*, pp. 1a, 3b, 5b, 13a.

74. Ibid., p. 30a.

75. Zhongxiang zhuren, *Zhongxiang guo*, in *QYLS*, p. 1030.

76. Zhou Yude, *Xiaohan xinyong*, p. 88. According to another source, every time the actor Xulun performed "Departure of the Soul" (Li hun) from *The Peony Pavilion*, "by the time he exited the stage, you could see that his sleeves and smock were drenched with tears; he is truly unparalleled"; *Guanju riji*, p. 29b.

77. On this audience dialectic between emotional involvement and critical alienation from the stories played out on the Qing opera stage, see, for example, Lu Yingkun, *Zhongguo xiqu yu shehui zhu se*; Zhao Shanlin, *Zhongguo xiju guanzhong xue*, pp. 164–70.

78. *Guanju riji*, pp. 1a, 12a.

79. See the treatment of the scene in Appendix 2, entries 3, 4, 8, 9, 18, 19.

80. *Zhan* is a common scribal abbreviation of the character *tie* in production scripts. It designates a tie dan role type, and here indicates Cui'er. In *Feicui yuan* Cui'er is played by the tie dan; Ma Feiying, by the dan role type. Although Cui'er's is the heftier part, her lower social status relative to Feiying requires that she be played by a tie dan rather than a dan.

81. *Zheng* refers to the *zheng dan*, or lead woman; in this scene, with just two characters, it designates the role type for the character of Madam Wei. In scenes of the play that featured the three characters, Cui'er, Ma Feiying, and Madam Wei, Cui'er would have been the tie dan, Feiying the zheng dan, and Madam Wei the *lao dan*, or old woman's role.

82. Xu Nongbo edition of "You jie," p. 4b; see Appendix 2, entry 18. This passage is rendered with minimal variation in scripts 4, 8, 9; see Appendix 2 for full citations. Script 19 may also include this passage, but since it is a part script for the role of Cui'er, it lacks Madam Wei's dialogue.

83. Wu Changyuan, *Yanlan xiaopu*, in *QYLS*, p. 44.

84. Xiao tiedi daoren, *Rixia kanhua ji*, in *QYLS*, p. 59.

85. For the seventeenth-century ideal of companionate marriage, see Ko, *Teachers of the Inner Chambers*. As further evidence of the popularity of this scene, it was adapted to other regional musical styles, such as the western qinqiang genre, under the title "Selling Jade" (Mai cuihua); see Zhou Yude, "*Xiaohan xinyong* jumu shulüe," in *Xiaohan xinyong*, p. 132.

86. Records of Du Shuangshou's performance activities in the capital can be found in various mid- to late nineteenth-century huapu, such as Sibu toutuo, *Tanbo*, in *QYLS*, p. 398; Hanjiang xiaoren youxianke, *Jubu qunying*, in *QYLS*, p. 501; Luomoan laoren, *Huaifang ji*, in *QYLS*, p. 592. See also Zheng Zhiliang, "Du Buyun yu Ruihe shanfang chaoben 'Xiqu sishiliu zhong'"; Wang Zhizhang, *Qingdai lingguan zhuan*, 1:74–79.

87. An undated full script of *Feicui yuan* includes a scene entitled "The Reunion" (Xiang hui) in the final position, in which Feiying is brought into the marriage. It is unclear if (or in what context) this script might have been performed. The first volume of this two-volume hand-copied script includes the commonly performed scenes. Other scenes found in the *Guben* edition but rarely, if ever, performed are copied into the second book. "Xiang hui" is the last scene in the second book; see *Feicui yuan*, 2:38a–40a, Appendix 2, entry 3.

88. *Chou* is the designation for the clown role type.

89. This line is marked with brackets in the original script, an indication that this is an aside Steamed-Bun mutters during Cui'er's speech.

90. *Feicui yuan*, p. 24a, Appendix 2, entry 2. See also the same exchange in *Feicui*

yuan, p. 50b, Appendix 2, entry 8. The *Zhuibaiqiu* and Sanqing Troupe scripts do not include Steamed-Bun's quip about the dead perch.

91. Catherine Swatek has explored the implications of Suzhou dialect in the plays of Li Yu in "Onstage Life" and "Beating the Officers and Cursing the Manchus" and via personal communication.

92. On dialect in Southern Song drama, see West, "Shifting Spaces," pp. 83–107.

93. McMahon, "Sublime Love," pp. 70–109.

94. The gendering of Jiangnan vis-à-vis the court is also discussed in Chang, *A Court on Horseback*, pp. 332–37. On the gendering of Chinese theater, and especially kunju, see Li Siu Leung, *Cross-Dressing in Chinese Opera*, p. 173.

95. Berezin, "Cultural Form and Political Meaning," pp. 1237–68.

96. On the bowdlerization (or vulgarization) of *The Peony Pavilion* in scene-selection commercial productions in the eighteenth and nineteenth centuries, see Swatek, Peony Pavilion *Onstage*.

97. Recent work on the refiguration of qing in the Republican era includes Lean, *Public Passions*; and Lee, *Revolution of the Heart*.

98. Kai-Wing Chow, *Rise of Confucian Ritualism*; Elman, *From Philosophy to Philology*.

99. See, for instance, Kuhn, *Soulstealers*; the surveillance powers of the Qing state are also illustrated in Spence, *Treason by the Book*.

100. Studies by both Hua Wei and Shang Wei on an eighteenth-century husband-and-wife commentary edition of *The Peony Pavilion*, *Caizi Mudanting*, have also suggested that the late Ming fascination with theatricality, sensuality, and sex did not die out in the Qing; see Hua, "*Caizi Mudanting* zhi qingse lunshu ji qi wenhua neihan," in *Ming Qing funu zhi xiqu chuangzuo yu piping*, pp. 437–62; Shang, "Yi yin yi yang zhi wei dao: *Caizi Mudanting* de pingzhu huayu ji qi dianfu xing."

Chapter Five

1. Chen Moxiang, *Guanju shenghuo sumiao* (1930), p. 458. A manuscript version of this text dated to 1925 is housed in the Zhongguo yishu yanjiuyuan Library in Beijing. For a brief account of Chen's career as a playwright, see Liu Naichong, "Ji jingju zuojia Chen Moxiang," pp. 233–44.

2. Chen claims that "saozi wo" are the first words out of the mouth of the dan character in such plays, but I have yet to see a script that assigns to the dan this line. Chen Moxiang, *Guanju shenghuo sumiao*, pp. 433, 469–73.

3. "Sha pi" was the commonly used title for the opera Chen Moxiang identifies as "Pijiang sha qi" (The Cobbler Kills His Wife). Chen criticizes the common title as confusing, suggesting that the cobbler is the victim rather than the murderer; Chen, *Guanju shenghuo sumiao*, p. 465.

4. On the evolution of this story material from historical legend to novelistic form, see Zheng Zhenduo, "Shuihu zhuan de yanhua," pp. 101–10; Hu Shi, "Shuihu zhuan kaozheng," pp. 505–47; Irwin, *Evolution of a Chinese Novel*; Plaks, *Four Masterworks*, pp. 280–302 passim.

5. See Zheng Zhenduo, "Shuihu zhuan de yanhua," pp. 101–10; Hu Shi, "Shuihu zhuan kaozheng," pp. 505–47; Irwin, *Evolution of a Chinese Novel*, p. 25.

6. *Xuanhe yishi* (ca. early fourteenth century), p. 29.

7. On the different recensions of the novel, see Plaks, *Four Masterworks*, pp. 280–302 passim; Irwin, *Evolution of a Chinese Novel*, pp. 61–86; Zheng Zhenduo, "Shuihu zhuan de yanhua," pp. 104–6; Hu Shi, "Shuihu zhuan kaozheng," pp. 505–11; Nie Gannu, *Zhongguo gudian xiaoshuo lunji*, pp. 96–204 passim.

8. Shi Nai'an and Luo Guanzhong, *Shuihu zhuan*, 1: 265–82.

9. Three out of four of these murders become fodder for later sister-in-law operas. On the ever-increasing violence directed against adulterous women in *Shuihu zhuan*, see Cheung, "Structural Cyclicity," pp. 1–15; Plaks, *Four Masterworks*, pp. 321–48 passim. On the code linking male heroism with misogyny in *Shuihu zhuan*, see also Hsia, *The Classic Chinese Novel*, pp. 105–7; Liu, *The Chinese Knight-Errant*, pp. 114–16; McMahon, *Causality and Containment*, pp. 52–59; Lü Xingchang, "*Shuihu zhuan* chutan: cong xing yu quanli de guandian lun Song Jiang," in Ke Qingming and Lin Mingde, *Zhongguo gudian wenxue yanjiu congkan*, pp. 21–48; Sun Shuyu, *Shuihu zhuan de laili, xintai yu yishu*, pp. 293–308; and Ma Youyuan, *Zhongguo xiaoshuoshi jigao*, pp. 225–32. On sexually potent women in *Shuihu zhuan*, see Eber, "Weakness and Power," pp. 13–15; Yenna Wu, *The Chinese Virago*, pp. 106–9; Sun Shouwei, "Mantan *Shuihu* li de funü xingxiang," in Hubei sheng *Shuihu* yanjiu hui, *Shuihu zhengming*, 3:417–25.

10. Jin Shengtan, in Chen Xizhong, Hou Zhongyi, and Lu Yuchuan, *Shuihu zhuan huiping ben* (1644), 1:380.

11. Sun Shouwei, "Mantan *Shuihu* li de funü xingxiang," 3:420; Sun Shuyu, *Shuihu zhuan de laili, xintai yu yishu*, p. 303; Plaks, *Four Masterworks*, p. 315; and Cheung, "Structural Cyclicity," pp. 4–8.

12. Plaks, *Four Masterworks*, pp. 304–21, chap. 4 passim; McMahon, *Causality and Containment*, pp. 52–59.

13. See Jin Shengtan's criticism of Song Jiang in his 1644 preface to *Shuihu zhuan* in Chen Xizhong, Hou Zhongyi, and Lu Yuchuan, *Shuihu zhuan huiping ben*, 1:6–8. Plaks, too, discusses Jin's critical stance toward the Liangshan gang in *Four Masterworks*, pp. 354–57.

14. Plaks, *Four Masterworks*, chap. 4 passim; McMahon, *Causality and Containment*, pp. 21–24, 52–56; Cheung, "Structural Cyclicity."

15. *Shuihu ji* was written between 1607 and 1623. Its first mention is in Qi Biaojia's early seventeenth-century catalog of plays, *Yuanshantang qupin*. The play is not listed in Lü Tiancheng's *Qupin*, whose preface is dated to 1610; Qi Biaojia, *Yuanshantang qupin*, in *ZGXLJ*, 6:59; and Lü Tiancheng, *Qupin*, in *ZGXLJ*, 6:201–64. Xu Zichang was also instrumental in the publication of the novel in the late sixteenth century. In his 1614 preface to the Yuan Wuyai edition of *Shuihu zhuan*, Xu praises the literary quality of *Shuihu zhuan* while criticizing its content; see Nie Gannu, *Zhongguo gudian xiaoshuo lunji*, pp. 83–84. For more on Xu Zichang, see also Lu Eting, *Kunju yanchu shigao*, pp. 63–64.

16. Xu Zichang, *Shuihu ji*, in *SHXQJ*, 1:278.

17. This section of the novel is often referred to as the "Wu Song *shi hui*" (Wu Song decicycle). On antecedents to the Wu Song story material, see Irwin, *Evolution of a Chinese Novel*, pp. 34–35. Although Hongzi Li Er's play is no longer extant, it was still in circulation in the early seventeenth century; see Qi Biaojia, *Yuanshantang jupin*, in *ZGXLJ*, 6:179.

18. *Gushu pi* means "the bark of the mulberry tree." The name refers to Wu Da's pockmarked and cratered face.

19. Shi Nai'an and Luo Guanzhong, *Shuihu zhuan*, 1:308.

20. Early seventeenth-century commentators litter these pages with gasps of "a painting" (*hua*) or "a living painting" (*huo hua*). See, for instance, the marginal comments in Chen Xizhong, Hou Zhongyi, and Lu Yuchuan, *Shuihu zhuan huiping ben*, 1:446–47.

21. Shi Nai'an and Luo Guanzhong, *Shuihu zhuan*, 1:315.

22. See the comments by Jin Shengtan in Chen Xizhong, Hou Zhongyi, and Lu Yuchuan, *Shuihu zhuan huiping ben*, 1:441.

23. The seventeenth-century commentator Jin Shengtan noticed certain similarities between Pan Jinlian and Wu Song. At the point at which Jinlian explains to Wu Song that she is "impetuous by nature," Jin remarks: "She suddenly divulges how similar she is to Wu Er"; see Chen Xizhong, Hou Zhongyi, and Lu Yuchuan, *Shuihu zhuan huiping ben*, 1:436. Throughout the Wu Song decicycle Pan Jinlian's lack of scruples is associated with feline imagery. On the association of shrewish women with lions and tigers in the Chinese literary imagination, see McMahon, *Misers, Shrews, and Polygamists*, esp. chaps. 1–3; Yenna Wu, "Inversion of Marital Hierarchy," pp. 363–82; Epstein, *Competing Discourses*, chap. 3.

24. On the dating of *Jin Ping Mei*, see Plaks, *Four Masterworks*, pp. 55–61; and Roy, *The Plum in the Golden Vase*, 1:xvii–xlviii.

25. The exact date of authorship of this drama is not known. The preface to the first extant published edition of *Yixia ji* is dated to 1607, but in that preamble the writer mentions that the play had already been in circulation in performance for some time; see the preface by Lü Tiancheng in *SHXQJ*, 2:160. An entry dated to 8 November 1602 in Feng Mengzhen's diary records having witnessed a performance of *Yixia ji*. See Feng, "Kuaixuetang ji," juan 59, p. 25b, in Siku quanshu cunmu congshu bianzuan weiyuanhui, *Siku quanshu cunmu congshu*, ser. 4, 165:58.

26. Since Shen Jing's play most likely predates Xu Zichang's, I suspect the latter's invention of a wife for Song Jiang was influenced by Shen's creation of Miss Jia.

27. Wang Jide, *Qulü* (1624), in *ZGXLJ*, 4:165. On the Wujiang style of playwriting, see Liu Jingzhi, "Yuandai zhihou de *Shuihu* xi," in *Shuihu zhengming*, 3:270; Aoki Masaru, *Zhongguo jinshi xiqu shi*, pp. 211–17.

28. Lü Tiancheng, another playwright associated with the Wujiang School, panned Shen Jing's addition of the Miss Jia scenes: "[The play] is full of excitement and pathos, capturing a heroic ethos. But the addition of a fiancée for Wu Song is gratuitous"; Lü, *Qupin*, in *ZGXLJ*, 6:229. Another seventeenth-century commentator gave the play a rating of 6 on a scale of 1 to 9 (with 1 the highest mark); see Wu Zhensheng, *Lige piping jiu ximu*, in *ZGXLJ*, 7:308. Qi Biaojia categorized

the play as "elegant"; Qi, *Yuanshantang qupin*, in *ZGXLJ*, 6:127. Zheng Zhenduo is one of the few modern critics to comment—approvingly—upon Shen Jing's choice to pair Wu Song with a wife. Zheng argues that this breaks the mold of misogyny, machismo, and sexual abstinence that characterizes the righteous bandits in *Shuihu zhuan*; see Zheng, "Wu Song yu qi qi Jia shi," in Zheng, *Zhongguo wenxue yanjiu*, 2:761–62.

29. The role of Pan Jinlian is played by a secondary dan; her lover, Ximen Qing, by a jing actor.

30. *Xuanhe yishi*, p. 30.

31. The title and authorship of this zaju drama is listed in Zhong Sicheng, *Lu gui bu* (ca. early fourteenth century), in *ZGXLJ*, 2:113; see also Irwin, *Evolution of a Chinese Novel*, p. 35.

32. C. T. Hsia has aptly characterized this scene as the sworn brothers cementing their bond through a blood ritual; Hsia, *Classic Chinese Novel*, p. 87.

33. Plaks, *Four Masterworks*, pp. 313–18, 321–48; Cheung, "Structural Cyclicity," pp. 1–15; on recurrence and rhetorical linkage in Ming-Qing vernacular fiction, see also McMahon, *Causality and Containment*, chaps. 1, 2.

34. Jin Shengtan, in Chen Xizhong, Hou Zhongyi, and Lu Yuchuan, *Shuihu zhuan huiping ben*, 2:831.

35. Ibid., 2:848, 849. Even those late Ming commentators who express admiration for Shi Xiu observe that Yang Xiong is a sorry excuse for a hero. See, for instance, the Yu Xiangdou commentary on the scene in which Yang Xiong believes his wife's slander against Shi Xiu. The commentator remarks: "See how Miss Pan manipulates Yang Xiong with her words, and how Yang Xiong, believing his wife, has no more affection for Shi Xiu. See how lacking is Yang Xiong's resolve compared with Shi Xiu's. I sigh for Shi Xiu; I am embarrassed for Yang Xiong"; from the Yu Xiangdou edition of *Shuihu zhuan* (ca. late sixteenth century), in Chen Xizhong, Hou Zhongyi, and Lu Yuchuan, *Shuihu zhuan huiping ben*, 2:848.

36. Jin Shengtan, in Chen Xizhong, Hou Zhongyi, and Lu Yuchuan, *Shuihu zhuan huiping ben*, 2:853.

37. As with the other two *Shuihu*-based plays, there is no definitive date of creation or publication for *Cuiping shan*. We know that the drama had to be written prior to 1636, because in that year Qi Biaojia makes note in his diary of having seen a performance of the play. See Qi Biaojia, *Qi Zhongmin gong riji*, 4:6b. In the earliest extant complete version of the script, dated to 1731, it comprises twenty-seven scenes. But I suspect that, like most chuanqi scripts, this drama originally had an even number of scenes. The late Ming drama miscellany *Zuiyiqing* contains a selection of scattered scenes from *Cuiping shan*; later scripts divide one of these, "Qu zhan," into three scenes—"Jiao zhang," "Xi shu," and "Song li." Other scenes, too, may have been combined or separated in later redactions of *Cuiping shan*, which would explain why this chuanqi drama has an odd number of scenes. See also Lu Eting, *Kunju yanchu shigao*, p. 102.

38. The term *shushu* means "brother-in-law." I have left the term untranslated because the English translation lacks the sense of familiarity conveyed by the Chinese.

39. From "Qu zhan" (Spying a Weakness) in *Cuiping shan* scene selections in Qingxi gulu diaosou, *Xinke chuxiang dianban shishang kunqiang zaqu Zuiyiqing* (Qianlong-era reprint of late Ming Zuiyiqing [Zhihetang, Suzhou], juan 3, 8a–b. Hereafter abbreviated as *Zuiyiqing*. The four scenes from *Cuiping shan* in *Zuiyiqing* represent the earliest extant partial versions of the script—perhaps closest to the playwright's original. In later performance scripts, this exchange is slightly different. See, for instance, scene 8, "Xi shu," in *Cuiping shan*, in *GBXQCK*, ser. 2, 76:14a–b.

40. This stage direction is interpolated from the 1731 edition of *Cuiping shan*, in *GBXQCK*, ser. 2, 76:14b.

41. Shen Zijin may also have included the flirtation scene between Qiaoyun and Shi Xiu because audiences found the equivalent scene in *Yixia ji* between Pan Jinlian and Wu Song extremely entertaining, and the younger playwright wished to capitalize on this popularity. Lü Tiancheng claims that *Yixia ji* was performed frequently in the Wu region in the early seventeenth century; see Lü, *Qupin*, in *ZGXLJ*, 6:229.

42. *Cuiping shan*'s earliest full recension shows signs of having been altered for the stage; Shen Zijin, *Cuiping shan*, in *GBXQCK*, ser. 2, vol. 76; also *Cui A*. See also Lu Eting, *Kunju yanchu shigao*, p. 102.

43. It is hard to know to what extent these scripts were ever performed in full. Even when late Ming catalogers of chuanqi drama allude to performance, rarely do they indicate whether the complete drama was being enacted. Shen Jing, author of *Yixia ji*, raised his own troupe of actors; we can assume that he had them perform his plays in full; see Lu Eting, *Kunju yanchu shigao*, pp. 60–63, 95–116 passim.

44. The scene "Da hu," originally scene 4 in Shen Jing's complete drama, is entitled "Chu xiong" in Shen's play; see Shen, *Yixia ji*, in *SHXQJ*, 2:165–68.

45. On illustrated literature and its readers during the Ming and Qing, see Hegel, *Reading Illustrated Fiction*.

46. A dual system of scene titles coexisted for the most popular scenes from *Cuiping shan* until the end of the eighteenth century. The anonymous *Guanju riji* (ca. 1773–1816) lists performances of both "Qu zhan" and "Xi shu." Likewise, the journal entries record performances of "Fen su" and "Jiulou," both referring to the same scene, just as "Qiao zan" and "Fan kuang" both refer to the same scene in *Cuiping shan*. "Qiao zan," the older title, was displaced by "Fan kuang" beginning in the eighteenth century.

47. Shen Jing, *Yixia ji*, in *SHXQJ*, 2:180.

48. In this version, the character of Pan Jinlian is played by a tie dan, abbreviated here as *tie*. In manuscript-production scripts the character *tie* becomes further abbreviated as *zhan*, scribal shorthand, in which the left-side radical is dropped from the character.

49. This added bit of stage directions comes from the 1770 edition of *Zhuibaiqiu*. See *SBXQCK*, 62:1736. Otherwise, the 1764 and 1770 editions of this scene are identical.

50. The wooden-fish percussion block (*muyu*) is the woodblock instrument used in Buddhist prayer ceremonies.

51. From "Tiaolian," in *ZBQ*, in *SBXQCK*, 64:375–76.
52. The joke about using the fu's head as a wooden fish is used also (almost word for word) in the scene "Zuo yi" in *ZBQ*, in *SBXQCK*, 64:382.
53. Xu Zichang, *Shuihu ji*, in *SHXQ J*, 2:185.
54. From "Zuo yi," in *ZBQ*, in *SBXQCK*, 64:385.
55. *Cui* B (copy dated to 1841), p. 16b.
56. Shen Jing, *Yixia ji*, in *SHXQ J*, 2:182.
57. In the original script this is the second-to-last aria of the scene. In the *Zhuibaiqiu* script it serves as the last aria but is then followed by some new dialogue between Mama Wang and Ximen Qing.
58. From "Tiaolian," in *ZBQ*, in *SBXQCK*, 64:379.
59. Although the copy date on this script is equivalent to 1731, another copy held in the Traditional Drama Research Institute (Xiqu yanjiusuo) archives has a new cover page dated to 1855. The name chop on this newer title page links this script with the Cao Family. The Cao Family produced several generations of career actors—some of whom were frequently called upon to perform at court; thus, they may have had access to court scripts (see the scripts in Appendix 3). The full copy of *Cuiping shan* included in *Guben xiqu congkan*, ser. 2, is based on the 1731 script.
60. "Fan kuang," in *ZBQ*, in *SBXQCK*, 58:319–30. Compare with Shen Zijin, *Cuiping shan*, in *GBXQCK*, ser. 2, 76:31b–33b; and *Cui* A, pp. 31b–33b. A discussion of the complete version of this play can be found in Lu Eting, *Kunju yanchu shigao*, pp. 102–3.
61. From "Qiao zan," in *Zuiyiqing*, in *SBXQCK*, 54:216. One strong bit of evidence suggesting that this version is closest to the author's original is that the ending couplets are preserved in this script.
62. From "Fan kuang," in *ZBQ*, in *SBXQCK*, 58:330.
63. Qi Biaojia, *Yuanshantang qupin*, in *ZGXLJ*, 6:9.
64. Wang Jide, *Qulü*, in *ZGXLJ*, 4:164. See also Lu Eting, *Kunju yanchu shigao*, pp. 60–63; Aoki Masaru, *Zhongguo jinshi xiqu shi*, p. 215.
65. Xu Zichang, *Shuihu ji*, in *SHXQ J*, 2:275.
66. From "Hou you," in *Shui* A (ca. mid-nineteenth century), p. 27a. A slight variation on this line is used in the same scene in *ZBQ*, in *SBXQCK*, 61:1156: "Aiya, . . . Sit and let me kneel down to call you my nearest, dearest, hot Mama."
67. Swatek charts the development of this middlebrow sentiment in commercial kunju performance of *Mudan ting* in Peony Pavilion *Onstage*, esp. chap. 4.
68. From "Xi shu," in *ZBQ*, in *SBXQCK*, 62:1721.
69. Lu Eting dates the practice of having the clowns speak in Wu dialect to the late sixteenth century, reaching its greatest ascendancy during the Qing; Lu, *Kunju yanchu shigao*, pp. 107–9, esp. p. 108n1.
70. Kunju scholars such as Lu Eting maintain that clown-dialect scenes became so popular that just about every play came to have at least one such dialogue-only scene; Lu, *Kunju yanchu shigao*, p. 107.
71. From "Qian you," in *ZBQ*, in *SBXQCK*, 61:1145–46.
72. Ibid., p. 1146.

73. From "Hou you," in *ZBQ*, in *SBXQCK*, 61:1157.

74. Volume 6 contains the scene "Banchang guaiqi" (While Moving Shop, the Wife Is Kidnapped), which features Wu Da and Pan Jinlian. It emanates from a probably less literate source and is lumped together with other bangzi opera scenes, to which two volumes of the 1770–77 *Zhuibaiqiu* edition are devoted. The great majority of the opera scenes in *Zhuibaiqiu* are from kunju plays; for more on the changing content of the *Zhuibaiqiu* anthology over time, see Wu Xinlei, "*Zhuibaiqiu* de lailong qumai."

75. For additional comparison of the sequence of selected scenes in *Zhuibaiqiu* with eighteenth-century performance practice, see Yan Changke, "Zhengui de xiqu shiliao: du 'jiaqing dingsi wuwu guanju riji' shougao," pp. 250–80; see also Lu Eting, *Kunju yanchu shigao*, pp. 174–83.

76. "Fan kuang" is featured in vol. 1; "Jiao zhang," "Xi shu," and "Song li" in vol. 3; and "Jiulou" and "Sha shan" in vol. 8.

77. Anon., *Guanju riji* (ca. 1773–1816), manuscript held in the Zhongguo yishu yanjiuyuan Library, Beijing.

78. Ibid., pp. 6b, 16a, 19a.

79. Ibid., pp. 6a, 11a.

80. Ibid., p. 5a.

81. Ibid., p. 2b.

82. Ibid., p. 12a.

83. *Leifeng ta* is a dramatic rendition of the *White Snake*, or *Baishe*, legend.

84. Older and newer scene titles seem to be used interchangeably for some of these performances, possibly suggesting that the performance of the selected scenes from *Cuiping shan* was still in flux at the time.

85. "Fan kuang" was published without any accompanying scenes from *Cuiping shan* in volume 1 of the 1770 edition of *Zhuibaiqiu*.

86. This performance consisted of the three linked scenes, "Fan kuang," "Jiulou," and "Sha shan," *Guanju riji*, p. 2a.

87. Ibid., p. 16a.

88. Judging from five huapu produced between 1785 and 1810, the overlap between plays listed in *Guanju riji* and in other contemporaneous texts of opera connoisseurship was considerable. All of the *Shuihu*-related operas listed in *Guanju riji* are also listed in these huapu. The huapu texts record a slightly expanded repertoire of *Shuihu*-based dramas, occasionally mentioning "Sha Xi," the scene of Yan Poxi's murder from *Shuihu ji*, as well as the pair of scenes from *Yixia ji* in which Wu Da catches the adulterers Pan Jinlian and Ximen Qing ("Zhuo jian" and "Fu du") and is then poisoned. Scenes with the clown Wu Da were also apparently quite popular, and even his death scene was milked for comedy, with the hapless Wu Da rising ghostlike several times from under the covers after his killers thought he had been finished off.

89. The clowns who played older women were situated at another terminus of the qing-burlesque continuum—their exaggerated and comic impersonations of "femininity" spoofing the cross-dressing conventions of Qing performance. Swatek has observed that, when repackaged for performance in the commercial theater, even

romantic scenes from *Mudan ting* were made sillier; see Swatek, Peony Pavilion *Onstage*, esp. chap. 4.

90. Li Dou, *Yangzhou huafang lu*, p. 124.

91. Wu Changyuan, *Yanlan xiaopu*, in *QYLS*, p. 38. There seems to have been some slippage in the characterization of the xiao dan role over time. In the chuanqi dramas the sisters-in-law are played by xiao dan, but by the eighteenth century the xiao dan role was used for depicting romantic young girls; the women of questionable repute were played instead by tie dan. Lu Eting categorizes actors who specialize in these types of roles—maids or lower-class heroines (often given more comic business)—as *liu dan*. Because of the stage fighting required in some of the scenes from these plays, these actors also sometimes double as *cisha dan* (fighting dan). See Lu Eting, *Kunju yanchu shigao*, pp. 194–95.

92. Xiao tiedi daoren, *Rixia kanhua ji*, in *QYLS*, pp. 78–79.

93. See, for instance, the description of the actor Chen Guilin, who excelled as the maid Chunxiang in the schoolroom scene of *Mudan ting*, as the nun in "Si fan," and as the sister-in-law in "Xi shu," in ibid., p. 59. Or the actor Li Yuling, who was particularly adept at the roles of Hong Niang (Red Maid) from *Xixiang ji*, Sekong in "Si fan," and Pan Qiaoyun in "Xi shu" from *Cuiping shan*, in Zhou Yude, *Xiaohan xinyong*, pp. 57–58.

94. See my "The Nun Who Wouldn't Be," pp. 107–13.

95. From Shiping jushi in Zhou Yude, *Xiaohan xinyong*, p. 55.

96. Liuchunge xiaoshi, *Tingchun xinyong*, in *QYLS*, p. 174.

97. From Tieqiao shanren, in Zhou Yude, *Xiaohan xinyong*, p. 56.

98. Xiao tiedi daoren, *Rixia kanhua ji*, in *QYLS*, p. 91.

99. From Tieqiao shanren, in Zhou Yude, *Xiaohan xinyong*, p. 62.

100. Li Dou, *Yangzhou huafang lu*, p. 132.

101. From a Qing manuscript edition of "Shi jin," with full musical and choreography scores, in *Shui A*, p. 8b. Note that the aria that accompanies these stage directions is not in the playwright's original text. It seems to have been copied from an aria in the earlier scene "Jie cha."

102. Lu Eting describes these plays as the "three little" plays (*san xiao*), featuring the flirtatious female lead (*xiao dan*), the romantic male lead (*xiao sheng*), and the little clown (*xiao chou*). By the end of the eighteenth century san xiao plays predominated in commercial performance in Beijing; Lu, *Kunju yanchu shigao*, pp. 234–35.

103. It was observed of the actor Shen Sixi that he "narrowed his eyes into slits when he gazed out; they were full of passion, without giving the sense that he was nearsighted"; from Wenjin yuzhe, in Zhou Yude, *Xiaohan xinyong*, p. 74.

104. Wu Changyuan, *Yanlan xiaopu*, in *QYLS*, p. 38.

105. From Wenjin yuzhe, in Zhou Yude, *Xiaohan xinyong*, p. 75. This particular gesture can be mapped to a specific line in the scene "Jie cha." As Yan Poxi walks offstage to fetch tea for Zhang San, Zhang remarks, "When she went in just now, the way she swayed her skirt was LIKE A LIGHT BREEZE WAFTING CHARM, A FLUTTERING OF CHANCE WONDER; WITH A SMILE THAT WOULD CONQUER ALL OF YANGCHENG

AND XIACAI, IT PROVOKES LONG THOUGHTS OF YEARNING." From "Jie cha," in *ZBQ*, in *SBXQCK*, 59:389; see also the same passage in "Jie/Huo" A, p. 3a; and in "Jie," p. 2b.

106. Chen Sen, *PHBJ*, chap. 30, pp. 17a–18a.

107. See, for instance, Yu Zhi's list of licentious plays in "Yihuatang tiaogui" in his *Deyi lu* (ca. 1849), juan 11.2, cited in Wang Liqi, *YMQ jinhui xiaoshuo xiqu*, pp. 196–200; see also "Tongzhi qinian Jiangsu xunfu Ding Richang chajin yinci xiaoshuo," in ibid., pp. 142–44.

108. For a brief account of Yu Zhi, his philanthropic activities, and his writings promulgating morality, see You Zian, *Quanhua jinzhen*, pp. 99–103.

109. Laolang was the patron saint of actors; from Yu Zhi, *Lingtai xiaobu*, cited in Wang Liqi, *YMQ jinhui xiaoshuo xiqu*, p. 361.

110. From Yu Zhi, *Deyi lu*, juan 11.2, cited in Wang Liqi, *YMQ jinhui xiaoshuo xiqu*, pp. 196–200.

111. *Lianhuan ji* is a drama based on the *Romance of the Three Kingdoms* (*Sanguo*) story cycle.

112. Li Dou, *Yangzhou huafang lu*, p. 124.

113. Anon., *Guanju riji*, pp. 5a, 20b.

114. See, for instance, an edict of 18 April 1754 prohibiting the publication of the novel *Shuihu zhuan*, cited in Wang Liqi, *YMQ jinhui xiaoshuo xiqu*, pp. 44–45; also an edict of 27 August 1753 ordering the confiscation of Manchu-language copies of *Shuihu zhuan* and *Xixiang ji*, cited in ibid., pp. 43–44.

115. Although no date is given for the completion of this opera, it had to have been created after the composition of another court grand opera entitled *Quanshan jinke* (based on the Mulian story cycle), written by Zhang Zhao (1691–1745) in the early 1740s. The ending of *Zhongyi xuantu*, in which all the characters are judged in the underworld, was clearly inspired by Zhang Zhao's treatment of the penultimate Hell scenes in his grand script. That would put the earliest possible creation date for *Zhongyi xuantu* at mid-decade of the 1740s. Many of the drama-related court publications were created under the auspices of the emperor's uncle Yinlu (1695–1767). If Yinlu oversaw the composition of *Zhongyi xuantu*, that would suggest a latest date of completion coinciding more or less with his death. The edicts proscribing publication of *Shuihu* stories and plays date from the 1750s. It seems that the Qianlong emperor chose to remold this material to his liking at precisely the time that he was stamping out seditious and pernicious versions of it.

116. Zhaolian, *Xiaoting xulu*, pp. 377–78.

117. The title for vol. 3, scene 21 of *Zhongyi xuantu*, "Lingzhuo shuangfeng xian bingtou," recalls that of the no longer extant Yuan drama about Wu Song's revenge, *Shuang xiantou*.

118. Zhou Xiangyu and Zou Jinsheng, *Zhongyi xuantu*, in *GBXQCK*, ser. 9, no. 10, vol. 2, scene 92; vol. 3, scene 82. For a detailed analysis of the changes in lyrical structure from *Shuihu ji* to the corresponding scenes in *Zhongyi xuantu*, see Xie Bixia, *Shuihu xiqu ershi zhong yanjiu*, pp. 277–83.

119. The four scenes are "Pan Jinlian chiqing you shu," "Wu Erlang chulu bie

xiong," "Wei tiaolian wuyi chuan qing," and "Cai yiliao Jinlian ye he"; they correspond to vol. 3, scenes 15, 16, 17, and 18 in *Zhongyi xuantu*.

120. The actor who played Wu Da usually walked on his haunches while onstage to create the illusion of dwarfish stature. His costume was made to partially hide the actor's knees pulled up to his chest—but only partially, because half the clown's entertainment value lay in the skill with which he moved nimbly about the stage on his haunches.

121. From "Xi shu," in *ZBQ*, in *SBXQCK*, 62:1724.

122. Zhou Xiangyu and Zou Jinsheng, *Zhongyi xuantu*, in *GBXQCK*, ser. 9, no. 10, 3:119b.

123. Ibid., 6:63b–64a.

124. Ibid., p. 73a.

125. For scholarship on this tension within late imperial fiction, see, for instance, McMahon, *Causality and Containment*; and Epstein, *Competing Discourses*.

126. A court script of *Yixia ji* in the Kun opera genre, with a copy date of December 1861, also covers the entire Wu Song decicycle. A court version of *Cuiping shan*, with a copy date of November 1861, also more closely follows the scenes in Shen Zijin's original. These scripts were hand-copied by Du Shuangshou, a commercial kunju actor brought into service at court in the final year of the Xianfeng reign (1861). See the scripts in Appendix 3, *Cui* Bb, and *Yi* Aa.

127. On the simpler phrasing and structure of pihuang plays, see, for example, Yan Quanyi, *Qingdai jingju wenxue shi*, pp. 57–66.

128. I have no direct evidence of the influence of the eighteenth-century imperially commissioned script of the *Shuihu* story cycle, *Zhongyi xuantu*, on later pihuang versions of the *Shuihu* sister-in-law plays. But it is known that the court version of another eighteenth-century grand opera, *Zhaodai xiaoshao* (*Heavenly Music of an Illustrious Age*), which tells the story of the famous Song-dynasty Yang family generals (*Yangjia jiang*), was the immediate source for the creation of some 105 new pihuang operas in the late nineteenth century; see Zhou Mingtai, "Zhaodai xiaoshao zhi sanzhong jiaoben," cited in Ma Shaobo et al., *Zhongguo jingju shi*, 1:233–34. See also Yan Quanyi, *Qingdai jingju wenxueshi*, pp. 393–94; Chen Moxiang, *Guanju shenghuo sumiao*, pp. 480–81. For more on the relationship between court scripts and operas popular in the commercial milieu, see Qi Rushan, *Qi Rushan huiyi lu*, in *QRSQJ*, 8.2:217–22.

129. This opera is also known as "Zuolou sha Xi" (Sitting in the Loft and Murdering Yan Poxi).

130. "Wulong" A, pp. 9b–13b. In "Wulong" C, the punch line of this joke is explained slightly differently. In that script, the combination of "cold water" and "garlic" means that her feelings for him are watered down, or weak; see "Wulong" C, p. 4b.

131. For the use of andian ben within the court, see Zhu Jiajin, "Qingdai luantan xi zai gongzhong fazhan de youguan ziliao," in Ma Shaobo et al., *Zhongguo jingju shi*, 1:643; Qi Rushan, *Qi Rushan huiyi lu*, in *QRSQJ*, 8.2:217–22.

132. To distinguish Shen Zijin's *Cuiping shan* from later pihuang opera adapta-

tions of the same name, I indicate the chuanqi title in italics and that of the pi-huang scripts in roman within quotation marks.

133. Here the script uses the role type to designate Pan Qiaoyun; she has become a nameless, generic dan, in contrast to the male characters, who are identified by their surnames.

134. "Cui" D, pp. 2b–3a; the full guessing game continues through p. 4a.

135. In this version of the play Old Man Pan is given the following monologue when he first enters: "I'm Old Man Pan. I have one son born to me named Pan Chengmei, who is stationed at the defenses of the Yanmen Pass. Later I had two daughters born to me. The eldest was named Pan Jinlian, and she was married to Wu Dalang. Later, she did some shameless things and was killed by Wu Song. My second daughter is named Pan Qiaoyun. She is married to Yang Xiong. I've come to live with them, and I lead a comfortable life. Today, they've called me out, and I don't know what it's all about"; see "Cui" E, p. 11b.

136. See "Cui" C, "Cui" D, "Shi part script" A, and "Shi part script" B. "Shi part script" A belonged to the professional actor Li Xinfu (1882–1918), a student of the famous lao sheng actor Tan Xinpei. "Shi part script" B lacks an owner's name, but its text is the same as that of "Shi part script" A.

137. Because the nicknames of the lead actors have been written faintly on the title page of the script, it is possible to date the script to ca. 1891–93. Tan Xinpei (1847–1917) is identified in the script by the nickname "Jiao tian"; and Yu Yuqin (1868–1939), by his stage name "Yu zhuang." Because it is known that Yu Yuqin was brought into the court to perform when he was twenty-three and performed for the palace for two years, the script can be dated to that time. For a brief biography of Yu Yuqin, see Ma Shaobo et al., *Zhongguo jingju shi*, 1:499–502. Yu Yuqin rose to fame in the mid-1880s, performing with Tan Xinpei in, among others, the pihuang opera "Cuiping shan."

138. The script indicates that each time Shi Xiu utters the word "kill," the orchestra underscores it with a clash of cymbals. Percussive music heightens the dramatic tension throughout the scene.

139. "Cui" C, pp. 43b–45a.

140. Chen Moxiang, *Guanju shenghuo sumiao*, p. 461.

141. Ibid., p. 470.

142. See *Yi* A, which comes from the collection of the twentieth-century dan actor Yu Lianquan, and also *Yi* B, with a copy date of 4 September 1931. According to the short biography of Yu Lianquan in *Zhongguo jingju shi*, in 1931 Yu performed a "complete" version of *Yixia ji* with his Qingsheng Troupe inside the rump court. Based on the dating and ownership of *Yi* A and *Yi* B, it is highly likely that both these scripts reflect the text for that 1931 performance. For information on the 1931 performance, see also Ma Shaobo et al., *Zhongguo jingju shi*, 1:674.

143. "Shizi lou" was performed in the palace twice in 1896, once on 6 May and once on 27 June; see Zhu Jiajin, "Qingdai luantan xi," in Ma Shaobo et al., *Zhongguo jingju shi*, 1:631, 632.

144. "Shizi lou." The version of "Shizi lou" published in the *Xikao* anthology is nearly identical with "Shizi lou"; *Xikao*, 2:527–34.

145. Zhu Jiajin, "Qingdai luantan xi," in Ma Shaobo et al., *Zhongguo jingju shi*, 1:631, 632.

146. See, for instance, a late nineteenth-century "capital melody" script of "Jinlian xi shu," in *Jingdiao Yi scenes*, pp. 5a–10b; and "Xi shu," in *Xikao*, 3:243–49.

147. Sometimes "Huo zhuo" was paired with a simplified pihuang version of "Jie cha."

148. A late nineteenth-century hand-copied edition of a script with the title "Jiaozheng 'Zuolou sha Xi' jingdiao quanben" covers just the second half of the plot, eliminating Zhang's flirtation with Yan and the first argument between Yan and Song; see "Zuolou." Another script hand-copied in 1912 by the Zhenglü xingwen she (likely an amateur performance group) bears the title "Wulong yuan" and encompasses only the first half of the plot; see "Wulong" C. The *Xikao* anthology version of "Wulong yuan" (published ca. 1915) also covers only the first half of the story, similar to the content encompassed in "Wulong" C; *Xikao*, 1:156–66. See also the scattered comments by Chen Moxiang, which suggest that "Wulong" had come to refer to the first half of this story and "Sha Xi" to the second; Chen, *Guanju shenghuo sumiao*, p. 425.

149. The *Xikao* script of "Jie cha, huo zhuo" preserves the Wu-dialect colloquialisms of the clowns; *Xikao*, 4:933–42.

150. My discussion here is based on two Shengping shu pihuang editions of "Huo zhuo"—one andian ben (copy for imperial review) and one *kuben* (storage copy). The andian ben, entitled "Huo zhuo," adds four opening scenes that introduce the full cast of characters of the Song Jiang–Yan Poxi story before launching into Yan Poxi's return as a ghost ("Huo" B). The kuben text, entitled "Jie cha, huo zhuo," presents the full cycle of female betrayal and male retribution. It begins with Song Jiang's initial encounter with the Liangshan bandits. A boldface notation following scene 5 reads: "play 'Wulong yuan' and 'Sha Xi' to the end." This is then followed by the same contents as in the andian ben version of "Huo zhuo" ("Jie/Huo" B). (Entire miniplays—"Wulong yuan" and "Zuolou sha Xi"—are slotted into the longer dramatic cycle in modulelike fashion in this script.) The kuben were copies of the full script of performances enacted at court, but unlike the andian ben, these texts were not for imperial review but for use by the actors. They tend to be written in a slipshod, cursive hand (unlike the neat, careful calligraphy of the andian ben). But like the andian ben, the kuben give full stage directions (and often costume notation). For more on the distinction between these two types of court "full-production scripts," or *zongben*, that is, kuben and andian ben, see Zhu Jiajin, "Qingdai luantan xi," in Ma Shaobo et al., *Zhongguo jingju shi*, 1:643; Qi Rushan, *Qi Rushan huiyi lu*, in *QRSQJ*, 8.2:217–22.

151. Yan Poxi is identified by the last syllable of her given name, here rendered as Xuejiao.

152. "Huo" B, n.p., but equivalent to p. 9b.

153. Luomoan laoren, *Huaifang ji*, in *QYLS*, p. 595.

154. Qi Rushan claims that the pihuang version of "Cuiping shan" was highly influenced by the bangzi version of the same story line; Qi, *Qi Rushan huiyi lu*, in *QRSQJ*, 8.2:293.

155. See *Xikao*, 2:649. Zhang San uses this same line in "Wulong" A, p. 1b. See also "Wulong" D, p. 31a.

156. Chen Moxiang, *Guanju shenghuo sumiao*, p. 459.

157. See the records of plays enacted by Tian Guifeng, in Zhou Mingtai, *Dao Xian yilai liyuan xinian xiaolu*, pp. 46, 79, 87, 88. Another dan actor active in the mid-1880s specialized in the roles of "the cobbler's wife," Pan Qiaoyun, and Yan Poxi; see *Jutai jixiu lu*, in *QYLS*, p. 639.

158. Zhou Mingtai, *Dao Xian yilai liyuan xinian xiaolu*, pp. 60, 64, 87.

159. One scholar has estimated that only 5 percent of the scene was given over to singing; the rest of the lines were delivered as dialogue; see Guo Jingrui, *Che wangfu quben yu jingju de xingcheng*, p. 94. Chen Moxiang claims that these saozi wo roles were more stigmatized than most dan roles. According to Chen, although the Republican-era actor Xun Huisheng (1900–1968) specialized in flirtatious dan operas, he refused to learn the part of the wife in "Sha pi." Chen, *Guanju shenghuo sumiao*, pp. 418–19, 503.

160. Xu Ke, *QBLC*, 11:5024.

161. Ibid., p. 5135.

162. Ibid.

163. Ibid., p. 5132. Another late nineteenth-century account concurs that actors without special talent would not be good in plays such as "Black Dragon Courtyard" and "Cuiping Mountain"; see Wu Tao, *Liyuan jiuhua*, in *QYLS*, p. 826.

164. "Cui" D, p. 2b. See also "Cui" E, p. 5a; and "Cuiping shan" in *Xikao*, 1:381, which simply refers to this bit with the phrase, "the three wash their faces." In still other scripts this bit is accompanied by direction to the orchestra to underscore some unspoken action here; see, for instance, the Shengping shu script "Cui" C, p. 7a.

165. See, for instance, the frontispiece to a 1912 edition of "Cuiping Mountain," in "Cui" G.

166. Chen Moxiang expressed disappointment that few amateurs—that is, men of status and education—dared attempt the flowery dan role type. He was an exception to the rule; Chen, *Guanju shenghuo sumiao*, pp. 401, 411, 418–19.

167. Emphasis mine.

168. Chen Moxiang, *Guanju shenghuo sumiao*, pp. 460–61.

169. Wu Tao, *Liyuan jiuhua*, in *QYLS*, p. 826.

170. Chen Moxiang, *Guanju shenghuo sumiao*, pp. 461–63.

171. Luo Ying'an, *Jubu congtan*, in *QYLS*, pp. 787–88. See also Chen Yanheng, *Jiuju congtan*, in *QYLS*, p. 879.

172. On the emergence of a strong male hero aesthetic in Peking opera, see also Mackerras, *Rise of the Peking Opera*; Darrobers, *Opéra de Pékin*, pp. 443–48.

173. I have found Carol Clover's folklore-analysis approach to modern slasher films useful in thinking through some of the issues of gender, violence, and audience reception; see Clover, *Men, Women, and Chain Saws*.

174. See Mann, *Precious Records*; Sommer, *Sex, Law, and Society*; Theiss, *Disgraceful Matters*.

175. Sommer, *Sex, Law, and Society*, p. 310.

Coda

1. Anecdote shared by former Peking University history student Qitao Guo; personal communication.

2. Qi Rushan claims that the eroticism quotient for romantic comedies in salon performance venues was greater than that within the commercial playhouses. I am not convinced that Qi's assertion is supported by the other sources; see Qi, *Qi Rushan huiyi lu*, in *QRSQ J*, 8.2:223–27.

3. Catherine Swatek discusses the comedic rendering of the love scenes in commercial productions of *Mudan ting* in Peony Pavilion *Onstage*.

4. On the concept of "self-fashioning" in early modern England, see Greenblatt, *Renaissance Self-Fashioning*.

5. My concept of "unreliable partners" has been influenced by Janet Theiss's discussion of the role of elites in the Qing state's project to shore up patriarchy. Writing on the eighteenth-century Qing state, Theiss has observed that the state looked to the local elites as partners in upholding patriarchy; in the end, the Qing state found the elite to be unreliable partners in its civilizing project; see Theiss, *Disgraceful Matters*.

6. See especially the arguments presented in Crossley, *Translucent Mirror*; Elliott, *The Manchu Way*; and Chang, *A Court on Horseback*.

7. The post-Taiping reconfiguration of political legitimacy has been discussed at length in Wright, *Last Stand of Chinese Conservatism*; Kuhn, *Rebellion and Its Enemies*; and Rhoads, *Manchus and Han*. I see this embrace, and then dissemination, of lowbrow culture via opera as the final (and perhaps most effective) stage in the Qing court's social-leveling agenda. The irony here is that this state-building project was finally achieved not at the seeming height of state power in the eighteenth century but at the nadir of Qing stability and legitimacy in the mid- to late nineteenth century. For more on the social-leveling argument, see Sommer, *Sex, Law, and Society*; Bernhardt, "A Ming-Qing Transition in Chinese Women's History?"; Mann, *Precious Records*.

8. On the predominance of strong masculine heroes in pihuang opera, see also Mackerras, *Rise of the Peking Opera*.

9. Cf. Wright, *Last Stand of Chinese Conservatism*. On the devolution of state power to localities, see, for example, Kuhn, *Rebellion and It Enemies*; Rankin, *Elite Activism*.

Bibliography

Ahern, Emily M. "The Power and Pollution of Chinese Women." In *Women in Chinese Society*, ed. Margery Wolf and Roxane Witke, pp. 193–214. Stanford, CA: Stanford University Press, 1975.
Aoki Masaru 青木正兒. *Zhongguo jinshi xiqu shi* 中國近世戲曲史. 2 vols. Translated by Wang Gulu 王古魯. Shanghai: Shangwu yinshuguan, 1936.
Beijing wangshi tan 北京往事談. Edited by Zhongguo renmin zhengzhi xieshang huiyi Beijingshi weiyuanhui wenshi ziliao yanjiu weiyuanhui. Beijing: Beijing chubanshe, 1988.
Belsky, Richard David. *Localities at the Center: Native Place, Space, and Power in Late Imperial Beijing*. Cambridge, MA: Harvard University Asia Center, 2005.
Berezin, Mabel. "Cultural Form and Political Meaning: State-Subsidized Theater, Ideology, and the Language of Style in Fascist Italy." *American Journal of Sociology* 99.5 (1994): 1237–68.
Bernhardt, Kathryn. "A Ming-Qing Transition in Chinese Women's History? The Perspective from Law." In *Remapping China: Fissures in Historical Terrain*, ed. Gail Hershatter et al., pp. 42–58. Stanford, CA: Stanford University Press, 1996.
Berry, Mary Elizabeth. "Public Life in Authoritarian Japan." *Daedalus* 127.3 (1998): 133–65.
Bevington, David, and Peter Holbrook, eds. *The Politics of the Stuart Court Masque*. Cambridge: Cambridge University Press, 1998.
Birch, Cyril. *Scenes for Mandarins: The Elite Theater of the Ming*. New York: Columbia University Press, 1995.
Bourdieu, Pierre. *Distinction: A Social Critique of the Judgement of Taste*. Translated by Richard Nice. Cambridge, MA: Harvard University Press, 1984.
———. *The Field of Cultural Production*. New York: Columbia University Press, 1993.
Brokaw, Cynthia. *The Ledgers of Merit and Demerit*. Princeton, NJ: Princeton University Press, 1991.
Brook, Timothy. *The Confusions of Pleasure*. Berkeley: University of California Press, 1998.
Brooks, Peter. *The Melodramatic Imagination: Balzac, Henry James, Melodrama, and the Mode of Excess*. New Haven, CT: Yale University Press, 1995.

Cao Xueqin 曹雪芹. Honglou meng sanjia pingben 紅樓夢三家評本. Shanghai: Shanghai guji, 1988.
Chang, Michael G. *A Court on Horseback: Imperial Touring and the Construction of Qing Rule, 1680–1785*. Cambridge, MA: Harvard University Asia Center, 2007.
Chang Renchun 常人春. *Lao Beijing de fengsu* 老北京的風俗. Beijing: Yanshan, 1993.
Chen Fang 陳芳. *Qianlong shiqi Beijing jutan yanjiu* 乾隆時期北京劇壇研究. Beijing: Wenhua yishu, 2001.
Chen Moxiang 陳墨香. "Guanju shenghuo sumiao" 觀劇生活素描. 1925, with revisions added in 1930. Manuscript held in the Zhongguo yishu yanjiuyuan Library, Beijing.
——— . *Guanju shenghuo sumiao*. Appended to Chen Moxiang and Pan Jingfu 潘鏡芙, *Liyuan waishi* 梨園外史. 1930. Reprint, Beijing: Baowentang, 1989.
Chen Moxiang and Pan Jingfu 潘鏡芙. *Liyuan waishi* 梨園外史. Ca. 1930. Reprint, Beijing: Baowentang, 1989.
Chen Sen 陳森. *Pinhua baojian* 品花寶鑒. 20 vols. N.p.: 1849.
Chen Xizhong 陳曦鐘, Hou Zhongyi 侯忠義, and Lu Yuchuan 魯玉川, eds. *Shuihu zhuan huiping ben* 水滸傳薈評本. 2 vols. Beijing: Beijing daxue, 1981.
Cheung, Samuel H. N. "Structural Cyclicity in *Shuihu zhuan*: From Self to Sworn Brotherhood." *Chinoperl Papers* 15 (1990): 1–15.
Chong Tianzi 蟲天子 (Zhang Tinghua 張廷華), comp. *Xiangyan congshu* 香豔叢書. 5 vols. 1909–11. Reprint, Beijing: Renmin wenxue, 1994.
Chong Yi 崇彝. *Dao Xian yilai chaoye zaji* 道咸以來朝野雜記. 1947. Reprint, Beijing: Beijing guji, 1982.
Chow, Kai-Wing. *The Rise of Confucian Ritualism in Late Imperial China: Ethics, Classics, and Lineage Discourse*. Stanford, CA: Stanford University Press, 1994.
Clifford, James, and George E. Marcus, eds. *Writing Culture: The Poetics and Politics of Ethnography*. Berkeley: University of California Press, 1986.
Clover, Carol. *Men, Women, and Chain Saws: Gender in the Modern Horror Film*. Princeton, NJ: Princeton University Press, 1992.
Clunas, Craig. *Superfluous Things: Material Culture and Social Status in Early Modern China*. Urbana: University of Illinois Press, 1991.
Cranmer-Byng, J. L., ed. *An Embassy to China: Being the Journal Kept by Lord Macartney during His Embassy to the Emperor Ch'ien-lung, 1793–94*. London: Longmans, 1962.
Crossley, Nick, and John Michael Roberts, eds. *After Habermas: New Perspectives on the Public Sphere*. Oxford: Blackwell Publishing, Sociological Review, 2004.
Crossley, Pamela Kyle. *Orphan Warriors: Three Manchu Generations and the End of the Qing World*. Princeton, NJ: Princeton University Press, 1990.
——— . *A Translucent Mirror: History and Identity in Qing Imperial Ideology*. Berkeley: University of California Press, 1999.
Da Qing lichao shilu 大清歷朝實錄. 94 vols. Taipei: Wenhua shuju, 1964.
Dai Lu 戴璐. *Tengyin zaji* 藤陰雜記. Beijing: Beijing guji, 1982.

Dames, Nicholas. *Amnesiac Selves: Nostalgia, Forgetting, and British Fiction, 1810–1870*. Oxford: Oxford University Press, 2001.

Darrobers, Roger. *Opéra de Pékin: Théatre et société à la fin de l'empire sino-mandchou*. Paris: Bleu de Chine, 1998.

Desai, Gaurav. "Old World Orders: Amitav Ghosh and the Writing of Nostalgia." *Representations* 85 (2004): 125–48.

Ding Ruqin 丁汝芹. "Qing gong yanxi shishi" 清宮演戲史事. *Yanjing xuebao* 燕京學報 4 (1998): 209–32.

———. *Qingdai neiting yanxi shihua* 清代內廷演戲史話. Beijing: Zijincheng, 1999.

Dolby, A. E. W. *A History of Chinese Drama*. New York: Harper & Row, 1975.

Dong Caishi 董蔡時. *Taiping tianguo zai Suzhou* 太平天國在蘇州. Nanjing: Jiangsu renmin, 1981.

Dong Han 董含. *Chunxiang zhuibi* 蓴鄉贅筆. In *Shuoling* 說鈴 (1799), comp. Wu Zhenfang 吳震方. 1705. Reprint, Taipei, 1968.

Dray-Novey, Alison. "Spatial Order and Police in Imperial Beijing." *JAS* 52.4 (1993): 855–922.

Dun Lichen 敦禮臣. *Yanjing suishi ji* 燕京歲時記. 1900. Reprint, Beijing: Beijing guji, 1981.

Dutton, George. *The Tây Son Uprising: Society and Rebellion in Eighteenth-Century Vietnam*. Honolulu: University of Hawaii Press, 2006.

Eber, Irene. "Weakness and Power: Women in *Water Margin*." In *Woman and Literature in China*, ed. Anna Gerstlacher et al., pp. 3–28. Bochum, Germany: Studienverlag, 1985.

Elliott, Mark C. *The Manchu Way: The Eight Banners and Ethnic Identity in Late Imperial China*. Stanford, CA: Stanford University Press, 2001.

Elman, Benjamin A. *A Cultural History of Civil Examinations in Late Imperial China*. Berkeley: University of California Press, 2000.

———. *From Philosophy to Philology: Intellectual and Social Aspects of Change in Late Imperial China*. Cambridge, MA: Council on East Asian Studies, Harvard University, 1984.

———. "The Hsüeh-hai Tang and the Rise of New Text Scholarship." *Ch'ing-shih wen-t'i* 3.7 (1977): 105–13.

Elvin, Mark. "Female Virtue and the State in China." *Past and Present* 104 (1984): 111–52.

Epstein, Maram. *Competing Discourses: Orthodoxy, Authenticity and Engendered Meanings in Late Imperial Chinese Fiction*. Cambridge, MA: Harvard University Asia Center, 2001.

Fan, Limin 范麗敏. *Qingdai Beijing xiqu yanchu yanjiu* 清代北京戲曲演出研究. Beijing: Renmin wenxue, 2007.

Fei, Si-yen. *Negotiating Urban Space: Urbanization and Late Ming Nanjing*. Cambridge, MA: Harvard University Asia Series, 2009.

Feng Guangyu 馮光鈺. "*Jiugong dacheng* de chuanbo yu 'jiugong dacheng xue' de xueke jiangou" 九宮大成的傳播與九宮大成學的學科建構. *Renmin yinyue* 人民音樂 6 (2003): 20–23.

Feng Menglong 馮夢龍. *Qingshi lei lüe* 情史類略. Changsha: Yuelu shushe, 1984.

Feng Mengzhen 馮夢禎. "Kuaixuetang ji" 快雪堂集 (1616). 64 juan. In *Siku quanshu cunmu congshu* 四庫全書存目叢書, comp. Siku quanshu cunmu congshu bianzuan weiyuanhui, ser. 4, vols. 164–65. Jinan: Qilu shushe, 1997.

Finnane, Antonia. *Speaking of Yangzhou: A Chinese City, 1550–1850*. Cambridge, MA: Harvard University Asia Center, 2004.

Fu Xihua 傅惜華. "Baiben Zhang xiqu shuji kaolüe" 百本張戲曲書籍考略. In *Zhongguo jindai chuban shiliao* 中國近代出版史料, ed. Zhang Jinglu 張靜廬, pp. 317–29. Shanghai: Qunlian, 1954.

———, *Shuihu xiqu ji* 水滸戲曲集. 2 vols. Shanghai: Gudian wenxue, 1958.

Geiss, James. "The Cheng-te Reign, 1506–1521." In *The Cambridge History of China*, vol. 7, *The Ming Dynasty, 1368–1644, Part I*, ed. Frederick W. Mote and Denis Twitchett, pp. 403–39. Cambridge: Cambridge University Press, 1988.

Goldman, Andrea S. "Actors and Aficionados in Qing Dynasty Texts of Theatrical Connoisseurship." *HJAS* 68.1 (June 2008): 1–56.

———. "Boy Heroines, Manchu Villains, and the Curious Tale of a Frenchman in Peking in the Twilight of the Empire." Conference paper delivered at Stanford University, April 2008.

———. "The Nun Who Wouldn't Be: Representations of Female Desire in Two Performance Genres of 'Si Fan.'" *LIC* 22.1 (2001): 71–138.

Goldstein, Joshua. *Drama Kings: Players and Publics in the Re-creation of Peking Opera, 1870–1937*. Berkeley: University of California Press, 2007.

Gong Zizhen 龔自珍. "Shu Jinling" 書金伶. In *Ding'an quanji* 定盦全集, *xuji* 續集, juan 4, pp. 7b–8a. N.p.: Baozhen zhai, 1898.

Goodman, Bryna. *Native Place, City, and Nation: Regional Networks and Identities in Shanghai, 1853–1937*. Berkeley: University of California Press, 1995.

Greenblatt, Stephen. *Renaissance Self-Fashioning: From More to Shakespeare*. Chicago: University of Chicago Press, 1980.

Grimsted, David. *Melodrama Unveiled: American Theater and Culture, 1800–1850*. Chicago: University of Chicago Press, 1968.

Gu Duhuang 顧篤璜. *Kunju shi bulun* 崑劇史補論. Nanjing: Jiangsu guji, 1987.

Gu Lu 顧祿. *Qingjialu* 清嘉錄. Shanghai: Shanghai guji, 1986.

"Guan Gong zhan Qin Qiong" 關公戰秦瓊. In *Chuantong xiangsheng huiji* 傳統相聲匯集, 6 vols., 1:318–21. Shenyang: Shenyang shi wenxue yishu jie lianhehui, 1980.

Guanju riji 觀劇日記. Manuscript, ca. 1773–1816. Zhongguo yishu yanjiuyuan Library, Beijing.

Guben xiqu congkan 古本戲曲叢刊. Shanghai: Shangwu yinshuguan, ser. 2, 1955; ser. 3, 1957; ser. 9, 1964.

Guo Anrui 郭安瑞 (Andrea S. Goldman). "Kunju de ouran xiaowang" 崑劇的偶然消亡. In *Kunqu, Chun san er yue tian—miandui shijie de kunqu yu* Mudanting

崑曲・春三二月天－－面對世界的崑曲與牡丹亭, ed. Hua Wei 華瑋 et al., pp. 354–66. Shanghai: Shanghai guji, 2009.

Guo Jingrui 郭精銳. *Che wangfu quben yu jingju de xingcheng* 車王府曲本與京劇的形成. Chaoyang: Shantou daxue, 1999.

Guo, Qitao. *Ritual Opera and Mercantile Lineage: The Confucian Transformation of Popular Culture in Late Imperial Huizhou.* Stanford, CA: Stanford University Press, 2005.

Guo Yingde 郭英德. *Ming Qing chuanqi zonglu* 明清傳奇綜錄. Shijiazhuang: Hebei jiaoyu, 1997.

Guy, Kent R. *The Emperor's Four Treasuries: Scholars and the State in the Late Ch'ien-lung Era.* Cambridge, MA: Council on East Asian Studies, Harvard University, 1987.

Habermas, Jürgen. *The Structural Transformation of the Public Sphere: An Inquiry into a Category of Bourgeois Society.* Translated by Thomas Burger with the assistance of Frederick Lawrence. Cambridge, MA: MIT Press, 1991.

Hadley, Elaine. *Melodramatic Tactics: Theatricalized Dissent in the English Marketplace, 1800–1885.* Stanford, CA: Stanford University Press, 1995.

Hayden, George A. *Crime and Punishment in Medieval Chinese Drama: Three Judge Bao Plays.* Cambridge, MA: Council on East Asian Studies, Harvard University, 1978.

Hays, Michael, and Anastasia Nikolopoulou, eds. *Melodrama: The Cultural Emergence of a Genre.* New York: St. Martin's Press, 1996.

He Gangde 何剛德. *Huameng ji* 話夢集. In *Huameng ji, Chunming menglu, Donghua suolu* 話夢集、春明夢錄、東華瑣錄. 1925. Reprint, Beijing: Beijing guji, 1995.

Hegel, Robert E. *Reading Illustrated Fiction in Late Imperial China.* Stanford, CA: Stanford University Press, 1998.

Hershatter, Gail. *Dangerous Pleasures: Prostitution and Modernity in Twentieth-Century Shanghai.* Berkeley: University of California Press, 1997.

Hevia, James L. *Cherishing Men from Afar: Qing Guest Ritual and the Macartney Embassy of 1793.* Durham, NC: Duke University Press, 1995.

Hinsch, Brett. *Passions of the Cut Sleeve: The Male Homosexual Tradition in China.* Berkeley: University of California Press, 1990.

Ho, Ping-ti. "The Salt Merchants of Yangchow." *HJAS* 17.1 (1954): 130–68.

Hostetler, Laura. *Qing Colonial Enterprise: Ethnography and Cartography in Early Modern China.* Chicago: University of Chicago Press, 2001.

Hou Baolin 侯寶林 and Guo Qiru 郭啟儒. "Guan Gong zhan Qin Qiong" 關公戰秦瓊. On "Xin Zhongguo wutai, yingshi, yishu jingpin xilie—xiangsheng" 新中國舞台，影視，藝術精品系列－－相聲, vol. 2, track 1, re-released recording. Beijing: Zhonghua wenyi yinxiang, 1999.

Hsia, C. T. *The Classic Chinese Novel: A Critical Introduction.* Bloomington: Indiana University Press, 1980.

Hu Ji 胡忌 and Liu Zhizhong 劉致中. *Kunju fazhan shi* 崑劇發展史. Beijing: Zhongguo xiju, 1989.

Hu Shi 胡適. "*Shuihu zhuan* kaozheng" 水滸傳考正. In *Hu Shi wencun* 胡適文存, pp. 500–547. Taipei: Yuandong tushu gongsi, 1953.

Hua Wei 華瑋. *Ming Qing funu zhi xiqu chuangzuo yu piping* 明清婦女之戲曲創作與批評. Taipei: Zhongyang yanjiuyuan zhongguo wenzhe yanjiusuo, 2003.

Hua Wei 華瑋 and Wang Ayling 王愛玲. *Ming Qing xiqu guoji yantaohui lunwenji* 明清戲曲國際研討會論文集. 2 vols. Taipei: Zhongyang yanjiuyuan zhongguo wenzhesuo yanjiusuo choubeichu, 1998.

Huang, Martin W. *Literati and Self-Re/presentation: Autobiographical Sensibility in the Eighteenth-Century Chinese Novel*. Stanford, CA: Stanford University Press, 1995.

Huang Tongsun 黃桐孫. "Weilang shuoshu ge" 魏郎說書歌, from *Guyuting shiji* 古于亭詩集. In *Qingren shiji xulu* 清人詩集敘錄, ed. Yuan Xingyun 袁行雲, 3:1993. Beijing: Wenhua yishu, 1994.

Huang Wei 黃暐, comp. *Hanfenlou miji erji* 涵芬樓秘笈二集. Shanghai: Shangwu yinshuguan, 1917.

Huang Yufu 黃育馥. *Jingju, qiao he zhongguo de xingbie guanxi* 京劇，蹺和中國的性別關係. Beijing: Sanlian shudian, 1998.

Huang Zongxi 黃宗羲. *Ming ru xuean* 明儒學案. Taipei: Mingwen shuju, 1991.

Hummel, Arthur W., ed. *Eminent Chinese of the Ch'ing Period*. 1943. Reprint, Taipei: Ch'eng Wen Publishing Company, 1972.

Idema, Wilt L. "Performances on a Three-Tiered Stage: Court Theatre during the Qianlong Era." In *Ad Seres et Tugusos: Feschrift für Martin Gimm*, pp. 201–19. Wiesbaden: Harrassowitz Verlag, 2000.

Idema, Wilt L., and Stephen H. West. *Chinese Theater 1100–1450: A Source Book*. Wiesbaden: Franz Verlag Steiner, 1982.

Im Ki-jung 林基中, comp. *Yŏnhaengnok chônjip* 燕行錄全集. Seoul: Tongguk taehakkyo, 2001.

Irwin, Richard G. *The Evolution of a Chinese Novel: Shuihu chuan*. Cambridge, MA: Harvard University Press, 1953.

———. "*Water Margin* Revisited." *TP* 48.4–5 (1960): 393–415.

Israel, Larry. "The Prince and the Sage: Concerning Wang Yangming's 'Effortless' Suppression of the Ning Princely Establishment Rebellion." *LIC* 29.2 (2008): 62–128.

"Jifang ban ximu" 集芳班戲目. Zhongguo yishu yanjiuyuan 中國藝術研究院 Library, 1829.

Jin Dengcai 金登才. *Qingdai huabu xi yanjiu* 清代花部戲研究. Beijing: Zhongguo xiju, 2006.

Jin Ping Mei cihua 金瓶梅詞話. 6 vols. 1617. Facsimile reprint, Taipei: Lianjing, 1979.

Johnson, David, ed. *Ritual Opera, Operatic Ritual*. Berkeley, CA: Publications of the Chinese Popular Culture Project 1, 1989.

———. *Spectacle and Sacrifice: The Ritual Foundations of Village Life in North China*. Cambridge, MA: Harvard East Asian Monographs, 2010.

Johnson, David, Andrew J. Nathan, and Evelyn S. Rawski, eds. *Popular Culture in Late Imperial China*. Berkeley: University of California Press, 1985.

Johnson, James H. *Listening in Paris: A Cultural History*. Berkeley: University of California Press, 1995.

Judge, Joan. *Print and Politics: "Shibao" and the Culture of Reform in Late Qing China*. Stanford, CA: Stanford University Press, 1996.

Kahn, Harold. *Monarchy in the Emperor's Eyes: Image and Reality in the Ch'ien-lung Reign*. Cambridge, MA: Harvard University Press, 1971.

Kang Baocheng 康保成. *Suzhou jupai yanjiu* 蘇州劇派研究. Shanghai: Huacheng, 1993.

Karl, Rebecca E. *Staging the World: Chinese Nationalism at the Turn of the Twentieth Century*. Durham, NC: Duke University Press, 2002.

Kasten, David Scott, and Peter Stallybrass, eds. *Staging the Renaissance: Reinterpretations of Elizabethan and Jacobean Drama*. New York: Routledge, 1991.

Ke Qingming 柯慶明 and Lin Mingde 林明德, eds. *Zhongguo gudian wenxue yanjiu congkan* 中國古典文學研究叢刊. 3 vols. Taipei: Juliu, 1977.

Ko, Dorothy. *Teachers of the Inner Chambers: Women and Culture in Seventeenth-Century China*. Stanford, CA: Stanford University Press, 1994.

Kroen, Sheryl. *Politics and Theater: The Crisis of Legitimacy in Restoration France, 1815–1830*. Berkeley: University of California Press, 2000.

Kuhn, Philip A. *Rebellion and Its Enemies in Late Imperial China: Militarization and Social Structure, 1796–1864*. Cambridge, MA: Harvard University Press, 1970.

———. *Soulstealers: The Chinese Sorcery Scare of 1768*. Cambridge, MA: Harvard University Press, 1990.

Lam, Joseph S. C. "Kunqu: The Civilized/Civilizing (*ya*) Music from Late Ming to Early Qing." Unpublished conference paper, Berkeley, California, 2006.

———. "Notational Representation and Contextual Constraints: How and Why Did Ye Tang Notate His Kun Opera Arias?" In *Themes and Variations: Writings on Music in Honor of Rulan Chao Pian*, ed. Bell Yung and Joseph S. C. Lam, pp. 31–44. Hong Kong: The Institute of Chinese Studies, The Chinese University of Hong Kong, 1994.

———. *State Sacrifices and Music in Ming China: Orthodoxy, Creativity, and Expressiveness*. Albany: SUNY Press, 1998.

Lean, Eugenia. *Public Passions: The Trial of Shi Jianqiao and the Rise of Popular Sympathy in Republican China*. Berkeley: University of California Press, 2007.

Lee, Haiyan. *Revolution of the Heart: A Genealogy of Love in China, 1900–1950*. Stanford, CA: Stanford University Press, 2007.

Legge, James, trans. *Confucius: Confucian Analects, The Great Learning and The Doctrine of the Mean*. New York: Dover Publications, 1971.

———, trans. *The Works of Mencius*. New York: Dover Publications, 1970.

Levine, Lawrence. *Highbrow/Lowbrow: The Emergence of Cultural Hierarchy in America*. Cambridge, MA: Harvard University Press, 1990.

Li Ciming 李慈銘. *Yuemantang riji* 越縵堂日記. Beijing: Zhejiang gonghui, 1920.

Li Dou 李斗. *Yangzhou huafang lu* 揚州畫舫錄. 1794. Reprint, Beijing: Zhonghua shuju, 1960.

Li Guangting 李光庭. *Xiangyan jieyi* 鄉言解頤. 1849. Reprint, Beijing: Zhonghua shuju, 1997.

Li Lüyuan 李綠園. *Qilu deng* 歧路燈. Annotated and edited by Luan Xing 欒星. Zhengzhou: Zhongzhou shuhuashe, 1980.

Li Mei 李玫. *Ming Qing zhi ji Suzhou zuojiaqun yanjiu* 明清之際蘇州作家群研究. Beijing: Zhongguo shehui kexue, 2000.

Li, Siu Leung. *Cross-Dressing in Chinese Opera*. Hong Kong: Hong Kong University Press, 2003.

Li, Wai-yee. "The Collector, the Connoisseur, and Late-Ming Sensibility." *TP* 81.4–5 (1995): 269–302.

———. *Enchantment and Disenchantment: Love and Illusion in Chinese Literature*. Princeton, NJ: Princeton University Press, 1993.

Li Xiaoti 李孝悌. *Qingmo de xiaceng shehui qimeng yundong, 1901–1911* 清末的下層社會啟蒙運動, 1901–1911. Taipei: Zhongyang yanjiuyuan jindaishi yanjiusuo, 1992.

Li Xiusheng 李修生 et al., comps. *Guben xiqu jumu tiyao* 古本戲曲劇目提要. Beijing: Wenhua yishu, 1997.

Liao Ben 廖奔. "Guanyu jingqiang liuda mingban" 關於京腔六大名班. Unpublished manuscript.

———. *Song Yuan xiqu wenwu yu minsu* 宋元戲曲文物與民俗. Beijing: Wenhua yishu, 1989.

———. *Zhongguo gudai juchang shi* 中國古代劇場史. Zhengzhou: Zhongzhou guji, 1997.

———. *Zhongguo xiju tushi* 中國戲劇圖史. Zhengzhou: Henan jiaoyu, 1996.

Lin Baochun 林保淳. "Zhongguo gudai xiaoshuo zhong de 'nüxia' xingxiang" 中國古代小說中的「女俠」形象. *Zhongguo wenzhe yanjiu jikan* 中國文哲研究集刊 11 (1997): 43–87.

Lin Sumen 林蘇門. *Hanjiang sanbai yin* 邗江三百吟. 1809. Reprint, Yangzhou: Jiangsu Guangling guji keyinshe, 1988.

Liu, James J. Y. *The Chinese Knight-Errant*. Chicago: University of Chicago Press, 1967.

Liu Liemao 劉烈茂 and Guo Jingrui 郭精銳. *Che wangfu quben yanjiu* 車王府曲本研究. Guangzhou: Guangdong renmin, 2000.

Liu Naichong 劉迺崇. "Ji jingju zuojia Chen Moxiang" 記京劇作家陳墨香. *Xiju luncong* 戲劇論叢 1.5 (1958): 233–44.

Liu Wenfeng 劉文峰. *Shan-shan shangren yu bangzi xi* 山陝商人與梆子戲. Beijing: Wenhua yishu, 1996.

Liu Xiaomeng 劉小萌. *Manzu de shehui yu shenghuo* 滿族的社會與生活. Beijing: Beijing tushuguan, 1998.

Lowe, H. Y. *The Adventures of Wu: The Life Cycle of a Peking Man*. Princeton, NJ: Princeton University Press, 1983.

Lu Eting 陸萼庭. *Kunju yanchu shigao* 崑劇演出史稿. Shanghai: Shanghai wenyi, 1980.

———. *Qingdai xiqu yu kunqu* 清代戲曲與崑曲. Taipei: Guojia, 2005.

Lu Gong 路工, ed. *Qingdai Beijing zhuzhici* 清代北京竹枝詞. Beijing: Beijing chubanshe, 1962.

Lu Yingkun 路應昆. *Zhongguo xiqu yu shehui zhu se* 中國戲曲与社會諸色. Changchun: Jilin jiaoyu, 1992.

Lu Xun 魯迅. *Zhongguo xiaoshuo shilüe* 中國小說史略. Shanghai: Shanghai guji, 1998.

Luo Suwen 羅蘇文. "Lun jindai xiqu yu dushi jumin" 論近代戲曲與都市居民. *Shanghai yanjiu luncong* 上海研究論叢 9 (1993): 207–30.

Ma Shaobo 馬少波 et al., eds. *Zhongguo jingju shi* 中國京劇史. 4 vols. Beijing: Zhongguo xiju, 1990.

Ma Youyuan 馬幼垣. *Zhongguo xiaoshuoshi jigao* 中國小說史集稿. Taipei: Shibao wenhua, 1978.

Mackerras, Colin P. "The Growth of Chinese Regional Drama in the Ming and the Ch'ing." *JOS* 9.1 (1971): 58–91.

———. *The Rise of the Peking Opera, 1770–1870: Social Aspects of the Theatre in Manchu China*. Oxford: Clarendon Press, 1972.

Mann, Susan. *Precious Records: Women in China's Long Eighteenth Century*. Stanford, CA: Stanford University Press, 1997.

———. "Widows in the Kinship, Class, and Community Structures of Qing Dynasty China." *JAS* 46.1 (1987): 37–56.

Mao Jin 毛晉, comp. *Liushizhong qu* 六十種曲. 6 cases. Mid-seventeenth century. Reprint, Shanghai: Wenxue guji kanxingshe, 1955.

Mark, Lindy Li. "*Kunju* and Theatre in the Transvestite Novel *Pinhua baojian*." *Chinoperl Papers* 14 (1986): 37–59.

———. "The Role of Avocational Performers in the Preservation of *Kunqu*." *Chinoperl Papers* 15 (1990): 95–114.

McMahon, Keith. *Causality and Containment in Seventeenth-Century Chinese Fiction*. Leiden: E. J. Brill, 1988.

———. *Misers, Shrews, and Polygamists: Sexuality and Male-Female Relations in Eighteenth-Century Chinese Fiction*. Durham, NC: Duke University Press, 1995.

———. "Sublime Love and the Ethics of Equality in a Homoerotic Novel of the Nineteenth Century: *Precious Mirror of Boy Actresses*." *Nan Nü* 4.1 (2002): 70–109.

Mei Lanfang 梅蘭芳 and Xu Jichuan 許姬傳. *Wutai shenghuo sishinian* 舞臺生活四十年. 3 vols. Shanghai: Pingming, 1952.

Meng Yuanlao 孟元老. *Dongjing menghua lu* 東京夢華錄. In *Dongjing menghua lu wai si zhong* 東京夢華錄外四種, ed. Zhou Feng 周峰. Beijing: Wenhua yishu, 1998.

Meng Yue. *Shanghai and the Edges of Empires*. Minneapolis: University of Minnesota Press, 2006.

Meyer-Fong, Tobie. *Building Culture in Early Qing Yangzhou*. Stanford, CA: Stanford University Press, 2003.

Miles, Steven B. "Celebrating the Yu Fan Shrine: Literati Networks and Local Identity in Early Nineteenth-Century Guangzhou." *LIC* 25.2 (2004): 33–73.

Mingshi 明史. Edited by Zhang Tingyu 張廷玉 et al. Beijing: Zhonghua shuju, 2005.
Naquin, Susan. *Millenarian Rebellion in China: The Eight Trigrams Uprising of 1813*. New Haven, CT: Yale University Press, 1976.
———. *Peking: Temples and City Life, 1400–1900*. Berkeley: University of California Press, 2000.
Nie Gannu 聶紺弩. *Zhongguo gudian xiaoshuo lunji* 中國古典小說論集. Shanghai: Shanghai guji, 1981.
Olivová, Lucie, and Vibeke Børdahl, eds. *Lifestyle and Entertainment in Yangzhou*. Copenhagen: Nordic Institute of Asian Studies Press, 2009.
Orgel, Stephen, ed. *The Illusion of Power: Political Theater in the English Renaissance*. Berkeley: University of California Press, 1975.
———. "What Is a Text?" In *Staging the Renaissance: Reinterpretations of Elizabethan and Jacobean Drama*, ed. David Scott Kasten and Peter Stallybrass, pp. 83–87. New York: Routledge, 1991.
Pan Lizhu 潘麗珠. *Qingdai zhongqi Yandu liyuan shiliao pingyi sanlun yanjiu* 清代中期燕都梨園史料評藝三論研究. Taipei: Liren shuju, 1998.
Pan Rongbi 潘榮陛. *Dijing suishi jisheng* 帝京歲時紀勝. 1758. Reprint, Beijing: Beijing guji, 1981.
Peng Xinwei 彭信威. *Zhongguo huobi shi* 中國貨幣史. 2 vols. Shanghai: Qunlian, 1954.
Perng, Ching-hsi. *Double Jeopardy: A Critique of Seven Yuan Courtroom Dramas*. Ann Arbor: Michigan Papers in Chinese Studies 35, 1978.
Pien, Rulan Chao. *Sonq Dynasty Music Sources and Their Interpretation*. Hong Kong: The Chinese University Press, 1999.
Plaks, Andrew H. *The Four Masterworks of the Ming Novel*. Princeton, NJ: Princeton University Press, 1987.
Polachek, James. "Gentry Hegemony: Soochow in the T'ung-chih Restoration." In *Conflict and Control in Late Imperial China*, ed. Frederic Wakeman Jr. and Carolyn Grant, pp. 221–56. Berkeley: University of California Press, 1975.
———. *The Inner Opium War*. Cambridge, MA: Harvard University Press, 1992.
Poole, Ralph J., and Ilka Saal. "Passionate Politics: An Introduction." In *Passionate Politics: The Cultural Work of American Melodrama from the Early Republic to the Present*, ed. Poole and Saal, pp. 1–26. Newcastle upon Tyne, UK: Cambridge Scholars Publishing, 2008.
Qi Biaojia 祁彪佳. *Qi Zhongmin gong riji* 祁忠敏公日記. 10 vols. 1937. Reprint, Hangzhou: Hangzhou gujiu shudian, 1982.
Qi Rushan 齊如山. *Qi Rushan quanji* 齊如山全集. 8 vols. Taipei: Chongguang wenyi, 1964.
———. "Xiguan" 戲館. Unpublished manuscript. Ca. 1930.
Qi Senhua 齊森華. "Shi lun mingdai jiayue" 試論明代家樂. In *Ming Qing xiqu guoji yantaohui lunwenji* 明清戲曲國際研討會論文集, ed. Hua Wei 華瑋 and Wang Ayling 王愛玲, 1:305–26. Taipei: Zhongyang yanjiuyuan zhongguo wenzhesuo yanjiusuo choubeichu, 1998.

Qi Senhua et al., comps. *Zhongguo quxue dacidian* 中國曲學大詞典. Hangzhou: Zhejiang jiaoyu, 1997.
Qinding Da Qing huidian shili 欽定大清會典事例. Pt. 2, vol. 11. 1909. Reprint, Shanghai: Shangwu yinshuguan, 1991.
Qing Che wangfu chaocang quben: zidi shu ji 清車王府鈔藏曲本—子弟書集. 2 vols. Edited by Liu Liemao 劉烈茂 and Guo Jingrui 郭精銳. Nanjing: Jiangsu guji, 1993.
Qinqiang jumu chukao 秦腔劇目初考. Edited by the Shaanxi sheng yishu yanjiusuo 陝西省藝術研究所. Xi'an: Shaanxi renmin, 1984.
Qiu Huiying 丘慧瑩. *Qianlong shiqi xiqu huodong yanjiu* 乾隆時期戲曲活動研究. Taipei: Wenjin, 2000.
Qixiang shi 緝香氏. *Pinghua* 評花. Zhongguo yishu yanjiuyuan Library, 1816.
Rancière, Jacques. "Good Times or Pleasure at the Barriers." In *Voices of the People: The Politics and Life of 'La Sociale' at the End of the Second Empire*, ed. Adrian Rifkin and Roger Thomas, trans. John Moore, pp. 45–94. London: Routledge & Kegan Paul, 1988.
Rankin, Mary Backus. *Elite Activism and Political Transformation in China*. Stanford, CA: Stanford University Press, 1986.
———. "Some Observations on a Chinese Public Sphere." *Modern China* 19.2 (1993): 158–92.
Ravel, Jeffrey S. *The Contested Parterre: Public Theater and French Political Culture, 1680–1791*. Ithaca, NY: Cornell University Press, 1999.
Rawski, Evelyn S. *The Last Emperors: A Social History of Qing Imperial Institutions*. Berkeley: University of California Press, 1998.
Ren Xiaowen 任孝溫. "Ming Qing Jiangnan quhui yu kunqu yanchang lilun de fazhan" 明清江南曲會與崑曲演唱理論的發展. *Xiqu yishu* 戲曲藝術 29.4 (2008): 17–20.
Rhoads, Edward J. M. *Manchus and Han: Ethnic Relations and Political Power in Late Qing and Early Republican China, 1861–1928*. Seattle: University of Washington Press, 2000.
Robertson, Maureen A. "'. . . To Convey What Is Precious': Ssu-K'ung T'u's Poetics and *The Erh-shih-ssu Shih-P'in*." In *Transition and Permanence: Chinese History and Culture*, ed. David C. Buxbaum and Frederick W. Mote, pp. 323–57. Hong Kong: Cathay Press Limited, 1972.
———. "Voicing the Feminine: Constructions of the Gendered Subject in Lyric Poetry by Women of Medieval and Late Imperial China." *LIC* 13.1 (1992): 63–110.
Rowe, William T. *Hankow: Commerce and Society in a Chinese City, 1796–1889*. Stanford, CA: Stanford University Press, 1984.
———. *Hankow: Conflict and Community in a Chinese City, 1795–1895*. Stanford, CA: Stanford University Press, 1989.
———. "The Problem of 'Civil Society' in Late Imperial China." *Modern China* 19.2 (1993): 139–57.
———. "The Public Sphere in Modern China." *Modern China* 16.3 (1990): 309–29.

Roy, David, ed. and trans. *The Plum in the Golden Vase or, Chin P'ing Mei*. Vol. 1. Princeton, NJ: Princeton University Press, 1993.

Rozman, Gilbert. *Urban Networks in Ch'ing China and Tokugawa Japan*. Princeton, NJ: Princeton University Press, 1973.

Schneider, Laurence A. *A Madman of Ch'u: The Chinese Myth of Loyalty and Dissent*. Berkeley: University of California Press, 1980.

Scott, Joan W. "Gender: A Useful Category of Historical Analysis." *American Historical Review* 91.5 (1986): 1053–75.

Seaman, Gary. "The Sexual Politics of Karmic Retribution." In *The Anthropology of Taiwanese Society*, ed. Emily Martin Ahern and Hill Gates, pp. 381–96. Stanford, CA: Stanford University Press, 1981.

Shanben xiqu congkan 善本戲曲叢刊. 104 vols. Compiled by Wang Qiugui 王秋桂. Taipei: Taiwan xuesheng shuju, 1984–87.

Shang Wei 商偉. "Yi yin yi yang zhi wei dao: *Caizi Mudanting* de pingzhu huayu ji qi dianfu xing" 一陰一陽之謂道：才子牡丹亭的評註話語及其顛覆性. Unpublished conference paper, Berkeley, California, September 2006.

Shi Dian 史典. *Yongxing bian* 庸行編. Danningtang, 1691.

Shi Nai'an 施耐庵 and Luo Guanzhong 羅貫中. *Shuihu zhuan* 水滸傳. 3 vols. Beijing: Renmin wenxue, 1995.

Shixing yadiao Zhuibaiqiu xinji hebian 時興雅調綴白裘新集合編. 48 vols. Compiled by Wanhua zhuren 玩花主人 and Qian Decang 錢德蒼. 1770–77 reprint by Hongwentang 鴻文堂 of the Baorentang 寶仁堂 edition. In *SBXQCK*, vols. 58–72.

Shuihu zhengming 水滸爭鳴. 3 vols. Edited by Hubei sheng *Shuihu* yanjiu hui 湖北省水滸研究會. Wuhan: Changjiang wenyi, 1984.

Skinner, G. William, ed. *The City in Late Imperial China*. Stanford, CA: Stanford University Press, 1977.

Sommer, Matthew H. *Sex, Law, and Society in Late Imperial China*. Stanford, CA: Stanford University Press, 2000.

Spence, Jonathan D. *Treason by the Book*. New York: Penguin, 2001.

Stallybrass, Peter, and Allon White. *The Politics and Poetics of Transgression*. Ithaca, NY: Cornell University Press, 1986.

Starr, Chloe. "Shifting Boundaries: Gender in *Pinhua Baojian*." *Nan Nü* 1.2 (1999): 268–302.

Staunton, George L. *An Authentic Account of an Embassy from the King of Great Britain to the Emperor of China*. 2 vols. London: Nicol, 1797.

Strand, David. *Rickshaw Beijing: City People and Politics in the 1920s*. Berkeley: University of California Press, 1989.

Strassberg, Richard E. "The Singing Techniques of K'un-ch'ü and Their Musical Notation." *Chinoperl Papers* 6 (1976): 45–81.

Struve, Lynn A. "Ambivalence and Action: Some Frustrated Scholars of the K'ang-hsi Period." In *From Ming to Ch'ing: Conquest, Region, and Continuity in Seventeenth-Century China*, ed. Jonathan D. Spence and John E. Wills, pp. 321–66. New Haven, CT: Yale University Press, 1979.

———, ed. and trans. *Voices from the Ming-Qing Cataclysm: China in Tigers' Jaws*. New Haven, CT: Yale University Press, 1993.
Su Yi 蘇移. *Jingju erbainian gaiguan* 京劇二百年概觀. Beijing: Beijing yanshan, 1995.
Sun Chongtao 孫崇濤. "Zhongguo xiqu xieben shulüe" 中國戲曲寫本述略. *Xiqu yishu* 5.4 (2005): 62–73.
Sun Chongtao 孫崇濤 and Xu Hongtu 徐宏圖, eds. *Qinglou ji qianzhu* 青樓集淺注. Beijing: Zhongguo xiju, 1990.
Sun Kaidi 孫楷弟. *Cangzhou ji* 滄州集. 2 vols. Beijing: Zhonghua shuju, 1965.
Sun Shuyu 孫述宇. *Shuihu zhuan de laili, xintai yu yishu* 水滸傳的來歷、心態與藝術. Taipei: Shibao wenhua, 1981.
Swatek, Catherine C. "Beating the Officers and Cursing the Manchus: Suzhou Dialect and Kun Opera." Unpublished manuscript.
———. "The Onstage Life of Two Politically Sensitive Plays by the Suzhou Playwright Li Yu." Unpublished paper presented at the 2006 Association of Asian Studies (AAS) annual meeting, San Francisco, California.
———. *The Peony Pavilion Onstage: Four Centuries in the Career of a Chinese Drama*. Ann Arbor: University of Michigan Center for Chinese Studies Monograph Series, 2002.
Tanaka Issei 田仲一成. *Chūgoku engeki-shi* 中國演劇史. Tokyo: Tōyōdaigaku, 1998.
———. *Chūgoku saishi engeki kenkyū* 中國祭祀演劇研究. Tokyo: Tōyōbunka kenkyūjo, 1981.
Tang Long 唐龍. *Yushi ji* 漁石集. Shanghai: Shangwu yinshuguan, 1935.
Tao Junqi 陶君起, ed. *Jingju jumu chutan* 京劇劇目初探. Beijing: Zhongguo xiju, 1963.
Tao Zongyi 陶宗儀, comp. *Shuofu* 說郛. 40 vols. Edited by Zhang Zongxiang 張宗祥. Tao Zongyi, fl. 1360–68. Reprint, Shanghai: Shangwu yinshuguan, 1927.
Terzioğlu, Derin. "The Imperial Circumcision Festival of 1582: An Interpretation." *Muqarnas* 12 (1995): 84–100.
Theiss, Janet M. *Disgraceful Matters: The Politics of Chastity in Eighteenth-Century China*. Berkeley: University of California Press, 2004.
Tianjin shi guji shudian 天津市古籍書店, ed. *Quhai zongmu tiyao* 曲海總目提要. Tianjin: Tianjin guji, 1992.
Timovsky, Egor F. *Travels of the Russian Mission through Mongolia to China, and Residence in Peking, in the Years 1820–1821*. 2 vols. Translated by H. E. Lloyd. London: Longman, Rees, Orme, Brown, & Green, 1827.
Vitiello, Giovanni. "Exemplary Sodomites: Chivalry and Love in Late Ming Culture." *Nan Nü* 2.2 (2000): 207–57.
Volpp, Sophie. "Classifying Lust: The Seventeenth-Century Vogue for Male Love." *HJAS* 61.1 (2001): 77–118.
———. "The Literary Circulation of Actors in Seventeenth-Century China." *JAS* 61.3 (2002): 949–84.

Wakeman, Frederic, Jr. "Boundaries of the Public Sphere in Ming and Qing China." *Daedalus* 127.3 (1998): 167–89.
———. "The Civil Society and Public Sphere Debate: Western Reflections on Chinese Political Culture." *Modern China* 19.2 (1993): 108–38.
———. *The Great Enterprise: The Manchu Reconstruction of Imperial Order in Seventeenth-Century China*. Berkeley: University of California Press, 1985.
———. "The Price of Autonomy: Intellectuals in Ming and Qing Politics." *Daedalus* 101.2 (1972): 35–70.
———. "Romantics, Stoics, and Martyrs in Seventeenth-Century China." *JAS* 43.4 (1984): 631–65.
Walkling, Andrew R. "The Apotheosis of Absolutism and the Interrupted Masque: Theater, Music, and Monarchy in Restoration England." In *Politics, Transgression, and Representation at the Court of Charles II*, ed. Julia Marciari Alexander and Catharine MacLeod, pp. 193–231. New Haven, CT: Yale University Press, 2007.
Wang Anqi 王安祈. "Li Xuanyu juqu shisan zhong yanjiu" 李玄玉劇曲十三種研究. Master's thesis, Guoli Taiwan daxue, 1980.
———. *Mingdai chuanqi zhi juchang ji qi yishu* 明代傳奇之劇場及其藝術. Taipei: Taiwan xuesheng shuju, 1986.
Wang Ayling 王瓊玲. *Ming Qing chuanqi mingzuo renwu kehua zhi yishuxing* 明清傳奇名作人物刻畫之藝術性. Taipei: Taiwan shudian, 1998.
Wang Chang'an 王長安. *Xu Wei sanbian* 徐渭三辨. Beijing: Zhongguo xiju, 1995.
Wang, David Der-wei. *Fin-de-Siècle Splendor: Repressed Modernities of Late Qing Fiction, 1849–1911*. Stanford, CA: Stanford University Press, 1997.
Wang Liqi 王利器, ed. *Yuan Ming Qing sandai jinhui xiaoshuo xiqu shiliao* 元明清三代禁毀小說戲曲史料. Rev. ed. Shanghai: Shanghai guji, 1981.
Wang Qiang 王強. *Huiguan xitai yu xiju* 會館戲臺與戲劇. Taipei: Wenjin, 2000.
Wang Shipei 汪詩佩. *Qian Jia shiqi kunju yiren zai biaoyan yishu shang yinying zhi tantao* 乾嘉時期崑劇藝人在表演藝術上因應之探討. Taipei: Xuehai, 2000.
Wang Shunu 王書奴. *Zhongguo changji shi* 中國娼妓史. Shanghai: Shenghuo shudian, 1935.
Wang Yongen 王永恩. "Shi lun Mingmo Qingchu xiqu zhong de nujie xingxiang" 試論明末清初戲曲中的女傑形像. *Xiqu yishu* 27.4 (2006): 45–51.
Wang Yongkuan 王永寬. "Mingmo Qingchu Suzhou diqu xiqu chuangzuo fanrong de shehui yuanyin" 明末清初蘇州地區戲曲創作繁榮的社會原因. *Xiqu luncong* 戲曲論叢 2 (1989): 165–86.
Wang Yufu 王玉甫. *Longfu chunqiu* 隆福春秋. Beijing: Zhongguo shehui, 1995.
Wang Yunwu 王雲五, ed. *Jiaofang ji ji qita jiu zhong* 教坊記及其他九種. Shanghai: Shangwu yinshuguan, 1939.
Wang Zhengyao 王政堯. *Qingdai xiju wenhua shilun* 清代戲劇文化史論. Beijing: Beijing daxue, 2005.
Wang Zhizhang 王芷章. *Qing Shengping shu zhilüe* 清昇平署志略. 2 vols. Beiping: Guoli Beiping yanjiuyuan shixue yanjiu hui, 1937.
———. *Qingdai lingguan zhuan* 清代伶官傳. Beiping: Zhonghua yinshuju, 1937.

———. *Zhongguo jingju biannian shi* 中國京劇編年史. Beijing: Zhongguo xiju, 2002.
Wen Kang 文康. *Ernü yingxiong zhuan* 兒女英雄傳. Edited by Er Gong 爾弓. 1888. Reprint, Ji'nan: Qilu shushe, 1989.
West, Stephen H. "Playing with Food: Performance, Food and the Aesthetics of Artificiality in the Sung and Yuan." *HJAS* 57.1 (1997): 67–106.
———. "Shifting Spaces: Local Dialect in *A Playboy from a Noble House Opts for the Wrong Career*." *Xiju yanjiu* 戲劇研究 2 (2008): 83–107.
West, Stephen H., and Wilt L. Idema, trans. *The Moon and the Zither: The Story of the Western Wing*. Berkeley: University of California Press, 1991.
Widmer, Ellen. "Xiaoqing's Literary Legacy and the Place of the Woman Writer in Late Imperial China." *LIC* 13.1 (1992): 111–55.
Widmer, Ellen, and Kang-I Sun Chang, eds. *Writing Women in Late Imperial China*. Stanford, CA: Stanford University Press, 1997.
Wong, Isabel K. F. "The Printed Collections of K'un-ch'ü Arias and Their Sources." *Chinoperl Papers* 8 (1978): 100–129.
Wong, R. Bin. "Great Expectations: The 'Public Sphere' and the Search for Modern Times in Chinese History." *Chugoku shigaku* 中國史學 3 (1993): 7–50.
Wright, Mary Clabaugh. *The Last Stand of Chinese Conservatism: The T'ung-chih Restoration, 1862–1874*. Stanford, CA: Stanford University Press, 1962.
Wu Changyuan 吳長元. *Chenyuan shilüe* 宸垣識略. 1788. Reprint, Beijing: Beijing guji, 1981.
Wu Cuncun. *Homoerotic Sensibilities in Late Imperial China*. New York: Routledge, 2004.
Wu Cuncun 吳存存. *Ming Qing shehui xing'ai fengqi* 明清社會性愛風氣. Beijing: Renmin wenxue, 2000.
Wu Cuncun and Mark Stevenson. "Speaking of Flowers: Theatre, Public Culture, and Homoerotic Writing in Nineteenth-Century Beijing." *Asian Theatre Journal* 27.1 (2010): 100–129.
Wu Jingzi 吳敬梓. *Rulin waishi* 儒林外史. Beijing: Renmin wenxue, 1995.
Wu Mei 吳梅. *Zhongguo xiqu gailun* 中國戲曲概論. Hong Kong: Xianggang taiping shuju, 1976.
Wu Renshu 巫仁恕. "Ming Qing zhi ji Jiangnan shishiju de fazhan ji qi suo fanying de shehui xintai" 明清之際江南時事劇的發展及其所反應的社會心態. *Zhongyang yanjiuyuan Jindai yanjiusuo jikan* 中央研究院近代研究所集刊 31 (1999): 1–48.
Wu Shuyin 吳書蔭. "Shu 'Qing Qianlong jian Yangzhou guan xiu *Xiqukao*' hou" 書《清乾隆間揚州官修戲曲考》後. *XQYJ* 28 (1988): 245–48.
Wu Xinlei 吳新雷. *Zhongguo xiqu shilun* 中國戲曲史論. Nanjing: Jiangsu jiaoyu, 1996.
———. "*Zhuibaiqiu* de lailong qumai" 綴白裘的來龍去脈. *Nanjing daxue xuebao* 南京大學學報 3 (1983): 36–42.
Wu, Yenna. *The Chinese Virago: A Literary Theme*. Cambridge, MA: Council on East Asian Studies, Harvard University, 1995.

———. "The Inversion of Marital Hierarchy: Shrewish Wives and Henpecked Husbands in Seventeenth-Century Chinese Literature." *HJAS* 48.2 (1988): 363–82.
Wu Yuhua 吳毓華. "Shi lun qingguan xi de sixiang yiyi" 試論清官戲的思想意義. *XQYJ* 1 (1980): 245–61.
———, ed. *Zhongguo gudai xiqu xu ba ji* 中國古代戲曲序跋集. Beijing: Zhongguo xiju, 1990.
Xie Bixia 謝碧霞. *Shuihu xiqu ershi zhong yanjiu* 水滸戲曲二十種研究. Taipei: Guoli Taiwan daxue wenshi congkan, 1981.
Xikao daquan 戲考大全. 5 vols. 1915–25. Reprint, Shanghai: Shanghai shudian, 1990.
Xinke chuxiang dianban shishang kunqiang zaqu Zuiyiqing (Qianlong-era reprint of late Ming *Zuiyiqing* [Zhihetang, Suzhou]). Compiled by Qingxi gulu diaosou, juan 3, 8a–b, in *SBXQCK*, 54:207–8.
Xu Gan 徐榦, comp., *Shaowu Xu shi congshu* 邵武徐氏叢書. Hangzhou?: Shaowu Xu shi, 1882.
Xu Ke 徐珂, ed. and comp. *Qing bai leichao* 清稗類鈔. 13 vols. 1916. Reprint, Beijing: Zhonghua shuju, 1996.
Xu Yusheng 徐余生. *Yanshi jibi* 燕市積弊. 1913. Reprint, Beijing: Beijing guji, 1995.
Xuanhe yishi 宣和遺事. Shanghai: Shangwu yinshuguan, 1939.
Yan Changke 顏長珂. "Zhengui de xiqu shiliao: du 'jiaqing dingsi wuwu guanju riji' shougao" 珍貴的戲曲史料——讀《嘉慶丁巳戊午觀劇日記》手稿. *XQYJ* 9 (1983): 250–80.
Yan Quanyi 顏全毅. *Qingdai jingju wenxue shi* 清代京劇文學史. Beijing: Beijing chubanshe, 2005.
Yan Xu 延煦 et al., comps. *Qinding taigui* 欽定臺規. 42 juan. 1892. Reprint, Beijing: Quanguo tushuguan wenxian suowei fuzhi zhongxin, 1989.
Yang Shaoxuan 楊紹萱. "Lun *Shuihu zhuan* yu shuihu xi" 論水滸傳與水滸戲. In *Shuihu yanjiu lunwenji* 水滸研究論文集, pp. 336–61. Beijing: Zuojia, 1957.
Yao Shuyi 么書儀. *Wan Qing xiqu de biange* 晚清戲曲的變革. Beijing: Renmin wenxue, 2006.
———. "Xiqu shi xushuzhong de Beijing 'tangzi'" 戲曲史敘述中的北京堂子. *Da xiju luntan* 大戲劇論壇 2 (2004): 47–60.
Ye Changhai 葉長海. *Wang Jide Qulü yanjiu* 王驥德《曲律》研究. Beijing: Zhongguo xiju, 1983.
Ye Xian'en 葉顯恩. *Ming Qing Huizhou nongcun shehui yu dianpu zhi* 明清徽州農村社會與佃僕制. Hefei: Anhui renmin, 1983.
Ye Xiaoqing. "Imperial Institutions and Drama in the Qing Court." *European Journal of East Asian Studies* 2.2 (2003): 329–64.
———. "Unacceptable Marriage and the Qing Legal Code: The Case of Yang Yuelou." *Journal of the Oriental Society of Australia* 27–28 (1995–96): 195–212.
Yeh, Catherine. "Playing with the Public: Late Qing Courtesans and Their Opera Singer Lovers." In *Gender in Motion: Divisions of Labor and Cultural Change in*

Late Imperial and Modern China, ed. Bryna Goodman and Wendy Larson, pp. 145–68. Lanham, MD: Rowman & Littlefield, 2005.

———. "The Press and the Rise of Peking Opera Singer as National Star: The Case of Theater Illustrated (1912–17)." *East Asian History* 28 (2004): 53–86.

———. *Shanghai Love: Courtesans, Intellectuals, and Entertainment Culture, 1850–1910*. Seattle: University of Washington Press, 2006.

———. "Where Is the Center of Cultural Production? The Rise of the Actor to National Stardom and the Beijing/Shanghai Challenge (1860s–1910s)." *LIC* 25.2 (2004): 74–118.

You Zian 遊子安. *Quanhua jinzhen* 勸化金箴——清代善書研究. Tianjin: Tianjin renmin, 1999.

Yu Jiao 俞蛟. *Meng'an zazhu* 夢庵雜著. Shanghai: Shanghai guji, 1988.

Yu, Pauline. "Ssu-k'ung T'u's *Shih-P'in*: Poetic Theory in Poetic Form." In *Studies in Chinese Poetry and Poetics*, ed. Ronald C. Miao, 1:81–103. San Francisco: Chinese Materials Center, 1978.

Yu Zhibin 于質彬. *Nanbei pihuang xi shishu* 南北皮簧戲史述. Hefei: Huangshan shushe, 1994.

Yuan Xingyun 袁行雲. "Qing Qianlong jian Yangzhou guan xiu *Xiqukao*" 清乾隆間揚州官修戲曲考. *XQYJ* 28 (1988): 225–44.

Zeitlin, Judith T. *Historian of the Strange: Pu Songling and the Chinese Classical Tale*. Stanford: Stanford University Press, 1993.

———. "The Petrified Heart: Obsession in Chinese Literature, Art, and Medicine." *LIC* 12.1 (1991): 1–26.

———. "Shared Dreams: The Story of the Three Wives' Commentary on *The Peony Pavilion*." *HJAS* 54.1 (1994): 127–79.

Zhang Cixi 張次溪, ed. and comp. *Qingdai Yandu liyuan shiliao: zhengxu bian* 清代燕都梨園史料——正續編. 4 vols. 1934 and 1937. Facsimile reprint, Taipei: Taiwan xuesheng shuju, 1965.

———, ed. and comp. *Qingdai Yandu liyuan shiliao: zhengxu bian*. 2 vols. 1934 and 1937. Reprint, Beijing: Zhongguo xiju, 1988.

Zhang Dai 張岱. *Tao'an mengyi* 陶庵夢憶. In *Ye hang chuan* 夜航船. Chengdu: Sichuan wenyi, 1996.

Zhang Dechang 張德昌. *Qingji yige jingguan de shenghuo* 清季一個京官的生活. Hong Kong: Xianggang zhongwen daxue, 1970.

Zhang Faying 張發穎. *Zhongguo jiayue xiban* 中國家樂戲班. Beijing: Xueyuan, 2002.

———. *Zhongguo xiban shi* 中國戲班史. Beijing: Xueyuan, 2003.

Zhang Geng 張庚 and Guo Hancheng 郭漢城, eds. *Zhongguo xiqu tongshi* 中國戲曲通史. Beijing: Zhongguo xiju, 1992.

Zhang Zhengzhi 張正治. *Jingju chuantong xi pihuang changqiang jiegou fenxi* 京劇傳統戲皮簧唱腔結購分析. Beijing: Renmin yinyue, 1992.

Zhao Jingshen 趙景深. *Zhongguo xiaoshuo congkao* 中國小說叢考. Ji'nan: Qilu shushe, 1980.

Zhao Shanlin 趙山林. *Zhongguo xiqu guanzhong xue* 中國戲曲觀眾學. Shanghai: Huadong shifan daxue, 1990.
Zhao Yi 趙翼. *Yanpu zaji* 檐曝雜記. Ca. late eighteenth–early nineteenth century. Reprint, Beijing: Zhonghua shuju, 1997.
Zhaolian 昭槤. *Xiaoting zalu* 嘯亭雜錄, and *Xiaoting xulu* 嘯亭續錄. 1815 and 1826. Reprint, Beijing: Zhonghua shuju. 1997.
Zheng Xuan 鄭瑄 (js 1631). *Zuofeian rizuan* 昨非菴日纂. Beijing: Beijing tushuguan, 1996.
Zheng Zhenduo 鄭振鐸. "*Shuihu zhuan* de yanhua" 水滸傳的演化. In *Zhongguo wenxue yanjiu* 中國文學研究, by Zheng Zhenduo, pp. 101–57. Beijing: Zuojia, 1957.
Zheng Zhiliang 鄭志良. "Du Buyun yu Ruihe shanfang chaoben 'Xiqu sishiliu zhong'" 杜步雲與瑞鶴山房抄本戲曲四十六種. *XQYJ* 68 (12 July 2008). Available online at "Zhongguo zhiwang" 中國知網, http://mall.cnki.net/magazine/Article/OXQY200502018.htm.
Zhi Chaozi 枝巢子. *Jiujing suoji* 舊京瑣記. Taipei: Chun wenxue, 1972.
Zhongguo gudian xiqu lunzhu jicheng 中國古典戲曲論著集成. 10 vols. Beijing: Zhongguo xiju, 1982.
Zhongguo xiqu zhi 中國戲曲志. 30 vols. Beijing: Wenhua yishu [some volumes published by Beijing: Zhongguo ISBN zhongxin], 1990–99.
Zhou Chuanjia 周傳家. "Wei Changsheng lun" 魏長生論. *XQYJ* 21 (1986): 172–92.
Zhou Miaozhong 周妙中. *Qingdai xiqu shi* 清代戲曲史. Kaifeng: Zhongzhou guji, 1987.
Zhou Mingtai 周明泰. *Dao Xian yilai liyuan xinian xiaolu* 道咸以來梨園系年小錄. Beijing: Zhongguo xiqu yishu zhongxin, 1985.
———. *Qing Shengping shu cundang shili manchao* 清昇平署存檔事例漫抄. Taipei: Wenhai, 1971.
Zhou Weipei 周維培. *Qupu yanjiu* 曲譜研究. Nanjing: Jiangsu guji, 1997.
Zhou Yibai 周貽白. *Zhongguo xiqu shi* 中國戲曲史. 3 vols. Shanghai: Zhonghua shuju, 1953.
Zhou Yude 周育德, ed. and annot. *Xiaohan xinyong* 消寒新詠. Compiled by Tieqiao shanren et al. Beijing: Zhongguo xiqu yishu zhongxin, 1986.
Zhou, Zuyan. *Androgyny in Late Ming and Early Qing Literature*. Honolulu: University of Hawaii Press, 2003.
Zhu Chongzhi 朱崇志. *Zhongguo gudai xiqu xuanben yanjiu* 中國古代戲曲選本研究. Shanghai: Shanghai guji, 2004.
Zhu Jiajin 朱家溍. *Gugong tuishi lu* 故宮退食錄. 2 vols. Beijing: Beijing chubanshe, 1999.
Zhu Jiajin and Ding Ruqin. *Qingdai neiting yanju shimo kao* 清代內廷演劇始末考. Beijing: Zhongguo shudian, 2007.
Zhu Wanshu 朱萬曙. *Shen Jing pingzhuan* 沈璟評傳. Beijing: Zhongguo xiju, 1992.

Zhu Yixuan 朱一玄 and Liu Yuchen 劉毓忱, eds. Shuihu zhuan *ziliao huibian* 水滸傳資料匯編. Tianjin: Baihua wenyi, 1981.

Zhuang Yongping 莊永平 and Pan Fangsheng 潘方聖. *Jingju changqiang yinyue yanjiu* 京劇唱腔音樂研究. Beijing: Zhongguo xiju, 1994.

Zu, Baoquan 祖保泉. *Sikong Tu* Shipin *zhushi ji yiwen* 司空圖詩品注釋及譯文. Hong Kong: Shangwu yinshuguan, 1966.

Zurndorfer, Harriet T. *Change and Continuity in Chinese Local History: The Development of Huizhou Prefecture, 800–1800*. Leiden: E. J. Brill, 1989.

Zwicker, Jonathan E. *Practices of the Sentimental Imagination: Melodrama, the Novel, and the Social Imaginary in Nineteenth-Century Japan*. Cambridge, MA: Harvard University Asia Center, 2006.

Index

Italicized page numbers indicate illustrations.

Abstracts of the Complete Titles of the Sea of Drama (*Quhai zongmu tiyao*), 148, 159
actors and acting troupes.
   boy actresses (*see* dan actors)
   connoisseurs focused on performance of, 104–5
   genre restrictions, response to, 117
   Huiban, 84, 85, 104, 127–29, 136, 138, 249, 305n56, 305n60, 305n68, 306n70
   imperial court and, 106, 111–12, 119, 121, 134, 136–40
   performance role types, 251
   popularity of qinqiang style affecting, 126
   princely sponsorship of, 304n49
   private or household troupes, 68, 97–99, 287–88n10
   resistance, opera as site of, 241
   salon performances, actor-audience dynamic at, 101–4
   status of, 102, 139, 293n87
   See also specific troupes and actors by name
Actor's Guild, Jingzhong Temple, Beijing, 69, *90*, 91, 117, 136–37, 140
actress/courtesan texts, borrowed discourse of huapu from, 21, 25–28, 31–33
All-China Drama Gazetteer (*Zhongguo xiqu zhi*), 2
All Nine Modes (*Great Compilation of Musical Scores from the Southern and Northern Arias in All Nine Modes*) (*Jiugong dacheng nanbeici gongpu*), 116, 117, 121–23, 132, 302–3n23
Alum-Paper Winehouse or Fanlou, Kaifeng, 54, 285–86n144
andian ben, 111, 329n150

Annals of the Tripartite Division (*Dingzhi chunqiu*), 214
apartheid regime, Qing state as, 68–69
Assorted Notes toward a Dream of Splendors Past (*Menghua suobu*) (Yang Maojian, 1842), 36, 37, 38, 40, 45, 54
audience
   connoisseurs (*see* connoisseurs of opera)
   lao dou (sugar daddies), 18–20, 22, 31, 53–58
   pihuang versions of "I, Sister-in-Law," audience responses to, 226–33, *229*, *230*
   playhouses, audience-actor dynamics in, 66, 83, 84–86
   salon performances, actor-audience dynamic at, 101–4
   salon performances, social homogeneity of audience at, 98
   temple fairs and temple stages, social and ethnic mixing at, 65, 87, 91–95
"bamboo-branch ditties" (zhuzhici), 17, 20, 53, 73
Bamboo-Branch Ditties from the Capital (1814), 17, 63
bangzi opera, 49, 57, 84, 116, 119, 133, 249
banner population
   ethnic identity of, 288n19
   as opera attendees, 4, 65–66, 86
   playhouses, efforts to forbid attendance at, 71–76
   salon performances and, 98
Beijing Actor's Guild, Jingzhong Temple, 69, *90*, 91, 117, 136–37, 140
Beijing opera during Qing dynasty. *See* opera in Qing Beijing

Beijing, urban plan of, 69, *70*, *71*
bense, 158, 313n37
Berezin, Mabel, 173
Blue Tower Collection (*Qinglou ji*) (Xia Tingshi, fourteenth century), 26, 27
Bourdieu, Pierre, 301n8
Boxer Uprising (1900), 10
boy actresses. *See* dan actors
Brief Register of Foam on the Sea, A (*Haiou xiaopu*) (Zhao Qiugu; 1704), 26–27, 28, 278n20
Brief Register of Songbirds and Flowers, A (*Yinghua xiaopu*), 28
Brief Register of the Orchids of Yan, A (*Yanlan xiaopu*) (Wu Changyuan, 1785)
   civic guidebook / urban memoir literature influencing, 37, 280n64
   connoisseurship in, 40–44, 46–50
   courtesan/actress texts, borrowed discourse from, 26–28, 31
   on *The Garden of Turquoise and Jade* performances, 145, 147, 167
   huabu, enthusiasm for, 132, 307n87
   on "I, Sister-in-Law" operas, 210
   on lao dou, 54–57
   on playhouses, 77–78
   popularity and prominence of, 18, 23, 283n105
   on qinqiang performers, 126, 305–6n69
   on tie dan roles, 208
   on Zha playhouse (Zhalou), 290n52
Brooks, Peter, 155, 163, 311n22, 311n24, 315n62
Bureau of Ascendant Peace (Shengping shu). *See* Shengping shu

Cao Family, 323n59
capital melody. *See* jingqiang
"chaotic strumming" (luantan), 116, 119, 132, 136, 224, 250, 306n70, 307n94
character or clown roles
   in "I, Sister-in-Law" operas, 192, 198, 201–2, 209–10, 324–25n89
   Suzhou dialect used by (*see* Suzhou dialect of clown/character parts)
Chen Guilin, 167
Chen Moxiang, 134, 175, 223–24, 229–31, 232, 318n1–3, 330n166
Chen Sen, 133, 210–11, 280n53
Chen Weisong, 284n115
Chen Yinguan, 124–25, 127, 128
Cheng Changgeng, 137

Chong Yi, 92–93
Chronicle of Lovers and Heroes, A (*Ernü yingxiong zhuan*), 82, 158
Chronicles of the Northern Quarter (*Beili zhi*) (Sun Qi, ca. 888), 21, 26, 278n20
chuanqi dramas
   adaptation of Kun opera from, 84, 218–19
   defined, 249
   Water Margin story cycle rewritten as, 176
Chubby Zhu the Ninth (Zhu Jiu Pangzi), 47–48
Chuntai troupe, 48, 165, 226, 249
civic guidebook / urban memoir literature, borrowed discourse of huapu from, 21–22, 35–39
civil service examinees
   as opera connoisseurs, 4, 44–45, 47
   at playhouses, 76–78
   sons and nephews of sitting officials allowed to take provincial-level exam in Shuntian Prefecture, 290n48
Cixi (Empress Dowager), 106, 109, 112, 134, 136, 218, 221
Clifford, James, 38
Cloak of Patchworked White Fur, A (*Zhuibaiqiu*) (Qian Decang)
   on *The Garden of Turquoise and Jade*, 161, 162, 169, 171, 172
   genre delineation and, 130
   "I, Sister-in-Law" operas and, 192, 196–98, 200, 202, 204–5, 215
   on salon performances, 105, 106
Clover, Carol, 330n173
clown or character roles
   in "I, Sister-in-Law" operas, 192, 198, 201–2, 209–10, 324–25n89
   Suzhou dialect used by (*see* Suzhou dialect of clown/character parts)
Clunas, Craig, 25
Cobbler Kills His Wife, The (*Pijiang sha qi*), or "The Cobbler Killer" (Sha pi), 175, 226, 227, 232, 318n3
Collected Publications of Rare Editions of Drama (*Guben xiqu congkan*), 148, 167, 169
Collection of Goose-Tracks from the Yan Stage, A (*Yantai hongzhua ji*) (Yang Cuiyan), 44, 281n86
Commentary of Master Zuo (*Zuo zhuan*), 23
commercial playhouses. *See* playhouses
companionate marriage, 167, 299n160

INDEX

Compendium of Trustworthy Words and Prudent Deeds, A (*Yongxing bian*), 149
Complete Works of the Four Treasuries (*Siku quanshu*), 43–44
Concise Sketch of the Imperial Enclosure, A (*Chenyuan shilüe*) (Wu Changyuan, 1788), 43–44, 280n64
Confucianism and neo-Confucianism, 10, 38, 157, 239, 245, 246, 312n33–34
Congshen (Patriarch of Zhaozhou), 309n1
connoisseurs of opera, 22, 39–52
    career disappointments and outsider status, 22, 43–47, 58, 172
    companionate marriage couple as, 299n160, 318n100
    dan actors, aesthetic criteria for, 50–52
    dan actors, identification with, 172, 241
    eccentricity, cultivation of, 47–48, 57
    eclecticism of opera preferences, 48–49, 57, 117, 131–34
    historical and nostalgic voice of, 36–39, 59
    identifying, 42–43, 281n86
    lao dou (sugar daddies), self-distinction from, 22, 53, 57, 78, 241
    legitimizing, formalistic style combined with sensually indulgent content by, 29, 59
    literary tradition of connoisseurship texts and, 23–24
    resistance, opera as site of, 239–40
    salon performances and, 104–5
    sex market for dan actors and, 33–34, 51, 280n50, 285n132
    textual community created by, 40–42
    writing huapu as mark of connoisseurship, 58
Country Chats on Flowery Opera (*Huabu nongtan*) (Jiao Xun), 132
court. *See* Qing court
courtesan/actress texts, borrowed discourse of huapu from, 21, 25–28, 31–33
Crossley, Pamela, 121
Cuiping Mountain (*Cuiping shan*) (Shen Zijin, before 1636), 176, 178, 186–91, 196, 200, 204–8, 213, 216, 321n37, 322n46, 327n126
"Cuiping Mountain" (pihuang version), 222-23, 226, 228-31, 328n137, 329n154, 330n163, 330n164
cult of qing, 33–34, 155, 158, 173, 208, 234, 280n49, 313n39
"cultural field," concept of, 301n8

Dai Lu, 304n49
Daily Records from the Cottage of Yesteryear's Mistakes (*Zuofeian rizuan*), 149–50
dan actors (boy actresses)
    aesthetic criteria of huapu authors for, 50–52
    age range of, 52, 285n140–42
    circumstances of, 84–85
    commodification of, 25
    condescension of huapu authors towards, 50–51
    connoisseurs' identification with, 172, 241
    courtesan/actress texts, borrowed discourse of huapu from, 21, 25–28, 31–33
    demographic expansion and supply of, 4
    depictions of, *Plates 1 and 2*
    flower metaphors for, 28–31, 283n110
    flower registers or huapu devoted to, 17–20, 21, 25, 28–31
    in *The Garden of Turquoise and Jade*, 145, 165
    gender and status hierarchy, superimposition of, 66, 85
    hierarchy of, 286n156
    in "I, Sister-in-Law" operas, 207–11, 227
    pathos of, 33, 34–35, 50–51
    performance role types, list of, 251
    playhouses, audience-actor dynamics in, 66, 83, 84–86
    primary (zheng) and secondary (xiao and tie) performers, 181, 207–8, 325n91
    purchased out of service contracts by lao dou, 54
    qiao shoes, wearing, 124, 138, 229, 303n38
    resistance, opera as site of, 240
    sex market, association with, 31–34, 51, 280n50, 285n132
    stage-left balcony seats, desirability of, 18–20, *19*
    in temple-fair performances, 96–97
    women as audience and, 96–97, 106
Daoguang emperor, 112, 135
Dark Snow Catalog (*Xuanxue pu*) (ca. 1628–44), 192, *193*, *194*
Donglin partisans, 156
Dream of Nanke, 46, 283n107
Dream of Splendors Past in the Eastern Capital, A (*Dongjing menghua lu*) (Meng Yuanlao, 1147), 22, 35–36, 38
Dream of the Red Chamber (*Honglou meng*), 98
Du Fu, 47, 283–84n112

Du Mu, 26, 27, 278n19
Du Shuangshou, 167, 317n86, 327n126

eccentricity, opera connoisseurs' cultivation of, 47–48, 57
Eight Trigrams Uprising (1813), 290n44
elites. *See* banner population; Jiangnan elites; official elites; Qing court
Elliott, Mark, 68
Epstein, Maram, 158
erhuang, 119, 128, 133–34, 136, 307n89
Ershisi shipin (Sikong Tu), 277n10
Established Pitches for Southern Lyrics (*Nanci dinglu*), 121, 303n24
ethnicity issues.
  apartheid regime, Qing state as, 68–69
  banner population, ethnic identity of, 288n19
  at opera venues generally, 11, 64, 65–67
  playhouses
    efforts to restrict location of and attendance at, 74–75
    social and ethnic mixing at, 11, 64, 65–67, 78, 82, 240–41
  salon performances and, 98, 102, 298n144
  Taiping rebellion and ethnic identity of Qing court, 243–45
  temple fairs, social and ethnic mixing at, 65, 87, 91–95
  venues, general social and ethnic mixing at, 65, 112–13, 240–41
  See also Jiangnan elites
evaluative classification (pin), concept of, 21, 24–25, 29
Expanded and Corrected Scores for Northern Lyrics (*Beici guangzheng pu*), 121, 303n24
Extended Record of Dream Splendors (*Menghua wailu*), 41

Fan Chengda, 277n11
Fanlou or Alum-Paper Winehouse, Kaifeng, 54, 285–86n144
Fei, Si-yen, 7
Feng Menglong, 97, 155
Feng Mengzhen, 320n25
Fifteen Strings of Cash (*Shiwu guan*) (Zhu Suchen), 155
flower registers or huapu, 9–11, 17–60
  aesthetic criteria for dan actors, 50–52
  aesthetic eclecticism of authors, 48–49, 57
  civic guidebook / urban memoir literature influencing, 21–22, 35–39

connoisseur authors of (*see* connoisseurs of opera)
courtesan/actress texts, borrowed discourse from, 21, 25–28, 31–33
dan actors, devotion to, 17–20, 21, 25, 28–31
defined, 17–18
"ethnographic mode" in, 33, 37–38, 53
evaluative classification (pin), concept of, 21, 24–25, 29
flower metaphors for dan actors in, 28–31, 283n110
historical and nostalgic voice in, 36–39, 59
on "I, Sister-in-Law" operas, 207–12, 324n88
lao dou (sugar daddies) in, 18–20, 22, 31, 53–58, 241, 277n3
organization and contents, 22
pathos of dan actors, 33, 34–35, 50–51
percentage of kunju and pihuang actors in, 134
production history, 20–21
readers of, 59–60
sex market and, 31–34, 51, 280n50, 285n132
significance of, 20, 58–60
stage-left balcony seats, desirability of, 18–20, *19*
flowery opera. *See* huabu opera
Forbidden City. *See* imperial palace
Forgotten Events of the Xuanhe Reign (*Xuanhe yishi*), 178, 180, 186
"Fourth Son Visits His Mother" (Silang tanmu), *Plates 1 and 2*

Garden of Turquoise and Jade, The (*Feicui yuan*) (attrib. Zhu Suchen, ca. 1620–1701), 12, 145–74
  authorship, dating, and sources of, 148–50, 310n19
  on commercial stage, 160–71
  dan actors, appeal of, 145, 165
  happy ending, use or disuse of, 147, 164, 166–67
  production scripts, 161–63, *162*, 165–71, *168*, *170*, 314–15n55, 314n50
  seamstress character Zhao Cui'er as main attraction, 145, 161, 163, 165–67
  selection of scenes staged, 147, 160–61

sentimentality and sensationalism, importance of, 163–65, 169, 172
Steamed-Bun character, use of dialect by, 169–71
as courtroom drama, 157–58
female audience for, 316n69
gender and class politics of, 146–48, 155–60, 164, 172–74, 238–39
"I, Sister-in-Law" operas compared, 177, 202, 234
migration of plot to other genres, 311n25
modern revival of, 311n25
plotline of, 145–46, 150–55, 159–60
Qing court script, double marriage preserved in, 167–69, *170*
resistance, opera as site of, 238–39
scripts, list of, 252–54
gender and gender representation, 8–9. *See also* dan actors; women
companionate marriage, 167, 299n160
The Garden of Turquoise and Jade,
gender and class politics of, 146–48, 155–60, 164, 172–74, 238–39
in "I, Sister-in-Law" operas, 176, 177, 217, 218, 228–34, 238–39
resistance, opera as site of, 237–42
genres of opera, 12, 115–41.
diversity of, 116
hybridization and delineation, 129–34
Qing court's efforts to control, 5, 12, 115–18, 140–41
before 1860, 119–28, *120*
after 1860, 134–40
qinqiang opera, suppression of, 115, 124–27
scholarly research on opera, patronage of, 121–24
state power, opera patronage as sign of, 119–22, *120*
yabu versus huabu categories, 118–19 (*see also* huabu opera; Kun opera)
See also specific genres
Goldstein, Joshua, 287n6
Gong Zizhen, 130, 306n81
Gong'an School, 157
Grimsted, David, 315n62
Gu Lu, 121
Guangxu emperor, 244
Guanju Daoren, 307n95
guidebook literature. *See* flower registers or huapu

Habermas, Jürgen, 6–8
Han. *See* ethnicity issues; Jiangnan elites
Handful of Snow, A (*Yipengxue*) (Li Yu), 156, 311–12n29
hanxu, 51
He Liangjun, 97
Hechun Troupe, 226, 249
Heshen (Manchu Grand Councilor), 164, 316n64
Hexun (imperial censor), 72, 73–74, 75
historical and nostalgic voice in flower registers or huapu, 36–39, 59
History of Flowers in the Phoenix City, A (*Fengcheng huashi*), 41
Hong Sheng, 205
Hongzi Li Er, 182, 186
Hsia, C. T., 321n32
Hu Ji, 306n70
Hua Wei, 318n100
huabu opera, 3, 118–19.
connoisseurs' eclecticism regarding, 48–49, 57, 117, 131–34
court sensibilities embracing, 134–38, 140–41
defined, 249
hybridization and delineation of genres, 129–34
lowbrow, regarded as, 117
proscription attempts, 5
See also specific types, e.g., pihuang opera
Huang Xiangjian, 149
huapu. *See* flower registers or huapu
Hui troupes (Huiban), 84, 85, 104, 127–29, 136, 138, 249, 305n56, 305n60, 305n68, 306n70
huidiao, 83

"I, Sister-in-Law" operas, 12. See also *Cuiping Mountain*; *Record of the Water Margin, The*; *Righteous Hero, The*
dan actors in, 207–11, 227
The Garden of Turquoise and Jade compared, 177, 202, 234
gender politics of, 176, 177, 217, 218, 228–34, 238–39
huapu commentaries on, 207–12, 324n88
kunju versions of, 13, 176–77, 205–12, 233, 234
pihuang versions of, 13, 177, 217–33
adaptation of chuanqi scripts to pihuang conventions, 218–26
audience responses to, 226–33, *229*, *230*

"I, Sister-in-Law" operas (*continued*)
  pihuang versions of (*continued*)
    sex and violence in, 217, 218, 223–26, 229–33, 234
  plotlines and themes, development of and variations on, 178–91
    from *Cuiping Mountain* (*Cuiping shan*), 186–91
    from *The Record of the Water Margin* (*Shuihu ji*), 178–82
    from *The Righteous Hero* (*Yixia ji*), 182–86
  popularity of, 205–7, 212
  progression from page to stage, 191–205
    clown or character roles and humor, increasing stress on, 192, 198, 201–2, 209–10, 324–25n89
    colloquial language and spoken dialogue, increasing use of, 192–200
    drama miscellanies showing, 191–98, *193–95*
    modifications to character, plot, and theme, 198–99, 200–201, 203–5
    production scripts showing, 13, 176–77, 198–205
    scene-ending couplets, revision of, 199–200
  Qing court and (*see under* Qing court)
  resistance, opera as site of, 238–39
  scripts, list of, 255–58
  sentimentality and sensationalism, importance of, 191–92, 196, 203–7, 232
  sex and violence
    didactic versus entertainment value of, 175–76, 232–35
    in kunju versions, 217, 218, 223–24
    in pihuang tradition, 217, 218, 223–26, 229–33, 234
    in Qing court's version, 217
    shifting sympathies regarding, 242
  temple performances of, 212
  Water Margin (*Shuihu zhuan*) story cycle, derived from, 12, 176, 178
imperial court. *See* Qing court
imperial palace (Forbidden City), Beijing
  Jacobean masque, court performances compared to, 65, 109, 300n173
  layout of, 69, *70, 71*
  salon performances at, 65, 66–67, 106–12, *110, 111*, 300n169
Imperial Textile Manufactories, 121, 134, 137
Inner City, Beijing, 69, *70, 71*, 98

Issei, Tanaka, 3

Jacobean masque, court performances compared to, 65, 109, 300n173
Jade Hairpin, The (*Yuchai ji*), 310n19
Jealousy-Curing Stew (*Liaodu geng*), 51, 89
Jiangnan elites
  as connoisseurs and taste-setters, 4, 5, 118
  gendered nature of position of, 172
  kunju opera genre favored by, 115
  Suzhou dialect, clown/character roles' use of, 171, 202
  Taiping Rebellion (1850–64) affecting, 139
Jiaqing emperor, 73, 111–12
Jifang Troupe, 161, 291n60, 314n54
Jin dynasty, 212
Jin Ping Mei cihua (1617), 192, *195*
Jin Shengtan, 180, 188, 320n23
jingqiang, 91, 116, 126, 250
Jingzhong Temple / Actor's Guild, Beijing, 69, *90*, 91, 117, 136–37, 140
Jinyu Troupe, 96, 166
Johnson, David, 282n91

Kangxi emperor, 71–72, 107, 119–21, *120*
kuben, 329n150
Kun-du-le, 75
Kun opera (kunju, kunqu), 3, 118
  commercial performance, attempts to exclude from, 117
  decline of, 12
  defined, 250
  favored position of, 115–16
  The Garden of Turquoise and Jade (*Feicui yuan*) (see *Garden of Turquoise and Jade, The*)
  huapu connoisseurs' eclecticism regarding, 48–49
  hybridization and delineation of genres, 129–34
  "I, Sister-in-Law" productions, 13, 176–77, 205–12, 233, 234
  Jiangnan, audience from, 4
  playhouse performances, nature of, 83–84
  romantic and sexually explicit plots in, 125

Lam, Joseph, 130
Lamp at the Fork in the Road, The (*Qilu deng*), 77, 103
lao dou (sugar daddies), 18–20, 22, 31, 53–58, 78, 241, 277n3

Last Word Studio (*Musical Scores from the Last Word Studio*) (*Nashuying qupu*) (Ye Tang), 117, 129–31, 306n79
Latter-Day Adept of the Iron Flute, The (Xiao tiedi daoren), 36, 41, 50
Lean, Eugenia, 8
Lee, Haiyan, 8
Lesser Yang Xiong, The (*Bing Yang Xiong*) (Hongzi Li Er), 186
Li Dou, 125, 127, 129, 209, 211–12, 305n60
Li Kaixian, 97
Li Lülin, 166
Li, Wai-yee, 25, 34
Li Xu, 121
Li Yu, 97, 148–49, 155, 310n13
Liao Ben, 67, 287n9
Liao dynasty, 212
Lingguanmiao (Temple to the Divine Agent), 1838 incident at, 92–95
Liu Langyu, 128
Liu Lixian, 44–45
Liu Zhizhong, 306n70
"Longing for the Secular Life" (Si fan), 163, 208
Lu Eting, 159, 314n48, 325n91, 325n102
Lü Tiancheng, 185, 319n15, 320n25, 320n28, 322n41
luantan ("chaotic strumming"), 116, 119, 132, 136, 224, 250, 306n70, 307n94
Luo Ying'an, 138, 232–33

Manchu. *See* ethnicity issues; Qing court
Mann, Susan, 234
Mao Xiang, 97
Master's Evaluation of Old Plays, The (*Lige piping jiu ximu*) (Wu Zhensheng and Cheng Qiong), 299n160, 318n100
McCartney, Earl George, 108–9
McMahon, Keith, 172
Mei Lanfang, 136, Plate 2
Mei Qiaoling, Plate 2
Meipu (Fan Chengda), 277n11
melodrama. *See* sentimentality and sensationalism of opera, importance of
merchants, as lao dou, 53–58, 78
Ming dynasty
    courtesan literature from, 32–33
    palace entertainment bureau of, 119
    pin, concept of, 24–25
    Qing drama influenced by values of, 10, 157, 158, 173, 234–35, 318n100
    reign periods, xi

salon performances in, 97
Suzhou dramatists on, 156-57
Water Margin story cycle in, 180
Miscellaneous Notes from the Wooden Bridge (*Banqiao zaji*) (Yu Huai, 1697), 26, 27, 278n20
Miscellaneous Records from Court and Society since the Daoguang and Xianfeng Reigns (*Dao Xian yilai chaoye zaji*) (Chong Yi), 92–93
Mulian story cycle (*Quanshan jinke*), 106, 120, 213, 326n115

Nanfu, 106, 119, 121, 135
Naquin, Susan, 7, 87
neo-Confucianism and Confucianism, 10, 38, 157, 239, 245, 246, 312n33–34
New Odes to While Away the Winter (*Xiaohan xinyong*) (1795), 28, 36, 42, 132, 279n42, 284n121
New Records on Listening to Youth (*Tingchun xinyong*), 41, 132
Ni Zan, 50
Northern Song dynasty, temple stages emerging during, 67
nostalgic and historical voice in flower registers or huapu, 36–39, 59

official elites
    civil service examinees, as opera connoisseurs, 4, 44–45, 47
    connoisseur authors of huapu, career disappointments and outsider status of, 22, 43–47, 58
    as lao dou, 53, 286n147
    pihuang sister-in-law operas and, 226
    playhouses, efforts to forbid attendance at, 71–76, 289n31
    salon performances and, 102
Old Talk about the Pear Garden (*Liyuan jiuhua*) (Wu Tao), 102
One Hundred Jingles for the City of Yan (Zha Kui, ca. 1800), 63
opera in Qing Beijing (1770–1900), 1–14, 237–46
    The Garden of Turquoise and Jade (*Feicui yuan*), 12, 145–74 (see also Garden of Turquoise and Jade, The)
    genres of, 12, 115–41 (see also genres of opera)
    guidebook literature, 9–11, 17–60 (see also flower registers or huapu)

opera in Qing Beijing (*continued*)
  "I, Sister-in-Law" operas, 13, 175–235 (*see also* "I, Sister-in-Law" operas)
  late Ming intellectual concerns and practices, survival of, 10
  Qing court's eventual co-optation of, 242–46 (*see also* Qing court)
  resistance, as site of, 237–42
  scholarly approaches to, 3, 5–9
  sentimentality and sensationalism in (*see* sentimentality and sensationalism)
  significance of, 2–5, 9–10, 13–14, 237
  social chaos, associated with, 1–2, 63, 116–17, 125, 126
  venues, 11, 63–114 (*see also* playhouses; salon performances; temple fairs and temple stages; venues)
Opium War, 295n115
Orchid Pavilion Collection (Wang Xizhi), 47, 283n111
Orchids of Yan. See *Brief Register of the Orchids of Yan, A*
Orgel, Stephen, 160
Outer City, Beijing
  playhouses restricted to, 69–74, 70, 71
  salon performances in, 98

Painted Boats of Yangzhou (*Yangzhou huafang lu*) (Li Dou), 211–12
Palace of the Dawn Star (*Weiyang tian*) (Zhu Suchen), 145–46, 148, 155
Palace of Eternal Youth (*Changshen dian*) (Hong Sheng), 205
Patriarch of Zhaozhou (Congshen), 309n1
Peking opera, 6, 140, 237, 276n19
  pihuang, relationship to, 140
Peony Pavilion, The (*Mudan ting*) (Tang Xianzu), 78, 206, 207, 298n141, 315n59, 316n76, 318n96, 331n3
Petty Historian of the Approaching Vernal Pavilion, 41
Petty Historian Who Feasts on Flowers, 29, 40
pihuang opera, 12, 217–18
  defined, 250
  "I, Sister-in-Law" productions (*see under* "I, Sister-in-Law" operas)
  playhouse performances, nature of, 83
  Qing court
    appeal of pihuang for, 117, 134–40, 218, 226, 235, 244–45
    court dramas influencing pihuang, 218, 327n128
  status of, 133–34
  as type of huabu, 119
  Peking opera, relationship to, 140
  xipi and erhuang, relationship to, 128
pin (evaluative classification), concept of, 21, 24–25, 29
Pinhua baojian (Chen Sen), 280n53, 298n144, 307n94
Plaks, Andrew, 180
playhouses, 64–65, 67–87
  audience-actor dynamics in, 66, 83, 84–86
  civil service examinees at, 76–78
  commercial nature of, 67
  development of, 67–68
  layout and seating at, 18–20, 19, 78–82, 79, 80
  Outer City, efforts to restrict to, 69–74, 70, 71
  performances, nature of, 83–84
  price of attending, 81–82, 86–87, 291–92n68–73
  public and private life, opera as border crossing between, 66, 114, 116–17, 174
  Qing court
    efforts at regulation, 11, 64–65, 69–76, 235, 240–41
    eventual co-optation of commercial theater by, 242–46, 331n7
  resistance, as site of, 237–42
  salon performances
    closing of playhouse due to, 104, 299n156
    rental of playhouse for, 98
  social and ethnic mixing at, 11, 64, 65–67, 78, 82, 240–41
  tea gardens as, 67, 68, 287n6
  terms for, 67
  winehouses
    possibly deriving from opera patronage at, 67, 287n164
    proximity to, 18, 53, 69
  women allowed to attend, 113, 292n77
  women forbidden from attending, 64–65, 82–83, 87
Playwatching Adept, 133
Playwatching Journal (*Guanju riji*), 69, 89, 161, 164, 165, 166, 205–7, 210, 212, 324n88

Plum in the Golden Vase, The (*Jin Ping Mei*), 102, 184–85, *195*
Polachek, James, 44, 47
Precious Mirror for Ranking Boy Actresses, A (*Pinhua baojian*) (Chen Sen), 42, 59, 78, 86, 103, 104, 133, 172, 211
Precious Raft of Exalted Peace, The (*Shengping baofa*), 214
Prince of Ning (Zhu Chenhao), rebellion of (1519), 150
private performances. *See* salon performances
public and private life, opera as border crossing between, 66, 114, 116–17, 174
public sphere, concept of, 6–8, 238
"pure-singing" (qingchang) style of Kun opera, 129–30

Qi Biaojia, 97, 185, 320–21n28, 321n37
Qi Rushan, 331n1
Qian Decang, 105–6
Qian Qiaoling, 166
Qianlong emperor, 73, 92, 106, 107, 109, 127, 134, 164, 213, 300n168, 302n20, 326n115
qiao shoes, 124, 138, 229, 303n38
Qing court, 4–5.
    actors employed by, 106, 111–12, 119, 121, 134
    apartheid regime, Qing state as, 68–69
    commercial actors used by, 136–40
    eventual co-optation of commercial theater by, 242–46, 331n7
    The Garden of Turquoise and Jade script, double marriage preserved in, 167–69, *170*
    genres of opera, exertion of control over (*see under* genres of opera)
    household troupes, discouragement of, 68
    "I, Sister-in-Law" operas
        appropriation and retelling of, 212–17
        commercial versions of, 226, 235
        proscription of, 211, 213
    Nanfu, 106, 119, 121, 135
    pihuang opera
        court dramas influencing, 218, 327n128
        court sensibilities embracing, 117, 134–40, 218, 226, 235, 244–45
        playhouses, efforts to control, 11, 64–65, 69–76, 235, 240–41
    reign periods for dynasty, xi

salon performances
    efforts to control, 68, 98–99, 113
    at imperial palace, 65, 66–67, 106–12, *110*, *111*, 300n169
scholarly research on opera, patronage of, 121–24
Shengping shu, reorganization of Nanfu into, 135
social-leveling agenda of, 331n7
state power, opera patronage as sign of, 119–22, *120*
temple fairs, efforts to control, *90*, 91–92, 95–97
venues generally, efforts to control, 11, 64–65, 112–14
Water Margin (*Shuihu zhuan*) story cycle, seditious overtones of, 212–14
See also imperial palace
qing, cult of, 33–34, 155, 158, 173, 208, 234, 280n49, 313n39
Qing dynasty, opera in Beijing during. *See* opera in Qing Beijing
qingchang ("pure-singing") style of Kun opera, 129–30
qinqiang, 49, 57, 84, 115, 116, 119, 124–28, 129, 250, 305n56
qiu dan (subtlety), 51
Qu Yuan, 47, 283m110
Qupin (Lü Tiancheng), 319n15

Rabinow, Paul, 39
Raconteur of the Western Hillocks (Xicheng waishi), 27, 46, 47, 50, 77
Realm of Many Fragrances, The (*Zhongxiang guo*), 40
Rebellion of the Three Feudatories (1683), 120
Recluse of the Drunken Bamboo, 41
Record of Appraising Flowers of the Yan Stage, A (*Yantai jiaohua lu*), 41
Record of Cherished Flowers (*Huaifang ji*), 30
Record of Collected Fragments, A (*Pianyu ji*), 43, 44
Record of Remembered Dreams of the Capital, A (*Chunming mengyu lu*) (Sun Chengze), 36
Record of Southern Flowers in the Mist, A (*Nanbu yanhua lu*) (attrib. Yan Shigu, ca. 581–645), 26, 278n18
Record of Tear Stains from the Golden Stage, A (*Jintai canlei ji*) (Zhang Jiliang, 1829), 32, 36–37, 38–39, 40, 44

362 INDEX

Record of Viewing Flowers in the Capital (Chang'an kanhua ji) (Yang Maojian, 1837), 28, 132–33
Record of Viewing Flowers in the Precinct of the Throne, A (Rixia kanhua ji) (Xiao tiedi daoren, 1803), 29, 316n71
Record of the Water Margin, The (Shuihu ji) (Xu Zichang, ca. 1607–1623), 176, 178–82, 185, 186, 190–92, 201, 203–4, 209, 213, 214–15, 319n15
Register of the Pure and Loyal, A (Qingzhong pu) (Zhu Suchen and Li Yu), 155–56
resistance, opera as site of, 237–42
Reunion of Ten Thousand Leagues, A (Wanli yuan) (Li Yu), 148–49
Righteous Hero, The (Yixia ji) (Shen Jing, after 1607), 89, 176, 178, 182–86, 190–92, 196, 198, 201, 204–6, 212–16, 224, 225, 320n25, 327n126
righteous servant characters, 159, 313n43
Rixia jiuwen (Zhu Yizun, 1688), 280n58
Ruan Dacheng, 97
Ruan Ji, 47
Rulan Chao Pien, 302n23

Sacrificing Two Heads, Wu Song Exacts Vengeance (Shuang xiantou Wu Song da baochou), 182
salon performances (tanghui), 65, 97–112
 actor-audience dynamic, 101–4
 circumstances and conduct of, 99–104
 closing of playhouse due to, 104, 299n156
 defined, 97
 ethnicity issues, 98, 102, 298n144
 at imperial palace, 65, 66–67, 106–12, *110*, *111*, 300n169
 in Inner and Outer Cities, 98
 male connoisseurs at, 104–5
 private or household troupes, 68, 97–99, 287–88n10
 Qing court
  efforts to control salon performances by, 68, 98–99, 113
  imperial palace, private performances at, 65, 66–67, 106–12, *110*, *111*, 300n169
 range in scale of, 98, *99*, *100*
 remuneration for performances at, 101–4
 rental of playhouse for, 98
 social homogeneity of audience at, 98, 297n133
 timing restrictions, lack of, 104, 299n158
 women's attendance at, 65, *99*, 102, 104–6, 113
Sanduo Troupe, 91, 165, 166, 206, 212, 305n58
Sanqing Troupe, 127–28, 136, 137, 161–63, *162*, 226, *230*, 249, 253n7
scholarly research on opera, court patronage of, 121–24
Scholars, The (Rulin waishi), 103
Scholars-and-Beauties Peony Pavilion (Caizi-Jiaren Mudan ting), 299n160, 318n100
School of Mind (xinxue), 157, 312n33–34
scions' tales
 "The Lament of the Fake Lao Dou" (Jia lao dou tan), 119
 "Pleasures in the Family Garden" (Jiayuan le), 99–103
 on Temple to the Divine Agent (Lingguanmiao) incident (1838), 93–95
 "The Wealthy Young Mistress Goes to the Holy Festival Plays" (Kuoda nainai ting shanhui xi), 95–96
sentimentality and sensationalism
 The Garden of Turquoise and Jade on commercial stage, 148, 163–65, 169, 172
 genre delineation and control and, 8
 in "I, Sister-in-Law" operas, 191–92, 196, 203–7, 232
 importance of, 8
 public and private life, opera as border crossing between, 66, 114, 116–17, 174
 venue control and, 66
sexuality.
 companionate marriage, 167, 299n160
 courtesan/actress texts, borrowed discourse of huapu from, 21, 25–28, 31–33
 cult of qing, 33–34, 155, 158, 173, 208, 234, 280n49, 313n39
 dan actors and sex market, 31–34, 51, 280n50, 285n132
 in "I, Sister-in-Law" operas (*see under* "I, Sister-in-Law" operas)
 Kun opera, romantic and sexually explicit plots in, 125
 youwu, 24–25, 30, 277n11
 See also gender and gender representation; women
Shang Wei, 318n100
Shanghai, as opera center, 139

Shen Defu, 33
Shen Jing, 97, 185, 186, 321n43
Shen Shixing, 97
Shen Zijin, 189–90, 196, 327n126
Shengping shu (Bureau of Ascendant Peace), 81, 135–37
Shu Fa, 149–50, 310n16
Shu Fen, 149, 310n15
Sikong Tu, 277n10
Sixi Troupe, 136, 165, 226, 249
Sketches from a Life of Watching Theater (Chen Moxiang, 1930), 175
So Hosu, 108
Sommer, Matthew, 9, 235
Song Yu (poet), 47, 283–84n112–113
Song Yulin, 165
Southern Song dynasty, catalogues or registers of collectibles during, 24
Southern Story of the Western Wing (*Nan Xixiang ji*), 298n147
Spring Purification Association (zhanchun ji), 44, 47
Stallybrass, Peter, 164
Stars of Loyalty and Righteousness (*The Plan of the Stars of Loyalty and Righteousness* or *Zhongyi xuantu*) (Zhou Xiangyu and Zou Jinsheng, ca. mid-1740s), 213–17, 223, 326n115, 327n128
Story of the Western Chamber (*Xixiang ji*) drama cycle, 163, 312n35
String of Rough Pearls, A (1809), 17
Study of Ancient Accounts from the Precinct of the Throne, A (*Rixia jiuwen kao*) (1785), 36, 44, 280n58
su and ya, 130–31, 315n59
Su Shi, 30
Sui Yangdi, 26
Sun Chengze, 36
Sun Qi, 21, 278n20
Suzhou dialect of clown / character parts
 in *The Garden of Turquoise and Jade*, 169–71
 in "I, Sister-in-Law" operas, 192, 201–2
 Jiangnan elites and, 171, 202
 pihuang operas abandoning, 219
Suzhou writers' group, 145, 148, 155–60, 309n5, 312n31, 314n50
Swatek, Catherine, 315n59, 324–25n89, 331n3

Taiping Rebellion (1850–64), 10, 139, 234, 243–45, 331n7

Taizhou School, 157
Tan Xinpei, 136
Tang Xianzu, 306n75, 315n59
tanghui. *See* salon performances
teahouses and tea gardens
 playhouses and, 67, 68, 287n6
 storytelling teahouses, 82, 89, 287n6
 teahouse culture, 7–8, 287n6
temple fairs and temple stages, 65, 87–97
 community and religious/ritual aspects of, 65, 67
 content and style of performances, 89–91, 96
 dan actors at, 96–97
 emergence of, 67
 festivals and ritual calendar of performances, 87–89
 "I, Sister-in-Law" operas performed at, 212
 Qing court's efforts to regulate, 65, 92–95
 social and ethnic mixing at, 65, 87, 91–95
 on temple grounds without permanent stages, 88, 89
 troupes performing at, 89–91
 wealthy patrons sponsoring plays at, 295n106
 women's attendance of performances at, 90, 91–92, 95–97, 113
Temple to the Divine Agent (Lingguanmiao), 1838 incident at, 92–95
"tent-arena" (goulan) theaters (1050–1450), 67
Theiss, Janet, 9, 331n5
Thorn Hairpin, The (*Jingchai ji*), 89
Three Kingdoms saga (*Dingzhi chunqiu*), 106
"Three Top Candidates Make the Grade, The" (San yuan jidi), 101, 297–98n140
Thunder-Wind Pagoda (*Leifeng ta*), 206
Tianning Monastery, 91, 295n108
Tieqiao shanren, 57
Timovsky, Egor F., 289n31
Tongzhi emperor, 244, 245
Treatise of the Three Kingdoms, 214
Tu Long, 97

unicorn, capture of, 38, 281n70
urban memoir / civic guidebook literature, borrowed discourse of huapu from, 21–22, 35–39

variety plays (zaju), 157, 182, 199, 249
variety-skit houses (zashua guan), 72, 77, 82, 84
Vast-Sky Pagoda (*Haotian ta*), 298n148
venues, 11, 63–114.
    Qing court's efforts to control, 11, 64–65, 112–14
    social and ethnic mixing at, 65, 112–13, 240–41
    "tent-arena" (goulan) theaters (1050–1450), 67
    See also playhouses; salon performances; temple fairs and temple stages
Viewing Flowers in the Precinct of the Throne (*Rixia kanhua ji*, 1803), 40–41, 46, 51–52, 57, 208–9
violence and sex in "I, Sister-in-Law" operas. *See under* "I, Sister-in-Law" operas
Volpp, Sophie, 33

Wang Da, 74
Wang Jide, 185
Wang Wenzhi, 131, 306n84
Wang Xizhi, 47, 283n110–11
Water Margin rebels, legends regarding, 106, 178
Water Margin (*Shuihu zhuan*) story cycle, 12, 176, 178, 212–14. *See also Cuiping Mountain*; "I, Sister-in-Law" operas; *Record of the Water Margin, The*; *Righteous Hero, The*
Weber, Max, 7
Wei Changsheng, 124, 125–27, 128, 304n53, 306n69
Wei Liangfu, 118
Wei Zhongxian, 156
Wen Zhengming, 97
White, Allon, 164
winehouses
    lao dou and dan actors at, 18, 53–57, 285–86n144
    number of, and frequency of visits by bannermen and officials to, 73
    payment for actors' entertainment services at, 104
    playhouses possibly deriving from opera patronage at, 67, 287n164
    prohibition of bannermen from entering, 289n24
    proximity to playhouses, 18, 53, 69
With Only a Broken Staff, Wu Song Fights a Tiger (*Zhe daner Wu Song da hu*) (Hongzi Li Er), 182
women.
    attendance at opera performances by *The Garden of Turquoise and Jade*, female audience for, 316n69
    playhouses, women allowed to attend, 113, 292n77
    playhouses, women forbidden from attending, 64–65, 82–83, 87
    salon performances, 65, 99, 102, 104–6, 113
    temple performances, 90, 91–92, 95–97, 113
    companionate marriage, 167, 299n160
    courtesan/actress texts, borrowed discourse of huapu from, 21, 25–28, 31–33
    elimination as actresses from palace performance, 119
    See also gender and gender representation
Wu Changyuan. *See Brief Register of the Orchids of Yan, A*
Wu Cuncun, 20
Wu Tao, 102, 104, 231–32
Wu Zhensheng, 320n28

Xia Tingshi, 27
Xianfeng emperor, 135–36, 244
xianggong, 32, 33, 279n48
Xiao tiedi daoren (The Latter-Day Adept of the Iron Flute), 128, 316n71
Xiaosheng (Empress Dowager), 107
xinxue (School of Mind), 157, 312n33–34
xipi, 119, 128, 305n63
Xu Daling, 237
Xu Zichang, 180–81, 186, 192, 201, 203, 214, 319n15
Xue Dan, 148, 314n48

ya and su, 130–31, 315n59
yabu opera, 118–19, 250. *See also* Kun opera
yamen runners, 81, 92, 94, 95, 138, 150, 152, 220, 238
Yan Shigu, 26, 278n18
Yang Cuiyan, 44–45, 77, 281n86, 282–83n98–100
Yang Guiyun, 227–28
Yang Maojian
    Assorted Notes toward a Dream of Splendors Past (*Menghua suobu*) (1842), 36, 37, 38, 40, 45, 54

as connoisseur, 45, 47–48, 51, 52
as huabu author, 32, 36, 37, 38, 282n89, 283n105
huabu, enthusiasm for, 133
on lao dou, 54, 56–57
on playhouses, 73, 78, 83, 84
Record of Viewing Flowers in the Capital (Chang'an kanhua ji) (1837), 28, 132–33
Yangzhou, opera in, 5
Yao Ying, 44
Ye Tang, 117, 129–31, 306n75, 306n79, 306n83
Ye Xiaoqing, 137
Yi Lansheng, 133
Yinlu (editor-in-chief of *All Nine Modes*), 122, 123, 303n25
Yiyang, 91, 116, 126, 128, 129, 250, 301n2
Yongqing Troupe, 127
Yongzheng emperor, 73
youwu, 24–25, 30, 277n11
Yu Huai, 27, 278n20
Yu Ji, 43–44
Yu Xiangdou, 321n35
Yu Zhi, 211, 245
Yu Zhibin, 305n68
Yuan drama, 157, 313n36
Yuan dynasty, 178
Yuan Haowen, 43, 282n90
Yuan Zhen, 43, 282n90

zaju (variety plays), 157, 182, 199, 249
zashua guan (variety-skit houses), 72, 77, 82, 84

Zha Kui, 63
Zha playhouse (Zhalou), 77, 290n52
Zhang Dai, 33, 97
Zhang Jiliang
as connoisseur, 44, 45, 47
on court regulation of qinqiang, 305n56
on dan actors, 84–85
The Garden of Turquoise and Jade and, 164
as huapu author, 36–37, 38–39, 280n66, 282n98, 283n105, 285n132
on lao dou, 54, 55, 57
A Record of Tear Stains from the Golden Stage (Jintai canlei ji) (1829), 32, 36–37, 38–39, 40, 44
Zhang Zhao, 214, 326n115
Zhao Qiugu, 26–27, 28, 278n20
Zhao Yi, 107–8, 125
Zhaodai xiaoshao (Heavenly Music of an Illustrious Age), 327n128
Zhaolian, 108, 125, 132–33, 213–14
Zheng Zhenduo, 320–21n28
Zhengde emperor, 156, 312n30
Zhou Shunchang, 156
Zhou Xiangyu, 122
Zhu Chenhao (Prince of Ning), rebellion of (1519), 150
Zhu Jiajin, 136
Zhu Suchen, 145–46, 148, 155, 156, 310n11, 311n27, 314n47. See also *Garden of Turquoise and Jade, The*
Zhu Yizun, 280n58
Zou Jinsheng, 122

The authorized representative in the EU for product safety and compliance is:
Mare Nostrum Group
B.V Doelen 72
4831 GR Breda
The Netherlands

www.ingramcontent.com/pod-product-compliance
Lightning Source LLC
Chambersburg PA
CBHW061929220426
43662CB00012B/1842